FOR THE
GOOD
of the
HORSE

FOR THE
GOOD
of the
HORSE

MARY WANLESS

Trafalgar Square Publishing

First published in the United States of America in 1997 by Trafalgar Square Publishing, North Pomfret, Vermont 05053

Printed and bound in Great Britain by Hillman Printers (Frome) Ltd

Library of Congress Catalog Card Number: 96-62093

ISBN 1-57076-083-7

Typeset in 11/13 Bembo
Illustrations by Christine Bousfield (except p31, p33, p34, p166, p247, p248 Kenilworth Press; p128-129 Sadddletech Ltd)
Design, typesetting and layout by Rachel Howe at Kenilworth Press

QUOTATION PERMISSIONS/ACKNOWLEDGEMENTS
Chapter 2: Quantum Healing - Deepak Chopra 1988, Bantam Books, 1540 Broadway, New York, NY 10036, USA.
Chapter 12: Kinship With All Life – J. Allen Boone. © 1954 by Harper & Brothers, renewed © 1982 by Daniel U. Boone, Jr. and Lois Boone Ragsdale.

Contents

To the map makers – those pioneering people who see beyond
convention, and risk going out on a limb as they take on
the task of honing their skills and bringing their
vision to public awareness.

....

When they don't know they don't know,
They think that they know;

When they know they don't know,
They don't think they know.

....

Acknowledgements

M Y THANKS ARE due to many people who all played a part in the development of this book. Firstly, I would like to thank Ann Mansbridge, my editor on *Ride with Your Mind* (*The Natural Rider*, USA) and *Ride with Your Mind Masterclass,* who shared the vision of this book from its inception. Although it became impossible for Ann to maintain her formal role of editor, I have so appreciated her continuing commitment to the book, and her practical help − and I thank her more than anything else for believing in me back in those early days.

My thanks as well to Lesley Gowers, who took over the role of editor with great skill and tact, and to all at Kenilworth Press, who made the transition to a new publisher as painless as possible. Caroline Robbins and Martha Cook of Trafalgar Square Publishing also gave me valuable assistance, and I particularly thank Martha for providing me with useful resource material, as well as finding answers to my seemingly impossible questions. As always, my illustrator Christine Bousfield did a superb job, working from a confusing plethora of resource material, including my own sketches which are all but incomprehensible!

My close friends have tolerated my absorption in this task with great good humour, and in some cases with significant personal self-sacrifice. I particularly thank Otto Rheinschmiedt, and also Clare Lester, Liz Mason and Helen Poynor, who have all enriched my life beyond measure.

Many people whose skills I particularly admire have helped with this manuscript. Some have answered very specific questions in their area of expertise. Others have allowed me to observe their practice, and to bombard them with questions. Some have looked once at their small sections of the manuscript, and others have trawled their way through whole chapters on more occasions than they will care to remember! I could not have produced this book without their thorough and insightful feedback. This has been a significant amount of work in lives which were already full to the brim. Thank you.

Mary Wanless

Special thanks are due to:

Chapter 2 Dr Sue Walker; Clare Lester

Chapter 3 Bob Livock; Chris Morris; Philip Lindley BHSI; Todd Williams MEqD BSc

Chapter 4 Gail Williams PhD; David Nicholls AWCF; Robbie Richardson RSS; Tony and Caroline Gonzales; Terry Richmond BSc, BHSI(SM), Post Grad. Dip. Eq. Sci. (Dublin)

Chapter 5 Lindsey Drewell CGCRS, L.; Sara Barnes MCSP, SRP; Andrew Foster; Barry Richardson; the Balance team – Carol Brett, Lesley Ann Taylor and Maureen Bartlett; Lavinia Mitchell; Yvonne Tyson; Auriol Lawson-Baker

Chapter 7 Michel Kaplan; Sarah Culverwell MCSP; Tex Gamble RSS; AFCL, ATF, B1. VET, RAVC; Kay McCarroll DHP, MC, AMC, MMCA; Gavin Schofield DOMRO; Pennie Hooper SMT, JMI; Dorothy Marks BSc(Hons), BSc(Chiro); Joyce Harman DVM, MRCVS; Julia Martin Grad. Dip. Phys, MCSP, SR; Linda Tellington-Jones

Chapter 8 Sherry Scott; Theresa Leehy NAAT; Julia Martin Grad. Dip. Phys, MCSP, SRP

Chapter 9 Hilary Page Self; Brian Jackson; Keith Allison; Joyce Harman DVM, MRCVS; Megan Kierney BVSc, MRCVS; Caroline Ingraham MRQA; Tom O'Hanlon; Ian Mole; and the 'help lines' of a number of UK feed companies.

Chapter 10 Trixie Williams BVSc, MRCVS; Mark Elliot BVSc, VetMFHom, MRCVS; Joyce Harman DVM, MRCVS; Christopher Day MA, VetMB, VetFFHom, MRCVS; Grace Gawler; Ann Mansbridge; Nicky Castle; Dr Sue Walker

Chapter 11 Monty Roberts; John Lyons; Tom Dorrance; Linda Tellington-Jones; Robert Miller DVM

Chapter 12 Kate Reilly, Kate Solisti; Nicci Mackay

Author's Note

IN WRITING THIS book it has been my intention to be as international as possible, and to use terminology that can be easily understood throughout the English-speaking world. In some cases it is not possible or necessary to 'internationalise' a word. I trust this will not lead to any confusion nor spoil your enjoyment of the book.

Throughout this book I have generally used 'she' to refer the rider or trainer, and 'he' to refer to the horse. I do this for ease of writing and in acknowledgement of a predominately female readership. In doing so I mean no offence to male readers!

Introduction

IN OCTOBER 1991 I held a one-day conference at West Wilts Equestrian Centre, in the south west of England. I called it 'For the Good of the Horse', feeling that much of what we do in our rather crude attempts to keep and train horses is often *not* for their good, and sometimes not for ours. Whilst a proportion of riders are in blissful ignorance of the damage they inflict, others are aware of the need to minimise the stresses that we inevitably place on the fit, stabled horse. In recognition of this, I chose speakers whom I felt offered some new solutions to the age-old problems inherent in riding and keeping horses. I included approaches which shed new light on the issues of learning and teaching, and of persuading an inept body to behave as one knows it ought to. I also included the supporting arts – farriery and saddlery – which have such a huge and often unseen role as they help or hinder our horse's performance. Finally, several speakers talked about some of the 'complementary' medical approaches which have recently come to the fore, offering solutions to some of the more subtle problems which seem to defy orthodox medicine.

At the time, organising this conference seemed like a stab in the dark. Friends and pupils had shown considerable interest in the idea, but I had little sense of how wide an appeal it would have. I did know, however, that a desperate enough horseman will try anything to get herself and her horse on the road! During the lead-up time I was almost reduced to biting my fingernails, but the eventual response was much greater than I had dared to hope for – as was the receptiveness and enthusiasm of the audience. Many people overcame our typical British reticence and travelled unbelievable distances to come. It was exciting to discover that the country contained enough curious, open-minded (or possibly desperate) people to justify my risk, and to ensure that the conference would become an annual event.

I was sitting with a friend a few days afterwards, casually talking through the impressions I had been left with, when he remarked, 'I bet there's a book in that.' I immediately knew he was right, and my heart sank at the enormity of the task which has indeed occupied me for much of the time since. You are now reading this over five years later, during which time the world has changed: saddlery in particular has become a 'hot' issue, and farriery may be about to do the same. Complementary treatments are much more widely available – with more vets undergoing post-graduate training in homoeopathy and acupuncture, and with equine physiotherapists, chiropractors and massage therapists becoming almost mainstream. More and more riders are using the techniques of bodywork to improve their own body awareness. Studies in sports psychology and biomechanics are affecting how we think about learning, and about choosing and riding the performance horse. Our traditional ways of handling and starting horses are under question. This is, I suspect, the beginning of a quiet revolution in riding and horse care.

My personal area of expertise lies in teaching, and in my ability to communicate the 'how' of riding to others. The methods I use have developed from my own experiences as a rider, and from my research into how people learn, and how mind and body interact. As I developed, tested and refined my approach, it gradually became clear to me that the seemingly magical skill of riding actually has a structure, with laws of cause and effect which determine just how the rider/horse interaction will work out. Understanding these laws makes riding far easier – and far more fun – both to learn and to teach. To date, this has been a sixteen-year research project, whose results have been charted in my books and video tapes. *Ride With Your Mind* was published in the UK in 1987 and in the USA (where it was entitled *The Natural Rider*) in 1988. *Ride With Your Mind Masterclass* was published in both countries in 1991, with video tape series following in 1993 and 1997. My next book (to be published in 1998) will take this process further.

During the course of a year's teaching I probably work with over three hundred horses, and watch their movement patterns change as their riders discover more effective ways to sit. Riding many of these horses myself gives me another perspective on how they hold patterns of tension, and how the restrictions in their movement are not always rider-induced. Through my own observation – and through liaising with some extremely astute professionals – it has become clear to me that the supporting arts of saddlery and farriery can have tremendous impact on our horses' well-being and performance. A large number of the riders and horses I see are coping relatively well despite the shortcomings of the horses' saddles and their shoes; but I also see some extremely well-intentioned riders who have failed to notice that their horses are all but crippled by them.

Over the last few years I have come to believe that *at least 60 per cent* of the horses I see show signs of pain or discomfort which could be alleviated through attention to their saddles, feet or teeth. Many more would benefit from a thorough check from a physiotherapist, chiropractor, or massage therapist who can trace patterns of tension throughout the horse's body. (Other authorities have suggested that over 85 per cent of competitive horses have their performance compromised by such physical problems.) Sadly, I once watched a horse buckle at the knees when mounted, whilst a veterinary surgeon insisted that the state of his back was 'nothing to worry about'. An equine bodyworker (this term includes chiropractors, osteopaths, massage therapists, and others) would take a very different view, however, as would an equine physiotherapist. For their particular expertise is the stresses and strains which limit the efficiency of muscles and joints, and which all too easily turn us – or our horses – into the 'walking wounded'.

Many years ago, as a rather green BHSAI (British Horse Society Assistant Instructor), I never even saw the gait abnormalities which are obvious to me now. I was in the blissful state of being 'unconscious of my incompetence', and was looking at horses with far too crude an eye. I had a textbook knowledge of lameness, and naively thought that my examination studies had taught me all I would ever need to know about saddlery and farriery. But my more recent experiences have led me to believe that these supporting arts are by no means as straightforward as I had once supposed, and that our general knowledge about both of them is inadequate. Since virtually all of those unfortunate riders with crippled horses have had their saddles fitted and their horses shod by supposedly reputable professionals, it follows that the knowledge of those professionals may also be open to question.

Once upon a time it seemed to be enough to throw on a saddle, be sure that it cleared the wither, and set off on your ride. Perhaps we demanded less of our horses; or perhaps we never related their high head carriage and hollow back to the state of their back and to *pain*. Perhaps we never stopped for long enough to notice the state of their muscle development, or the wear on their shoes. We were blissfully ignorant. The post-World War II period changed saddlery: competition and fashion became the dominant elements in a swiftly developing industry, and as a result saddles gradually became more comfortable for us, and *less* comfortable for the horse. Eventually, a few of the more observant saddlers could no longer ignore his plight. It is fortunate that saddlery – like every field – has a number of extremely far-sighted and knowledgable practitioners whose perceptions are much more circumspect than most. They have bravely sought solutions which lie beyond the conventional, transcending the dictates of fashion and putting current trends in perspective. This has enabled them to design, make and fit saddles with the eye for detail which every horse deserves.

It would be an extremely naive view of farriery to suggest that it merely consists of hammering a piece of metal onto the horse's foot so that we can ride him along the road without harm. I have seen the damage done by bad trimming and shoeing; but much more than this, I have seen the incredible change for the better which can be created in a horse's movement by trimming an apparently tiny piece of horn off one side of one foot. In reality, this rebalancing of the hoof rebalanced the limb and thus the whole horse, creating a difference that was obvious even to the untrained observer. Yet to the average farrier, the horse barely exists from the knee up; and the average horse owner has little idea of the impact of his work. Indeed she settles for very little – her major concern is probably to keep shoes on for as long as possible and to keep her shoeing bills down to a minimum.

I have had to persuade myself to learn all I can about these arts, and to become a much more discerning consumer – for I am one of those rather eager, impatient riders who is tempted to assume that all is well, and to leap on board with a minimum of fuss. But it is inevitable that we, as consumers, will get what we are willing to accept – and in this, our horses get not what they deserve but what *we* deserve. Whilst you might describe your latest piece of equipment as 'cheap and cheerful', your horse is unlikely to agree – although, to complicate the issue, expense is no guarantee of a well-designed and well-fitted product.

Some aspects of the horse industry are ready for an overhaul, and it is important that we, as riders, help this along. For in a market economy, the most impactful, positive changes will undoubtedly be consumer-led. We tend to expect that dutifully learning the basics of horse care should be sufficient to protect both us and our horses; but a little knowledge is a dangerous thing. If the average rider understood what 'normal riding' can do to horses, she would probably be guilt-stricken – especially when she appreciates that a 'rogue' horse is rarely more than one of the few who is not willing to quietly endure it all, and to perpetuate 'the silence of the lambs'.

. . . .

My sixteen-year quest to discover all that I could about riding and learning led me to appreciate the complex interaction between mind and body. I became so fascinated by this that I trained in a number of body-mind disciplines, including psychotherapy, martial arts and biofeedback. But this aspect of my learning had another dimension, and another motivation – my health. Although I could never persuade my doctor to take my condition seriously, I was convinced that something was sapping my energy. In desperation I dabbled in many of the techniques of complementary medicine, and it took a very long time for me to track down what was really wrong and to begin to heal myself. But during that process I gained a fairly good overview of the scope and limitations of many different approaches. This has served me well in writing this book, and in using complementary treatments with my horses.

Inevitably in all of these fields, I came across practitioners and methods that did not gel with me, and others that profoundly influenced my life. Different approaches, too, were right at different times, and I discovered that any technique was only as effective as the person performing it. Thank goodness I gave some of them a second chance, and realised retrospectively that to judge a technique on the performance of the first practitioner one meets may well be to do it a disservice. This is equally true in treating horses. In contrast, most people place blind faith in mainstream medical practice (although they commonly have less faith in vets), and they usually follow the directives of their vet, doctor or consultant without question. Indeed we are *expected* not to question, and to be a 'good patient' who respects the doctor's authority. In the traditional medical model we are the sick ones who patiently wait for the doctor to dispense his pills and make us well. We are supposed to be passive.

In complementary medicine the patient is much more actively engaged in her healing. She may be asked to change her diet, her lifestyle, and even how she thinks. This latter is not so easy with horses – although lifestyle changes, and attention to diet and to the supporting arts are often part of the holistic approach to a veterinary problem. In the UK and USA only vets with further training are legally allowed to practise homoeopathy, herbalism and acupuncture on animals, so these treatments are not so widely available as they are for people. Since our practitioners do not have to be medical doctors, they do not have to be 'converts' from the established system. Thus there are many more of them, and legally, they have much more room to manoeuvre than the practitioners of the healing arts who would like to work with horses.

Complementary practitioners know that they are bound to be judged on their merits – that blind faith is not part of the contract. So inevitably, they all have stories about clients who did not give them enough time: and when the results are not yet obvious many people (myself included) find themselves wondering whether to stay with it or invest their hard-earned cash elsewhere. We all long for the miracle cure – and sometimes it happens – but a chronic condition which has taken many years to develop can hardly be expected to dissolve overnight. Biased by our culture and experience we often apply completely different expectations to the two systems of medicine, and do not fully embrace the philosophy of holism – which rests on the maintenance of health rather than the treatment of disease, and relies on mobilising the healing powers inherent within the body itself.

Typically, vets using complementary methods have been called out only as a last resort – which means, of course, that their successes are particularly impressive. Increasingly, however, the general public are not happy just dosing themselves and their horses with pills, for medicine's 'magic bullets' have too many side-effects to make their long-term use inviting. So many horse owners who have successfully used complementary techniques in their own healing now call on these approaches at the *beginning* of treatment – they no longer wait for orthodox veterinary medicine to fail, or for its side-effects to show.

Before I gained access to a vet trained in the complementary approaches, I found that choosing the medical care I gave to horses was much more difficult than choosing the care I gave to myself. In the past I have felt extremely unhappy about following veterinary advice and giving them antibiotics when I, in the equivalent situation, would not have taken them. We have been brought up to believe that we would be negligent not to use all the drugs on offer – and it would be much easier not to if our horses could give us moment by moment reports on their condition. It is because they cannot do this, and cannot choose their own treatment, that the law is there to protect them, requiring a veterinarian to perform or oversee complementary treatments (at least in Britain and America).

However, in the absence of a holistically trained veterinary surgeon who can advise about problems large and small, many people are developing their skills in using the better known homoeopathic or herbal remedies to treat everyday horse (and human) ailments. This is often a very non-invasive and appropriate form of treatment; but there are some dangers – the biggest being that an underlying condition goes undiagnosed. If this were to cause the horse undue suffering, it could put the horse owner on the wrong side of British (but not American) law. In paying for a veterinary diagnosis, one pays in part for peace of mind, which – for increasing numbers of people – is maximised in the ideal situation where a vet can draw from both orthodox and complementary approaches. Times are undoubtedly changing, but sadly there are all too few veterinarians with training in both. However, when the type of treatment given becomes a choice based on sound knowledge it can only be to the horse's benefit. For both systems are valid and useful when the appropriate choices are made.

....

It has been a delight in preparing this book to take on the role of an investigative journalist, to meet and talk with many extremely capable and fascinating practitioners. I have enjoyed writing as a *consumer*, and not as an expert. Some of the people I talked to are well-known names; others are known only within their local equestrian communities. But this does not necessarily imply that their work is of lesser quality. I am in an extremely privileged position, in that my frequent teaching trips to east and west coast America, and to Australia, have given me a much larger overview of the field that I could have had from England alone. Many of the people who have invited me abroad already had an interest in complementary medicine, and their interest in my work was kindled by the similarities they saw in my philosophical approach to people and their development. They introduced me to networks of people, and as one contact led to another, my vision broadened. But I know that there are many hundreds of practitioners who I have never met or even heard of who have equally important contributions to make to the field as a whole.

Before starting this book, I had visions of how much fun I would have meeting and interviewing different practitioners – and I was looking forward to it immensely. What I did *not* realise was just how much ground work I would need to do before I knew enough to ask them the right questions, to understand their answers, and to compare the perspectives of different approaches. One of my strengths is my great tenacity: when I do not understand something, I am like a bulldog and cannot let go until I do. I have needed that tenacity in getting to the bottom of some of the more complex material in this book – particularly concerning farriery and saddlery. I have never had much faith in my innate intelligence, and once *I* can understand something, I have always found that I can explain it to other people so that *they* can understand it too. I hope you will find this to be the case, but if these sections offer a more in-depth view than you need right now, skip them – the rest of the book is much less complicated.

My university degree, taken back in the early 1970s, was in physics. (It was my training ground in tenacity!) I have maintained a layman's interest in the advances of the 'new' physics – quantum mechanics, cosmology, and chaos theory. Even back in the seventies, physicists were beginning to look for a 'theory of everything' that would tie the different aspects of physics together and explain how the universe worked, right from the realm of the very big to the realm of the very small. Now, as I attempt to explain some of the many approaches to complementary medicine and bodywork, I find myself wanting to fit them into a 'theory of everything' that relates them to each other. I would love to be able to tell you about the 'ultimate method' which works for everything, and makes sense of a whole spectrum of 'sub-methods'. But this does not seem possible, for the body is a complex organism which can be approached in many different ways. These do not always fit neatly together and follow the same logic.

My hope in writing this book is that I will invoke your curiosity, and encourage you to move beyond the rather superficial ways in which we are taught to look at and think about riding and keeping horses. For this maintains the status quo in a world where even well-meaning people who think they are doing the right thing can unknowingly abuse their horses. Right across the equestrian spectrum – from the backyard horse owner to the ambitious, skilful rider – few people notice the restrictions in their horse's performance which are caused by pain. That horses tolerate us with so much equanimity is little short of a miracle; it convinces me that they really are God's greatest gift to mankind.

CHAPTER ONE

....

The Map is Not the Territory

....

Pᴇᴏᴘʟᴇ ᴀʀᴇ ᴅɪꜰꜰᴇʀᴇɴᴛ from horses. This may seem an obvious statement, but remarkably few riders appreciate just how significant those differences are. They are not limited to those we see on the outside; the most far-reaching and least honoured are those relating to the scope and the limitations of the human and equine senses, for these define how people and horses perceive the world.

Many of us live with the mistaken belief that the way in which we perceive the world is the way the world actually is. But in fact, information from the world – the 'reality' or 'territory' outside of us – comes in through our senses, which act as *filters,* screening out some pieces of information, and letting through others. Thus our supposed interactions with the world are not with the world itself, but with the *map* or representation of the world which we each create inside our heads. Human maps and horse maps are not the same, and within each species, much of our uniqueness as individuals lies in the idiosyncratic ways in which we have developed our maps. My aim in this chapter is to demonstrate this, and to show that many of our maps are extremely imprecise renderings of the territory. This is particularly true of the maps which guide us as we interact with horses, determining their care and their training.

All human beings share neurological and genetic constraints which have a tremendous influence on our map-making abilities: the human ear, for instance, cannot detect sound waves below 20 cycles per second or above 20,000 cycles per second. Our eyes only detect light waves that lie between 380 and 680 milli-microns. The phenomena that we call 'sound' and 'light' are but a small portion of the range in which these physical phenomena exist, and some other animals operate from such a different set of neurological constraints that their senses only begin to function in the range where ours no longer can.

Consider, for instance, how different our experience would be if we orientated ourselves in the same way as some bats and snakes, who cannot depend as we can on vision and hearing. Some bats continually emit high-frequency sounds as they fly, and these are inaudible to the human ear. By receiving – and making sense of – the echoes that come back to them from objects in the area, they locate their prey and know where they are. Some snakes have organs on the sides of their heads which are tremendously sensitive to heat, detecting temperature changes of only half a degree Celsius (or one degree Fahrenheit). Before they strike they move their head from side to side: this allows them to register subtle temperature changes, and to know the precise position of their prey.

These differences are so far reaching that it is all but impossible for us to conceive what it might be like to live from the map of a snake or a bat. But somewhat closer to home is the experience of a dog, and in his book *The Man Who Mistook His Wife For a Hat,* Oliver Sacks gives us some insight into what this might be like. He tells the story of a friend of his, who as a medical student was taking 'highs', mostly amphetamines and cocaine. One night he dreamt that he was a dog, and had a very rich, olfactory dream. He woke up to find himself with an extremely heightened sense of smell, in a new world, where he could distinguish all of his friends and patients by their smell, even before he saw them. 'Each had his own olfactory physiognomy, a smell-face, far more vivid and evocative, more redolent, than any sight-face.'

He could smell the emotions of people around him, recognising their contentment, fear, or sexuality. He could distinguish the smells of different shops and streets, and could find his way around New York by smell alone. He found a whole new immediacy and significance in his experience of the world, whose sensory richness sparked off an emotional eagerness and sensitivity; he talked about the smell of water as if it were 'happy', the smell of a stone as if it were 'brave'. Although he had previously been quite intellectual and introspective, he now found thought and abstraction somewhat unreal. Indeed, his sensory experience was so compelling that he had to restrain himself out of politeness from following the impulse to sniff and touch everything, for nothing seemed real until he did.

His other senses were heightened too, and he found that he could distinguish colours with a sensitivity that made him feel as if he had previously been colour-blind. He was able to distinguish a whole range of browns where he had simply seen brown before. He found, too, that he was able to see pictures in his mind's eye, which he had been unable to do previously, and this suddenly gave him the ability to do much more accurate anatomical drawings. It was as if the images were projected on his paper, enabling him to draw around them. (He had, in fact, stumbled upon the strategy used by good artists and spellers.)

His experience lasted three weeks, and then he found himself back again in his old map of the world, with its sensory faintness, and its capacity for abstraction. When Oliver Sacks wrote about his friend's experience some sixteen years later, nothing like it had ever recurred. Despite being relieved and happy to be back in the 'normal' world of human beings, his friend reported an occasional nostalgia for this lost world, the richer and more immediate map of a dog.

....

Of course, we cannot know how dog-like this experience really was, but it certainly gives us a glimpse of life beyond the confines of our senses. I know of no such ventures into the world of the horse, and I certainly could not begin to describe it with such richness. Indeed, much of our knowledge is guesswork, and it has only recently been shown that horses' eyes lack the chemicals which enable humans to see reds and greens. Thus their colour vision is much less differentiated than our own.

So, as a small experiment in map-creation, imagine yourself horse-shaped, with four legs, a very long neck, and a tremendous appetite for grass. You are, however, very discerning about what you eat (given the choice), and nature has equipped you with a very sensitive, mobile muzzle, and with whiskers which yield very precise information about your food and the environment around your nose. Your genetic constraints have not given you hands like a human; but your muzzle is so dexterous that the escapologists amongst your species (whose map of the world extends beyond its usual equine limits) can even impress humans with its intricate use!

Despite your strong teeth and your ability to kick out, you are no match for predators and are one of the flightiest animals on earth, always on the look-out for danger. Your keen senses are designed to keep you alert, and as you graze, you can see almost all the way around you, with only a 6° blind spot behind your tail. Thus you can scan the whole horizon – almost as if a wide-angled video camera were positioned on each side of your head. Having your eyes this wide apart, however, means that you have only monocular vision for most of your visual field, and cannot gauge the distance between yourself and any object you see. This inability is coupled with an extreme sensitivity to tiny movements, and near vision which is probably poor and slow to focus. All of this contributes to your suspicious nature. You have depth perception similar to a human for only 30° to each side of a line straight in front of you, where the visual fields of each eye overlap. However, you also have a blind spot just in front of your nose, and because of this you cannot see the centre of a jump after you have taken off.

Your night vision is extremely good, but your method of focusing is less sophisticated than that of a human eye, which focuses on near or far objects by changing the shape of the lens. You cannot do this: sections of your retina are automatically focused for different distances, so you must move your head into the best position to see each one. (To understand this in human terms, think of wearing a pair of bi-focal glasses, where you must look up to see distance, and look down to read.) With your head down to graze you see the horizon in focus, and to focus on a carrot placed just in front of your nose you must raise your head and tuck it in.

Your hearing is at least as acute as it is in humans, and your large ears are so mobile that you can more easily locate a sound. Your skin is so sensitive that you can feel a fly land anywhere on your body. Your sense of smell is far more important to you than to a human – you use it in the recognition of friend, foe, food, and place. It is rare for you to follow trails like a dog, but you can always find your way home. Some evidence suggests that you do this in the same way as migratory birds – by registering spatial changes in the earth's magnetic field, and navigating from a 'magnetic map'.

You are a creature of the herd, and a creature of habit. Your interests lie only in surviving, and (if you have not been neutered) in breeding. Your friendships – which in the wild are mostly within family groups – are extremely important to you, and rivalries are normally a lesser part of herd life. The exceptions to this are provided by stallions who vie for dominance, and situations (normally in captivity) which create competition for scarce resources. Social bonding is vitally important, for to be banished from the herd would be the worst possible punishment, and all your instincts tell you that this could result in death.

You have a tremendous memory – perhaps as good as an elephant's – enabling experiences involving intense pain or panic to be remembered for years. You know your territory extremely well, and within it, any little thing out of place disturbs you: you *cannot not* notice, for instance, something new on the ground, or a branch which has become dislodged from a tree. Furthermore, each of your three visual fields (the monocular one to each side, and the binocular one in front) are processed completely separately by the brain. Thus if you change direction and see a 'spook' out of the other eye, you see it as if for the first time. This only adds to your flightiness – and when human beings judge you by their own maps (as they almost always do) it makes them think of you as 'stupid'.

....

Clever Hans was a nineteenth-century horse with apparently exceptional intelligence, which enabled him to count and solve simple arithmetical puzzles, tapping out the answers with his hoof. His fame spread far and wide as he performed before large audiences, and he was finally presented before a group of academicians in Holland. They ascertained that no trickery was involved in his feats, since he could perform them even when his trainer was not present. But it transpired that he could *not* perform them when he could not see the audience. From this it was apparent that he knew the answer not through any mathematical ability, but by their reaction: he could 'read' the slight changes in their body language which accompanied their building anticipation as he reached the right number.

Furthermore, Clever Hans had taught himself to do this. His trainer had no idea how he did it, and he and other people could not perceive the subtle visual cues which were obvious to the horse – and which remained obvious even when the audience were told in advance how he did it. Interestingly, some of the pioneering trainers who speak 'Equus' (and who you will meet in Chapter 11) believe that whilst we gaily presume that horses are obeying our voice commands, they are actually reading our body language, and working – as they do within the herd – much more from visual and kinaesthetic cues than from auditory ones. For very little of their language is auditory; clamping a lip, moving an ear, shifting their weight, cocking a leg, or just looking at a different part of another horse's body, are all meaningful signals which we humans are often too 'dumb' to notice – until the unheeded warning escalates into (more) overt action.

'Whilst we gaily presume that horses are obeying our voice commands, they are actually reading our body language.'

It is often said that we have no chance of ever attaining the sensory awareness of the horse, and horses are often attributed with the best 'sixth sense' of any animal. But a number of strange experiences during my lifetime have left me questioning our 'sixth sense' and our apparent insensitivity. I was once riding on an escalator on the London underground during rush-hour, when I suddenly felt compelled to turn around and look behind me. Gazing at my back was someone I knew very slightly, who was trying to work out if she did indeed recognise me. Most people have a few stories like this – despite the fact that our established maps of the human senses do not allow for such phenomena. Yet in US army courses on survival and escape when captured, recruits are told never to focus their gaze on the back of the head of the guard they are trying to evade. So the question may not be whether we really do have 'extra sensory perception' but *why* such experiences do not appear to be a part of our everyday repertoire.

Although the horse's senses are more finely tuned than ours are, we can – if we choose – take significant steps towards matching his acuity. As a rider, I have deliberately trained my kinaesthetic sense, and its sophistication far outstrips that of my vision or hearing. Whilst watching a rider and horse, however, I see far more than most people, who ignore the more subtle signals of their interaction – having, perhaps, no map through which to give them meaning. But the few people who handle horses superbly from the ground have trained their visual acuity in this context far better than I have, and through this they have learned to train horses in the language 'Equus'.

The advantages of 'talking' to someone in their own language must surely be apparent; yet few of us realise that we have the option to step out of the map of 'human', to enter the map of 'horse', and to communicate with horses *beyond the limits* of our own language. But before you can learn 'Equus' (as a kinaesthetic language when mounted, or as a visual language when interacting from the ground), you have to appreciate that you will have to become the horse's *pupil* and not insist on being his *teacher*. This requires a humility which does not come easily to many. In fact, in the twenty-three centuries since Xenophon, only a handful of people have observed horses astutely enough to become really fluent in their language. They have become the 'horse whisperers' who appear (when viewed from our normal everyday maps) to do the 'impossible' with them. A dramatically new 'normality' is created by communicating with horses in their own terms.

....

We humans, with our enhanced capacity for abstraction, are much better than horses at *deleting* information which comes to us from the environment. This stops us from being overwhelmed by a mass of data, much of which is irrelevant – so, for example, we 'tune out' the cigarette packet lying in the grass verge which the horse *cannot* not notice. Our ability to delete information can be both positive and negative: if you are absorbed in reading this book whilst sitting in a room that is full of distractions, you are deleting background noise and activity to create a focused state – an ability that is useful on many occasions. Similarly, we want our horses to pay attention to their rider and to delete external stimuli, which is a far greater challenge for them than it is for us. But we also want them not to delete the stimuli *we* give them – unless they are riding school horses who must be patient with riders so inept that the 'noise to signal ratio' is extremely high.

Our deletions, however, can also have the negative effect of keeping us locked within the confines of a map which no longer serves us well, and it is because of our selective deletions that you and I will probably both remember the the same event in totally different ways. If you just read my last sentence as 'remember the same event' you too have used a deletion; for it read 'remember the *the* same event'. By doing this you were able to make sense out of what you saw: you literally deleted the piece that did not fit. The tendency to do this is so strong that proof-reading is a

> 'We have the option to step out of the map of 'human', to enter the map of 'horse', and to communicate with horses beyond the limits of our own language.'

notoriously difficult task – but this is the thin end of the wedge. If, for instance, your map of the world and yourself does not hold within it the possibility that others could value you enough to pay you a compliment, you might literally *not hear them* when they do. Thus your deletions serve an extremely important function – they enable you to preserve the integrity of your map.

I once reversed the positions of the hinges and door handles on a door in my house, and it was amusing to observe how the inmates – two humans and two cats – kept going to the wrong side of it, expecting it to open in the old way! But despite our supposedly superior intelligence, the cats adapted far faster than we did, for the here-and-now information coming from their senses was relatively more impactful than the there-and-then information coming from their map. Like horses and Oliver Sacks's friend, they live their lives much more in the rich world of sensory experience.

So instead of noticing what *is,* we commonly generate our behaviour according to what *has been.* This means that it is probably easier to rehabilitate traumatised horses than it is to rehabilitate traumatised people; for horses update their maps very quickly – except when there has been a tremendous amount of fear involved in their initial creation. Even then, the fluent speaker of 'Equus' will approach and ride the fearful horse in ways which can catalyse tremendous change in a remarkably short time.

....

When you make your map of the world, you also use generalisations. These too help us cope with the world, for once you have touched one hot stove, your ability to generalise stops you from repeating the experience. But supposing you were bitten by a German Shepherd Dog. Would you generalise to the extent that you would not go near that particular dog again, or would you avoid all German Shepherd Dogs, or even all dogs? I know some horses who have generalised from one bad experience with a farrier to all farriers, and to all men. The ability to generalise allows both humans and equines to learn many new behaviours much faster than we could if we had to begin each one 'from scratch', so it is a blessing as well as a curse. The majority of horses are better at generalising than autistic humans, who, even though they have learned how to cross *one* street, will not know how to cross *every* street. Teaching them to buy a candy bar in *one* store will not teach them how to buy a candy bar in *any* store. We always hope that our horses will be able to generalise from jumping one particular jump to jumping any jump in any place; but this requires an intelligence which cannot be taken for granted.

Along with deletions and generalisations, we also make distortions as we create our maps of the world, and we do this by changing our experience of sensory input. This is primarily a human rather than an equine trait (although my horse sees a snake in the most innocuous stick left lying on the ground!). Children at play do this all the time, or at least most do. One very pragmatic little girl I know has been rather a disappointment – in this one respect – to her parents, who were longing for their second childhood. 'Don't be silly,' she says to them, 'that's not a boat, it's a table!' Great artists all manipulate their perceptions of reality to create something different, whether it be water lilies as seen by Monet, or the sky as seen by Van Gogh. When you enjoy their works, or read the words of a good novel, you use distortion too. From symbols written on a page you create scenes and characters in your mind's eye – you may even *become* the heroine, and experience life through her eyes.

'It is as if we have on a certain pair of glasses that screen out any information which does not match our existing beliefs.'

But our distortions are not always so creative. Supposing you have been put down at some stage, and made the generalisation that you are not worthy of love and respect. As I said earlier, you may then literally not hear (i.e. you delete) any positive feedback that comes your way. But you may also distort it. When your boss compliments you on a job well done you may well find yourself thinking, 'I bet he's only saying that because he wants me to do something else.' As each person's life experiences are unique, so are our maps, and as well as allowing us to create and learn they all too easily blind us and cause us pain. To quote Richard Bandler and John Grinder, authors of *The Structure of Magic:* 'A person's generalisations or expectations filter out and distort his experience to make it consistent with those expectations. As he has no experiences which challenge his generalisations, his expectations are confirmed and the cycle continues. In this way people maintain their impoverished models of the world.' It is as if we have on a certain pair of glasses that screen out any information which does not match our existing beliefs.

....

Inevitably, these beliefs become our 'mind-set'. This is more or less rigid in each individual – and education, quite often, serves only to entrench it more. (My purpose in writing this, as you may have realised by now, is to try to loosen yours!) As someone who has dedicated over fifteen years to redrawing our traditional map of riding, I know all too well how strong a force our 'mind-set' can be, especially when we have all shared a map which has, in effect, become a 'consensus reality'. To challenge this is to challenge the pervasive force of culture – like asking a whole generation to take off the glasses they were handed by their parents and teachers, and to look at the territory as if for the first time.

This has happened at various times in history, and in many different fields. The makers of new maps – the fathers of the paradigm shifts which have completely changed our understanding of the world – have oftentimes met with attempts by the established hierarchy to 'delete' them. It was Copernicus who first put forward the idea that the earth moved around the sun, and later, when Galileo was seen to support it, the Catholic Church warned him not to 'hold and defend' the theory. But in his later writing he did: he was made to recant, and was sentenced to life imprisonment. Even this was not a completely effective 'deletion', for whilst there he was able to clarify the mathematics of the new theory, and even to get it published. It was not until 1979 – nearly three hundred and fifty years later – that Pope John Paul II finally took the step of declaring that the church might possibly have been mistaken in condemning him!

Einstein did unusually well with his theory of relativity, which could explain and predict far more than the existing scientific maps of his day, which were mostly the brainchild of Newton. On average, though, radical new ideas take around forty years to be accepted - and it took this long for 'flat-Earthers' to concede defeat and admit that the Earth must be round. In medicine, there have been many major map revisions: thanks to these, we no longer use poisonous mercury-based laxatives or cure diseases with blood-letting. Because we know about germs, and about penicillin and other antibiotics, there are few unexplained deaths from small wounds, or in childbirth. Whilst technology gives us more and more sophisticated weapons with which to fight disease, the most dramatic shift of our time is perhaps the emergence – or rather the re-emergence – of the maps used by practitioners of complementary medicine, who see both the body and disease in a very different light. Instead of being something that we 'fight' with outside agents, disease becomes a signal that all is not well with the body and its defences. Complementary treatment is aimed at strengthening these, easing out the imbalances which eventually manifest as illness or injury, and making the body a much less hospitable host to invasion.

'On average, radical new ideas take around forty years to be accepted.'

But the teachings of complementary practitioners are also often deleted, distorted, and generalised. One easy way to do this is to call them 'quacks'. Since any paradigm shift requires a break with old ways of thinking, the die-hards who wish to maintain their position in the established hierarchy will inevitably adopt a very protective position. The need to maintain established maps may even be part of the driving force behind the laws which define the scope of veterinary treatment, and limit the contexts in which complementary practitioners can legally treat horses. Whether these laws are primarily for the protection of the *public* and their animals, or for the protection of *veterinary surgeons/veterinarians* (and their income) may well be open to debate.

In their work with animals, physiotherapists and bodyworkers in both the UK and USA operate legally only if called in by a vet, and only a vet with the appropriate further training can practise homoeopathy, acupuncture and herbalism. The companies producing herbal products, and the bodyworkers – who unlike physiotherapists tend not to uphold the law – have the least easy truce with the vets. But there is more in question than the legalities of these practitioners, and the vets who practise complementary treatments have themselves gone out on a limb. They risk the wrath of other colleagues, and have to be absolutely meticulous in fulfilling their ethical obligations. For when called in as a second opinion, vets in the UK (but not the USA) are required to contact the vet who has previously been treating the horse, and to obtain a full case history before they begin treatment. Much to their consternation, many feel the need to cover themselves from the possible consequences of litigation by giving orthodox treatment alongside complementary treatment.

Whilst many vets remain sceptical, the tide of public opinion is increasingly behind complementary practitioners, and many people are tempted – especially when seeking bodywork for their horses – not to involve their vet. Strictly speaking, the practitioners they call in are breaking the law, and especially with regard to the lesser known therapies there are some grey areas in its interpretation. This is also true in the USA, where some states are more restrictive in their laws than others, making manipulative treatment as well as homoeopathy, herbalism and acupuncture the sole province of veterinarians. To keep us all within the limits of the law, I must suggest to you throughout this book that your horse must only ever be diagnosed by a vet, and never by a complementary practitioner. Furthermore, any complementary treatment which can be legally done by a non-veterinarian must be overseen by a vet.

The current stand-off between the veterinary and the complementary camps is an uncomfortable situation which is probably better resolved than left to fester, and I hope that public opinion can play its part in this. If the Royal College of Veterinary Surgeons were as restrictive as it has the legal right to be within British law, we and our horses could lose access to a variety of practitioners whom I believe offer tremendously valuable treatments. (I suspect, though, that they would continue to practise, and that we would continue to vote with our feet – whether or not we did so legally.) However, if a case were taken to the *European* court, the legalities of the monopoly held by the vets would be questioned, and the outcome could be very different. Neither side wants this legal battle – which would, in reality, be a battle over maps and incomes – and it is unlikely ever to happen. I only hope that wisdom prevails as solutions are sought to this complex and difficult problem.

It is undoubtedly true that a proportion of the people jumping on the complementary bandwagon do not have the skills and training that are needed to work safely and effectively – and we, the public, need ways of recognising them and weeding them out. It certainly could be argued that we are such a gullible bunch of consumers that we and our horses need to be protected from charlatans. But should we be protected just from unskilled practitioners, or from any map which does not follow established veterinary thought? Are all chiropractors trying to cheat us (by definition), or just some? The usual criticism levelled at complementary practitioners by the veterinary profession is that their training is not specific and detailed enough – so recognised qualifications within the complementary fields would seem to be the answer.

My hope is that the various disciplines which have not yet done so will come clean, opt for self-regulation, and put their houses in order. I also hope that they will avoid in-fighting, and that their standards will be set by their most skilful and ethical practitioners. However, even qualifications do not guarantee a uniform standard of practice (and even some vets are better than others!). One could even argue that they foster mediocrity – encouraging practitioners to sit on their laurels, and not to pursue the ideal of 'life-long learning'. So ultimately, only *we* can protect ourselves from the poor practitioners who exist in every profession, regardless of the training they have had and the certificates they hold. To make sensible decisions, and to find the best possible treatment for our horses, we need *information*, so that we too are working from viable maps – and we need to be astute.

'Ultimately, only we can protect ourselves from the poor practitioners who exist in every profession, regardless of the training they have had and the certificates they hold.'

· · · · · · · · · · · · · · · · · ·

As another example of vested interest and confused priorities, consider the case of equine dental specialists (who cannot legally call themselves equine dentists). In Britain, equine dentistry does not yet have any recognised qualification, or any regulating body. The best dental specialists are extremely well trained in their field but are not qualified as veterinary surgeons. They know – as the vets know, and as many people learn the hard way – that there are tremendous variations between the skill levels of different practitioners, for *anyone* can legally 'set up shop'. Consequently, there a large number of self-taught, self-professed specialists.

Inevitably this leads to animosity between the vets and the dental specialists. The vets commonly regard *all* the dental specialists with suspicion, so often, both the best and the worst practitioners are tarred with the same brush. However, the most skilful specialists spend much of their time clearing up the messes left by the 'experts', and also doing a more thorough, professional job than the vets – who rarely claim either to *like* rasping horses' teeth or to make a particularly good job of it.

As a purchaser of skills and services, who would you expect to have a more detailed map of the horse's teeth and all that can happen to them – someone who has trained extensively in this one area, and who deals with fifteen or more sets of teeth in each working day? Or someone who has to be a 'jack of all trades', who works with horses and probably other animals, and who at most rasps a few sets of teeth in a week? (Bear in mind too that during a five-year veterinary training, probably only one afternoon is dedicated to the practicalities of rasping horses' teeth.) Unlike other complementary practitioners, the dental specialists are not rocking the boat by putting forward radically different theories, and they themselves insist that they would be much happier if they could work with the blessing of vets.

In a few US states, Australia, and most European countries, the vets recognise equine dentistry as a profession, which they do not in Britain. (One could say, in fact, that many British vets do not want to rasp horses' teeth themselves – but neither do they want anyone else to rasp them!) In some countries the two professionals work alongside each other, with vets providing sedation when necessary, and the public willingly pay both practitioners for their services. We British are unwilling to do this, however, and our tardiness tempts the specialists to break the law by performing minor surgical operations, like removing wolf teeth. The short shrift which the dental specialists receive from the vets themselves only increases the temptation – and thus the animosity persists.

The situation is improving, however, for very recently a one-week training course in the basics of equine dentistry has been established in the UK, taught jointly by a vet and by a dentist who trained in America. It is modelled on the American training set up by the World Wide Association of Equine Dentistry, where two one-week courses (basic and advanced) teach the essentials of dentistry. Although these give a good theoretical background, they inevitably give very little practice in handling a rasp, and practical skill can only result from a long apprenticeship which offers hands-on experience with a wide variety of dental problems.

The most respected dentists actually teach veterinary students within the universities, where there have been preliminary discussions about setting up further training, leading to membership of an association. The vets and dental specialists will then have to decide how this will be regulated. Sadly, similar issues have blocked the establishment of a training in equine physiotherapy, for the vets and physiotherapists cannot agree on who should be teaching it! Many physiotherapists feel that they have walked an ethical and professional tightrope in their quest to gain the respect of vets, adopting a subservient attitude, and choosing their words with extreme care. For many veterinary surgeons seem unwilling to admit that they could ever be part of a two-way learning process. This is despite

Fig 1.1
See page 32.

the fact that they themselves are not specifically trained to recognise and treat the damage which so often results from wear and tear on the muscular system.

Back in the eighteenth century, farriers in Britain were also horse vets (albeit rather ignorant ones). This part of their practice declined after the first veterinary school opened in 1791, and it was finally made illegal in 1881. Perhaps vets too might reconsider whether the best interests of the horse-owning public are served by them alone, or through them enabling a team of suitably qualified and experienced practitioners to work together, pooling resources to look at the same problems from many different angles. (Since complementary practitioners must only work under veterinary referral and supervision, the law is currently only upheld if a *vet* convenes the team.) For whenever we have two descriptions of the same territory, we are infinitely better off than if we only have one. The overview gained from our changing perspectives gives us far more information than we could ever have if we were locked within the confines of one alone.

....

The medical and veterinary establishment often dismisses evidence of the success of complementary practitioners because it is anecdotal, and not the result of a statistical survey, carried out under strict conditions and written up in a medical journal. On a more personal note, I have even heard stories of people who went back to visit their consultant having cured themselves — by complementary means — of a cancer which had been diagnosed as terminal. They had hoped that the consultant would at least be pleased to see them, even if he could not manage to be openly curious about their story. But in each case they discovered that he was extremely disgruntled to find that they had violated the predictions of his map by managing to stay alive and well!

Complementary practitioners themselves are usually content to be judged on their merits, and rarely have the time, money, inclination, or expertise, to conduct statistical studies. Even if they did, it would still probably be extremely difficult to get them published, for medical journals only accept papers from researchers with a proven track record, who have previously had papers published in other journals. With no established on-the-map credentials, complementary practitioners have the disadvantage that they do not have the same ongoing respect as vets or doctors, and are often considered only as good or bad as their last treatment. So people will glorify them for their latest success, only to knock them off their pedestal the moment they appear to be failing. If the efforts of their own medical doctor were proving equally ineffective, they would undoubtedly bear with him longer. After all, he is the doctor.

As a map-maker myself, I have received a lot of flak over the years, as well as tremendous encouragement from those who have joined me in questioning our traditional map of riding. But it helps me to remember that the flak is always sent by those who would rather delete me than study the map, try it on for size, and see if it fits. It is the *professionals* within a given field who are the most guilty of this deletion; but even within the population at large, there is tremendous mistrust of anything so new that it lies off the edge of our established maps. A rather insightful chiropractor pointed out to me recently that if you discover that your lawyer or accountant is not doing his job well, you find yourself a better one. But if you discover that your *chiropractor* has not done his job well, you are likely to make a massive generalisation, and write off all chiropractors as charlatans.

....

Let me give you another experience of the pervasive effect that our established maps have on our vision and our thinking. Look at Fig. 1.1, the drawing on page 31. Then look at Fig. 1.2 on page 33, and describe the characteristics of the woman you see. How old would you say she is? What is she wearing? What kind of conversations do you imagine you might have with her? You probably see her as young, sophisticated, and attractive, someone who might be an actress or a model. But supposing I

Fig 1.2

tell you that I see her as an old woman, with a huge nose, and a rather sour expression. Would you tell me I must be crazy, would you be ready to have an argument with me, or would you be willing to try and see her as I see her?

We could even go to war over this, both of us convinced that we are 'right'. But we would become involved in what is, in effect, a 'map battle'. Consider this: when you go into a restaurant and read the menu, it is clear to you that the decision you make about what you will eat is based on a map. The restaurateur might tempt you with mouth-watering descriptions of his food, or with glossy pictures of full plates; but however clever or accurate these are, you would never make the mistake of eating the menu! However, when you operate from the misconception that your map of the world *is* the world, this is (metaphorically speaking) precisely what you do. It is done every day by individuals, institutions, and entire nations.

Look again at the drawing: can you see the old woman? If not, look at Fig. 1.3 on page 34, and then come back to this one. Can you see now that what you thought was a necklace could be seen as a mouth, that what you thought was a chin could be seen as a nose? So neither of us was wrong; our seeing was simply conditioned by our previous experience – even though it was little more than a glance. It is apparent from this that we can both see the same thing, disagree, and yet both be right. But given that the conditioning of a lifetime is hugely more pervasive than a short glance at a picture, it is not so surprising that history records rather few examples of such concord.

Fig 1.3

My whole aim in writing this chapter is to awaken in you the idea that your way of seeing the world is only your way of seeing the world – the map you have developed firstly through the inevitable genetic limitations of the human senses, and secondly through paying attention selectively. Added to this are the influence of your family and culture on the ways that you have deleted, distorted, and generalised as you received information from the territory out there. Yours is just *one* map out of an infinite number of possibilities – your own particular version of 'consensus reality'.

This book is intended to question and update our maps. It builds on a paradigm shift which has already begun in the horse world, and is my personal attempt to move it along. For this is a time of change, in which approaches once labelled 'alternative' are gradually becoming accepted, and so sought after that they could even become mainstream. The urge to look beyond our established practices and treatments began with a few: but it is becoming an unstoppable force backed by the many, who increasingly see the limitations of convention.

You will probably have heard and read little bits (and perhaps big bits) about some of the maps presented in this book. The most pervasive are the complementary approaches to the body, illness and medicine which are in some cases very new, and in others very old. Then there are refinements to the rather sketchy maps of dentistry, farriery and saddlery, which most of us work from. We will then explore maps which delineate the stresses and strains placed on the muscular and skeletal systems of the

'This is a time of change, in which approaches once labelled 'alternative' are gradually becoming accepted, and so sought after that they could even become mainstream.'

athletic horse, offering him the same care as is commonly given to human athletes. Finally, we will come back to the ethos of this chapter, questioning the assumptions which underlie our ways of handling and thinking about those 'dumb animals' we call horses. As you read about these maps, the belief systems held in your own established map will inevitably operate – but not so unquestioningly, I hope, as they would have done a few pages ago.

CHAPTER TWO

Body/Mind/Spirit – Challenging Our Accepted Notions

As CHILDREN IN school, on adult first-aid courses, or even as we learn how to care for our horses in sickness and in health, we are taught the traditional map of the body in its most basic form. As a result, most people have vague memories about muscles, tendons, ligaments and bones, even if they cannot clearly remember the function of each. These are the building blocks of our traditional Western view of the body, which developed alongside the industrial revolution, and Newton's understanding of the world. The parallel suggests that the body is a solid structure, behaving like some huge machine manipulated by the pulleys and levers which move its component parts through space.

The bones of the skeleton – as you undoubtedly once learned – form a rigid, supporting, moveable framework, which give shape and firmness to the body, and protect the organs within. Of itself, the skeleton has no power to move, but movement can take place at the joints where two or more bones come together. The body has several different kinds of joints, including the sutures between the bones in the skull, the cartilaginous joints between the vertebra of the spine, and the synovial joints in the limbs which allow much freer movement. These latter vary in type, and include the ball and socket arrangement which gives so much freedom to the human shoulder, and also to the human and equine hip joints. A hinge joint forms the human knee, and its equivalent, the horse's stifle (or 'back knee' as it is known to some), and other smaller more complex joints allow a pivoting or gliding motion.

In a synovial joint the ends of the bones are perfectly contoured to fit each other, and are covered with a very smooth substance called cartilage. But they do not actually touch, and the entire joint is encased in a capsule whose inner layer, the synovial membrane, secretes a viscous fluid rather like egg white (see Fig. 2.1). This lubricates the joint, and if the capsule is punctured and joint fluid is lost, it is time to start worrying. Joints are bound by ligaments which are more or less elastic: they stabilise the joint and limit its range of motion appropriately – it is these which get over-stretched and possibly torn when, for example, you go over on the side of

Fig. 2.1 A synovial joint.

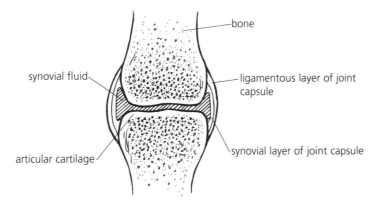

bone

synovial fluid

ligamentous layer of joint
capsule

articular cartilage

synovial layer of joint capsule

your ankle. Arthritic conditions in joints occur when the cartilage is damaged, or worn away. Cartilage cannot replace itself for it has no blood supply, but when it is damaged new bone will often grow, giving a roughened surface within the joint. When the ends of the bones touch each other in movement there will be pain, and the degenerative process can ultimately lead to the joint fusing, as sometimes happens when a bone spavin forms in the horse's hock.

Movement of the body is carried out by muscle, which is the flesh of the body, responsible for its contours and for one fifth of its weight. Muscles are workers which need to be well supplied with fuel, so they have an extremely good blood supply. The arteries bring oxygenated blood, and this reacts chemically with glycogen stored in the muscle (there as a result of digesting carbohydrates). This reaction creates the energy which fuels the muscle's contraction. If sufficient oxygen reaches the muscle it can work very efficiently; but shortage of oxygen leads to a build-up of lactic acid, causing muscle fatigue and stiffness the next day. The venous and lymphatic systems – which also need to be extremely efficient – carry away the waste products of muscular work, including carbon dioxide. This finally reaches the lungs and is exchanged for oxygen. Thus the rate and depth of our respiration, and also of our heart beat, are increased during effort in the attempt to get enough oxygen to the muscles and to remove waste products.

Muscles come in many different shapes and sizes. The abdominal wall and scalp are covered by flat, sheet-like muscles, but in the limbs they are mostly spindle shaped, having a thick belly of tissue which tapers away at either end forming an inelastic cord of fibrous tissue called a tendon. This attaches the muscle to bone. Where the muscle crosses a joint, its contraction causes the two bones to come closer together, and the joint closes (Fig. 2.2). Bones act as levers which are moved by the contraction

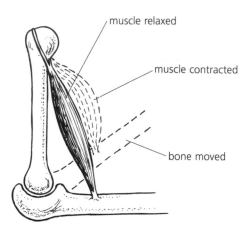

Fig. 2.2 The contraction of a muscle causes a joint to close.

of muscles: you can both see and feel this contraction, for as the muscle fibres shorten, the muscle concerned bulks out. Tendons are tremendously strong: it takes a very traumatic force to tear one away from its attachment to bone, or to damage its fibres – but mis-coordination due to muscle fatigue can sometimes be enough to make this happen. Tendons vary tremendously in length, with some of the longest, best known, and most frequently damaged being the flexor tendons that run down the back of the horse's cannon bone, from the knee and hock to below the fetlock.

Muscles themselves are made up of thousands of long thin fibres, each one enclosed in a fine sheath of connective tissue. Bundles of these are also bound together by connective tissue, and these bundles are bound together, forming the muscle belly itself, which is also enclosed in a sheath. Groups of muscles in various regions are enclosed in a common sheath known as the fascia. When you cut a muscle across its length, it looks rather like a coaxial cable, whose insulation-wrapped wires are gathered into insulation-wrapped bundles, all of which are wrapped in thicker insulation (see Fig. 2.3). The fascia occupies a far smaller proportion of the space involved than does the insulation between wires; the principle, however, is the same.

Fascia envelops just about everything in the body: it lines the thorax and the abdominal cavity which contain the organs. It covers the organs themselves, as well as every nerve, every blood vessel, and even the bones. If you could somehow dissolve everything in the body apart from this connective tissue, you could still discern all its parts, with the bones and organs left as holes in a delicate three-dimensional web of tissue.

Fascia is the whitish membrane that lies between the muscle and the skin on a chicken leg: in fact, if you go out and eat one, you can discover

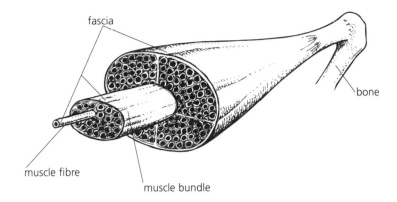

Fig. 2.3 The structure of a muscle, showing how fascia wraps its individual fibres, whilst also wrapping them into bundles, and wrapping those to form a muscle belly.

practically all you need to know about the structures I have been talking about! There is no substitute, however, for doing an actual dissection, and I would recommend any serious student of horse management to procure a horse's leg and take it apart. It is possible to do this armed with little more than a pair of rubber gloves, a few kitchen knives, and a sharp pair of scissors – and a good sized dustbin or trash can full of bleach will finally yield a set of bones in pristine condition. If the thought of this makes you squeamish, do not be put off. When you have recovered from the initial horror you are likely to be as fascinated as I was by the sheer beauty and intricacy of the structures in front of your eye. No amount of book learning can compare with the understanding gleaned from this experience.

....

Our very basic map here has mostly been concerned with the skeletal system and the muscular system. We have briefly mentioned the circulatory system, the nervous system, the digestive system, and the respiratory system – and you are probably extremely relieved (as I am) that we have not had to worry ourselves with the excretory system, the reproductive system, or the glandular system. If you were studying for a medical or veterinary degree, you would spend years learning about all of them in far more detail; the questions left unanswered by our simple map would be addressed, and many more questions would appear – including some that medical science is currently rethinking its answers to.

But however far you went along this road you would almost certainly still think about the body as a series of *systems*. You would eventually specialise in one of them, mapping it to the Nth degree – and perhaps adding to the many volumes of books and papers about each of them that fill the medical libraries. But in the process you would probably fall prey to the tunnel vision which inevitably goes hand in hand with such a reductionist approach. The closing in of your vision would be exacerbated by one of the fundamental difficulties of mapping: it is very hard to map something effectively unless you can freeze a moment in time and stop it from changing.

'Through the inheritance of Newtonian science we see the body as a machine – a system of gears, levers, pulleys and plates.'

Much of science has inherited its taste for rather static models from Isaac Newton, who regarded nature like some huge billiard game – a collection of solid objects that moved in straight lines and were propelled by fixed laws of motion. But to predict their path, speed and momentum, you have to stop the game and draw a map of it. This enables you to measure all the angles and distances involved, and then to apply formulas which yield information about the speed and trajectory of the objects. Through the inheritance of Newtonian science we see the body as a machine – a system of gears, levers, pulleys and plates – much more like a robot than a river.

Yet in its composition, the body is between 60 and 80 per cent water. We begin life as a single cell, the fertilised egg, which is – like all cells – basically a bag, enclosed by the outer membrane of the cell wall, and filled with water and swirling chemicals. It is generally accepted that the fully grown human body is composed of about fifty trillion cells (which is about ten thousand times the earth's present population count). Even the bones, which are the most solid components of the body, are filled with liquid marrow. The muscles, organs, nerves, and virtually every other part of the body are composed of fluid-filled sacs and semi-permeable membranes, which are continually crossed by flowing liquids. Only the circulatory system needs a pump – the heart – and in the ideal state the ordinary movement of breathing and living keeps all our juices flowing.

When we think of a muscle, we typically visualise it rather like a rubber band attached to two bones; but it is more viable to think of it as a fluid-filled sac which contracts and expands rather as a balloon changes shape under externally applied pressure. In the process it acquires and releases fluids across the walls of its membrane, exchanging them with the tissues around it. A fluid body which obeys the laws of fluid mechanics moves like flowing water – rippling like cornfields in a breeze, or like a cat stalking. Its laws are very different to those of solid mechanics: it is far more flexible and has many more possibilities than a ball game, or a system composed of pistons and pulleys.

A physical body which has this extra latitude is unfortunately not the norm. Perhaps this is the reason why we so much admire the skilled dancer, or the rider who can harmonise with the energy of a fluid and beautiful horse Perhaps they remind us of the fluidity which we have forgotten we have. In the course of aging most of us move less and less, becoming increasingly sedentary and confined. Not surprisingly, many of the diseases of aging are related to circulatory problems; for to function well both we – and our horses – are reliant on the passage of fluids, and this is stimulated by movement.

All of our cells, whether they appear 'en masse' as obviously liquid or apparently solid, are primarily water. Life, from its single-celled beginning, can be seen as a process of drying out – although by keeping ourselves fluid and mobile we can lessen the effects of aging. We go not from dust to dust, but from water to dust; beginning as 99 per cent water, we become, as adults, more than one third solid. It is as if we go from a plum to a prune, and finally, after death, all the body fluids evaporate, and our bodies desiccate.

Thus dissection views a *dehydrated* body, and makes it appear like a sculpture – non-functioning, with no movement, and no intelligence. Dissection is still an extremely useful tool: it revolutionised our understanding of the body in the Renaissance, and I strongly recommend that you do one. But realise that a huge amount of the knowledge in medical textbooks pertains not to life but to *death*: it has been discovered from autopsies, from the examination of tissue slides under microscopes, and from analysis of the body's by-products.

So it is not surprising that equine chiropractors and veterinary researchers argue about the validity of experiments which determine the amount of movement possible in a *dead* horse's spine. Recent research in the Netherlands has used very sophisticated strain gauges to measure the stress in the flexor tendons and suspensory ligament of live ponies during various phases of their stride. The results have conflicted with laboratory research using dead horses' legs, and shown that (within the limb at least) live joints and tendons work differently from dead ones. Undoubtedly, these results will give rise to debate; researchers will come up with new and different findings – and there will be continuing arguments between those who have a vested interest in the results.

....

....

'Realise that a huge amount of the knowledge in medical textbooks pertains not to life but to death.'

....

The mechanistic, Newtonian view of the body is incredibly outdated. Yet its inherent body/mind split – the idea of inert matter controlled by the smart technician inside your head – continues to permeate most people's thinking. The Chinese, however, have a very different philosophy, for they took a different route in creating their maps of the body. Instead of observing it from the *inside* they established their maps through incredibly astute observation from the *outside* – studying life instead of death. Whilst our maps date back about two hundred years, they have been collecting data for well over *two thousand*. Implicit in our everyday ways of describing the body lies the belief that it is fundamentally a solid object; implicit in theirs is the idea of fluidity, of energy flow, and vitality.

At any moment in life an infinite number of processes are being coordinated in our bodies: we breathe, eat, digest our food, fight off infections, talk, think, purify our blood of toxins, renew our cells, discard waste, ride our horses, and go about our business as if none of these were happening. Although our physiology may appear to operate in separate compartments – and it is convenient for medical science to think of them as such – they are all invisibly connected, and superbly orchestrated. In his wonderful book *Quantum Healing,* Deepak Chopra MD makes it clear that the intelligence of the body far outstrips that of Western medicine; for despite the sophistication of medical science, it cannot duplicate the healing powers of the body, and cannot coordinate them with anything like the same precision.

'Drugs lack the precision and the perfect timing of the body's in-built pharmacy, and the know-how of its intelligence.'

If, for instance, the mechanism of blood-clotting fails – as it does in haemophiliacs – a doctor can prescribe drugs that will indeed make blood clot. But they are temporary, artificial, and have numerous other functions too (which we term side-effects, attempting to imply that they are indeed secondary). Drugs lack the precision and the perfect timing of the body's in-built pharmacy, and the know-how of its intelligence: for example, when a red blood cell rushes to the site of a wound and begins to form a clot it knows exactly where to go and what to do when it gets there.

So, too, do the hormones, enzymes, and other biochemicals produced by our bodies, and for a drug to work (regardless of whether it was made in the laboratory or in the human body) it must in effect be a 'key' which fits precisely into the 'keyhole' present on the wall of the appropriate type of cell. These keyholes are made of complex molecular chains whose last links are open-ended. In the otherwise smooth wall of the cell it is as if they are 'sticky', and they alone are waiting for another molecule to come along and bind with them. But the drug must bind *only* with some precisely chosen receptor; and it is here that drugs made in the human body are far more discerning than those made in the laboratory.

The Newtonian view of the body was made to look very outdated in the 1970s, when a series of revolutionary discoveries showed that the neurological communication system of the body actually works *chemically* using molecules called neuro-peptides, and not *electrically* as was previously thought. It became clear that none of our emotions, desires, memories or dreams are confined to the brain itself; neither are they strictly mental – for no thought can exist without brain chemistry, and without its message being carried throughout the body.

Initially it was thought that there were just two neuro-peptides, one to activate a distant cell and one to slow its activity down. But it was soon discovered that there were many more, each with a different message. Our brains put our bodies to sleep with a chemical message, and if you remove some of the spinal fluid from a sleeping cat and inject it into the spinal column of a wide-awake cat, the latter will immediately fall asleep. Similarly, injecting the right 'wake up' signal into a sleeping cat will indeed wake it up. Camels have an exceptional tolerance to pain – they take no notice if they are beaten, and they happily chew on thorns. Researchers found their brain cells to contain a specific biochemical which, if injected into other animals, causes them to ignore pain too (and certain heavier horses seem to have it in good supply!). These are the now well-known endorphins and enkephalins – narcotics which are completely non-addictive, and two hundred times stronger than anything you can buy on the street. They block pain by fitting into a certain type of receptor site on the nerve cell, preventing the biochemicals which carry the message of pain from fitting in.

In the early 1980s, researchers naively thought they had developed a viable map of brain chemistry, but then their hopes were dashed rather suddenly. Much to their surprise, receptors for neuro-peptides were found on cells of the immune system which travel throughout the bloodstream. This means that the brain does not only use nerve cells to convey its signals, and it is not limited to the set pathways of the nervous system – it sends its messages throughout the body. So if you are having happy, sad, or excited thoughts, and you produce the neuro-peptides that go with them, you will, in effect, have happy, sad, or excited immune cells.

People who are depressed produce unusually high quantities of a neuro-transmitter called imipramine, and receptors for this are found not only on brain cells, but also on skin cells: so their skin gets depressed too. (I once had a stand-up argument with my veterinarian about whether my cat was depressed, and still maintain that I have seen both depressed cats and depressed horses – complete with their depressed skin and hair. It seems highly likely that they too are 'not feeling high' on imipramine.) Two specific chemicals were found in high quantities in the brains and adrenal glands of people who complain of feeling jittery all the time; but high concentrations of them were also found in blood platelets, implying that they had jittery blood cells as well! Looking beyond the nervous system and the immune system, researchers have since found the same neuro-peptides, and the receptors for them, in various organs, including the kidneys, intestines, stomach, and heart. These organs actually *produce* the same neuro-peptides found in the brain, which suggests that the whole of your body produces brain chemicals and can think.

'The whole of your body produces brain chemicals and can think.'

Given all this, it becomes difficult to maintain the illusion of the smart technician living inside your head. There now seems very little reason to keep body and mind apart, for it becomes blatantly clear that the body really is a three-dimensional print-out of our thoughts. Few of the changes in it are visible to the naked eye, but in subtle, biochemical ways it is changing in every moment. The discovery of neuro-peptides is perhaps medicine's most recent and important paradigm shift, and the neat medical division into systems may soon be outmoded, for we have (at the very least) brought together the brain, the nervous system, and the immune system. The field now known as psychoneuroimmunology is very new; yet it could, quite literally, be the herald of a new age in medicine.

....

In *Quantum Healing* Deepak Chopra talks through the physiology of the startle reflex, a complex internal event that takes place whenever you jump at a loud noise. The same changes occur when your horse suddenly leaps in the air at the sight of a hidden tiger, and you fall prey to the foetal crouch. Externally, you hold your breath, tip forward, grab on with your knees, curl up your toes, and clutch at the reins in terror. But what happens internally is a rather more complex – both for you and your horse. Dr Chopra describes it thus: 'The trigger for the event is a burst of adrenalin from your adrenal glands. Carried into the bloodstream, this adrenalin signals reactions from your heart, which starts to pump blood faster; from your blood vessels, which contract and force up your blood pressure; from your liver, which puts out extra fuel in the form of glucose; from your pancreas, which secretes insulin so that more glucose can be metabolised; and from your stomach and intestines, which immediately stop digesting food so that more energy can be shunted elsewhere.'

'All this activity, happening at a furious pace and with powerful effects everywhere in your body, is coordinated by the brain, which uses the pituitary gland to guide many of the hormonal signals just described, not to mention various other chemical signals that go racing down your neurons...'

'To make this whole reaction happen and then to make it go away again (for the body, unlike a man-made drug, knows how to reverse every one of these processes just as neatly as it began), the same key-in-the-lock mechanism is employed everywhere. It is all so deceptively simple, yet if you attempt to duplicate this event with a drug, the results are nowhere near as precise, orderly, and beautifully orchestrated. In fact, they are chaotic. Injecting adrenalin, insulin, or glucose separately into the body gives it a crude jolt. The chemicals immediately flood all the receptor sites without coordination from the brain. Instead of talking to the body, they assault it with single-minded insistence. Even though the chemical make-up of adrenalin is identical no matter where it is derived, the critical ingredient of intelligence must be present; otherwise the drug's action is a mockery of the real thing.'

Drugs act like counterfeit keys, and when they fit into the 'keyhole' of a particular type of cell, they either stop the body's natural messengers from fitting in – thus preventing the cell from working normally – or they mimic the chemicals which 'turn on' the cell. Acepromazine ('Ace' or ACP) is a tranquillising drug, commonly used to calm nervous horses, and it blocks dopamine, the neurotransmitter responsible for acute awareness. So the horse can still move normally whilst having an emotional 'edge' removed. But it also lowers blood pressure, and stimulates the release of prolactin, the reproductive hormone needed for a mare to let down milk. Its long-term use in stallions can lead to infertility.

Anti-inflammatory drugs like phenylbutazone (bute) interfere with a cell enzyme involved in the production of chemicals which generate a supersensitivity to pain. These chemicals are nature's way of stopping the horse from overusing some part of its body and compounding the damage. They also play a role in producing fevers, so the drug helps to reduce high temperatures; but the blocked chemicals have so many other beneficial functions that damage to the digestive tract and kidneys can accompany the long-term use of bute. In contrast to the highly sophisticated drugs which mimic the action of neuro-peptides, the success of antibiotics like penicillin lies in the fact that they only have to be aimed at the bloodstream. The limitation of any 'magic bullet' depends, at least in part, on how precisely it needs to hit its target.

'The limitation of any 'magic bullet' depends, at least in part, on how precisely it needs to hit its target.'

....

Just as you can never step into the same river twice, so you never *are* the same body twice. Your skin is new every month, and your stomach lining replaces itself every four days, with the surface layer of cells that are in contact with your food being replaced every five minutes. Liver and bone cells are replaced much more slowly, but atoms of all kinds pass through them in both directions, so that the liver is new every six weeks, and the skeleton every three months. Carbon, oxygen, hydrogen and nitrogen pass through us very quickly – none of these atoms that are in your body now were there a month ago – whilst other elements like calcium and iron are replaced much more slowly. To quote Deepak Chopra again, 'It is as if you lived in a building whose bricks were systematically taken out and replaced every year. If you keep the same blueprint, then it will still look like the same building. But it won't be the same in actuality. The human body also stands there looking much the same from day to day, but through the processes of respiration, digestion, elimination, and so forth, it is constantly and ever in exchange with the rest of the world.' It is as if the body is 'non-change being preserved in the midst of dynamic change.'

If we could map the body in every moment, and keep up with the incredibly intricate web of life, we would not be so tempted by the static, Newtonian view of it. In fact, the realisation that there is indeed so much change leaves us marvelling that so much 'non-change' is somehow preserved within it. But inside the body there is always a structure waiting for the next atoms to arrive, and it would appear that the *memory* which encodes this structure is more permanent than matter itself.

'An arthritic bony growth is not the same as the one which was X-rayed even a few months ago.'

If an addict is detoxified, and kept off alcohol or drugs for several years, all the old cells that were 'chemically addicted' (if indeed they were) are gone. Yet the *memory* of the addiction persists, and if you put him back into the context of his life as an addict, he is highly likely to become hooked. If a doctor discovers a malignant tumour by X-ray, and then X-rays the same tumour a year later, it is *not* the same tumour, for all of the atoms which were there a year ago have now been replaced. An arthritic bony growth is also *not* the same as the one which was X-rayed even a few months ago (and thus it may not be as immutable as it appears). What has persisted – as in the addict – is a *distorted cellular memory*, which has recreated the new growth again and again.

If we can find a way to influence *this*, we have found a far more sophisticated form of healing than any which addresses actual physical change, whether it is provided by drugs or by surgery. In fact, many pioneering workers in the field of complementary medicine would suggest that terminally ill people who have experienced spontaneous remissions have indeed succeeded in changing the blueprint or memory that their cells were simply conforming to. Mystical experiences and meditation are usually cited as the pathways to this change; but however it happens, medical science has had to admit that its effects are undeniable.

....

The experimental discovery of this energetic blueprint began in the 1940s with Harold Burr, a neuro-anatomist working at Yale University who studied the electrical energy fields surrounding living plants and animals. In his work with developing salamanders, he showed that their energy field was shaped roughly like the adult animal, with an electrical axis aligned with the brain and spinal cord. He then wanted to know when this axis formed, and discovered that it was already present in the unfertilised egg! In fact, the direction of this axis within the egg predicted exactly where the spinal cord would form. He also worked with the electrical fields that surrounded tiny seedlings, showing that the field was shaped like the *adult* plant, and not like the seedling itself. By measuring the energy field he could predict how strong the plant would become. Put together, these findings suggest that the electromagnetic field of an organism acts as a 'growth template', giving a blueprint which the physical form is destined to follow. Also in the 1940s a Russian researcher named Kirlian actually photographed the energy fields of living organisms positioned in an electrical field. This caused them to show spark discharges which he captured on a photographic plate, creating an image which has been called the 'Kirlian aura'. Many variables can affect the picture, and this has led medical researchers to dismiss the technique. But Kirlian and many others have shown that the discharge patterns surrounding the human fingertips change according to the health of the individual, and can even be used to predict the presence of cancer, cystic fibrosis and other diseases.

Although mainstream medicine has never embraced these findings, both medicine and physiotherapy use electromagnetic energy in diagnosis and treatment. Most people have heard of the electrocephalograph (EEG), which detects electrical currents within the brain, the electrocardiograph (ECG) which measures electrical currents in the heart, and lie detectors which measure the electrical potential of the skin. Even animals can be used as sophisticated 'measuring instruments', able to 'read' our energy fields. (Thus they know far more about us than we know about ourselves!) Some dogs are able to predict when their epileptic owners are about to have a fit, and dogs are now being trained to provide an early warning system for sufferers.

Electromagnetic radiation has also allowed us to see inside the body. It was X-rays which first enabled doctors to see its bony structure, and these have been followed by CT (computerised tomography) scanners, PET (positron-emission tomography) scanners, and MRI (magnetic resonance imaging), each able to yield more and more precise pictures of soft tissues as well as bones. But doctors are still looking – albeit in more detail – at the *biochemical abnormalities* which accompany disease, and not at the *energetic cause* of the disease.

Moving beyond diagnosis, one of the most profound uses of electrotherapy in treatment came about through pioneering research in Sweden. This suggested that electrotherapy can be used successfully in treating certain kinds of cancer, leading to tumour regression and even complete remission in a significant number of cases which were considered untreatable by other therapies. Bone fractures heal faster when placed in an externally applied electromagnetic field (some of the early research into this was done using fractures in horses). The most common use of electrical stimulation is in pain relief, with the TENS (transcutaneous electrical nerve stimulation) machine helping many women through childbirth.

All of this work has led some researchers to believe that there is a bioelectrical network in the body, whose functioning is affected by injury, infections and tumours. But if we want to look at the *energetic cause* of disease, we have to leave behind the thinking of Western medicine. In a strange blend of old and new, we find the experimental results of Burr, Kirlian and many others more in sympathy with ancient Chinese philosophy, with the work of Samuel Hahnemann (the eighteenth-century physician who discovered homoeopathy), and with physics and metaphysics.

....

Metaphysical thinkers have long recognised the existence of the body's energy field, needing only their subjective experience as justification. But the leading thinkers in 'new age' medicine have drawn on the work of Einstein and the principles of quantum mechanics to explain phenomena which we, as Newtonian thinkers, find hard to grasp. Einstein's famous equation $E=Mc^2$, proved that matter and energy are synonymous – two different expressions of the same universal substance. The conversion of matter into energy is an everyday occurrence (as well as the basis of the atom bomb), and physicists can watch energy being converted into matter in their experimental 'cloud chambers'.

This suggests that the physical matter of the body can also be viewed as energy, and there is, in fact, much experimental evidence to support the idea of matter-as-energy, and energy-as-matter, within and around the physical body. Early in this century, when experiments into the nature of light marked the birth of quantum mechanics, physicists were left struggling with an equivalent duality. For with only a small change in their experimental conditions they could *prove* that light was a wave, and then *prove* that it was a particle. Instead of adopting an either/or philosophy, they had to come to terms with the idea that it was *both* a wave *and* a particle (both energy *and* matter) depending on how they looked at it.

Richard Gerber MD, author of *Vibrational Medicine,* suggests that you think of the body as a specialised energy field, a packet of light that has been slowed down and 'frozen', giving it the appearance of solid matter – its wave-like properties hidden, except in certain experimental situations. Superimposed on the physical body is the energy field which scientists like Burr and Kirlian have measured. This is often known as the etheric body. But metaphysical thinkers believe that the human energy system does not end here – it continues with the 'higher energy bodies'. You can think of them like a piano keyboard: it is as if the etheric body vibrates at a frequency one octave up from the physical body. Above this are another five octaves, giving the *seven* octaves of vibration which are believed to make up the entire human energy field. Our instruments cannot currently detect these, but some physicists believe that fully solving Einstein's equations *predicts* their existence, incorporating the phenomena of the subtle energy bodies into the existing framework of physics.

....

Mystical experiences, however, are not the only way to influence the subtle layers of the body's blueprint, and (fortunately for our horses) these can be addressed directly by various forms of 'energy medicine'. Homoeopathy and acupuncture work on the interface between the etheric and the physical bodies; the Bach flower remedies and radionics influence the more subtle levels. (We will learn more about all of these forms of medicine in Chapter 10.) The Chinese theory for the way in which information passes from the etheric octave to the physical stems from the oldest medical textbook in existence, the *Huang Ti Nei Jing Su Wen* or *Yellow Emperor's Classic of Internal Medicine* (whose exact publication date is unknown). Acupuncture is one of the oldest treatment systems in the world: it began to evolve up to four thousand years ago in China, although it may have existed in India as long as seven thousand years ago. The Chinese view the acupuncture meridian system as the conduit of life energy or Qi, which enters the physical body from the etheric via the acupuncture points, making its way along meridians to the internal organs.

In the early 1970s when President Nixon visited China and opened up its philosophies to the West, doctors were forced to admit that acupuncture is not just 'mumbo jumbo', for they observed its use with pain disorders, and saw it producing anaesthesia in surgery. But initially the acupuncture meridians could not be found under the microscope. This put them outside the realm of Newtonian medicine, and made them the subject of ridicule. Thus Western minds were faced with a difficult dilemma.

The TENS machine was already known to have much greater pain-relieving effects when the electrodes were placed on specific areas of the skin. It was subsequently realised that these are classical acupuncture points, and that stimulating them with needles in the traditional way also produced pain relief. Research has now proved the existence of the acupuncture points, showing that their electrical resistance is nearly *ten times* less than elsewhere, giving them much greater conductivity than the surrounding skin. Most of the research into acupuncture in the Western world has centred on the relief of pain (for only this use of it seemed to make any scientific sense) and it has shown that at least part of its pain-relieving mechanism lies in the release of the now familiar endorphins within the central nervous system.

However, research conducted in Korea during the 1960s focused on the meridians themselves. Early experiments on rabbits showed that a radioactive isotope injected into an acupuncture point migrated through the body following the classic acupuncture meridian system, with negligible levels of the isotope being found in the surrounding tissue. Later work on human subjects showed that a radioactive substance injected into an acupuncture point could travel a distance of 1 foot/30cm along traditional Chinese acupuncture meridians in four to six minutes. Injecting the isotope into random parts of the skin, or into veins and lymph vessels, did not produce any similar results.

Microdissection techniques finally showed the meridians to exist in the body as very fine duct-like tubules. (Although Western thinkers commonly like to equate them to the nerve pathways, they exist as a completely separate system.) Repeated experiments showed that when the liver meridian of a frog was severed, the liver cells degenerated seriously within three days. On humans, an acupuncture needle inserted into the point Stomach 36 will cause the stomach to secrete digestive juices, and will make the intestines increase their peristaltic movement. Inserting a needle into the skin a short distance from the acupuncture point produces no such response.

'The meridian system may influence the migration of cells as they develop.'

Further studies focused on discovering when a developing embryo formed the meridians, and in the chick, this was found to be within *fifteen hours* of conception, before the formation of the organs. These findings, along with Harold Burr's studies of the electrical fields of developing salamanders, suggest that the meridian system may influence the migration of cells as they develop into the internal organs. So research into the Chinese philosophies of health support the idea that growth and development may be guided by the body's energetic template and its 'cellular memory'. Thus disease may begin as an energetic dysfunction in the 'higher energy bodies', then becoming a distortion in the etheric body (as observed in the Kirlian photographs). It next becomes an imbalance in the energy flow within the acupuncture meridians – and only then does it finally manifest as dysfunction in the physical body.

....

Homoeopathy is another technique which treats the 'energy body'. It is a clear example of a 'vibrational medicine', for homoeopathic remedies are so dilute that in many cases not a single molecule remains of the substance they have been made from! Furthermore, the more dilute they are, the stronger they are in their action. This makes it easy for conventional

Newtonian thinkers to dismiss homoeopathy completely, yet its effectiveness has been proved in many studies. Double-blind studies have shown homoeopathy to be twice as effective as placebos in treating influenza in people; and people with allergies respond better to homoeopathic treatment than they do to orthodox treatment.

Homoeopaths believe that 'the energy signature' of the original substance remains throughout its dilutions, and that a good homoeopathic physician matches the energetic frequency of his remedy with the frequency of the patient's illness, thereby promoting healing. Before you laugh at the simplicity of their thinking, realise that it is supported by scientific enquiry: homoeopathic substances have been shown to give off measurable electromagnetic signals, and a study using magnetic resonance imaging showed distinctive readings of subatomic activity in twenty-three different homoeopathic remedies. Placebos, however, showed no such activity.

The 'vibrational signature' of the remedy is stored in water. This also constitutes 99 per cent of the molecules which make up the human body, and experiments have shown that water can be 'charged' with a particular subtle energy, and can then store that energy. Some of the most interesting work on this, performed in the 1960s at McGill University in Montreal, was originally designed to show whether healers evoked any real energetic change in their patients, or whether their effects might be regarded as 'faith healing'. The 'patients' were barley seeds, which were to be germinated in salty water (known as a growth retardant) before being grown in incubators. Prior to germinating the seeds, some of the containers of salt water were treated by healers, and the seeds were subsequently placed in the containers by people who did not know which ones had been treated.

In the two groups, the percentage of germinated seed was calculated and compared statistically. The results showed that more of the seeds germinated in the healer-treated water sprouted. After several weeks of growth the plants were again compared for height, weight, leaf size, and chlorophyll content. Those germinated in the healer-treated water were of greater height and contained more chlorophyll. Interestingly, other seedlings germinated in salt water which had been held by psychiatric patients had their growth rate *suppressed* compared to the control group.

Interestingly, treating water with magnets also led to enhanced growth rates in the seedlings. Other experiments have also suggested that the forces emanating from healers are magnetic in nature, for both healers and high-intensity magnetic fields have been shown to accelerate the reaction rates of enzymes, and to repair damaged enzymes. Healers can both see and touch the 'energetic blueprint', adjusting it so that the cells of the physical body no longer have to conform to a distorted template. So in

'Experiments have suggested that the forces emanating from healers are magnetic in nature.'

each of these cases, as well as in homoeopathy, we have a curative medicine which does not contain any physical molecules of a drug.

....

Within the human energy field *each part contains information about the whole*. This is an example of the holographic principle. Many people have seen a three-dimensional hologram, which forms a bewitchingly life-like image. If you took the negative of an ordinary photograph and cut away one corner, it would only show a small proportion of the total picture. But if you did this with the photographic plate of a hologram (and viewed it with the laser light which was also used in producing it), you would see *a smaller, hazier version of the complete image*.

One also sees the same phenomena with DNA, the chemical mastermind of the body, which is present in the nuclei of all of our cells except the red blood cells. DNA is the source of all the proteins that repair cells and heal our body, and also of the neuro-peptides. But DNA itself is made up of essentially the same building blocks as the proteins and neuro-transmitters it manufactures and regulates. As Deepak Chopra says, 'the human body is nothing more than variants of DNA built by DNA.' This remarkable, and extraordinarily complex molecule has encoded in it all the information necessary to create and sustain human (or equine) life. When the fertilised egg first splits into two cells, DNA begins the process of reproducing itself to form all the body's cells, and all its inherent capabilities. The DNA in each body cell *contains all the information needed to produce an identical clone of that individual*, and DNA is the most stable chemical in the body – hence our ability to inherit and pass on genetic traits.

The holographic principle, whether applied to energy fields or DNA, makes it seem less outrageous that radionics practitioners use a 'witness' – say, a hair from a horse's mane – to determine the energetic state of the whole body-mind-energy system. If we extend the holographic principle beyond the energy field of each individual, we can even conceive of the *holographic universe*, in which each part (including us) contains information about the whole. Again, physicists endorse this idea, with 'Bell's theorem' proving that there is no such thing as 'local reality'. It shows that a change at one end of the universe will have a corresponding change at the other end, with all of the necessary information getting there faster than the speed of light. Thus it provides a rationale for human intuition and for extra-sensory perception.

Mystics insist that in the higher realms of energy, we are all inter-connected. However far-fetched this seems, it is undeniable that animals demonstrate this connectedness more easily than we do. One of the most dramatic examples has become known as 'The Hundredth Monkey

Principle'. Lyall Watson, author of the book *Lifetide: The Biology of Consciousness,* watched a group of island-dwelling monkeys learn how to wash yams in sea water before eating them. Very soon, other monkeys living on other islands had also leant to wash their yams, even though they could not communicate with the first group by 'normal' means.

In arriving at the holographic universe, we have travelled a very, very long way from our original Newtonian map of the body – the bones, muscles and tendons which constitute the levers and pulleys which are controlled by the smart technician inside your head. This simplistic view of the body is made much less tenable by the discovery of neuro-peptides, and of the energy fields which surround and permeate it, pre-dating the body, and forming the energetic blueprint that it conforms to. The discoveries of quantum mechanics also make both the universe and the body seem much less solid; but it is when we can *move easily between maps* that we can deal with many different situations in the most appropriate way. So the next chapter will see us safely back in our everyday world, looking at horse's teeth – which are best viewed from a good, solid Newtonian viewpoint. But later we will look at issues where the more esoteric treatments can be viable alternatives to their Newtonian counterparts.

Inevitably – and perhaps ironically – it is medics and vets who have the biggest investment in the Newtonian map. Often they forget that the Newtonian, mechanistic map of the body is only a *map;* moreover, it is a map based on concepts which are over two hundred years old. To the human eye and the microscope it is extremely convincing – but, as physicists have been forced to admit, our observations are determined by how we look. To act as if the Newtonian map is *reality* limits us hugely, and makes us 'Newtonian thinkers'. We make the mistake of 'eating the menu'.

CHAPTER THREE

Equine Dentistry

MOST HORSE OWNERS are aware that they should have their horse's teeth rasped at least once a year, but few realise what an important and specialised job this is, and just how frequently it should be done. Many top competition horses have their teeth rasped every three months, for the cost and inconvenience of this is minimal compared to the expense and trauma of travelling them across the world only to find that their performance is marred by a dental problem. Some top-class dressage riders insist that three-monthly treatments make a significant difference to their horse's performance – and if all horses were done every six to nine months they would be spared much anguish. But all too often we leave the horse to his fate – until the vet has to come for something else, or until the horse makes his discomfort so apparent that we are finally shamed into action.

Like us, the horse has incisor teeth at the front of his mouth which cut his food. Since they meet each other directly, they are much more effective cutters than ours are. The horse does not have the ability to advance and retract the lower jaw as we do – so although our normal resting position is, in effect, parrot-mouthed, we can advance our lower jaw to bite to bite into an apple. (Munching on fields of grass, however, would be a far more difficult problem!) Both humans and horses also have cheek teeth, the premolars and molars which lie further back in the jaw and have the function of grinding food. In the space between the horse's incisors and molars, stallions, geldings and some mares have a single tooth called the canine tooth or tush; but there is still plenty of space left for the bit to lie on the bars of the mouth – the flesh which covers the lower jaw. Although a number of factors may make bitting uncomfortable for the horse, nature's design at least makes it possible; for if the horse could hold the bit between continuous rows of teeth he could brace his neck against the rider, and would become impossible to ride.

Human molars, as you can confirm by feeling yours with your tongue, are indented, but the horse's have a flatter surface than ours do. Nature has adapted them superbly for their task, and the large grinding surfaces, or 'tables', are covered by a complicated maze-like pattern of enamel, with small indentations in the dentine which lies between the lines. Also like us, the horse's top jaw is wider than the bottom jaw, so the outside edges of the top teeth and the inside edges of the bottom teeth do not cover each other. Like us – and all mammals – the horse has both milk teeth and permanent teeth. The change from one to the other can bring its problems, and few owners appreciate the extent of these, or the effects they can have on the horse's early ridden work.

The biggest difference between human and equine teeth is that ours never wear away. In contrast, both the horse's incisor and molar teeth are continually worn down by the friction created in biting and grinding – which, in the ideal state, he does for about sixteen hours a day. So to compensate for this, and to ensure that the surfaces of the teeth continue to meet each other, the teeth are gradually pushed out of their sockets within the jaw bones. As this happens, the sockets fill with bone.

Once the adult permanent tooth has come fully into wear, the visible portion, known as the clinical crown of the tooth, begins to be worn away. As nature compensates for its loss the reserve crown or neck of the tooth becomes exposed. Originally this was encased within the jaw, along with the root of the tooth. But if the horse reaches the ripe old age of about thirty-five, the root itself will become exposed and brought into wear. An unworn, permanent incisor tooth has its maximum length in a five-year-old horse, and will measure about 7cm/2.75in. A permanent molar will measure about 8cm/3.1in. But if we extracted the teeth from the jaw of a very old horse, they would measure only about 3cm/1.1in., for all that remains is the bottom part of the root, and much of this is now exposed. (See Fig. 3.1.)

As the incisor teeth wear away and are pushed out from the jaw their shape changes, with the biting surface of the tooth becoming less rectangular and more triangular. In a very old horse it becomes circular, and as the horse ages the teeth begin to protrude forward more, meeting at a more acute angle. (This reflects the shape you see if you pull the horse's lips apart and expose the gums; for the neck of the tooth which is now exposed was once lying within them and following their contour.) The markings on the table of each tooth change too, and taken together these changes create differences which allow us to age the horse – albeit rather inexactly.

As the permanent molars wear away their shape alters much less than the incisors. But their gradual emergence is accompanied by the almost continual movement of the bottom jaw in chewing, and this is the most significant factor. For since the teeth do not meet each other directly, the movement of chewing creates sharp edges on the outside of the top teeth and the inside of the lower teeth.

'The biggest difference between human and equine teeth is that ours never wear away.'

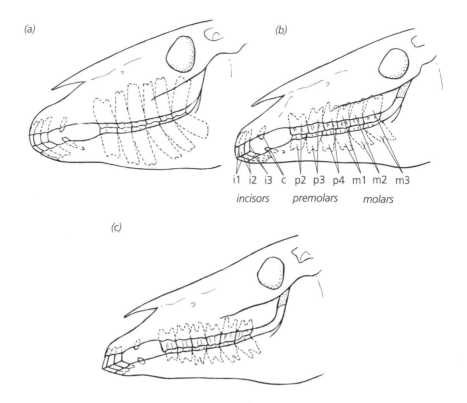

(a)

(b)

i1 i2 i3 c p2 p3 p4 m1 m2 m3

incisors   premolars   molars

(c)

Fig 3.1 The horse's upper and lower jaw seen from the side, showing both the visible portion of the teeth, and the part which is encased in the jaw: (a) on a five-year-old horse (b) on a ten-year-old horse (c) on an eighteen-year-old horse

'Young horses should see an equine dental specialist before they are ever ridden.'

Whilst all horses need regular dental care, it is of course, young and old horses who are most likely to need treatment which goes beyond a routine rasping of the sharp edges on the molar teeth, and it is unfortunate that the young horse is losing his milk teeth and gaining his permanent ones at the same time as he is doing his early work in a bridle. Young horses should see an equine dental specialist before they are ever ridden, which means that racehorses need treatment at two, and riding horses at three – although they can be accustomed to the feel of the rasp when they are even younger. Most people are aware that the horse loses the central and lateral incisor milk teeth at two and a half and three and a half respectively, so by the time he is four he has those permanent incisors in wear (but still has his corner milk teeth). The corner teeth erupt when he is four and a half, and are fully in wear at five. These changes allow us to age him more accurately at this time of his life than we ever can again, but dramatic as they are, they rarely cause him as much problem as the equivalent changes which take place in the molar teeth.

Three cheek teeth are present when the foal is born: these are temporary premolars. The first permanent molar erupts *behind* them at about one and a half years old, and over the next six months the grinding surface reaches their level. The next one back appears at two and a half, and after this the three temporary premolars are replaced by permanent ones. At three and a half the final molar erupts right at the back of the jaw. Nature has been extremely clever here, for this sequence allows additional cheek teeth to be added as the horse's jaw elongates with age, and it ensures a fairly evenly distributed rate of wear.

Horses lose their temporary premolars in a way very similar to humans. The adult tooth lies in the jaw directly beneath the temporary one, and as it begins to emerge, the root of the temporary tooth is reabsorbed. This shortens the tooth until it becomes a 'dental cap' which covers the grinding surface of the adult tooth when it erupts. These caps should then fall off: but if they do not, they meet with their opposite premolar, stopping it from growing as it should. So instead of growing upwards, the teeth in the lower jaw begin to protrude *downwards*, and in consequence three-year-old horses often have a bumpy appearance to the line of the lower jaw bone. This signifies that they are in desperate need of treatment.

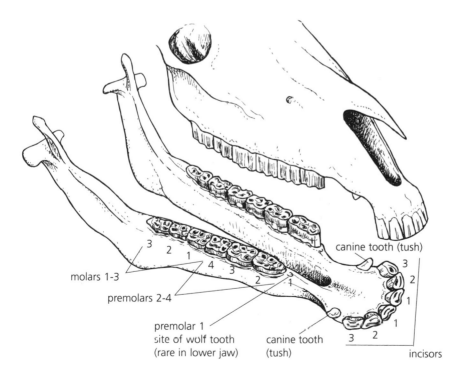

Fig. 3.2 The lower and upper jaw of an eight-year old horse, showing the pattern on the tables of the molar teeth.

Equine dental specialists sometimes find caps still present in *six-year-old horses*, by which time they have done tremendous damage. When the caps are removed (very often the dentist can pull them off with his hand) the tooth bleeds, for within the new tooth was a membranous sac which then bursts. It dries up very quickly, and the bumps in the lower jaw also disappear in time.

Anatomists number the horse's premolars not as one, two and three as one might expect, but as two, three and four. Tooth number one is the ubiquitous wolf tooth, commonly found lying in front of the premolars in the upper jaw and very occasionally in the lower jaw too. Equine dental specialists often use a different system, dividing the mouth into quadrants, as shown in Fig. 3.5 (page 61). Then they count the teeth in each jaw beginning with the central incisor as number one, and ending with the back molar as number eleven. This makes the canine tooth number four, and the wolf tooth number five.

Wolf teeth are the remains of teeth which were well developed in the ancestors of the horse who lived during the Eocene period. Occasionally a wolf tooth is found which resembles the shape of the premolars, albeit much smaller. But more often they are tubercular, and the variations in size and shape between different horses are tremendous. Wolf teeth appear at five or six months, but before eighteen months they are not developed enough to make removal easy. The tooth is sometimes shed at two and half

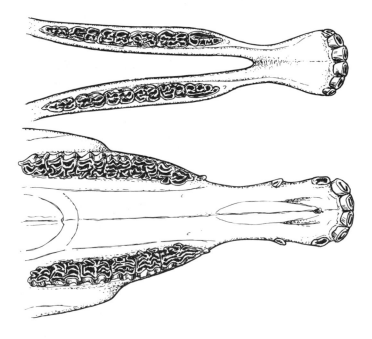

Fig. 3.3 Shows the upper and lower jaws of a four-and-a-half-year-old horse.

years old along with the premolar behind it, but often it remains. A wolf tooth in the lower jaw interferes with the bit far more than one in the upper jaw, where it may not in fact cause a problem. Theoretically wolf teeth should always have been removed by the time the horse begins work, but they are missed surprisingly often. One friend of mine recently took her ten-year-old quality horse to an equine dental specialist who discovered a wolf tooth in his lower jaw. The horse had changed hands at least twice: this means that the wolf tooth had remained undiscovered in two vettings prior to purchase, as well as in routine dental treatment. This becomes even more amazing when you consider that it was still causing difficulties in the horse's ridden work which should have alerted everyone to its presence.

Wolf teeth are usually removed with the use of a spray-on local anaesthetic, and an 'elevator', a tool with a cylindrical head which encases the tooth, and can gradually be worked right up around its root, ensuring that this is removed too. Down-market horse dealers have been renowned for attempting this job without the proper tools, and this can create really insidious problems. For if part of the root is left behind there is little visible evidence. But think of the kind of pain which would accompany pressure from the bit near the root of a tooth.

'Think of the kind of pain which would accompany pressure from the bit near the root of a tooth.'

In the space between the incisor and premolar teeth lie the canine teeth or tushes, which are the same shape as our eye teeth. But they are usually only present in male horses, although females may have small rudimentary ones. The tushes do not develop until the horse is three, and they are fully grown at four and a half to five – so there is no temporary tush. The top tooth is further back than the bottom one, so they do not contact each other, and are not worn away by friction. Thus they do not continue to emerge from their socket. They rarely cause any problem, although older horses many have a build up of tartar around the tooth, which can be removed using a dental tool.

The biggest danger with the tush is that it might get caught up in something. Because of this, and because the canine teeth leave so little room for the tongue, some dentists clip them to about half of their original length, and then smooth them off. This also helps to stop the rider from banging the bit against them as she removes the bridle – an experience not relished by horses. One of the most common dental emergencies is the horse who has caught a tush in the clip of a lead rope or in a link of a chain that has been left hanging in the stable. Removing the tooth is difficult enough since 60–70 per cent of it lies within the jaw. But removing the chips of bone that have become dislodged with it is an extremely difficult task, and any free floating pieces that are left behind could cause the horse a lot of pain.

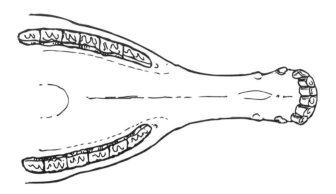

Fig. 3.4 A jaw with a more convex shape bulges out against the cheeks and makes them more vulnerable to damage.

'Only an idiot would put his hand in a horse's mouth without using a gag to hold it open.'

The horse's molars reach far back into his mouth towards the point where the lower jaw hinges. The further back they are, the closer they are to the sides of the mouth, and the more tightly the flesh of the cheek is stretched over them. (We humans have far looser, more mobile cheeks than horses do.) Thoroughbreds tend to suffer from the effects of sharp teeth more than warmbloods because the skin of their cheek is pulled even more tightly over the jaw. A horse will also be more prone to damage to the flesh on the inside of the mouth if the shape of the jaw is more convex, making the upper teeth curve out against the skin. (See Fig. 3.4.)

As a horse owner, you can really only assess the state of the first two premolars; but a cursory glance at these may well not reveal the extent of the sharp edges on the *back* molars, and the damage to the sides of the mouth that these are inflicting. (In other words, your investigation may only provide you with a false sense of security.) The safest way to examine the premolars is to hold the jaws shut by encasing them with both hands, and to slip the thumb of the hand which lies on the horse's nose into the side of his mouth. As you feel back from the corners of the lips, you can run your thumb along the bottom outer edge of the upper teeth and feel how sharp they are. (But beware – they could be like razors.) Pulling the horse's tongue out to the side, as is often done, can have terrible consequences, for the horse's tongue is attached differently to ours. If its connection to the inner ear is damaged, the horse can develop bizarre symptoms. Also, once the tongue is hyperextended the horse may not be able to retract it again – and a continually lolling tongue will reduce his value drastically. One of the least consequential dangers of pulling the tongue out to one side is that it may well be lacerated if the teeth are sharp – and it needs only a small mishap for you to emerge with a squashed finger. In fact, many dental specialists insist that only an idiot would put his hand in a horse's mouth without using a gag to hold it open. It is clear

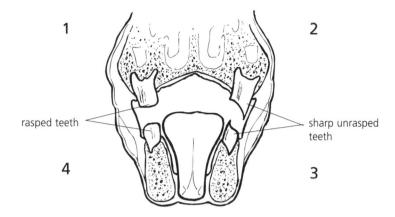

1

2

rasped teeth

sharp unrasped
teeth

4

3

Fig. 3.5 A cross-section of the jaw at the level of the first molar (i.e. the fourth tooth back from the bars). The teeth on the left of the diagram have been rasped. If we are looking straight at the horse's nose the quadrants (see page 58) would be numbered as shown.

that fools rush in where the specialists fear to tread.

Traditionally, textbooks tell us that sharp edges on the horse's molar teeth will lead to 'quidding', where food is mixed with saliva, partially chewed and rolled about in the mouth, until some of it is swallowed and some allowed to drop out into the manger. In this process wads of food may accumulate in the horse's mouth, held between the molars and the inside of the cheek. The biggest danger of this, we are told, is that food which has not been properly masticated cannot be well digested, for it is not broken up well enough for saliva and the digestive juices to act on it effectively. More rarely mentioned – and perhaps equally debilitating – is the pain which accompanies the process of eating.

Often, the first test which the dentist uses to assess the state of the teeth is to hold the horse's mouth shut and attempt to move the bottom jaw sideways across the top jaw in both directions. It should move quite easily, emitting the characteristic sound of tooth grinding against tooth; if it does not (or does not in one direction) he knows that sharp edges on the teeth are preventing this side-to-side movement.(See Fig. 3.5.) So the horse is restricted to *pounding* (rather than grinding) his food. To do this, he must keep opening his mouth, and hence food drops out. Another possibility is that the incisor teeth are so long that the molars do not meet – as yours will not if you put your incisors together. This then makes it impossible or extremely painful for the horse to close his mouth at all. Then even pounding his food becomes difficult.

Horses, however, are extremely inventive, and in this case they try to eat by taking in huge mouthfuls of food which fill in the gap, and/or by tipping their head to get all the food to one side of the mouth. The jaw muscles then work extremely hard in their attempt to bring the teeth together. This is turn stresses the temporomandibular joint (TMJ or jaw joint), which can only stay healthy if the molars meet correctly. So chiropractors who attempt to adjust the joint then find themselves doing so repeatedly – for they are addressing the symptom and not the cause.

The horse with sharp edges to the teeth will attempt to avoid the pain of cutting the inside of their mouth by stuffing their 'pouches' – small though they are – like a hamster. So the food (usually hay) which accumulates between the molars and the cheeks is put there by design not by default. 'You wouldn't believe what I've pulled out from there,' says dental specialist Chris Morris. 'Wads and wads of the stuff…'. As you can imagine, it soon becomes extremely unsavoury! Where Chris has expected to find two long teeth at the back of the jaw (this is common in an overshot jaw, which we will discuss later), he has at times found only *one* very long tooth, with its partner on the opposite side broken off. This leads him to think that horses will attempt to perform their own dentistry, and to break off the long tooth by chewing on a pebble. They also grind their teeth against earth, but have no really effective way of mitigating the effects of wear.

Many domestic horses look quite healthy at twenty or even twenty-five years old, and reach thirty, or even more. But in the wild, horses rarely live beyond sixteen. Equine dental specialist Bob Livock suggests that the difference lies in their teeth – basic and inadequate though our dental care usually is. For the wild horse will finally go beyond quidding: he will stop eating, and in effect he will starve himself to death. His loss of condition – were anyone to document it – would probably just be attributed to old age; but the question of old age must always be: 'Which of the body's systems wears out first?' The pattern of wear on the molar teeth and their resulting sharp edges is a built-in design fault: it has even been suggested that it is nature's own culling device – a way of keeping the herd down to a manageable size even in the absence of predators.

....

Textbooks which emphasise the dangers of quidding tempt us to think, 'My horse does not quid, he does not seem to eat particularly slowly, and when I ride he takes a fairly even rein contact, so he must be OK.' I personally have never seen a horse quid, and from the contact I have had with equine dental specialists, I am now convinced that the effects of sharp teeth can cause our horses significant distress without there being obvious symptoms either in their way of going or in their condition.

By telling us only about one of the most extreme symptoms of dental pain that a horse can show, our textbooks do not really bring home the point that the horse with sharp edges to his teeth may appear to the average owner to be in good shape, but he will have lacerations and ulcers on the inside of his mouth which are continually reopened as he eats. Inevitably these will not heal up until the teeth are rasped effectively. The tongue is likely to be cut as well, the culprit now being sharp edges on the insides of the bottom molars. But the horse's cheeks are the most vulnerable part, and if you have ever bitten the inside of your mouth (with your not-sharp molars, your more out-of-the-way cheek, and your tendency to eat for less than one hour a day) you will know how unpleasant it is. You will also know how the resulting swelling makes it far more likely that you will do so again. Perhaps my point is best made by telling you that dental specialists have been known to describe the state of a horse's cheeks by comparing them to 'raw hamburgers'.

Open wounds which never get to heal have other side-effects over and above their effect on mastication and digestion. For they are a ready site for low-grade bacterial infections, which enter the bloodstream. Elderly horses with Cushing's disease often succumb to infections in one part of the body after another, and the cycle continues until the teeth and mouth have been attended to. When an abscess forms under a tooth, British dental specialist Bob Livock believes that it is usually the result of infection being carried there by the bloodstream, and finding a place to abscess. This often results in the tooth being removed – even though it is actually healthy. Bob tells me that he has saved many a tooth from this fate, simply by getting right to the source of the problem. For this acute situation has only arisen because sharp edges on the horse's teeth and damage to his mouth have previously gone undiagnosed. Bob eradicates the problem simply by discovering these sore places and rasping the teeth – treating the underlying *cause* and not just the *symptom*. He also advises the use of a herbal remedy which boosts the horse's immune system whilst the mouth and the abscess heal themselves.

The fact that we cannot easily *see* the lacerations and ulcers that lie deep within a horse's mouth does not mean they do not exist, and although ignorance may be bliss for us, it most certainly is not for the horse. It is appalling that the damage which results from wear on the horse's teeth so often goes unnoticed; and I am sure that if the average owner could easily see the state of her horse's cheeks at the back of his mouth, she would be far more motivated to do something about it. We, the lay public, can perhaps be forgiven for our sins – especially as our textbooks are, I think, misleading. But the unfortunate fact is that this state of affairs is often self-perpetuating; for it is all too common for the professional who rasps the teeth *not to reach right to the back of the mouth*, so that he misses it too. Visiting an abattoir and looking at the state of the teeth of horses who have, in theory, had dental care is – I am told – an enlightening as well as sobering experience.

'The horse with sharp edges to his teeth may appear to the average owner to be in good shape, but he will have lacerations and ulcers on the inside of his mouth which are continually reopened as he eats.'

'The fact that we cannot easily see the lacerations and ulcers that lie deep within a horse's mouth does not mean they do not exist.'

Given that horses usually manage to eat somehow, we may only suspect a dental problem through our ridden work – especially in these days of manufactured combined feeds, which are often more easily chewed than grains. At the very least, pain on one side of the mouth can cause the horse to tilt his muzzle, or to take a stronger contact on one rein. The horse's contortions can become profound enough to affect his whole body, eventually creating the gait irregularities which necessitate treatment from a physiotherapist or chiropractor: but this will cause only

Fig. 3.6

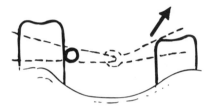

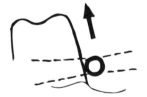

(a) The bit rests against a long bottom premolar on one side of the jaw, whilst it slips past the same tooth and into the corners of the lips on the other side. This horse will show a very uneven rein contact.

(b) The front edge of the bottom premolar slopes forward from the gum to the table, keeping the bit against the bars of the mouth.

(c) The front edge of the bottom premolar slopes backward from the gum to the table, so that the bit slides upwards towards the roof of the mouth.

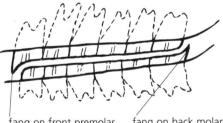

fang on front premolar   fang on back molar

(d) The overshot jaw results in a long portion of tooth on the top of the front premolar and the bottom back molar, which can extend to the opposite jaw and be extremely painful.

(e) The shape of the 'bit seat'.

temporary relief if the underlying cause is not addressed. Hence many bodyworkers become good at assessing the state of a horse's teeth and referring him on if they feel that only dental work will reach the root of the problem.

So if you keep having to take your horse back to the chiropractor, suspect his teeth (and also his feet), and be aware that the interplay of factors is so complex that each case can be extremely idiosyncratic. Some equine dental specialists (like some astute professional riders) have stables full of horses they acquired cheaply because they had the reputation for being 'rogues' – and it is quite common for a horse to suddenly rear or become a head-shaker immediately after the owner acquires a new noseband. By clamping the jaw tightly shut this forces sharp teeth against the flesh. However, the effects of dental pain can be much less extreme, and can account for many everyday forms of crookedness as well as some rather more strange forms of evasion. I remember one four-year-old horse who was brought to one of my courses, whose contorted way of going convinced me (both from watching and riding him) that he needed chiropractic treatment. However, I was wrong – the chiropractor gave him a clean bill of health, and the day after his teeth were rasped he was a very different ride: we caught him in time.

The shape of the first premolars (as well as the presence of wolf teeth) is often the critical piece in establishing dental-based evasions. It is not uncommon for the bottom premolar to be much longer on one side of the jaw than it is on the other; the bit can then sit against this long tooth, whilst it slips *past* the tooth and into the corners of the lips on the other side. (See Fig. 3.6.) Once the bit lies against the tooth, the horse can brace the whole of his neck against the contact, which can become extremely strong on that side. Sometimes the front edge of the tooth slopes *forward* from the gum to the table, which can have a very large hook on it – so large that it hits the roof of the horse's mouth and does untold damage. The slope, however, will hold the bit against the bottom of the mouth; but if the front edge of the tooth slopes *back* towards the table, the bit will slide upwards and hit against the upper gum. This can give the horse such a shock that his head carriage becomes very unsteady. (See Figs 3.6b and 3.6c.) Combine it with wolf teeth, and you could have a thoroughly traumatised animal.

Another variation on the theme occurs when the horse has an overshot jaw, so that his molars as well as his incisors do not meet each other as they should. With the top molars in advance of the bottom ones, a portion of the front top tooth and the bottom back tooth have no counterpart in the opposite jaw: without being worn away they grow long, and probably sharp. (See Fig. 3.6d.) (In the jaw which is undershot the long teeth will be at the bottom in the front of the jaw, and at the top in the back of the

> 'It is quite common for a horse to suddenly rear or become a head-shaker immediately after the owner acquires a new noseband.'

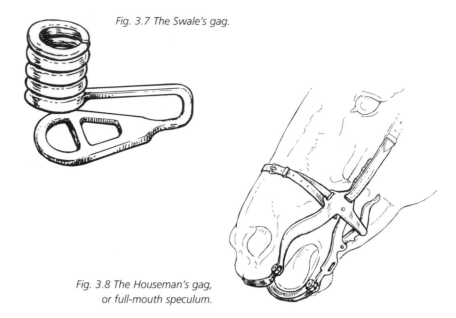

Fig. 3.7 The Swale's gag.

Fig. 3.8 The Houseman's gag,
or full-mouth speculum.

jaw.) The teeth at the back can be so long that they stop the horse from closing his mouth – and in a cursory treatment they are all too often missed. Eating would then become tremendously difficult; but imagine again what might happen if the horse's rider buys herself a flash noseband and straps it up tight.

Good dental specialists take great care to reach the teeth right at the back of the mouth. They also shape the front premolars very carefully, rounding them off to create the 'bit seat'. (See Fig.3.6e.) When this is even on both sides and all sharp edges are removed, many ridden problems (both the average and the highly traumatic) melt away. Horses have also been known to undergo a complete character change in the three days following a treatment, losing the short temper or general grumpiness which accompanies continual pain.

....

Rasping (known as 'floating' in the USA) a horse's teeth is a two–man job, needing a competent handler as well as the dental specialist, although some specialists prefer to work alone. Although ineffective – and potentially dangerous – it used to be common practice to rasp the teeth simply by having the assistant bring the horse's tongue out of the side of his mouth and hold onto it. Veterinary surgeons often use a Swale's gag (Fig. 3.7), which holds only one side of the mouth open at a time. When the horse bites down on it he stresses the temporomandibular joint, and can even split a molar tooth. It is also still possible for horse to clamp the back portion of his jaw shut, so that these teeth never get rasped. This is a situation which can continue over years, during which time the owner thinks she is doing the right thing and taking good care of her horse. If he does not look well, she is far more likely to increase his feed and perhaps review her worming programme than she is to suspect his teeth. But behind the scenes, their condition can only be worsening, and this will often continue until a well-trained equine dental specialist sees the horse.

The full mouth speculum, or Houseman's gag (Fig. 3.8), holds both sides of the jaw open and makes it impossible for the horse to clamp his jaw shut. Only with the gag on can the dental specialist see and feel enough to assess the state and balance of the jaw, which he needs to do both before and after his work. But the Houseman's gag has often been blamed for terrifying horses and causing accidents. My proposal (and that of most equine dental specialists, though not all veterinary surgeons) is that the gag itself is not to blame. Instead the problem lies in the way it is used. Put on quickly and wrenched open suddenly, it could cause any horse to panic. When put on slowly and skilfully, it is not a dangerous piece of equipment, and the more expensive gags have a finer ratchet which makes them inherently safer.

Dental specialist Bob Livock claims that he has had only *one* horse 'go berserk' in the many years that he has been using a Houseman's gag. It needs to be used on a headstall which holds it absolutely in place. There must, for instance, be a brow band, so that the headpiece cannot slip back from the ears down the horse's neck. Almost all dental specialists use this instead of a Swale's gag, believing that it provides the *only* way to assess the jaw and reach the back teeth. (A cheap one would cost around £150 ($225) – but a dental specialist could pay anything from £250 ($375) to £1,250 ($2000) for one which will withstand the rigours of his work. A Swale's gag at £50 ($50-$120) could at least give you an idea of the state of your horse's teeth, although its use for anything else is extremely dubious.

The dental specialists I have talked to in preparing this chapter pride themselves on the thoroughness with which they approach a task which is often not done thoroughly enough, both by poorly trained dental specialists and by veterinary surgeons. They tell horror stories about unqualified, and the state in which they have left horses' mouths. One such 'specialist' had failed to notice that a horse's tooth was split right down through the middle, with each half moving as he rasped it. (Imagine the pain involved in this. When told of his mistake he reflected back on the incident and said 'I had wondered why the horse was so fractious.' Removing the tooth was, of course, the job of a veterinarian.) In another case, vets who had removed the eye of a very successful competition pony had failed to notice that it had only become infected as a result of a tooth abscess. This had actually *moved* the tooth: the table was tilted towards the pony's cheek, cutting into him every time he turned that way and adding even more pain to that of the abscess.

On average, the best dentists probably take forty-five minutes to rasp the teeth of a horse they have never treated before – even though he may have had regular attention previously. This means that you should be wary of anyone who takes *less* than that time, especially if he does not use a Houseman's gag and has only one or two rasps. Some of my pupils, for instance, recently told me of a dental specialist who had visited the yard where they keep their horses, and done each of them in about ten minutes, charging £15 ($25) (You can expect to pay £25 to £30 for a good dentist in the UK and upwards of $50 in the USA – but you will save his fee in reduced feed bills.) Needless to say, the dental specialist who did them thoroughly whilst they were attending a course with me found all manner of undiscovered problems – a phenomenon which has happened again and again, and which makes me extremely suspicious of most dental treatment.

In later visits which are now routine maintenance a dental specialist would hope to treat the horse in about thirty minutes. No vet who has ever rasped my horses' teeth has taken even half that time: this is highly significant, for it is the difficult-to-get-to teeth at the back of the jaw which account for the extra time taken, along with the shaping of the front premolars so that they form the 'bit seat'.

....

Tooth enamel is extremely strong, and tooth rasps, of course, need to be even stronger. Their surface is like very coarse sandpaper, made sometimes of pieces of tungsten carbide – the same metal which is used in the heads of road nails. Some rasps are even made of small pieces of diamond (a good reason for not investing in one for your grooming kit!). Their shape varies slightly, making them appropriate for different size horses with different shaped jaws, and a good dental specialist will usually have at least six rasps – giving him a bigger choice than most veterinarians. They need to be wet when used, in order to minimise friction against the inside of the horse's mouth, and they are usually kept in a bucket of mild antiseptic which makes them safe to use on horse after horse. They often need a quick brush-over during use, for when they become caked with ground-up bits of tooth they are inevitably not so effective.

Rasping a horse's teeth is primarily a kinaesthetic task, and the dentist works from the feel of the rasp against the horse's teeth, and from the feel of the teeth themselves. The *sound* of the rasp also provides a guide, for this changes when the sharp edges have been removed. To get a visual perspective on the back of the mouth is not so easy – although I recently heard of one dentist who works wearing a helmet with a miner's light attached! Dentists develop their own style, with their own individual strengths and weaknesses, and in the UK they are a small enough community that many of them can put their hand in a horse's mouth and recognise who last rasped his teeth!

....

The really good equine dentists are rather special people with enormously high standards, and they are not affected by the temptation to 'botch it' and earn a lot more money a lot faster. The horse who is sore on the inside of his cheeks is rarely a good patient – for allowing someone to pass even the smooth side of the rasp backwards and forwards over the flesh (as will inevitably happen when the rough side is passed over the edges of his teeth) will be distinctly painful. The rasp will only act directly on the sharp edges of the teeth if it is placed at about a 45° angle to the grinding surface and the edge of the mouth, and its angle must be varied to round off the tooth. It would touch the cheek *less* if it was put in horizontally, but the dentist does not want to rasp the flat surface of the tables themselves, as would then happen. The more un-cooperative the horse is about the whole venture, the more likely he is to have deep seated damage – and the more likely his dental specialist is to back off from getting right to the source of the problem. This only has to happen once for the situation to become progressively worse.

> *'The horse who is sore on the inside of his cheeks is rarely a good patient.'*

Equine dentistry is a demanding job, for just handling a rasp for hours on end takes it toll on the body, as do fractious horses. The best dentists give the same care and attention to each patient – regardless of his value, regardless of his resistance to being treated, and regardless of how late in the day he appears for treatment. But the ideal dentist is not only a saint, he is also ambidextrous! In reality few are – and whichever hand they use, they have to be sure that they eventually get the same result on both sides, working harder with their weaker arm. Those who 'hang in' to the bitter end (and are not put off by the horse's antics), gain tremendous reward from leaving the horse able to eat and work without pain. They have to, or they could never do it.

Equine dental specialists become very astute readers not only of horses but also of their owners, who often present a much bigger problem than their charges! They know that approaching a horse slowly, kindly, but with complete confidence gains his trust, and is much more effective than displays of strength. The good ones soon learn where their limits lie, and if necessary they will leave the stable and cool down before they continue. Interestingly, horses who are extremely difficult on the first thorough rasping – and who are well handled throughout this – soon realise that this torture has a pay-off, and they become progressively easier to handle in future treatments.

Until recently there were not been very many equine dental specialists in existence. But times are changing, and in the UK a number of frighteningly unskilled self-taught practitioners have jumped on the dental bandwagon. Sadly, they have given the profession a bad name, and dental specialists as a whole are often not looked upon kindly by veterinary surgeons. The best of them, however, are immensely skilled, and eminently more meticulous in their practice than the vets themselves. Some vets will happily refer you to a specialist, whereas others will not. A handful of the better British specialists have qualified through training in Canada or America with the World Wide Association of Equine Dentistry or the International Association of Equine Dental Technicians. They will be registered members of one of these associations if they have attended its courses, fulfilled very stringent apprenticeship requirements, and passed its examinations. Others have learned only through an apprenticeship. Both associations provide a good monitoring system with good back-up for their graduates, but as yet, there is no British equivalent.

Thus dental specialists in the UK are probably a more diverse group than they are in the USA, and standards vary enormously both within the profession, and between dental specialists and veterinary surgeons. Hopefully in the UK the profession will find a way to legitimise and regulate itself, and to set high standards (which could then make it illegal for anyone who has *not* passed its examination to practise). At least there is now a short introductory training course running in the UK – but remember that it is impossible to become skilful in dentistry without serving a thorough apprenticeship. Your best guide when seeking a dentist in America is to contact the World Wide Association of Equine Dentistry or the International Association of Equine Dental Technicians. In the UK you may be well advised do the same. But if instead you go on personal recommendation, ask what kind of gag the dentist uses, how he learned his trade, how many rasps he has, and how long he typically takes to rasp a set of teeth.

CHAPTER FOUR
Farriery and Gait Analysis

AFTER CHEFS, FARRIERS are often reputed to be some of the most demanding prima donnas in existence. Whether they really are, or whether we – their clients – drive them to distraction is another matter: but the difference between throwing together a meal and creating a gourmet feast is not so unlike the difference between throwing on a set of shoes and practising farriery as a precision art. Yet many riders who would not consider themselves gourmands *do* believe themselves to be discerning observers of horse shoes. Most of us are well versed in the anatomy of the foot, and have spent hours studying the traditional guidelines about 'what to look for in a newly shod foot' and 'how to tell when a foot needs reshoeing'. (As I write this chapter I shall presuppose this knowledge – although, as we shall see, some of the foremost thinkers in the field are challenging even these long-held assumptions.) But whether education and experience really do provide us with enough knowledge to comment – favourably or otherwise – on a farrier's work is a moot point.

It is hardly surprising that our often ill-informed judgments about such a complex and demanding art can lead to some heated disputes between owners and farriers. One end of the spectrum is peopled by concerned horse owners who have arguments (or 'map battles') with their farriers about 'who knows best'. The other end is composed of owners who get what they are willing to pay for, and ultimately, what they deserve. (Inevitably, though, it is their *horses* who bear the brunt of their tight-fistedness.) For the main concern of many riders is that their horse's shoes stay on as long as possible, allowing them to extend the time between each shoeing and keep their farriery bills to a minimum. The fact that this might ultimately be false economy does not enter their heads.

At the very least, the 'slash and bash' shoeing which can take place at the bottom end of the market is not conducive to high performance. Even more devastating are the effects of the excessive horn growth which occurs between each shoeing, and which is highly likely to increase both the horse owner's veterinary surgeon's bill and her chiropractor's bill: in fact,

'After chefs, farriers are often reputed to be some of the most demanding prima donnas in existence.'

Dr Gail Williams, whose PhD study has examined factors related to shoeing, foot balance, lameness, and navicular disease in particular, estimates that within any one year, for every extra £5 ($8) that you spend in each shoeing on a good farrier, you save £100 ($165) on veterinary bills.

Seventy per cent of the horses who are out competing will go lame during any one year. Sixty-five to seventy-five per cent of these lamenesses might be avoided if horses were well shod every four to five weeks, and not left to go through excessively large cycles of growth, followed by the inevitable cutting back of the feet. For these lamenesses – wherever in the body they occur – are caused or contributed to by imbalances in the feet. The idea of not knowing if you are 'on your arse or your elbow' translates in the horse's body into not knowing if you are on your heels or your toes.

In human feet, our weight is supported by our bones, which lie very close to the ground, with relatively little flesh between them and it. The bones in the horse's foot, however, do *not* support his weight, and neither

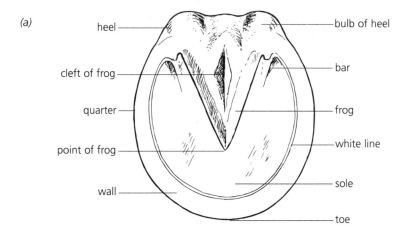

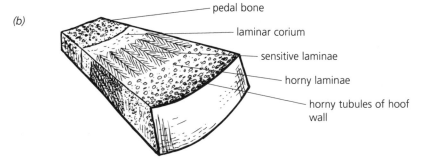

Fig. 4.1 (a) The ground surface of the foot. (b) A cross-section through the hoof wall (parallel to the ground) which shows how the sensitive and insensitive laminae interlock to suspend the pedal bone within the hoof capsule.

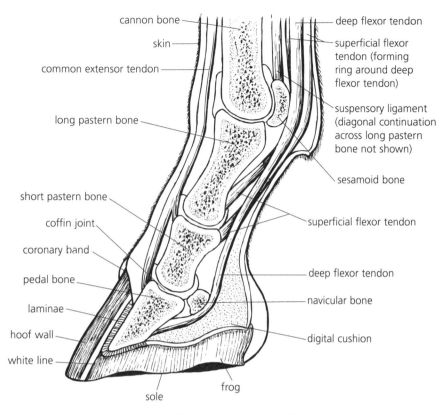

Fig. 4.2 A cross-section through the fetlock, pastern and hoof.

does the sole, except at the bars. (See Fig. 4.1a.) Since the bars are an extension of the hoof wall as it curves inwards around the frog, they should indeed be weight-bearing. The horse's weight is transmitted down through the bones of his leg to the pedal bone, which is approximately hoof-shaped; but this is cushioned from the ground by the thickness of the sensitive and the insensitive soles, and the plantar cushion. (See Figs 4.2 and 4.9.) More importantly, the pedal bone is *suspended* within the hoof wall by the interlocking laminae which cover both the bone and the inside of the wall (see Fig. 4.1b). This is an ingenious arrangement, for the laminae have a convoluted surface shaped like fern leaves, and this gives a tremendously large contact area between the pedal bone and its supporting structures. The bone is hung as if it were a circular hammock fixed to a circular wall; so the horse's weight is transferred from the bone to the wall and borne by its ground surface, which – at only ⅜ inch/9mm thick – is a very small surface to support a horse.

This means that if the horse's weight is not distributed evenly over the entire wall, there is a high price to be paid, and the wall itself can become distorted. One result of this is the all-too-frequent problem of 'undershot heels', where the horse's foot is permanently out of shape with his heels low and his toes long. The horn tubules which compose the wall are hollow, hair-like fibres, which grow down from the coronet lying parallel to each other. Think of them like a bunch of drinking straws: if they were aligned vertically, and you put pressure on their ends, they would be very strong. If they were arranged between 90° and 45° to the horizontal they could still bear weight adequately. But once the angle became *less* than 45° they would begin to bend (see Fig. 4.3).

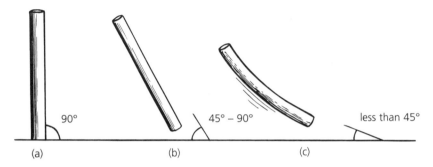

Fig. 4.3 The horn tubules which make up the hoof wall would be at their strongest if they grew vertically as in (a). As long as they are angled between 90° and 45° to the ground as in (b) they can still bear weight effectively. As soon as the angle becomes less than 45°, as in (c), the tubules begin to bend.

Horn tubules never grow down vertically, and most farriers aim to keep the line of the toe (i.e. the line of growth) at 45° to 50° to the ground on the front feet and 50° to 55° to the ground on the hind feet. However, in wild horses, the line of the toe is 50° to 55° in the front feet, and 55° to 60° in the hind, suggesting that the ideal is even steeper. If these angles become *less than 45°* the horn tubules become squeezed between the weight of the horse acting downward and the upthrust of the ground acting upward. As the 'drinking straws' are brought closer towards the horizontal, they are weakened considerably – and as they begin to grow forward rather than down, the hoof wall at the toe bends outwards and upwards. If you imagine the pain you would inflict on yourself if you had a rather long fingernail and you bent it backwards, you are imagining a state not dissimilar to the horse's plight.

Leverage forces cause the separation of the laminae at the toe (see Fig. 4.4), both in the piece of horn that protrudes beyond the sole in a foot which needs reshoeing, and higher up within the foot – so the damage can be far more extensive than it first appears. Separation of the laminae within a small area can also occur when grit or dirt works its way into the white line (the line on the sole which marks the meeting of sole and wall, and therefore of the laminae – see Figs 4.1 and 4.2), but this is more likely to be an *effect* rather than a *cause* of separation.

The separation caused by a long toe is insidious; and whilst we dread laminitis – which is indeed the most devastating form of separation – we do not pay enough attention to the chronic, ongoing damage caused by long feet. Even laminitis can be mechanical in its origins, occurring after overgrown feet have been subjected to the concussive forces of prolonged road work. It may also occur if the placenta is retained after foaling, or after ingesting foods rich in carbohydrate. Both of these lead to a build-up of toxins in the blood, and this increases blood pressure, triggering a mechanism which causes the blood supply to by-pass the sensitive laminae. Thus 'toxic shock' is the cause of their separation.

Horn takes from nine months to one year to grow from the coronet band down to the ground, growing about ³⁄₈ inch/9mm in a month. So it could take several shoeings before all of the wall which was damaged as the toes grew too long becomes exposed and can be trimmed away by the farrier. The toes and heels grow equally fast, but the heel is simultaneously worn away by the expansion of the foot which should take place each time the heels touch the ground. So after shoeing it takes about four weeks of growth before the hoof wall at the toe begins to extend beyond the sole, giving the extra piece that is nipped off by the farrier when he next prepares the foot. This differential has a huge impact on the horse who is left too long between shoeings; for the toe becomes relatively longer than the heel, changing the slope of the hoof and rocking the horse's weight back towards his heels.

In the extreme situation of the long toe and low heel, the whole hoof begins to grow forward, for the 'drinking straws' which lie towards the heels are also pulled forward, keeping them parallel to those at the toe. They may, however, even begin to bend under the weight of the horse, curving downwards. Most people are familiar with the way that new

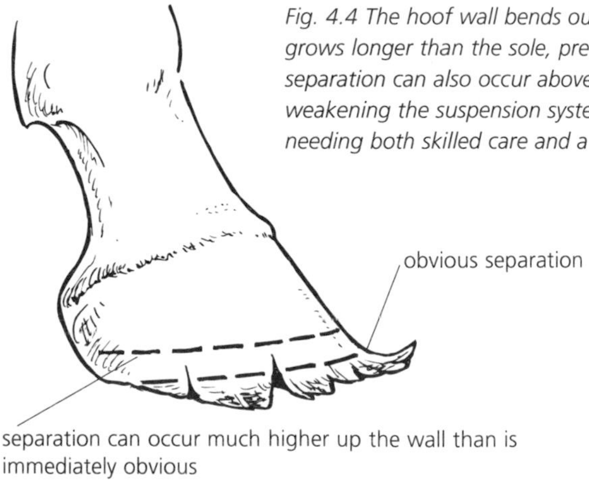

'We do not pay enough attention to the chronic, ongoing damage caused by long feet.'

Fig. 4.4 The hoof wall bends outwards and upwards as it grows longer than the sole, predisposing it to crack. But the separation can also occur above the level of the sole, weakening the suspension system of the pedal bone and needing both skilled care and a long time before it grows out.

obvious separation

separation can occur much higher up the wall than is immediately obvious growth pulls the *shoe* forward with it, making the heels of the foot grow down around the heels of the shoe, which now press on the horse's sole and can cause corns. (We often do not take these seriously enough, however, for the commonly held belief that 'all hunters get corns' belittles the damage which is actually occurring within the sensitive tissues of the heels.) But when the horn tubules at the heels are pulled forward along with the shoe, the result can be a broken back hoof/pastern axis: in other words, the hoof slopes forward more than the pastern. (See Fig. 4.5.)

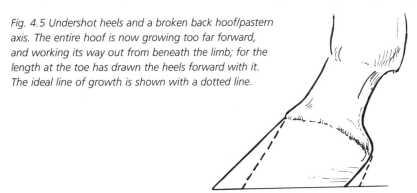

Fig. 4.5 Undershot heels and a broken back hoof/pastern axis. The entire hoof is now growing too far forward, and working its way out from beneath the limb; for the length at the toe has drawn the heels forward with it. The ideal line of growth is shown with a dotted line.

When the hoof/pastern axis is correctly aligned, the long pastern bone, short pastern bone, and pedal bone form one continuous line, and a line drawn through their centre passes through the pastern joint and the coffin joint. (See Fig. 4.6.) Ideally, they should also be parallel to the line of the shoulder blade. Also, a vertical line from the centre of the coffin joint to the ground should bisect the hoof from front to back. This means that an equal amount of the horse's weight is borne in front of and behind the line. Also, ideally, an equal amount of weight is borne to the inside and the outside of a line drawn at 90° to it. This means that the horse's weight acts through the centre of the foot. If the line from the toe to the vertical line from the centre of the coffin joint is *longer* than the line from the vertical to the heel, the back 'half' of the foot which is in contact with the ground is subject to greater pressure.

If the horse's shoe does not extend right back to his heels (either in its initial fitting, or by being left on for so long that it has been pulled forward by the growth of the toe) the weight-bearing surface is decreased even further, and the pressure in the heel region becomes greater still. The effect is exaggerated if the shoe has a tapered heel; for this reduces still further the length of the line from the vertical to the last point of contact of the shoe with the ground. Dr Gail Williams reacts very strongly to this, saying, 'If I could introduce one law that would be for the greater benefit of horses it would be to ban hunter shoes.'

Farriers are often tempted to shoe a horse short because owners do not

Dr Gail Williams: 'If I could introduce one law that would be for the greater benefit of horses it would be to ban hunter shoes.'

like the look of shoes which extend beyond the heel and appear likely to be pulled off by the hind foot. (And if indeed a shoe *is* lost, the farrier may well lose this person as a client.) However, in reducing the support of the heels, the farrier creates a far more insidious problem than the one he is attempting to cure – especially if that shoe is left on for too long. However, unless horses are jumping out of very muddy ground, those with balanced feet rarely pull shoes off from the heels; if anything, they *forge* them off. With a short toe, the fore foot can leave the ground faster than it does if the toe is long; since the heels are already elevated as the hind shoe advances, its toe strikes the *branches* of the front shoe instead of the heels.

In the broken back hoof/pastern axis, it is as if the hoof capsule is working its way out from underneath the horse instead of remaining in its correct position beneath the limb. We no longer have a foot with a long toe: the foot is now out of balance in its entirety. Sadly, this process can begin whilst the horse is still a foal, and some authorities in the UK suggest that 75 per cent of horses have heels which are more or less collapsed. The horse's weight is then *permanently* taken towards his heels, which in the unshod foot causes them to wear excessively, thus worsening the situation. Only if the farrier can transfer the weight of the horse forward by raising his heels and keeping his toes short can the angle of the foot be changed over time, so that the horn tubules begin to grow *down*

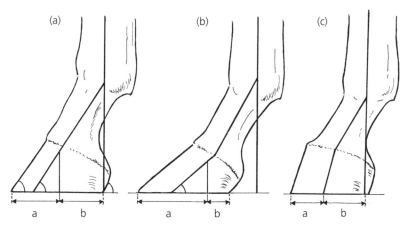

*Fig. 4.6 The ideal hoof/pastern axis is one straight line as in (a), with equal angles at the heel and toe. A vertical line from the centre of the fetlock joint should in theory touch the final point of weight-bearing at the heels, something one rarely sees in practice. As shown in (a), a vertical line from the centre of the coffin joint should bisect the hoof, so that lengths **a** and **b** are equal. (b) A broken back hoof/pastern axis is indicative of a long toe and a low heel, reducing the length of **b** and the weight-bearing surface behind the coffin joint. (c) A broken forward hoof/pastern axis, which makes the foot so upright that it is subjected to increasing concussion; shortening the distance **a** concentrates the weight towards the front of the foot.*

instead of *forward*. He needs to shoe the foot not to perpetuate the shape that it already *is* but to reinstate the shape that it *ought to be*.

The obvious answer seems to lie in raising the heels of the shoe, creating a wedge which changes the angle of the foot. But (like so many of the apparently logical solutions in farriery) this does not work in the way one might expect. The wedge gives the horse the impression that he is always walking down hill, and since the fetlock has been artificially raised it now descends more in each stride, *increasing* the strain on the joint, the tendons which support it, and the back third of the foot. As a result, the horn at the heel is compressed more, which again pushes the 'drinking straws' forward.

The back of the foot is actually given much more support by a shoe which is longer at the heels. This extends the weight-bearing area (equalising lengths *a* and *b* in Fig. 4.6), thus reducing the pressure on the heels whilst keeping the foot level. In theory, it might be possible for the farrier to reinstate the horse's heels within the time that it takes to grow one complete hoof. But the inevitable weakness of the heels and the horn are likely to lead to set-backs which will cause it to take twice as long – requiring a time span of eighteen months to two years.

'It is the tired, unbalanced horse who over-reaches and pulls shoes off.'

In very severe cases the branches of the shoe can be joined together behind the foot, creating a full bar shoe or an egg-bar shoe. Both stabilise the heel area by reducing its expansion, and the egg bar, by extending further back, gives more support to the heels at the cost of being suitable only for dressage work. (See Fig. 4.7.) (However, some very good riders have successfully hunted and evented horses wearing egg-bar shoes; but they are able to keep their horses balanced, never letting them get fatigued. It is the tired, unbalanced horse who over-reaches and pulls shoes off.) The addition of support for the frog, which creates the heart-bar shoe, spreads the horse's weight over an even bigger surface, and is useful in remedial shoeing when weight cannot be borne by a portion of the wall. Heart-bar shoes, however, require great skill to make and use.

The farrier faced with the long toe and low heel has the options of increasing the effective length of the heels and decreasing the length of the toe. One apparently very radical attempt to shorten the toe is the 'four point trim', which, in its most extreme form, leaves the wall bearing weight *only* at both heels and at two 'pillars', lying at the junction of the quarters and the toes. (See Figs. 4.8 a–c.) One might imagine that this would stress the foot beyond tolerance; but in fact it enables the horse (especially if he is left unshod) to reproduce the natural foot shape of the feral horse, which – with its steeper angles and denser horn – withstands conditions that would cripple domestic horses.

During an initial trim, the foot shape is changed dramatically, and the look of the 'four points' really shocks the eye. The sole and the wall lying towards the toe are rasped at an angle to the ground surface, with the sole then being given a slight ground clearance. This creates a much wider, rounder toe which looks rather strange; but this foot shape improves the biomechanics of motion by reducing the distance between the point of the frog and the breakover point at which the hoof leaves the ground. In the traditionally shod horse this is commonly over 2 inches/50mm, but the four-point trim reduces it to between 1 and 1½ inches/25-37mm. (Remember the analogy to the long fingernail; reducing this distance decreases the leverage forces which tear the 'nail' away from the 'finger'.) Taking the quarters out of contact with the ground also reduces the leverage forces acting there, which are particularly strong on turns. If the horse is to be shod, however, this is done extremely carefully so as to keep continuous contact between the foot and the shoe.

Although a normal shoe can be adapted to fit the new hoof shape, special shoes are available whose ground surface has only a four-point contact. In each case the shoe is squared off at the toe and the fullering (the groove which contains the nail heads) is closed. In fitting, it is set back from the horse's toe, and the trim rounds off the 'overhang' as shown in

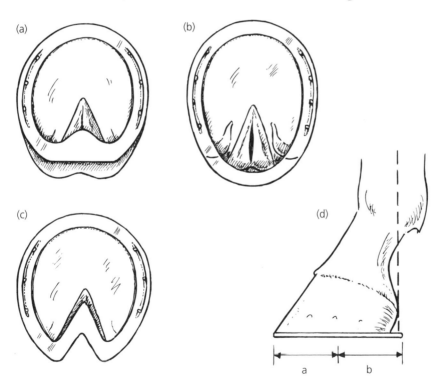

Fig. 4.7 (a) The bar shoe, (b) the egg-bar shoe, and (c) the heart-bar shoe, which all support the horse's heels and give varying degrees of support to the frog. The last point of weight-bearing is brought further back as shown in (d).

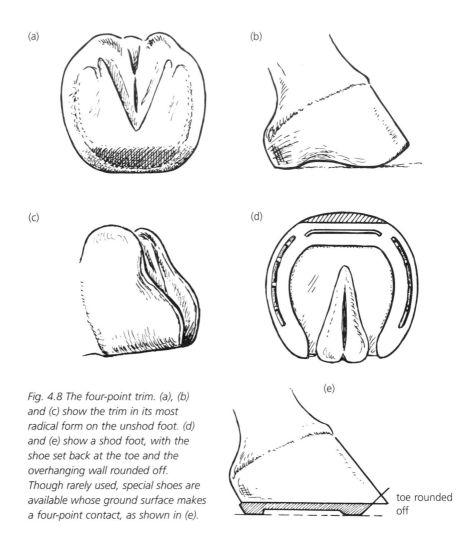

(a)

(b)

(c)

(d)

(e)

Fig. 4.8 The four-point trim. (a), (b) and (c) show the trim in its most radical form on the unshod foot. (d) and (e) show a shod foot, with the shoe set back at the toe and the overhanging wall rounded off. Though rarely used, special shoes are available whose ground surface makes a four-point contact, as shown in (e).

toe rounded off

Figs 4.8d and e. With so much strain taken off the laminae, cracks in the wall become much less likely; but perhaps more significant is the way that this foot shape somehow triggers the growth of denser, tougher horn. Over only a short period of time, the hoof grows in a way which makes it look less dramatically 'wrong'. Its shape rounds out, an increase in strength is soon apparent, and future trims do not need to be so radical.

Advocates of the trim believe that it improves both the mass and the structural integrity of the foot. This immediately makes the foot more 'shoe-able', and many other problems relating to foot balance are simultaneously solved. It becomes much easier to keep the hoof capsule in place under the limb, so that the lengths *a* and *b* in Fig. 4.6 are equal. Problems with the moisture balance of the foot, and with its side-to-side balance (which we will talk about later) seem to take care of themselves.

The enthusiasts feel that they have found 'the answer'. Inevitably, others question the wisdom of such dramatic changes, and whether one can so easily cross the great divide between the feral and the domestic horse.

Older farriers have all witnessed a number of cycles in which ideas that were supposedly 'new' have come and gone in turn. As a result, they often become cynical; but farrier David Nicholls (who regards himself as one of the most cynical) states that 'In all the thirty years that I've been shoeing horses, this is the first thing that has really made sense to me, and has really made a difference.' Of course, it should not be such a surprise to discover that *nature* provides the most appropriate blueprint for how a horse's foot should be shaped – and in converse to discover that what 'looks right' to us through the conditioning of our traditional map is really not 'right' at all.

'It should not be such a surprise to discover that nature provides the most appropriate blueprint for how a horse's foot should be shaped.'

The overall shape and growth direction of the foot, along with the increasing weakness which this generates, is only one of the problems which arise in the long-toe-low-heel syndrome. Traditional writings have, perhaps, made us more aware of the strain placed by excessive horn growth on the flexor tendons at the back of the leg. To illustrate this, place the tips of your fingers on a flat surface with your hand (which represents the horse's foot) at about 45° to it. Then lower your palm until it lies flat, with your forearm vertical. As you do this, you put progressively more strain on the tendons which run down the back of your arm and over your wrist (and you can increase the strain even more by moving your elbow over your hand). As the horse's toe lengthens and his heels come closer to the ground he too suffers from this effect.

Something has to hold up the horse's fetlock joint, and in theory, this is the job of his heels. A perpendicular line dropped from the centre of rotation of the fetlock joint should ideally touch the final weight-bearing point of the heels — something one rarely sees in practice. (See Fig. 4.6.) So when the heels lie forward of this point, increased strain is placed on the suspensory ligament and the superficial digital flexor tendon, and both structures become much more vulnerable to injury. The superficial tendon runs down the back of the cannon bone, over the fetlock joint, and attaches into both pastern bones. The deep digital flexor tendon passes over the navicular bone and finally inserts into the pedal bone. (See Fig. 4.2.) But the repercussions of stressing these structures extend all the way from the navicular area to the horse's back, because his protective stance may well take the strain off one part of his body only to place it in another.

Any increase in pressure in the area of the navicular bone can, as so many horse owners have discovered, prove deadly. But full-blown navicular disease is actually very rare, and recent research suggests that it

'Full-blown navicular disease is actually very rare.'

is found in horses who have an abnormal way of loading the forelimb. This increases concussion in the navicular area, and by the time the bone has holes in it, or has tiny 'avulsion fractures', remedial shoeing can at best make the horse more comfortable. (These fractures occur when the ligaments attaching into the weakened navicular bone pull so strongly on it that small pieces of bone are pulled off.) By this time, compression has caused a chronic reduction in the blood supply to the area, and it is this which is addressed by most of the drugs used in veterinary treatment. But many diagnoses of navicular disease are in reality diagnoses of pain in the rear third of the foot. For a positive response to nerve blocks can only tell us that the horse is experiencing the pain which accompanies damage to the soft tissues in this region, *not* that he has navicular disease.

I personally know a number of people who feel that their doomed horse has had a reprieve – even after they had come to terms with owning an equine invalid, and had received an insurance payment for loss of use, good trimming and shoeing has been enough to restore their horse to soundness and full work. Indeed, some research papers discussing the treatment of navicular disease have reported success rates of up to *86 per cent* using only remedial farriery. But these success stories were *not* cases of true navicular disease, and rebalancing the foot was sufficient to relieve the horse's discomfort. This suggests that the discomfort might not have happened in the first place if the horse had been regularly shod in a way which kept the hoof capsule in its right place beneath the limb, and gave ongoing support to the heels.

'Some research papers discussing the treatment of navicular disease have reported success rates of up to 86 per cent using only remedial farriery.'

Pain in the rear third of the foot may also be located around the laminae. As the hoof capsule is drawn forwards and the horse supports more weight than he should with the rear third of the foot, his heels usually collapse inwards. This increases the compression in this area and contributes to the reduction in its blood supply; but in some heavier topped horses with large flat feet the heels splay *outwards* as the toe extends forward. These horses (who are often obese) have feet which can barely support their body weight. The heel area is over-functioning, showing so much expansion in each step that the sensitive and insensitive laminae in the heel area are pulled apart.

With the shoe on, this is not obvious – and the symptoms are so similar to navicular syndrome that a wrong diagnosis is commonly made. In each case the horse will put his toe to the ground before his heels, and be bilaterally lame. He will react to hoof-testers, and go sound when nerve-blocked. Since pain and lameness actually result from the separation of the laminae, the farrier has to stabilise the foot and to stop it from 'running away with him'. As the foot gets bigger, he is tempted to shoe it bigger – so it then gets bigger, and he then shoes it bigger… To tighten it up takes skilful trimming and shoeing, and the return to soundness will also require a strict diet and good stable management practices. He shoes the foot according to the shape that it *ought to be*, instead of perpetuating the shape that it is.

Whilst it is primarily bad management which causes all the problems associated with the long toe and low heels, we have stacked the odds against our horses by selectively breeding Thoroughbreds with lower, weaker, heels and longer, more sloping pasterns (or as a well-known vet once said, 'The vehicle's all right, but don't ask about the wheels!'). In the quest to produce a faster horse – which has not met with any significant success – we have used too much inbreeding, and British horses rarely have the line of the heels parallel to the line of the toe. Often, the coronary band comes very close to the ground in the heel region, and the heels slope forward excessively. When George Stubbs painted his beautiful pictures of Thoroughbreds in the latter half of the eighteenth century, he drew exactly what he saw, and his background in anatomy precluded any artistic licence. If you look at his horses, you can see that their heels are much deeper than those of their modern-day counterparts, whose horn tubules commonly grow forward at an angle of less than 45° to the ground. Much of the damage was done in the late 1930s and early 1940s; but it is time to remember that with no foot, we have no horse, and to reconsider our tactics.

> 'We have stacked the odds against our horses by selectively breeding Thoroughbreds with lower, weaker, heels and longer, more sloping pasterns.'

....

As we have seen, the broken back hoof/pastern axis puts tremendous strain on the structures towards the back of the foot. Much rarer (in Thoroughbreds) is the broken forward hoof/pastern axis, in which the angle of the hoof is *steeper* than the angle of the pastern. Upright feet bring with them a different set of problems, particularly an increase in concussion – for upright feet and pasterns do not allow the fetlock to sink so much in each stride and thus to absorb the force of the hoof impacting on the ground. In theory this predisposes the horse to ringbone, sidebone and pedal osteitis. But whilst the broken forward axis may not be ideal, it does at least put the hoof capsule more underneath the limb, making it the less damaging alternative.

The make and shape of Thoroughbred feet contrasts sharply with that of most warmblood horses, who have more upright feet with parallel toes and heels. The foot also has much more *mass*, with thicker horn and a thicker sole. So the farrier must use a shoe which also has increased mass as well as greater width, and he will probably appreciate having much more leeway for error as he positions his nails. But if the heels as well as the toes become long, there is a danger that the frog is no longer weight-bearing, reducing the expansion of the heels, their role in shock

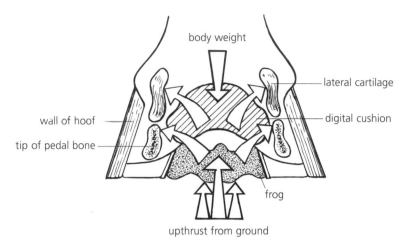

Fig. 4.9 The shock-absorbing mechanisms of the hoof, which transmit the upward force that results from impact with the ground through the frog, to the digital cushion and the lateral cartilages.

absorption (see Fig. 4.9) and the blood supply to the heel area. So, despite the more appropriate angle of both the heel and the toe, this horse too can become a candidate for pain in the rear third of the foot. Too much weight taken in the heel region can cause the heels to contract – but so too can too little weight. The balance must be just right.

'Very many horses have dysfunction in the heel region of the foot.'

The horse who genuinely *is* afflicted with navicular disease contrives to reduce the pressure in the heel area for himself, by 'pointing', i.e. standing with one front foot out in front of him. He also adopts a movement pattern which takes weight off his heels in each step, and this reduction in pressure encourages his feet to become 'boxy'. This further develops the upright heels which expand less and less in each step as the frog becomes non-functional, and the shock-absorbing mechanism of Fig. 4.9 ceases to function. But one sees these adaptations very much less than one used to, probably because diagnoses of pain in the rear third of the foot are made very much earlier, when there is a small reduction in performance and the horse becomes unwilling to jump or stride out. Very many horses have dysfunction in the heel region of the foot; but, as stated earlier, very, very few go on to develop full-blown navicular disease.

Moisture levels in the feet

The conditions in which the horse lives have a tremendous impact on the amount of moisture that his feet are exposed to. Whilst some horses stand day after day knee-deep in mud, others live in such arid conditions that any drop of water is a rarity. Some people smother their horse's feet every day in preparations designed to make them grow, to keep them moist, and/or to make them look good. Others ignore them completely. They are often, however, unknowingly making a continual application of straw or wood shavings soaked in urine – the substance which forms the upper as well as the lower layers of many deep-litter beds.

The horse evolved on semi-arid plains, and is suited to such conditions; but both too much moisture and not enough moisture can cause him problems. For both can destroy the delicate balance between the amount of water held within both the inner and the outer layers of the hoof. Horn is dense and hard, and it has a moisture content of 15 to 20 per cent. The inner layers of the sensitive laminae and the plantar cushion, however, have an average water content of about 45 per cent. When the horse's circulation is good, and both blood and lymph vessels are working efficiently, there is a constant flow of fluid which replenishes any moisture loss, for some diffuses outwards from the moist inner structures through the dry outer wall. But the inactivity forced on the horse who lives in confinement can reduce the circulation dramatically. The hoof diseases of navicular and laminitis both signal that further profound circulatory changes have taken place.

Whenever the horse puts its foot to the ground the inner layers expand, and push out against the wall and sole, whose hardness resists this expansion. The domed shape of the sole helps it to resist the forces acting on it, which tend to flatten it down towards the ground. The wall acts like a spring, expanding and contracting in each step, especially at the heels, and creating a brilliant mechanism for absorbing the shock of impact. But if the inner, sensitive, layers dry out, *they do not push outwards enough*; and if the outer insensitive layers dry out *they push inwards too much*. You can observe this happening if your farrier nips off a long piece of wall as he prepares the foot, and you leave it out in the sun to dry. It soon curls into a small circle, for there is no inner layer to combat the tendency of the dried-out wall to contract inward. It is exactly the same phenomenon which causes contracted heels; the moisture within the foot is not replaced as quickly as it diffuses out through the outer wall, and this reduces the pressure on the outer wall whose contractile strength wins the day.

However, if the outer structures of the hoof are *too moist*, they are unable to resist the outward push of the inner structures, and the whole hoof spreads. This creates the large, open-heeled flat feet which become so vulnerable to bruising, and which are, in some cases, barely capable of supporting the weight of the horse. The hoof can become too soft because the horse is continually standing in water; but it can also be made that way by the too-frequent application of hoof dressings, and hoof oil so disturbs the moisture-balancing mechanisms of the horn that it is better not to use it. Without the dynamic balance of the forces which keep the hoof in shape, the horn is likely to separate into layers, with the inner layer collapsing inwards, and the outer layer dropping outwards. If this happens in the heel region, the horse can even be left with no wall resting on the surface of the shoe to bear his weight.

However, the distinction between whether your horse's feet are *deprived* of moisture or are the recipients of *too much* moisture is not so obvious as you may think. For nice fresh mud – along with urine soaked bedding – can act like a poultice or a mud facial and draw moisture and oils *out of* the hoof. This can reduce its flexibility, and damage the cellular cement which holds the horn tubules together. But worse than this, the drying process tends to make the wall attempt to bend or warp; however, the laminae hold it in place so well that it cannot, so it cracks instead. When the cracks become filled with mud and dirt they cannot close, and they tend both to deepen and to extend up the wall. Thus both excessive dryness and (apparently) excessive moisture can cause the horn to crack.

Repeating cycles of dry and wet conditions also make it difficult for the hoof to maintain the ideal moisture balance between its two layers. So the horse who walks through the mud and then stands in the sun becomes vulnerable, as does the horse who lives in hot humid conditions, especially if he stays out overnight, has the dew on his hooves, and then has them dried out during the day by the sun or the bedding in his stall. Hooves can only adapt well if they can dry out slowly – like newly made clay pots and freshly cut timber, fast drying makes them crack. So in many climatic conditions it can seem impossible to win, although some of the new 'hoof hardener' paint-on products help to stabilise the situation by stopping both the take-up and the loss of moisture.

The strong natural foot of the feral horse appears much more able to maintain its own constant level of moisture, and is not so vulnerable to changing environmental conditions. It has been suggested that the amount of moisture in the wall affects its growth rate, and wild horses who live in the marshy conditions of the Camargue in France grow far less horn than horses of the dry, rocky western states of America. So hard, dry horn will maintain itself better, as will a hard dry sole. The use of sole pads can stop the sole from drying out, so that it too becomes soft and moist. Then, when the pad is first removed the horse can appear tender, becoming sound only as his sole hardens and dries out. A medicated hoof dressing like Stockholm tar (known as pine tar in the USA) has been the traditional way of discouraging the fungal infections which flourish in this environment, but (as we shall see later) both this and leather pads have been superseded by 'high-tech' materials.

Canker, and even thrush, are largely diseases of the past which many of us know from books and not experience. But recent discoveries have increased our understanding of the fungi which can attack the white line. Most authorities used to believe that separation of the laminae and any

'The distinction between whether your horse's feet are deprived of moisture or are the recipients of too much moisture is not so obvious as you may think.'

accompanying deterioration of the white line was always the result bad shoeing, so for many years 'white line disease' was a hypothesis which was frequently viewed with great scepticism. Attempts to make a culture out of any organisms which might be present in affected hooves repeatedly failed, until American farrier Burney Chapman consulted a friend who grew cultures in a laboratory used for human rather than veterinary diagnoses.

The increased time for which they kept their cultures eventually yielded two organisms. These same organisms affect humans with abnormal immune systems, and are present in AIDS sufferers and long-term drug abusers. They are anaerobic (without oxygen), are found in soils worldwide, and (now that we know what to look for) have been discovered to affect many more horses than anyone ever suspected. But they are not likely to affect healthy people, or to be transmitted by farriers' tools, and it is common for only one or two horses in a large group to be affected.

The fungi destroy the white line; it turns grey, has a cheesy appearance, and may smell bad. The fungi can be killed by disinfectants contained within a highly penetrating fluid: using a plastic syringe to inject this into old nail holes both prevents and cures the problem, and since reinfection occurs very easily this may need to be done on a ongoing basis. (Eucalyptus oil containing 3 per cent iodoform by volume also works well, and in the UK can be made up for you by a chemist; it is, however, a banned substance in the USA.) In severe cases, damage to the white line can extend so far up the hoof that the wall has to be removed, along with all the affected tissue and several centimetres of the apparently sound tissue which lies in front of the infection. The horse will then require specialist shoeing, and extremely good care. The damaged area should not be covered over with hoof filler, for this creates an anaerobic environment: so if any infected tissue remains, the problem flares up again.

One of my own horses has been quite severely affected with white line disease, although the use of a penetrating disinfectant has been enough to eradicate the problem. (I would not, however, dare to stop taking preventative measures.) The incidence of white line disease is increasing worldwide, and little is known about why it affects one horse and not another; so we horse owners need to be aware of its existence, and of the damage it can do.

The knock-on effects of foot balance

Whilst we have every excuse for being ill-informed about new discoveries, remaining so *unaware* of the damage that can be done by poor shoeing virtually amounts to burying our heads in the sand. An ill-fitting pair of shoes might ruin your night out (even if you do not have to run around in them!) but you can at least take them off, relieve your feet, and choose not to wear them again. The poor horse cannot. But his plight does not stop with sore feet, for as the old song says, 'the ankle bone's connected to the knee bone, the knee bone's connected to the thigh bone...', and the way the horse stands on his feet has repercussions which go all the way up his body, extending above and beyond their effect on the foot and the flexor tendons of the lower limb. Some researchers in the field of equine biomechanics go so far as to suggest that it is a waste of time calling out the chiropractor to the horse who is uncomfortable in his back. This is like fixing the roof when the foundations are crumbling; for unless you adjust his stance he will continue to make the same compensations, manoeuvring pain from one part of his body to another – and ensuring that the roof will collapse yet again.

Many farriers look no further than the foot itself, considering this as their target, but American farrier Tony Gonzales, author of *PBM: A Diary of Lameness*, and originator of the 'Proper Balance Movement' system of thinking, changed his approach to shoeing when he began to look at horses not just from the knee down (as he had been trained) but by assessing the entirety of their conformation and movement. When he considers the effects of the long-toe-low-heel syndrome on horses, he thinks as follows: if the weight of the horse is taken predominantly on his heels, then the fetlock is pushed back (closing the space in the front of the joint relative to the space at the back), the knee is pushed back (or hyperextended), the elbow is pushed back, the point of the shoulder is forced down, and the shoulder blade is rotated so that its top is brought forward. On the hind leg, as the fetlock drops down and back, the hock is pushed forward (closing the space at the back of the joint relative to that at the front), the stifle is pushed back (making the second thigh more vertical), the point of the buttock is pushed up, and the lumbar/sacral joint is pushed forward, with a rotation which creates the characteristic shape of the 'hunter's bump'. (See Fig. 4.10a.)

So consider the converse. When the weight of the foreleg passes through the centre of the foot, the fetlock can move forward and up, making the pastern slightly more upright. The knee is then brought forward (taking it out of hyperextension), the elbow is brought forward, the point of the shoulder is brought up, and the top of the shoulder blade brought back. On the hind leg, as the fetlock is brought forward and up, the hock moves back, the stifle moves forward, the point of the buttock moves down and the lumbar/sacral joint is brought back and up. (See Fig. 4.10b.) This stops the weight of the horse's quarters pressing forward and down onto his lumbar spine and thus through to his forehand, and down through his chest.

The horse whose front feet are hurting as a result of this will find ways to transfer weight to his hind limbs, and may do so by adopting an almost

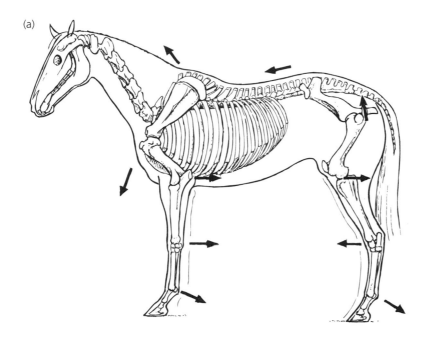

Fig. 4.10 (a) When the long toe and low heel leave the fetlock unsupported, the joints are affected as shown, leading to a movement pattern which badly affects muscle development; (b) shows the converse, occurring when rebalancing the foot brings the whole body into balance.

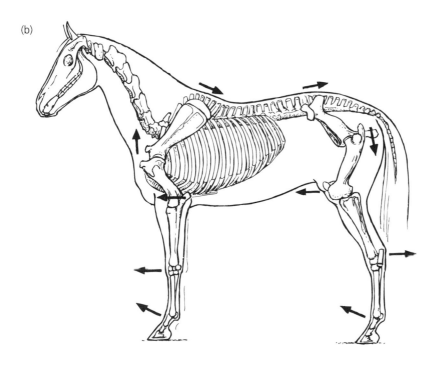

laminitic pose, with the front feet out in front of him and the hind feet brought forward under his belly. Horses with more acute pain sometimes stand as if on a pedestal, with both sets of limbs brought underneath the body. They then become very stiff behind, and since they do not want to bring the hind leg out behind them, they become difficult for the farrier to shoe. Sickle hocks are rarely a conformation fault; more often they represent the attempt of a horse with pain in both front feet to keep himself more comfortable. Normally, 60 per cent of the horse's weight is supported by his front legs, and 40 per cent by the hind, and this reduced weight-bearing gives them greater propulsive ability. But if they are made to weight-bear *more*, they inevitably propel *less*, and then the forelimbs take over this role. The engine is now at the wrong end of the horse, and he *pulls* himself along instead of *pushing* himself along. To compensate for this the horse may move with his head up in the air; and/or he may pull his chest up and in, using the pectoral muscles between his forelegs, and creating a chronic tension here which stops him from feeling as if his weight is continually being thrust down onto his forefeet.

'In severe cases of maladaptive movement pattern the horse begins to hurt all over – and then, he may even learn to rear.'

This way of moving develops the muscles under his neck, stresses the muscles above the elbow and around the girth area, weakens the horse's top line, and often puts his long back muscles into spasm. It also contributes to forging, especially in the short-coupled horse with long legs. If the horse's front feet are long they remain on the ground for longer, so the breakover (when the toe leaves the ground) is delayed and forging becomes more likely. So keeping the hoof capsule more under the limb helps the foot to break over more quickly and to get out of the way of the hind foot. To address the foot balance in front is vital, since the part played by the hind legs is secondary: for they are only being brought more under the body to help take weight off the aching forelegs. They can, however, be retarded by keeping the hind shoes long at the heels, or fitting egg-bar shoes. In severe cases of this maladaptive movement pattern the horse begins to hurt all over – and then, he may even learn to rear. The knock-on effects of transferring pain through his body have made him virtually unrideable – and it all began with a broken back hoof/pastern axis.

When we see the horse standing still, we commonly make the mistake of viewing these chronic patterns of tension as part of his conformation. I feel privileged to have watched Tony trim and shoe a horse who looked, when viewed from the front, as if he had 'both legs coming out of the same hole'. The difference when Tony had finished was unbelievable, and the horse's chest had dropped and widened, as if he had finally taken a deep breath and stopped his attempt to defy the effects of gravity. It forced me into the realisation that 'conformation' is a static concept, and – as with sickle hocks – a factor which I had assumed to be an indelible part of this horse's body was merely the result of his *use*. In the same way, round

(a)

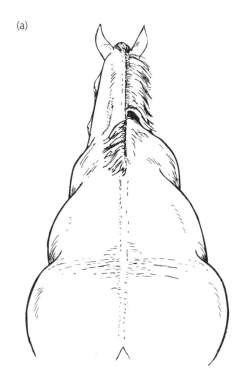

(b)

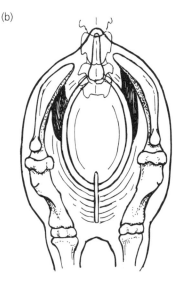

Fig. 4.11 (a) Uneven shoulders are most
obvious when the horse is observed from
above and behind. (b) The muscle sling
supporting the rib cage is inevitably also
asymmetrical.

shoulders are a common result of human use, and not a part of our
conformation (not, at least, until we reach the age and stage when our
muscles have rigidified and pulled on our bones to such an extent that it
becomes impossible to straighten out again!).

Tony developed his approach by working on horses who were destined
for the knacker's yard unless he could perform a miracle on them – and
often he did. With nothing to lose, he also dared to be extremely radical.
Gradually he realised that he had to look at horses not only from the
bottom up but also *from the top down*. He discovered that many of the
lameness problems which afflict horses result from them having a long or
a short leg, and the odd-leg-out can be either in front or behind. The leg
may not be *structurally* a different length, but it is certainly *functionally*
different – perhaps because of a chiropractic problem, or because of
unequal muscle development.

If the difference lies in the functional length of the forelegs, it follows
that there must be a difference in the muscle development around the
shoulder blades, which are only attached to the rib cage by muscles and
ligaments (Fig. 4.11b). If you climb up onto something and view the
horse from above and behind you get a very interesting view of his
shoulder development, which can show one shoulder to be higher, more
forward, and more developed than the other (see Fig. 4.11a). There is also
often an obvious difference in muscle development which you can see if

*'Many of the
lameness
problems which
afflict horses
result from them
having a long or a
short leg, and the
odd-leg-out can
be either in front
or behind.'*

Fig. 4.12

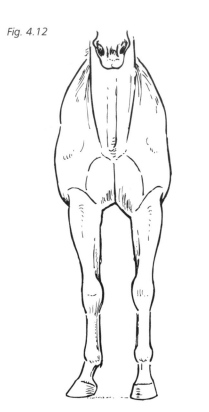

Fig. 4.13

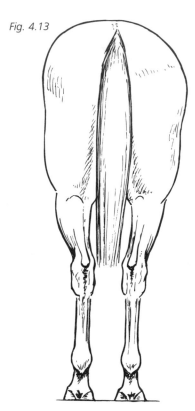

Fig. 4.12 Uneven development in the pectoral muscles in between the forelegs. This shows one leg which has an outward rotation.

Fig. 4.13 Uneven development of the muscles of the pelvis and second thigh.

'The horse's mane in the region of the wither will always fall towards the side of the lower shoulder and the functionally shorter leg.'

you can safely squat down and look at the horse's chest, viewing the line in between his forelegs (see Fig. 4.12). Looking up from this position at the shoulders and the underside of the neck can also be very revealing. One of Tony's big breakthroughs came when he realised that the horse's mane in the region of the wither will always fall towards the side of the lower shoulder and the functionally shorter leg. (How delighted I was, on discovering this, to come home and find that the bottom of my horse's mane goes straight up in the air!)

When the functional difference is in the hind legs, one side of the croup is raised relative to the other, and one point of hip is higher (see Fig. 4.13). The whole of one quarter may appear more muscled than the other, with the unequal development extending down the second thigh, and also showing if you look at the line between the buttocks. Owners who observe this kind of difference in their horse usually seek veterinary referral to a physiotherapist or chiropractor and would not involve their farrier – but when Tony was developing his ideas he was the only available option. Now that we have more choices, the question about which end of the horse is best treated first remains open to question, although my personal bias veers more and more towards the feet (and getting the best out of a horse who has been in pain will probably require a team effort from several professionals).

Tony has found differences of as much as 1½ inches/37mm between the (functional) length of the front or hind legs. If the horse's odd-leg-out is shorter, the hoof grows more upright and boxy, helping to create more height. (This, as we shall see later, may also be the result of 'ballerina syndrome'.) If the odd leg out is longer, the heels of that foot will be lower, with the growth of the horn happening more at the toe. The horse often stands and also grazes with the longer foreleg leg out in front of him, and when he stands square, a close inspection can show his knees to be unlevel.

These discrepancies can create a pressure point within one foot, or within one of the limbs (probably in a joint), and this eventually becomes the seat of lameness. Tony's answer was to trim the foot of the longer limb as much as possible, and put on a very thin shoe. By using pads to lengthen the shorter limb, he found that the horse's muscle development evened up, allowing the height of the pads to be gradually reduced over six months or so. (To understand his system more fully, you will need to read his book, *PBM: A Diary of Lameness,* which, as a series of case histories, shows how he puts theory into practice.) But he has used these tactics only on the most drastic cases which do indeed show lameness.

This approach is extremely controversial – although progressively more farriers are willing to think in this way. If you know you are dealing with marked asymmetries you will need to send the horse to the best farrier you can find, and also call in professionals from other disciplines. But nonetheless there is much to be learned from the way that Tony teaches riders to become more astute observers of conformation and movement. Skilful farriers and physiotherapists look at the horse's movement with a much more astute eye than the average observer, and to help you develop your skill you can attach coloured stickers onto horses at strategic points which help their asymmetries to show up.

The following exercise needs at least three people to make it worthwhile, but it repays the effort expended. If you do it with two friends and your three horses you will learn a lot, as long as you take your time, *simply observing and reporting* what you see, and not what you think you *ought* to be seeing. Do not expect yourself to see everything first time round, and be prepared for many repetitions as you walk the horses past you, and also towards and away from you. Be prepared to discuss what you are seeing in depth, without glossing over any discrepancies in your observations, and without giving up until you are sure of the patterns that are emerging. Observe one limb at a time – and if you progress

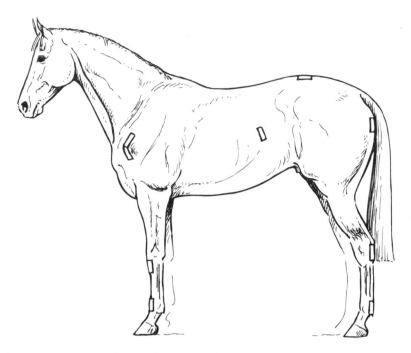

Fig. 4.14 Positioning stickers on the horse so that you can observe his movement patterns more easily.

to watching the trot be aware that you are rushing in where many professionals fear to tread!

Place the stickers on the front of the horse's knees (lining them up precisely with the bottom of the joint), and on the front of the fetlock (see Fig. 4.14). Place two oblong stickers so that they make a 'V' shape which lies approximately horizontally, with its point precisely at the point of each shoulder. Place a sticker on each side at the highest point of the croup, on the point of the buttock, on the hock, and on the bottom of the flexor tendons as they pass behind the fetlock joint. Also place a sticker on each side of the ribcage at its widest part. Putting your thumb or little finger on the point of the hip, use the span of your hand to help you find the right place. Make sure that each sticker precisely matches its counterpart in the way it is placed relative to the joint it delineates. As you may discover, this does not necessarily mean that they are exactly the same height from the ground.

When you observe your horse walking, from the side, it may be apparent that the point of one shoulder moves *up* as the forelimb advances, whilst the point of the other shoulder moves *down*. You may find that either the toe leads the fetlock forward, or that the fetlock leads the toe forward, and see that the foot comes to the ground flat, that the heels land first, or that the toe lands first. As you watch the horse coming towards you, focus on one forelimb at a time: they are highly likely not to move straight, and you might see one or both of them make either a C- or an S-shaped path. It may also be apparent that the last point of the shoe to leave the ground is off to one side, so the foot does not breakover exactly at the toe.

Watching from behind, the hind limbs are again unlikely to move straight, and the feet may well twist as they come to the ground. One side of the croup (that of the functionally longer leg) may be *raised* as that hind limb is brought forward, dropping to level as it hits the ground. In comparison, the croup on the side of the functionally shorter leg will appear to be *lowered* as the leg leaves the ground, coming up as the hoof strikes the ground. You may also find that the sticker on one side of the ribcage is visible for much more of the time than the sticker on the other side, suggesting that the rib cage is carried permanently to one side, and perhaps even that the horse's spine has an in-built curvature.

If you walk the horse on a raked or rolled sand surface, you can see from the hoof prints where each hind foot lands relative to the forefoot on the same side, and you can also measure the stride length of each limb. If you walk the horse on a concrete or tarmac surface, you can use your hearing as well; the foot should, in theory, land with both heels at the same time, followed less than one hundredth of a second later by the toe – a discrepancy which it is impossible to see with the naked eye, or hear with the naked ear. (This means that if we could see the foot land in slow motion, it would land rather like an aeroplane, which touches down with its rear wheels first.) At each footfall, you should hear a crisp 'plop'; if you hear 'kuh-lops', you know that the heels touched down first, with so much time elapsing before the toe lands that you can indeed discern it. With one heel landing first, and yet more twisting and sliding, the sound becomes even more slurred; and if the toe lands first it sounds more like a scrape than a 'plop', and the chances are that the horse has extremely long feet.

....

The previous exercise is extremely useful in helping to develop your eye, and to show you that nothing is as straightforward as it appears. The patterns that emerge from this gait analysis, however, can be extremely complex. Furthermore, as the horse walks or trots he utilises the compensations which help to keep him pain-free, so you may well not be seeing his body in its natural state, moving in the way that his conformation dictates. Because of this, some remedial farriers prefer to shoe the horse according to how he *stands* (which is, of course, how he spends most of his time), rather than how he *moves*.

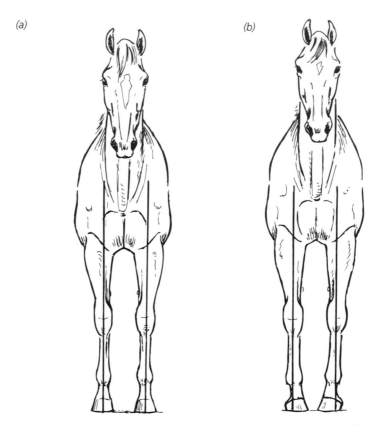

Fig. 4.15 (a) A plumb line from the chest should pass through the knee, fetlock, and the centre of the hoof; but as shown in (b) (and also in Fig. 4.12), it may not.

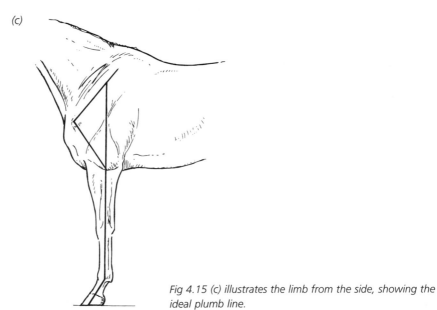

Fig 4.15 (c) illustrates the limb from the side, showing the ideal plumb line.

So for an easier assessment of the horse's limbs (which you can do alone), observe the standing horse. Most people are aware of how the limbs should line up in relation to a plumb line (see Figs 4.15 and 4.16), and of the most common deviations – over and back at the knee on the forelimb, and sickle hocks, or cow hocks on the hind limb. But few people actually bother to make a plumb line, and to look at their own horse. This may reveal far more subtle deviations, which in a foreleg can include either a twist in the limb and the foot (as shown in Fig. 4.12) or a lateral displacement of the knee. If the toes turn in, the elbows turn out, which gives the limb much greater freedom of movement than it has if the elbows turn in and the feet turn out. In the hind limbs it is common for the hocks to turn in (cow hocks) and the toes to turn out, and this allows the stifle to swing forward clear of the belly.

Viewing the hock from above and looking down the cannon bone, your eye should trace a line which passes down a straight stack of bones to the centre of the hoof – but it may well not. Also, if you view the horse from behind each hind leg, you should ideally find that he has a leg at each corner, and that the hind limb blocks your view of the forelimb. Standing

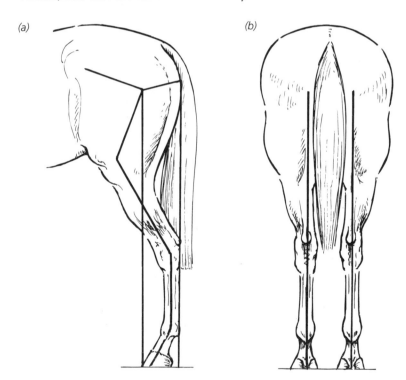

(a)   (b)

Fig. 4.16 A plumb line dropped down the back of the hind limb from the point of the buttock, should run down the line of the back of the limb as in (a). It should bisect the hock, the fetlock, and the hoof as in (b).

slightly to the inside and the outside of the hind limb and viewing the forelimb from behind also gives another view of whether it, too, is a straight stack of bones. We all know how difficult it is to find a horse with ideal conformation (and how costly that horse will be!); but remarkably, it is all but impossible to find a horse with *straight legs*, and when looked at closely, virtually all horses deviate from the textbook norm.

You can also learn a lot by 'hanging' the forelimbs (see Fig. 4.17). Pick up one foot, and facing forward, hold the foreleg above the knee so that the lower limb drops freely. Then look down it, and see if it hangs straight

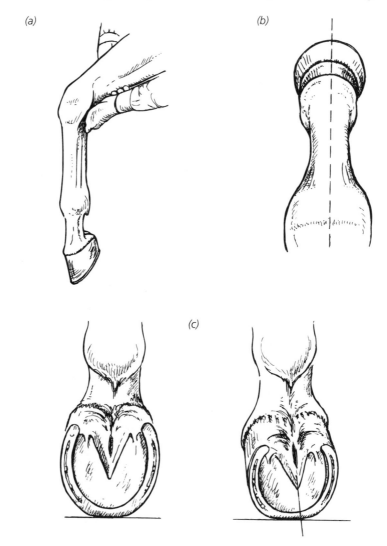

(a)　　　　　　　　　(b)

(c)

Fig. 4.17 (a) and (b) Hanging the forelimbs allows you to look down them and observe if they are straight. (c) If you then lower the toe to the ground, it will make contact at the breakover point, which may not be at the centre of the toe.

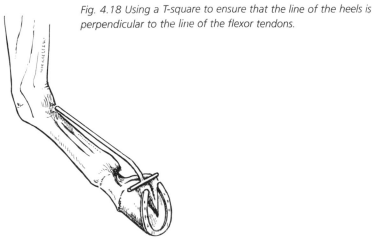

Fig. 4.18 Using a T-square to ensure that the line of the heels is perpendicular to the line of the flexor tendons.

– the most probable place for deviations is the hoof. If you can, lower the limb to rest the toe on the ground (a relaxed horse will allow you to do this, especially if you swing the lower limb gently backwards and forwards as you lower the toe to the ground). The hoof will touch the ground at the breakover point – which may turn out not to be dead in the centre of the hoof. You can also find the breakover point by standing the horse square and pinching him gently midway down the flexor tendons, so that he lifts his heel up off the ground, and rests his foot on the toe. A well-worn shoe will also show the breakover point, and whether one side of the foot weight-bears more than the other.

Some farriers assess the leg and foot by using a T-square with a long stem which curves around the fetlock (see Fig. 4.18). They let the horse pick his foot up naturally, hold the leg under the cannon bone, and then lie the stem down the line of the flexor tendons. This allows them to check whether or not the ground surface at the heels lies at a right angle to them, and to observe the foot and limb lying as they do in their normal flight pattern. In a straight leg, the heels should be at 90° to the limb, and if they are not, one of them will strike the ground before the other. But if the leg is not straight the picture becomes more complicated, and reading the T-square requires a very sophisticated understanding of the dynamics of movement.

....

The advantage of paying attention to the patterns of motion is that it really makes you think about *function*, and not just about *structure*. When lameness becomes apparent, the aim of veterinary diagnosis is to identify the presenting problem and to treat it using drugs or surgery. It is not always customary to back up a stage and consider the evolution of cause and effect: but since any chain is only ever as strong as its weakest link, there must always be a reason *why* this particular spot has become the presenting difficulty. Within the bony columns of the horse's legs, margins for error have been virtually eliminated in a trade-off designed to create a lightweight structure which enables the horse to escape quickly from predators. So the stresses created by bad and/or infrequent shoeing can have devastating effects over time, affecting bones and joints as well as tendons and ligaments.

Lameness is usually the culmination of forces which have been pulling different parts of the limb in different directions, until the compression or tension this creates eventually causes it to give out somewhere. The joints of the leg are designed to allow a little sideways movement, for without this the horse would not have enough leeway to move over rough ground and go around corners. This is facilitated by the curved shape of the joint surfaces and the spaces between them; and it is limited by the collateral ligaments situated on each side of the joint capsule (see Fig. 4.19). When the horse's limb is in the air, the joint spaces will be even; and instinctively, the horse will want to move in a way which keeps them even as the hoof strikes the ground.

In the short term, the limb can tolerate some unevenness; but in the long term, the compression of one side of the joint capsule, along with the stretching of the collateral ligaments on the other side, and the stress placed on their attachment to the bone, are likely to lead to lameness. This

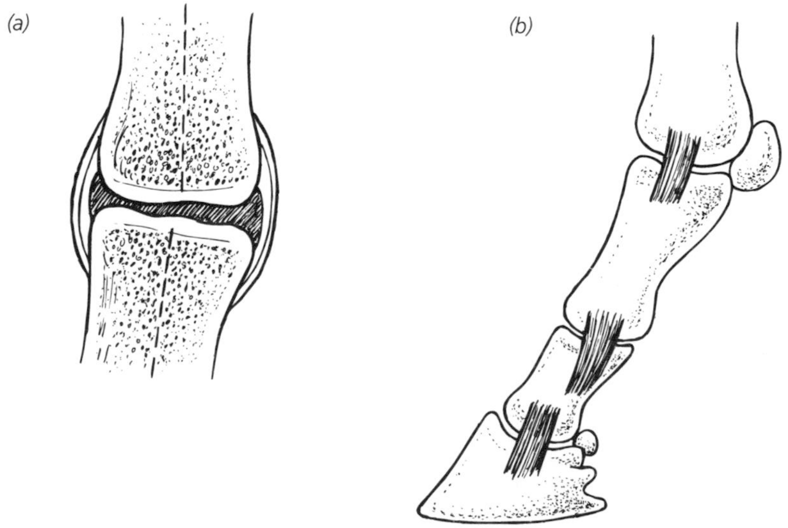

> '*When the horse's limb is in the air, the joint spaces will be even; and instinctively, the horse will want to move in a way which keeps them even as the hoof strikes the ground.*'

(a)   (b)

Fig. 4.19 (a) The distortion of the joint spaces between the bones of the limb and (b) the positions of the collateral ligaments.

makes it easy to understand why circling in one direction exaggerates the problem and shows the horse as lame, whilst going in the other direction mitigates it, and leaves the horse sound. Since this will be the result of a long period of foot imbalance, you – as the distraught owner – are unlikely to associate the lameness with the foot. But a good farrier who can help you discover the cause of the problem (and not merely treat the symptoms) could give your horse a new lease of life.

Our traditional ways of waiting until trouble occurs and then thinking about the 'what' more than the 'why' are rather like shutting the gate after the horse has bolted. It is in the light of a *functional* way of thinking that farriery can become preventative medicine at its best; in fact, Haydn Price and Rod Fisher, in their book *Shoeing for Performance,* go so far as to suggest that skilful farriery can extend your horse's useful working life by five years, an estimate which Dr Gail Williams regards as conservative.

....

From your observations, it may well have become apparent that each limb can be out of balance both from toe to heel (known as dorso–palmar balance), and from side to side (known as medio–lateral balance). If you have indeed scrutinised your horse and analysed his movement patterns, you may well have learned a tremendous amount about him which you did not know before – but what you then *do* with the information you have gleaned is a rather tricky question! It comes into its own when you are about to purchase a horse, and when you are hunting down the origins of an obscure lameness. But before you start arguing with your farrier about the ramifications of your observations, please appreciate that a fundamental dilemma faces every farrier who cares to look further up the limb than the foot itself. For he can create a textbook set of feet which adhere to the ideals of conformation and shoeing: he can trim the foot so that the coronet is the same distance from the ground on each side of the foot, and on each pair of feet. The hoof/pastern angles can be perfect, and the breakover point made to lie exactly in the centre of each toe. When the foot is picked up, the inside and outside halves of the foot can be made to look identical in shape. But in response to this, the horse may well go hopping lame.

You can think of the hoof capsule as if it were made of plasticine or modelling clay. It is a malleable medium, which changes shape in response to the demands placed upon it. So the unshod horse roaming in the wild can sculpt himself the perfect set of feet for his particular limb conformation. The coronary band, which manufactures the hoof wall, is able to sense which parts of it wear away faster as a result of landing heavier or earlier than the rest of the hoof, and in response it secretes more

....

'The unshod horse roaming in the wild can sculpt himself the perfect set of feet for his particular limb conformation.'

....

horn. On a suitably abrasive surface, this makes the feet self-maintaining: for if the horse is to produce mile after mile of trouble-free movement, what is required is that the feet land *flat*, contacting the ground as described earlier, with both heels landing at the same time, just a fraction of a second in front of the toe. They must also take a straight-line path over the ground, or make a simple arc, curving outwards or inwards (without, hopefully, doing so to such an extent that the horse interferes with the other leg in each stride).

The naturally sculpted hoof is much more adaptable than the shod hoof, responding to changes in the horse's weight, muscle development and way of going; but the result of this is that each pair of feet is rarely an exact pair, and the wall on one side of the foot (usually the inside) is nearly always more upright and shorter than that on the other side, making the coronary band closer to the ground on that side. Since the inside of each leg is closer to the horse's centre of gravity, more weight is transmitted through it, and this reduces the blood supply to that side, compressing the hoof wall and making it more upright. The outside of the hoof, in contrast, suffers more from the forces of *concussion* than from *compression* making it more likely to crack. The hoof breaks over at the 'functional toe' which may not be dead centre; for this would require a perfectly straight limb to be stacked up above the perfectly aligned hoof.

'In the shod hoof, the coronet still produces extra wall in the areas that land early or are overburdened; but the shoe stops it from wearing away faster, and nature's master plan is thwarted.'

In the shod hoof, the coronet still produces extra wall in the areas that land early or are overburdened; but the shoe stops it from wearing away faster, and nature's master plan is thwarted. The more deviation there is from the ideal foot fall, the more complex the situation becomes: many horses, for instance, land first on the outside quarter of the front feet and then twist to bring the inside heel down. The growth rings on the hoof can even become distorted, for faster growth in hard-hitting areas causes them to be wider apart than they will be anywhere else. In extreme cases, the coronary band too can become distorted, for as the fast-growing horn is not worn away the coronary band is pushed *up* (see Fig. 4.20.).

Any farrier who attempted to force the 'physically challenged' horse to break over in the centre of the toe would introduce a *twist* into the flight path of the hoof, so that it no longer makes a simple C-shaped arc. This attempt to better nature creates the S-shaped path which significantly increases the chance that the horse will interfere with his opposite leg. The strain on joints and ligaments is increased hugely, and so are the chances of lameness, for the upper and lower limbs are working against each other. It is as if tension is being wound into the joints, and through this the horse can even be induced to dish in front and to brush behind. As the foot is brought to the ground the ligaments surrounding the joints are put under an abnormal twisting, and as the foot leaves the ground they 'ping' back into their natural state, altering the flight path of

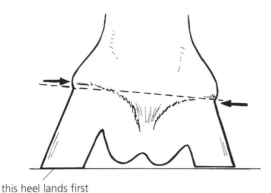

this heel lands first

Fig. 4.20 When one heel of the foot lands before the other, the horn grows faster but the shoe stops it from being worn away; so the hoof wall can be pushed up on that side.

the hoof. This also implies the converse: that dishing and brushing are often the result of medio–lateral foot imbalances, and are not always the result of conformation.

The shoe will gradually wear in a way which makes the footfall more level, creating a ground surface which comes closer to that which the horse would have if left unshod. In the process one branch of the shoe may well wear more than the other. His actual foot, however, with the shoe removed, would *not* land level, for it needs these custom-made compensations in order to do so. The worn shoes provide important clues for the farrier; for if the foot were trimmed to resemble the surface of the worn shoe, it would make a more level footfall (landing with both heels at the same time), and the wear on the new shoe would become more even. The shoes would then last a lot longer, for when the foot is in the best possible balance to support its limb, no one part of the shoe is consistently overloaded. (It is normal, however, for the outside branch of the hind shoes to wear more quickly than the inside branch, for the distance between the thigh bones is bigger than the distance between the hooves, and the horse attempts to place the foot at 90° to the axis of the limb, which is not actually vertical. The loading will only be even when the horse moves wider behind in the faster gaits, which he naturally does to maintain balance and avoid interfering with his front feet.)

This means that if you or your farrier ever become tempted to mitigate the effects of uneven wear on a shoe by applying a hard surface like tungsten carbide to parts of the shoe, you go completely *against* nature, and make any limb imbalance worse. It also means that it pays you, as the horse's owner, to keep track of how he wears his shoes – for any abnormal wear could be the first sign of an impending problem. On an old set of shoes, the 'body reading' you did earlier encompasses the hoof plus its compensations, coming close to the hoof that the unshod horse would sculpt for himself; on new shoes it tells you whether the foot itself has been trimmed to encourage a level footfall, or to adhere to the ideals of perfect conformation.

If the horse's footfall is observed with his shoes removed, it is *the parts of the hoof which meet the ground first* that need to be trimmed, for this simulates the wear which would have happened to the horse if he had been left unshod. In preparing the foot, one side may have to be trimmed more in order to create medio–lateral balance. If the heels of the unshod horse land noticeably before the toe, they are too long and need trimming; and if the toe lands before the heel, the toe is too long. When the foot of the shod horse lands toe first, the shoes have probably been left on for far too long (see Fig. 4.21). Alternatively, the horse is already experiencing pain, and is adopting a compensatory movement pattern designed to keep weight *off* his heels.

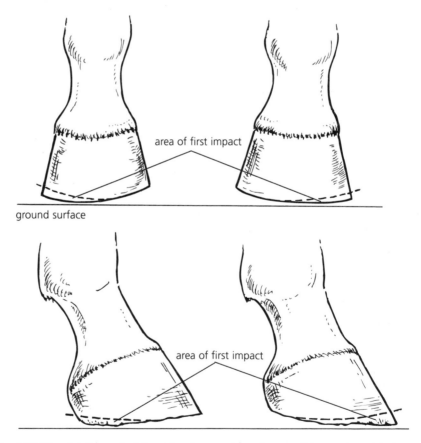

area of first impact

ground surface

area of first impact

Fig. 4.21 Trimming the unshod foot. The diagram shows four possible ways in which the unshod foot could land on the ground: with the inner or outer branch first (top), or the heel or toe first (lower). The dotted line shows the hoof that should be rasped away in each case.

So if the horse's plight is appearing to become ever more complex (and if you despair of understanding my appraisal of it), please appreciate that it *really is* extremely complex. It was the Romans who first shod horses, and throughout the centuries since we have committed many, many sins. Today, we have reached a point where the discrepancy between the foot which is deemed perfect by the textbooks and that which is deemed perfect by the horse's limb can be immense. The 'map makers' at the forefront of farriery are making more astute observations than ever, with progressively more of them becoming united behind the principles of the 'four-point trim' (which, of itself, helps to mitigate medio-lateral foot imbalances). Their less radical colleagues, however, do not see the need for change, or for such precise thinking. From 'slash and bash' to 'gourmet shoeing', farriers' understanding and their application of the principles involved vary hugely.

....

The skill needed for a farrier to create a level footfall should not be underestimated, and there is even more to it than correctly analysing the patterns of the horse's movement. For every farrier, as he rasps the foot, will have his own predisposition towards creating a certain unlevelness. The farrier is more effective when he pushes the rasp away from him than when he draws it towards him, and apprentices are often guilty of 'rocking-horse trimming', which rasps away more at each end of their sweep and than it does in the middle. To leave one side of each foot lower than the other is one of the most commonly made mistakes in shoeing, and I was horrified recently to see a horse who was, quite literally, walking as if on the left side of all four feet.

> 'The skill needed for a farrier to create a level footfall should not be underestimated.'

Given the complexity of both horses and people, it is perhaps not surprising that about *95 per cent of horses* show a medio-lateral foot imbalance, with one heel landing before the other. Ultimately, this is associated not just with dishing and brushing. (These opposite rotations of the front and hind limbs occur because the way in which the farrier holds the limb and the rasp in each case encourages him to take too much horn off the inside of the front feet, and off the outside of the hind feet.) The joints are stressed so much by this that the eventual outcome could well be degenerative joint disease in the coffin joint, fetlock joint or knee joint, as well as sesamoiditis, sesamoid fractures, and chip fractures in the long pastern bone. Thus there is an extremely high price to be paid for forcing the horse to move in a way that is different to the one which nature intended!

> '95 per cent of horses show a medio-lateral foot imbalance.'

When the foot is not balanced to its limb and one heel lands before the other, there will often be a very deep cleft in the centre of the frog. As the first heel hits the ground the frog on that side is pushed up; but the second heel is still dropping *down*, and this discrepancy creates a shearing force which deepens the cleft. This, and/or the uneven forces acting on the limb, will often create lameness (see Fig. 4.22). When the foot *twists* as it hits the ground (which happens much more commonly in hind feet), the frog is often overdeveloped. It has, however, much more flexibility than the rest of the limb in its response to the stresses involved.

So it also makes absolutely no sense to carefully trim the foot for a level footfall, and then to add a stud. For the stud, which stands proud of the shoe, contacts the ground first, and unless it sinks straight into the ground, the footfall is again uneven. But even if it *does* sink in, one stud placed in the outer heel of the hind foot causes that heel to be retarded relative to the other one, so that the foot twists around it, bringing the toe out and the hocks closer together. Then, as the limb leaves the ground it 'unwinds' that twist to re-find its natural flight, but in the next landing the tension is wound into the joints again, only to be unwound during the next flight.

The pressure on the hoof wall directly above a stud is so intense that the wall can be pushed up, distorting the growth rings and crushing the coronet (see Fig. 4.23). Both the vertical force and the shearing forces created by the stud do so much damage that it is far better, whenever possible, to place a small stud nail back towards each heel (or even to use a stud in each side), for these will not alter the balance of the foot. Eventers and show jumpers in particular are often extremely reluctant to give up using studs, although – to their credit – they are usually very sensible about leaving them in for the shortest possible time. But it is questionable whether the gains exist just in their mind, or in the reality of a more secure and comfortable horse.

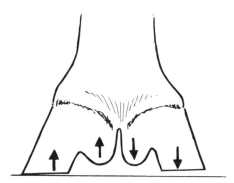

Fig. 4.22 The heel of the foot which lands first is pushed up, along with the frog on that side, whilst the other side of the frog and hoof are still dropping down. Thus a shearing force pulls the two sides of the frog apart, creating a very deep cleft which may become painful, and making the heels move independently of each other.

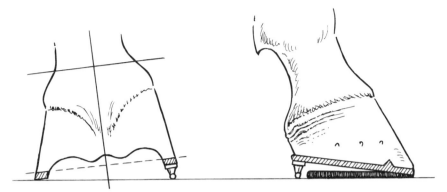

Fig. 4.23 The effect of placing a single stud in the outer heel of the shoe. The growth rings are pushed up, and the bones no longer stack up vertically.

The stress of weight-bearing on the hoof itself is hugely increased, as we have seen, by both the long toe and the low heel, as well as by the medio-lateral imbalances which cause one heel to land in advance of the other. The side of the foot which is longer lands first, and is subject to strong leverage forces which can tear the horn away from the laminae. This creates a *flare*, in which a portion of the horn bulges outwards. The way in which the farrier is naturally inclined to rasp the front and hind feet creates a different imbalance in each, making flares more common on the outside of the front feet and the inside of the hind feet. The farrier's job is to create a level landing, and by doing this he hopes to stop the hoof capsule from becoming more and more upright on one side (the side of greater compression) and splaying out more on the other side (the side of greater concussion and higher leverage forces). So if the situation were instead allowed to worsen, the hoof capsule would work its way out *sideways* from under the limb, losing the ideal line-up of Fig. 4.24a.

There is another factor at play, however, for nature – as well as poor farriery – can cause this to happen. Flares can be nature's response to poor conformation, and when the horse is base-narrow or base-wide, the hoof does not stand in the ideal position under the horse's body, and it cannot support weight as it should. So the wall splays outwards *in the section of the foot which lies beneath the unsupported weight.* So if the narrow-chested horse has his front feet too close together, flares develop on the outside of the hoof in an attempt to support the weight which lies further out. The cow-hocked horse whose hind feet are very close together will show the same phenomenon behind, and if you drop a plumb line from the side of the horse's shoulder near the elbow joint, or from the horse's greater trochanter of the femur, it will line up with the edge of the flare. (The greater trochanter of the femur is a fairly well-padded bony knobble which lies toward the back of the quarters on approximately the same

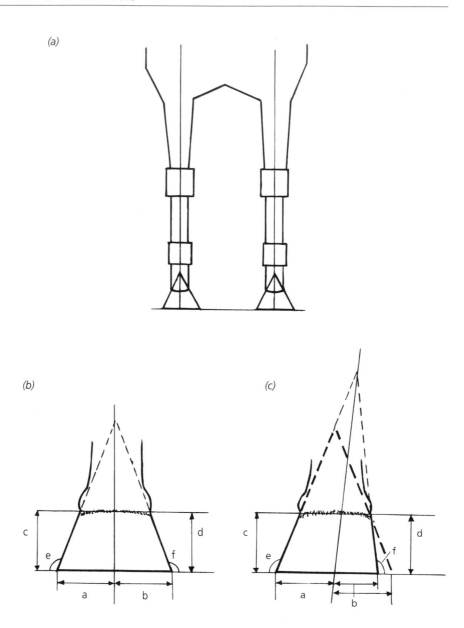

Fig. 4.24 (a) A schematic representation of a textbook pair of forelimbs, with the hoof capsule perfectly positioned under the limb. (b) Shows the symmetrical hoof of the textbook, which has equal lengths from the centre to each side (a and b), equal heights on each side (c and d) and equal angles at each side (e and f). If the lines of the wall were extended on each side they would meet in the centre of the leg as shown by the dotted lines, keeping the stresses on the limb symmetrical. (c) Extending the lines of the wall on this asymmetrical hoof does not cause them to meet in the centre of the leg, and this causes asymmetrical stresses on the limb; but these can be normalised by shoeing the foot wider on the more upright side, creating the same effect as the symmetrical hoof shown in (b). (My thanks to Robbie Richardson for permission to use these diagrams.)

level as the point of the buttock.) It is almost always the outside of the front feet which flare; hind feet are more variable, with different types of horse and different farriers creating different patterns.

Good shoeing aims to place the hoof capsule *directly beneath* the long axis of the limb, so that the horse's weight passes down from the point of the buttock or the point of the shoulder to the centre of the foot (Fig. 4.24a): in other words, the farrier has to shoe the limb, and not just the foot. So he may need to fit the shoe wide on the most upright side of the hoof, effectively creating symmetry in the weight-bearing surface. Again, he creates the shape that the foot *ought to be* instead of perpetuating the shape that it is (see Fig. 4.24b-c). On other side, he will dress back the flare in the lower part of the wall, so that he stops the foot from cracking and allows it to function more normally. If the flare is the result of bad shoeing he will fit the shoe tight, but if it is the horse's attempt to place his foot beneath body weight which is otherwise unsupported, he will want to maintain the required width.

With a horse who brushes, traditional practice has been to close the fullering on the inside branch of the shoe. This creates the narrowed ground surface of the feather-edged shoe, which is also made less obtrusive by fitting it in under the wall. But this attempt to minimise the damage addresses only the foot, and does not consider *why* it is taking that particular flight path. The problem cannot truly be solved without rebalancing the entire limb, and placing the foot under its long axis. The feather-edged shoe can, in fact, cause the horse to brush *more*, for it creates an imbalance between the inside and the outside of the foot which rotates the limb in towards the other as it swings forward. In contrast, *widening* the inside branch of the shoe tends to rotate the limb the other way, evening out the stresses on the limb, minimising the likelihood of brushing – and turning our established mode of thinking on its head. (See Fig. 4.24c.) Another point against the feather-edged shoe is that it leaves the wall on the inside with little support, and since it is already subject to tremendous compression, the damage that is done can be significant.

'The farrier has to shoe the limb, and not just the foot.'

· · · · · · · · · · · · · · · ·

Most limb and foot imbalances begin early, and when a skilful farrier works with foals, he can have a tremendous influence on their limb development. Conversely, this means that neglecting to have their feet trimmed can also have a tremendous influence on the straightness of their limbs and their long-term soundness. Both the cannon bone, and the bones of the upper limbs contain a growth plate towards each end. This is a soft area of cartilage from which new bone is secreted. There is also a growth plate toward the upper end of the long and the short pastern bones. The growth plates close from the bottom up: the short pastern is fully grown and set just before the long pastern, whose growth plate closes at three months. The bottom end of the cannon bone closes at six months. This means that the farrier has *three months* in which to balance the leg and influence the way it grows. During this time, he can adjust the hoof/pastern axis, and the straightness of the limbs.

The foal may be born with legs which are slightly or obviously crooked. But tremendous damage can be done if, for any reason, he keeps weight off a painful limb; then, the growth plates of its opposite pair become overloaded, especially on one side. This will slow down the growth of the limb, particularly on the more weighted side, and create a deformity. The growth plates themselves are easily damaged by trauma, and this will affect their functioning to such a degree that veterinary intervention will almost certainly be needed. But a far more insidious influence on the development of the foal's growing limbs is the diet of his dam, which must be carefully monitored, not just to ensure the foal's growth, but to ensure that there is not *too much growth too quickly.*

There is a tremendously high price to be paid for this: for 'ballerina syndrome' is the result of so much rich food that the bones grow faster than the growth of the tendons can accommodate. This requires one or more of the feet to compensate for the problem by becoming more upright in the heels, creating the so-called 'club foot'. Virtually every pair of uneven feet became that way during the first few months of life, and the closing of the growth plates signals the end of the influence that the farrier can have over the alignment of the limbs, and the evenness of the feet those limbs will sculpt.

Some vets, chiropractors and farriers believe that the unevenness can develop even without this dietary mistake, for the long-legged foal has to graze with his front feet apart, and if he always advances the same leg, the limbs develop under the influence of different stresses. These create asymmetries all the way from the feet to the shoulders and even back through the spine (contributing to the unevennesses of Figs 4.11 and 4.12). The heels of the weight-bearing leg become more crushed, whilst the forward leg which carries less weight will have a more upright heel. These differences will be exaggerated if the hooves are saturated with water, and will be less significant under dry conditions.

Growth and symmetry can even be affected by the stance taken when a youngster has a hoof abscess (for instance) which occurs during a fast growing period and goes undiagnosed for only a few days. Some practitioners find these explanations for right- or 'left-handed' horses far more convincing than the traditional ones of the way in which the foal lies in the womb, or the way in which we lead him. For so little leading is done during this formative time, and the foal can lie in the womb in so many different ways that one would not expect this to cause horse asymmetries which have such a uniform pattern.

....

As the farrier seeks to make the best of the legs the adult horse has developed, modern technology gives him many more options than ever before. We have come a long way since the days when sole pads were old pieces of leather, and disintegrating hoofs were held together with car repair kits. We now have many high-tech alternatives, and the latest pads are made of a dense plastic, beneath which the farrier can inject an anti-fungal silicon solution. It is undoubtedly true that if a horse becomes lame on hard ground, you are seeing evidence of a problem which already existed – but damaged walls and thin soles can now be protected with far less chance of creating the moist, anaerobic environment in which the sole could not dry out, and thrush and fungal infections could flourish. The leather pads, too, had their limitations, expanding and contracting so much that nails easily became loose, leading to the premature loss of the shoe.

At around £20 ($32) a pair, plastic sole pads may well be a worthwhile investment; but with glue-on plastic shoes running at £100 ($160) a pair, you might think twice before using them! Some horses, however, become reformed characters and show vastly improved performance when they do not have nails driven through their horn, so the shoes can become a worthwhile investment (and if a horse has hardly any wall they may be your only choice). As plastics and glues improve (and as solvents are found to dissolve the glues), we may well see synthetic shoes becoming much more common. But since most are currently over four times the price of a stainless-steel shoe, the benefits will not warrant the cost in a horse who only hacks out at weekends. Unless this changes significantly, they will probably remain the province of the high-performance horse.

Aluminium shoes (which are used most commonly as racing plates) have the advantage of being much lighter than steel, but they wear quickly and are easily bent out of shape. An alloy made of aluminium and magnesium has proved stronger, and holds great promise for the future. Titanium has also been tried: it is strong, light and non-corrosive, and it maintains its shape, but it does not absorb concussion well. 'Sneakers' are shoes designed to enhance the absorption of concussion, involving aluminium and a thick layer of rubber which began its life as an industrial tyre. Technology will doubtless expand our options, but there probably is no single ideal material for horse shoes, and time will tell whether we can find a robust, affordable shoe which is a significant improvement on steel.

A few years ago, a team of engineers who knew nothing about horses – but a lot about forces – were given the brief of designing a horse shoe.

'Time will tell whether we can find a robust, affordable shoe which is a significant improvement on steel.'

They came up with a basic stainless-steel shoe, to which one could fit various plastic inserts, each for a different job. But, to change one for another, you had to stand the horse on a firm surface, lift up the foot, put the insert in place, and then pick up the *opposite* foot so that the horse's weight would 'click' it into position. The only problem was that, at a one-day event, for instance, there is rarely a flat concrete surface to stand the horse on! Also, if you dropped the foot after removing the insert, you were in danger of damaging the channelling into which the new one was supposed to fit. The base shoes were intended to last for several shoeings, but in practice they were not as robust as expected, and the costs of the system were high. It never took off.

As well as the increasing number of materials used to create pads and horse shoes, there are a variety of materials which can be used to encase injured hooves far more effectively than the plastic bags and old bran sacks of yesteryear. We also have hoof fillers, hoof repair compounds, and hoof restructuring compounds. Weak and cracked walls can be reinforced, and if an accident or surgery has caused the removal of a large piece of wall, the hole can be patched with acrylic resin. Also, resin granules can be built up in layers using an acrylic adhesive, creating 'horn' which can, for instance, build up the short side of a hoof with a significant medio-lateral imbalance. It can then be rasped and shod as normal.

Not to be underestimated in all of these high-tech (and high cost) options is the skill to diagnose accurately – to use the appropriate technique at the appropriate time, and to use it *well*. This is extremely specialist work, and some approaches may require the hygienic conditions which are only to be found in a veterinary hospital – for sealing bacteria into the foot can create horrendous problems. But the dangers inherent in these techniques also include the deliberate masking of problems which then go unseen in breeding stallions or in the sale ring. As technology allows us, quite literally, to rebuild hooves, the wisdom to use our influence for good cannot be taken for granted.

....

The issues involved in updating our map of farriery are clearly very complex, and for every farrier who addresses the issue of how the horse's weight is balanced over his limbs, there are many who do not, and who trim the foot solely with the intention of removing the excess growth. In the UK our farriers undergo an extensive training, but the degree to which this addresses the finer points of their art depends a lot on the farrier with whom they have spent their apprenticeship, and on their own desire to think about the ramifications of foot balance and to provide a service which goes beyond the basics of 'slash and bash'. In the USA (where, historically, every cowboy worth his salt had to be able to shoe his horses), there is much less regulation, and a greater variety in standards.

It is undoubtedly difficult for the roving farrier to carry a stock of horse shoes which equips him for every occasion, and most shoe all horses in one style, regardless of their type and the job that they do. It is perhaps fortunate for them that so many horses are a 'jack of all trades' – and since each job ideally requires a different approach, compromises must be made. Inevitably, the more specialist remedial work is beyond the scope and training of many; but despite the long-term pay-offs of the balanced foot (an increase in the life span of your horse, along with a decrease in vet's bills and heartache) we are reluctant to travel our horses to a specialist, and to the more ideal conditions of his forge. For without good conditions to work in, even the best farrier has his hands tied. If he cannot stand the horse on a level surface, and cannot see him move, he cannot diagnose well. If he is working outside in the pouring rain, or he does not have good light, we cannot possibly expect him to do as good a job as he could in ideal conditions.

The farrier is always making compromises, and the need to provide what his (often ill-informed) customers want to see, and the need to earn his living (and thus to work rather quickly) may well conflict – for the more skilled and conscientious farrier – with the desire to provide what he believes the horses in his care really need. Indeed, the true cost of skilful and remedial work comes as a shock to many horse owners. The pressure on farriers comes from all directions – from recalcitrant horses, difficult owners, tradition, and fashion. All of these intermingle with the need to pay their bills, the sheer complexity of their craft, and the need to keep up with the leading-edge changes which update their maps. As their consumers become more discerning (demanding more than 'slash and bash' done as infrequently as possible), the pressure on some farriers will ease, and on others will increase. But they alone cannot make the changes from which our horses stand to gain so much. We too need to update our maps and do our share.

CHAPTER FIVE

Saddles and Saddle Fit

MANY RIDERS TREASURE their saddle (or saddles) more dearly than any other piece of equestrian equipment they own. After their horse and their trailer it is indeed their most expensive investment; but it is also the most difficult-to-get-right, potentially dangerous item in their tack room. I dread telling anyone that their saddle does not fit their horse, for the ramifications of this are so huge in terms of damage done, replacement cost and hassle generated. Yet it is a prospect I am often faced with. Buying saddles is really an exercise in 'damage limitation', and I have seen a number of people who unwittingly took themselves 'out of the frying pan, into the fire'. I myself have bought and sold more saddles than I care to remember (including one which was soon discovered to have a broken tree, purchased at auction during my student days when I was in desperate need of a bargain). There will always be people operating at the bottom end of the market who will saddle their horses with everybody else's rejects; but at the top end of the market there are also many sins committed, primarily in the name of fashion.

But these are not strictly the fault of horse owners, who almost invariably mean to do the best they can by their horses. Many people fall into the trap of *thinking they know more than they do* — and the traditional rules, although useful, are not sufficient as guides for their purchase. To their credit, however, most horse owners would not buy a saddle without advice from a reputable professional, and in the UK that 'reputable professional' may or may not have attended a saddle-fitting course. Until recently that course would have been a single day's training, which can hardly be regarded as comprehensive, and which did not lead to a recognised qualification; now it is a four-day course which does. But even the best fitter of saddles can only choose between those that are available on the market, so he is at the mercy of the saddle makers, who themselves are at the mercy of the tree manufacturers.

In the UK and Europe virtually everyone rides in a saddle which Americans would define as 'English' — using this term as a generic description of all of those saddles which are not Western. This being so, I have little experience of Western saddles, and this chapter is mostly confined to a discussion of the problems with beset English saddles. I have referred at times to the most obvious problems that I am aware of in Western saddles; I hope Western riders will forgive this scant attention, and be able to generalise from the principles outlined here and glean some useful information.

The actual *design* of trees and saddles is the province of a handful of people, who shape the direction of the whole industry. The vast majority of people employed in the saddlery industry are simply doing what they are told to do, and using the skills that they were trained in without regard for the design of the finished product. Sadly, there is a great divide between *riders*, and the saddlers who both design and make saddles. Many workers in the industry have little clue about what is involved in actually riding (many, in fact, have never set foot near a horse!). On the other hand, very few riders know anything about the design and production of the product which means so much to them. Relatively few people – usually saddlers who run a small, very personal, saddlery business and who also ride – have crossed this great divide.

The current trend at the top of the market is to consult with a known, successful rider, and to produce a product which bears her name. We can then presume that the shape and style of the saddle suits her body and her riding – which, of course, provides no guarantee that it will suit yours. And the overt or covert sales pitch that 'You too could ride like So-and-so if only you had a saddle like this,' will inevitably dangle a tantalising carrot in front of many riders – even though the transformation might require a saddle with magical powers! People buy and sell saddles in search of the one which possesses the hidden 'key' to riding, and what was once a purchase for life is often now just a stepping stone to greater things. This increased choice and turnover has revolutionised the saddlery trade and made it far more competitive, but it may now be time for a review – for whilst a bad saddle can indeed compromise your technique, a good saddle can never do the riding for you.

Since the Second World War, changes in saddle design have catered for a huge influx of recreational riders, and have created a (supposedly) more rider-friendly surface. The pre-War saddles used by the British cavalry and in the hunting field may not have been luxurious, but they were at least based on the idea of maximising the horse's comfort by spreading the rider's weight over a large surface area. The modern-day 'improved' (and usually smaller) versions have sacrificed the horse's comfort in a quest to maximise that of the rider – and to offer, perhaps, a competitive edge in an increasingly competitive industry, as well as the promise of that illusory hidden 'key'. Only now are the trends of fashion being reviewed and reversed in the horse's favour.

'Whilst a bad saddle can indeed compromise your technique, a good saddle can never do the riding for you.'

Consider, for instance, the case of recessed stirrup bars. For the rider, these are a great idea, as the bar no longer stands proud of the tree and interferes with her thigh. But the recessed bar has been placed so close to the horse that it often now becomes a pressure point on the *underside* of the saddle. No one consulted the horse about this change, and only now – with computer scanning of the pressures under the saddle – can we really see and appreciate the problems that maximising our own comfort has created for *him*. Dressage girths are another eminently sensible idea for the rider, as there are no more buckles beneath the leg; but they do have drawbacks for the horse. One might also question their necessity, for on a well-designed saddle with a girth of the appropriate length, the buckles will lie behind the rider's knee and not cause any problem.

The buckles of the dressage girth lie over the serratus ventralis, the muscle on the lower part of the rib cage behind the elbow, which draws the body forward over the leg. (See Fig. 5.1a.) This often becomes very tense and sore – especially in the horse who is over-using his forehand to compensate for poor use of his quarters. The mounted rider who is tightening a dressage girth can get a tremendous amount of leverage, pulling almost directly on the ribs and potentially affecting their attachment into the spine. This can cause a dysfunction which can only be righted by manipulative treatment – implying that the rider has already 'manipulated' her horse simply by tightening the girth! It helps to use a girth which is longer than the average dressage girth, which has elastic to each buckle, and a soft, padded buckle guard; but care is still needed.

A physiotherapist or equine massage therapist is the best person to assess the state of the muscles in the horse's back itself, for she will have a

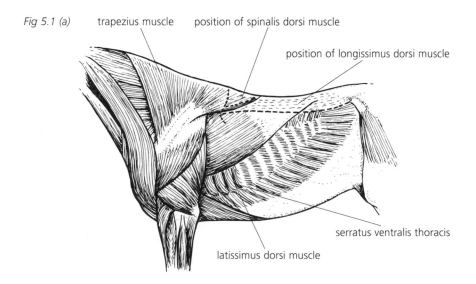

Fig 5.1 (a)   trapezius muscle   position of spinalis dorsi muscle

position of longissimus dorsi muscle

serratus ventralis thoracis

latissimus dorsi muscle

sophisticated touch through which she can diagnose whether a muscle is healthy, bruised, or in spasm. Her touch is likely to reveal soreness in the trapezius muscle which lies behind the shoulder blade, and in the longissimus dorsi lying on each side of the spine (Fig. 5.1b). There are various ways in which she can release that tension; but if the fit of the saddle (or even the state of the horse's feet) are compromising his stance and movement, it is highly likely to re-occur. The horse may even be sore over the spine itself, for the spinal processes and the ligament which covers them lie just beneath the skin, making them very vulnerable to damage from a narrow gullet and/or a gullet which does not give them enough height clearance. Felt pads are notorious for causing this type of

Fig. 5.1 (b)

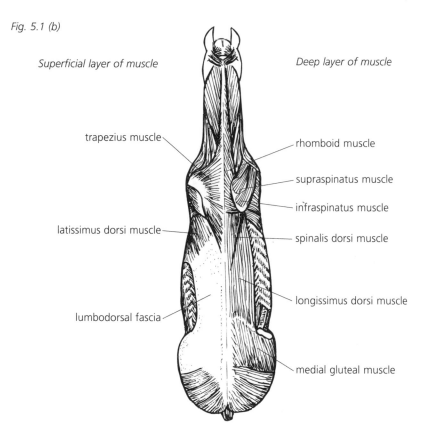

Superficial layer of muscle   *Deep layer of muscle*

trapezius muscle

rhomboid muscle

supraspinatus muscle

infraspinatus muscle

latissimus dorsi muscle

spinalis dorsi muscle

longissimus dorsi muscle

lumbodorsal fascia

medial gluteal muscle

Fig. 5.1 The muscles affected by the saddle: (a) from the side, (b) from above The area just behind the shoulder blades is affected the most by pressure from the tree points and stirrup bars, although the spinal processes can also be damaged if the saddle does not have a wide or deep enough gullet. The area towards the back of the saddle is often affected by friction and by the bruising which results from continued bouncing of the back of the saddle. The serratus ventralis muscle behind the elbow is often made sore by the girth, especially a dressage girth.

damage, and racing saddles with a half tree very often damage the spine at the point where the tree ends.

Yet the damage (from girths and saddles of all types) will be inflicted over and over again, despite the protestations of our horses, who do their best to tell us of their discomfort. Many short-striding horses who move with hollow backs, swishing tails, and their ears pinned back, are making their predicament very clear. But they tell us before we even mount – by refusing to be caught, laying their ears back when we approach with the saddle, and biting, swishing their tail, and kicking out as we girth up. They could not make their case much clearer – and since they only have one language, they have to resort to 'shouting louder at the natives'. But we (the natives) simply reprimand them for their ill-manners and persistently refuse to listen.

....

Despite the fact that modern English saddles have so many variations and innovations which supposedly help us ride better, my contention is that the changes in saddle design which would help our horses could prove equally beneficial for riders – for reasons extending beyond their horse's happiness. Umpteen versions of thigh rolls and knee rolls have created some distinctive designs in modern saddles, but overall they have become smaller than their old-fashioned counterparts, with deeper, more cushioned seats and higher pommels and cantles. So the large, flat surface of old has been replaced by a more hammock-shaped sitting surface. (See Fig. 5.2.) Some saddles have a sitting surface which is fairly symmetrical, with the lowest part in the centre of the saddle. Others slope gradually backwards, finally meeting a cantle which then rises up steeply. This resembles the shape of the seat of a Western saddle, which was designed as an armchair for a passive rider. To all intents and purposes, it appears that this is what we 'English' riders are seeking too.

'The hallmark of an 'independent seat' is that the rider herself generates the muscular forces which mould her onto the horse's movement.'

Both shapes encase the average rider's backside, and give her the illusion that she can sit reasonably well, for her backside is held in place by the cantle, which stops her from bumping backwards. The ultimate challenge of riding is to match the forces exerted on the saddle – and your own body – by the thrust of horse's hind leg. The hallmark of an 'independent seat' is that the rider herself generates the muscular forces which mould her onto the horse's movement. (Ironically, it is this which makes her sit so still that she looks 'relaxed'.) When the rider's body cannot generate enough force in each stride it becomes *inevitable* that she will either bump backwards, or use the reins and/or the cantle to hold herself in place.

At best, the cantle can offer only a false sense of security. Many people, however, perceive this as a viable alternative to an 'independent seat'. To ride without recourse to either the reins or the cantle is a noble ideal; however, the 'props' work well enough to stop many riders from appreciating that they do indeed have a problem. This in turn stops them from seeking the muscle-power which could genuinely hold them in place.

This means that saddle buying is an occasion where (as in riding lessons) what 'feels good' to the average rider is not necessarily a reliable guide, especially when considering her long-term progress. (I do not mean to imply that you should go and buy a saddle that 'feels bad', but when you are buying a saddle you should consider having someone with you who knows more about riding than either you or your saddler.) I was taught as a child that you should be able to place the flat of your hand on the saddle behind your backside; but this rule no longer seems to apply. It does, however, ensure that it is *you* – and not the saddle – who does the riding.

Over the last forty years the pendulum has swung from one extreme – maximising the horse's comfort at the expense of the rider's (although in reality, the old-fashioned saddles probably were pretty spartan for both parties) – right to the other – of maximising the rider's comfort at the expense of the horse. Only now is it beginning to swing back, hopefully to a point where we can learn from experience, combine the best of both worlds, and use modern technology to increase our options. But although saddlers have a huge responsibility, it is *riders* who need to understand the dynamics of riding and saddle fitting, for in this profit-conscious world, it is inevitable that large companies will cater for the demands of the market.

Purists argue that the advent of the modern deep-seated saddle coincided with the demise of the institutionalised cavalry training of riders, and that this lack of training is to blame for all our current problems. I am not so convinced that cavalry training ever achieved very lofty aims, but it is certainly true that modern saddles have made riding available to the masses whilst compromising its basic principles. But many people find themselves stuffed into their saddles by default not by design, since they went out and bought what the market has on offer. The saddle has become a crutch for the average rider, holding her in place and minimising the need for effort. One could argue that this is a much better solution than leaving her to flounder; but I would like riders to be able to make a much more informed choice about their saddle, and their approach to learning. Whilst they know no different, the situation is inevitably self-perpetuating.

'It is certainly true that modern saddles have made riding available to the masses whilst compromising its basic principles.'

....

It is rare, however, for top-class riders to have such small, deep-seated saddles, for many appreciate having room to manoeuvre. Less skilled riders

Fig. 5.2 Four saddles seen from the side, from above, and from underneath: (a) and (b) illustrate designs in common use; (c) and (d) are more modern designs, with (d) being a 'two layer' saddle.

(a)

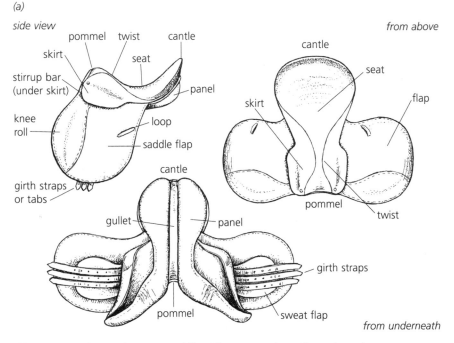

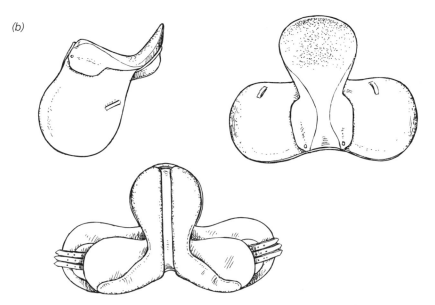

(a) Deep-seated general-purpose saddle with narrow twist, gullet and panels.

(b)

(b) Deep-seated general-purpose saddle. Note that the deepest part of the seat is very far back, and bounded by an extremely high cantle. The twist, gullet and panels are narrow.

(c)

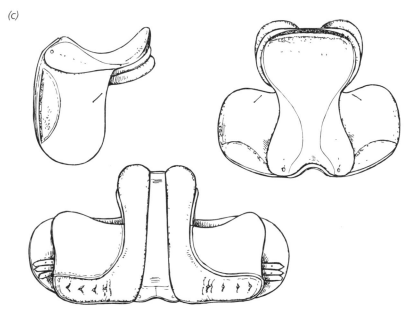

(c) Dressage saddle with flatter seat, wide twist, low cantle, a wide gullet and long wide panels which extend behind the seat.

(d)

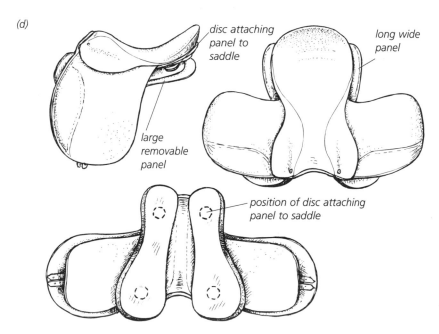

disc attaching panel to saddle

long wide panel

large removable panel

position of disc attaching panel to saddle

(d) Two-layer saddle with a flatter seat. The panels have an extremely large bearing surface, and are far enough apart to give the saddle a very wide gullet.

abhor this, however, since it gives them room to bounce backwards. Many accomplished riders talk of needing to move their centre of gravity forward or back slightly as the horse's evasions vary, and as the demands of different movements pose different biomechanical challenges. But many riders would find themselves unable to do this even if their skill level allowed it, for they are held immovable by saddles which are in reality far too small.

The small seat is often not the saddle's only problem, and many saddles do not have large enough flaps to accommodate the length of the rider's thigh bone, from her greater trochanter (the bony knobble at the top outside of the thigh, where the thigh meets the pelvis – see Fig. 5.12, page 123) to her knee. When you are choosing a saddle this, and the size of your backside, are extremely important variables. Some dressage saddles have such straight flaps that one assumes they were designed for the vertical thigh, which good riders do not in fact have. So riders do not have to be particularly long-legged to find that their knees are appearing over the knee roll when their stirrups are set at the right length. The length of the flap from top to bottom is another important variable, and as a small rider I often find that my feet barely appear beneath the flaps of taller people's dressage saddles! A flap so short that it catches the top of your boots, however, is an even greater annoyance, and one of the delights of having a saddle made for you is to get the optimum shape and length of flap. You can then have a knee roll which is available if you need it – not one that your knee is rammed into, or one that remains permanently out of reach!

Many people talk about the need for the rider to have a shoulder/hip/heel vertical line, and a vertical stirrup leather. But only when the stirrup bars are *correctly placed on the tree* can the rider easily sit like this. For the distance between the stirrup bar and the deepest part of the seat needs to match the distance between the ball of the rider's foot (where the stirrup should rest), and the knobble of her ankle bone (which, when she sits correctly, lies directly beneath the greater trochanter and the deepest part of the saddle). This is 6-7 inches/15-18cm. (See Fig. 5.3a.) The short, deep-seated dressage saddle in which the distance is not sufficient may make the rider sit with a hollow back, for with no room to put her backside down on the saddle she has to get it out of the way somehow! (See Fig. 5.3b.) Many general-purpose saddles have the stirrup bar too far forward, which automatically tempts the rider to adopt an armchair seat, especially if the seat of the saddle slopes backwards to a steep cantle. (Fig. 5.3c) But this distance from the stirrup bar to the deepest part of the seat is not simply a feature of design, as we shall see later; it is also affected by the front-to-back balance of the saddle.

Many older saddles have a groove where the stirrup leather has lain against the flap, and often, riders of old have stuck their feet forward to

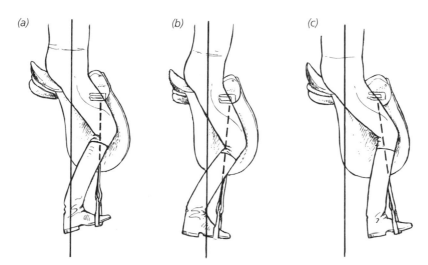

Fig. 5.3 (a) This saddle is an appropriate size for its rider, giving an appropriate distance between the stirrup bars and the deepest part of the saddle. (b) The short, deep seat in this saddle puts the rider onto her fork. (c) The long distance between the stirrup bar and the deepest part of the seat puts this rider into an armchair seat.

such a degree that this is in front of vertical. Inevitably, the leather has a homing instinct back into this groove; at the same time the rider's knees have a homing instinct forward and up into the knee rolls, and her feet gravitate towards the horse's shoulders. Only if she goes to the trouble of bringing the stirrup leather *back* so that it hangs on or even *behind* vertical, does she become able to sit with a shoulder/hip/heel line; but then, in many old-fashioned saddles, she suddenly finds that the leather lies right over the girth buckles.

Keeping the stirrup leather here is virtually impossible – although putting the girth on the first and third straps may create a groove for it to lie in. But this still leaves some uncomfortable knobbles under the rider's knees! The rider is, quite literally, fighting the effects of the saddle as she struggles to maintain a good alignment, and the odds are stacked very strongly against her. Many general-purpose saddles are much more forward cut than the average rider needs, and when you are positioned correctly for flatwork you could even find that the back of your leg is coming off the back of the flap, or being interfered with by the thigh roll. Unless you are really serious about jumping, a saddle whose cut lies between that of a general purpose and a dressage saddle (or a working hunter model) may provide a very good compromise, which still allows you to jump whilst making it easier to ride well on the flat. Even some dressage saddles are designed with too big a distance between the stirrup bar and the deepest part of the seat, making it impossible for the rider to have a shoulder/hip/heel line *and* a vertical stirrup leather. Although the

'Even some dressage saddles are designed with too big a distance between the stirrup bar and the deepest part of the seat, making it impossible for the rider to have a shoulder/hip/heel line and a vertical stirrup leather.'

(a)

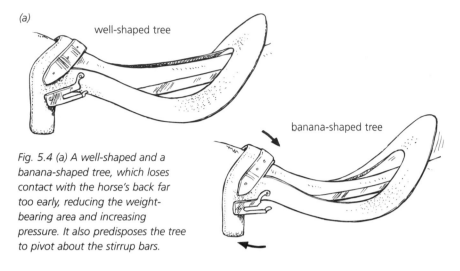

well-shaped tree

banana-shaped tree

Fig. 5.4 (a) A well-shaped and a banana-shaped tree, which loses contact with the horse's back far too early, reducing the weight-bearing area and increasing pressure. It also predisposes the tree to pivot about the stirrup bars.

(b)

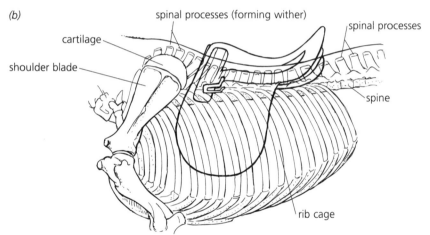

spinal processes (forming wither)

spinal processes

cartilage

shoulder blade

spine

rib cage

Fig. 5.4 (b) Shows how the saddle and tree sit above the horse's bones, clearing the spinal processes, and giving the shoulder blade freedom to move.

(c)

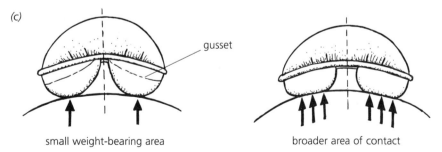

gusset

small weight-bearing area

broader area of contact

Fig. 5.4 (c) Panels which are stuffed and shaped like rolling pins, as in the left hand drawing, also reduce the weight-bearing area, and even a gusset which keeps the panels in contact with the horse's back for longer does not guarantee that the panel is well shaped.

hang of the stirrup leather has traditionally been used as a guide to the rider's alignment, it would be a reliable guide only in the ideal world of perfectly designed saddles!

The more obviously damaging problem – which riders never fail to notice – is the steep slope up to the pommel which leaves many women screeching in agony. The shape of seat and twist which best suits women is a topic we will come to later, but the most common problems I see with saddles that do not fit their riders are the small seat which puts the rider's backside up against the cantle, insufficient length in the flap to accommodate her thigh, a forward stirrup bar, and a steep pommel. These are the important points to look for in a saddle which is to fit *you*.

....

The small seat, in particular, also has ramifications for the horse, since it decreases the bearing surface of the saddle, concentrating the rider's weight over a smaller area. This increases the pressure in pounds per square inch that his back has to tolerate. Very often, the panels do not span the entire length of the seat, but curve up and away from the horse's back prematurely – and this makes the situation worse. (See Fig. 5.2 and compare the first two saddles with the second two saddles.) An important design facet which increases their bearing surface is a gusset, placed at the back of each panel, which keeps it in contact with the back for longer – although not many gussets are made in a shape which really matches the shape of the horse's back. (See Fig. 5.4c) However, it is *the shape of the tree* which ultimately dictates the shape of the panels, and fortunately banana-shaped trees are much less common than they used to be (see Fig. 5.4a).

If you decide that you *must* have a small, deep-seated saddle, and you do not want to bite off the challenge of stabilising yourself without 'props', the only possible way to accommodate both you and the horse is to keep the panels long, and build a small seat above them. A small number of saddlers who specialise in custom-made saddles will do this for you, and the design of the saddle then becomes reminiscent of the cavalry saddles of old. Pre-World War II hunting saddles were commonly 19 inches/48cm in length, and on a large horse, this still kept the weight-bearing area on the rib cage, for it should not extend beyond the last rib to the more delicate area of the loins. If a modern 16-inch/40cm saddle (which I believe is too small for all but the smallest of people) has only 13 inches/33cm of panel in contact with the horse's back, the pressure it must bear has increased substantially.

It is increased even more if the panels themselves do not present a surface which moulds to the horse's back. For often they lack *width* as well as length, and are so fully stuffed that their shape mirrors two rolling pins.

(See Figs 5.2 and 5.4c.) Then, only a very small proportion of the existing width lies against the horse's back, for you are putting a round surface on top of an almost flat surface, and the saddle will look as if it perches *on top of* the horse. A wider, flatter, and also a softer panel gives him a much easier time, and enables a saddle which fits well in other ways to look as if it is *part of* the horse.

....

Only now, after millennia of riding horses, are we able to measure the pressures generated by the saddle and the rider. This is made possible by the 'Saddletech' system, which consists of a thin pad containing pressure sensors, which connects to a computer giving a coloured print-out of the pressures beneath the saddle (see Fig. 5.5, pages 128-129). Ninety-nine times out of a hundred the reading simply confirms what a careful observer can see by eye, but it certainly does make us aware of the intense pressures generated by riding, and particularly by poor saddle fit.

The danger of pressure is that it squeezes the blood out of the capillaries, which are the most delicate blood vessels to permeate the muscles. The tissues can tolerate the resulting lack of circulation for only short periods of time, and starved of oxygen, they can even die. To date, no experimental work has been done with horses to determine their tolerance to pressure, and the results of experiments using dogs, pigs and humans are generalised to horses. At a pressure of $1oz/in^2$ ($0.004kg/cm^2$) the circulation is two thirds impeded. (This means that you do not have to press very hard on your skin before it turns white.) Pressures of between $1-2lb/in^2$ ($0.07-0.14kg/cm^2$) cut off the circulation completely; so it is usually considered that the static pressure of the rider sitting on the saddle should be kept below $2lb/in^2$ ($0.14kg/cm^2$). However, this can be very difficult to achieve, especially with heavier riders.

When the horse is moving, the pressures fluctuate, which means that blood intermittently flows into the tissues, giving him intermittent relief; but the pressures generated very often exceed *$4lb/in^2$ ($0.28kg/cm^2$)*, which is the maximum that the current 'Saddletech' machine can register. However, the constant but lesser pressure of just standing still does the most damage, and police horses in particular suffer from this. Perhaps one of the horse's saving graces is that squeezing the blood out of his tissues causes pain for the first ten to fifteen minutes of a ride, and then his back goes numb.

If you ride your horse for less than forty-five minutes to one hour he should tolerate even high pressures without long-term damage, but beyond this limit cutting off his circulation can lead to swellings, and the development of white hairs. These latter are indicative of cell damage. Soft 'squidgy' swellings rather like soft blisters result when the capillaries

'At a pressure of 1 ounce per square inch, the circulation is two thirds impeded.'

cannot withstand the sudden rush of blood that occurs when the saddle is removed. The damaged capillaries leak, creating a pocket of fluid which will disperse in anything from a few hours to a few days. This is particularly common in endurance horses, but on any horse it is wise to loosen the girth after you dismount and leave the saddle in place for a few minutes so that blood returns slowly to the back. The build-up of toxins in pressurised flesh is thought by many to play a part in the development of the hard and painless lumps which can appear under saddles. These have become more common over recent years, and are still the subject of much veterinary debate.

Even though the well-designed saddle reduces pressure by having long, broad, flat panels, it is not as easy as one might think to get the entire surface of the panels to bear their share of the load, as they do in Fig. 5.5a. When the rider stands up in the stirrups, the area of the stirrup bars and tree points bears virtually all of her weight and commonly registers pressures of over 4lb/in^2 (0.28kg/cm^2), as in Fig. 5.5b. This suggests that balancing permanently out of the saddle is not such a good idea as many endurance riders think it is. When the rider actually *sits*, a well-fitting saddle will distribute her weight: but this ideal cannot be achieved if the saddle is 'banana' shaped, if it sits to one side, or if it has such a long flat tree that it 'bridges' the back (only making contact at the front and rear).

The lessons to be learned from a computerised assessment of saddle fit are really that the intense pressures generated by riding, coupled with the sensitivity of the tissues involved, place on us a responsibility to put the horse's welfare before our own desire for ease and comfort. Saddle sores and girth galls should never happen, and should not be regarded as the standard definition that something is amiss; we are doing damage long before these signs are apparent.

. . . .

Whilst the shape of the panels is important if the saddle is to spread the load on the horse's back, the saddle can never compensate for deficiencies in the shape of the tree it is built on. The width of the tree is an issue we will return to again later; suffice it here to say that if one draws an analogy to shoe fitting, three sizes could not possibly accommodate every make and shape of foot, and it is questionable whether three sizes of tree (narrow, medium and broad) can really accommodate every make and shape of horse. But we have passed through the worst of the post-Second World War adaptations to the mass market, and many British and European companies now make *five* widths. Before the Second World War, however, it was established practice to offer *seven* widths, and many trees were made specifically for a certain horse.

'The saddle can never compensate for deficiencies in the shape of the tree it is built on.'

Fig. 5.5 Computer assessments of the pressure under a saddle. The pommel of the saddle is towards the right-hand side of the page in each case. The measurements are taken from below, as if viewed from underneath, so right and left are reversed.

On this scale the different shades of grey represent the different pounds per square inch pressure on the back, from 0.00psi on the far left to 4.35psi on the right.

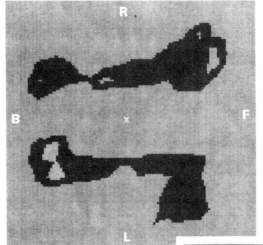

(a) Shows a well-fitting saddle with minimal pressure spread over a reasonably large contact area.

(b) A typical reading when the rider stands up in the stirrups, concentrating pressure beneath the tree points. If the backs of the panels do not remain in contact with the horse's back the reading might look quite similar to this even with the rider sitting.

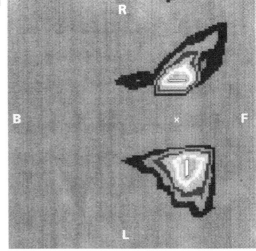

(c) A four-point contact, made by a tree which bridges the horse's back (and is likely to be too long for him). This is common in Western saddles. Pressure is highest beneath the tree points

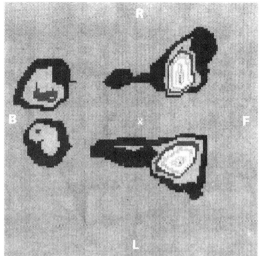

(d) A saddle which slips to one side (towards the top of the page), showing a line of pressure along the opposite side of the spine, and minimal pressure on the side it slips to.

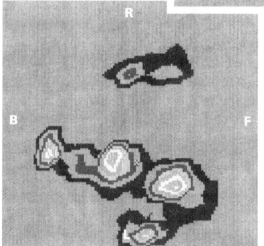

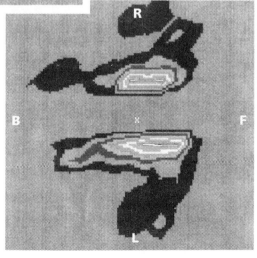

(e) A banana-shaped tree concentrates pressure under the tree points and the centre of the seat.

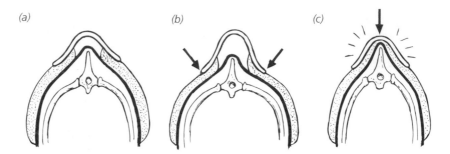

Fig. 5.6 The width of the tree needs to match the width of the horse, as in (a). If it is too narrow, as in (b) there will be pressure at the tree points. If it is too wide, the pressure points will be higher up on the points of the tree, and ultimately on the wither as in (c).

The saddle which is far too wide will press on the horse's wither. (See Fig. 5.6c.) This is a problem which few riders would miss, and clearance of the wither has traditionally been regarded as the most important point to watch for in saddle fitting. But many riders take the age-old test of putting three fingers in between the pommel and the wither to mean that the fit of the entire saddle must be good, and they look no further. However, this cannot assure us that the saddle has a sufficiently large bearing surface and that it remains still on the horse's back. Neither can it assure us the saddle is not in fact too narrow: so the saddle can satisfy this traditional criteria, and still be causing the horse a number of problems.

When a tree is indeed too narrow, the bottom of the tree points will dig into the horse, concentrating pressure in the area behind the shoulder blades (Fig. 5.6b). If it is slightly too wide, the pressure points will be higher up on the points of the tree; for we face an inherent problem when we attempt to put a saddle tree which is shaped like an inverted V onto a horse who is shaped like an inverted U. Few people realise that throughout the width fittings, the front arch of the tree remains the same width whilst the points of a wider tree curve outwards. As they extend down over the horse's musculature, it is rare for both tree and horse to be an exact match for each other in shape.

One way to check how closely your saddle tree and your horse match in shape is to take two long dressage whips, and to lie one along the line of the horse's rib cage just in front of the saddle (see Fig. 5.7). Then lie the other along the line of the point of the tree. You will have to search for this, lifting up the saddle flap and checking that you are not being deceived by the line of the stitching around the point pocket. For this may not be exactly in line with the point of the tree itself. If the saddle is narrower than the horse, the two whips will cross lower down than the saddle, and if it is wider than the horse they will cross up in the air. Ideally they will be parallel: but you are highly likely to find that this is not the

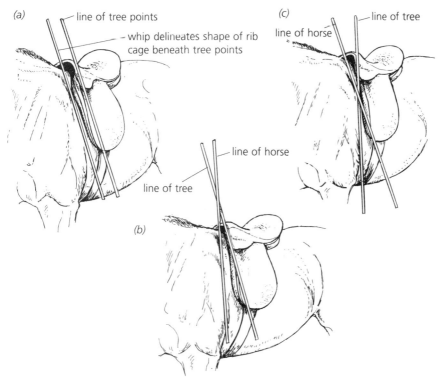

(a) line of tree points

— whip delineates shape of rib cage beneath tree points

(c) line of tree

line of horse

line of horse

line of tree

(b)

Fig. 5.7 Using two dressage whips to estimate the shape of the tree and of the horse. (Three different horses are illustrated.) When the shapes are the same the whips are parallel as in (a). If the tree is wider than the horse they will cross above the wither as in (b). If it is narrower they will cross below the wither as in (c).

case (and even if it is, some would argue that the saddle which passes this test only does so because the horse has adjusted his own shape to fit the saddle, an idea we will talk more about later).

Another simple assessment demonstrates how much of the saddle makes contact with the horse's back. If you ride a dirty horse in a well-soaped saddle with no pad beneath it, you can see which areas of the saddle become marked. If the marks are not even throughout the bearing surface, then the saddle is not making the ideal contact. Sweat marks on the horse can also give you an idea of this (especially if you dismount just as he is beginning to sweat), although they may be indicative of friction rather than pressure. Dry areas can occur when the movement of the horse's back under the saddle ventilates a specific area – usually just to each side of the gullet from the front to the middle of the saddle. They can also be the result of either too much pressure or not enough pressure – but either way, you know you have a problem. The commonest culprit is the saddle which takes pressure off the central part of the back by bridging it.

Fig. 5.8 'Mapping' the horse's back.

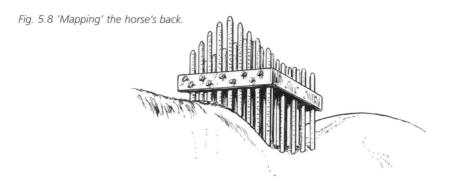

British saddler Andrew Foster has invented a very simple, but extremely clever way to get a 'read out' of each individual horse's back. The contraption he uses is somewhat similar to those executive toys which have a large number of metal pins, allowing you to make an impression of your face or hand. It has a number of vertical rods, held within a framework which allows them to be adjusted up or down. So he stands the horse square on a level surface, places the framework on the horse's back so that it too is horizontal, and raises or lowers each rod so that its tip rests on the horse's back. Tightening a screw allows each one to be fixed in that position, and as the rods are calibrated, the reading can be noted and then reproduced in his workshop. (See Fig. 5.8.)

The saddle is then built and stuffed to fit the shape which is made by the top of the rods, since this is a replica of the horse's back. This gives him much, much more information than a wither trace, made by moulding an artists' flexible curve to the line just behind the wither where the front of the saddle would sit. This is the place where individual horses differ the most, and there is less variation in their longitudinal profile, and in the shape of their back under the back of the saddle; but being able to 'map' the whole back is tremendously useful in ensuring the overall size and balance of the saddle. If you only have one seventeenth of the information you need to build a 17 inch/43cm saddle, you cannot expect to be absolutely precise!

Andrew takes great care that the horse's back is not hollowed as he makes his adjustments. Fitting a saddle to a static horse can be very deceptive: I remember attending a saddle-fitting symposium, and watching the horse in the demonstration drop his back more and more as various trees and saddles were shown. The one which was finally selected as the best fit was chosen when his stomach was virtually hanging down around his knees! Some saddlers (who show tremendous integrity) will not fit a saddle to a horse whose back dips away from contact; instead they refer him to a vet, who will ideally refer him to a physiotherapist or bodyworker.

The horse's back should be in its neutral position when the saddle is fitted. If he is standing with his back in extension (i.e. dipped), tickling him on the midline of his stomach just behind the girth area should cause his back to come up, and the saddle should, in theory, fit *this* shape, since it is the shape he will make when he is (well) ridden. This is a valuable test: if your horse's back seems immovable, or if it drops down again very quickly after you have lifted it, do *not* invest in a saddle until your vet and physiotherapist have sorted out the problem.

....

The post-War innovations which revolutionised the saddle industry probably began with the spring tree, which was again an attempt to make the rider more comfortable. Approximately 90 per cent of saddles are now made on them, but they have their critics, who claim that the spring adds another dimension of 'bounce' between horse and rider, and that *three* moving parts is one too many! The more modern ones are less springy and also less banana-shaped than they used to be – and in older saddles one sometimes sees a seat with cross-ways wrinkles, which is indicative not of a broken tree, but of a spring tree with metal fatigue!

In modern saddles there is now less difference than there would have been between a rigid and a spring-tree saddle, and as long as the shape of the tree fits the shape of the horse there is probably little to choose between them. A rigid tree, being flatter, is more likely to bridge the back of a hollow horse, making contact only at each end. This generates tremendous pressure at four points (see Fig. 5.5c). The banana-shaped tree will make virtually no contact at the back (Fig. 5.5e), and will concentrate pressure on the tree points at the front. In more complicated cases there can be one point which the saddle pivots about, or two points that it rocks between.

When the horse's muscle development shows a marked asymmetry the potential for the saddle to slide sideways, or to pivot or rock as the horse moves is tremendous – and he can become extremely difficult to fit. As we saw in the last chapter, one shoulder can be higher and much more muscled than the other, which is lower and more forward. Also, one quarter can be lower and less muscled than the other. (See Figs 4.11–13, pages 91–92.) Interestingly, about 80 per cent of saddles slip to the right, and only 20 per cent to the left. (Along with this, many more horses go lame in the right hind than in the left – two facts which may well be connected.) In considering these asymmetries we are entering a very specialist area, where the rider needs advice from someone with an unusually astute eye, and a very deep knowledge of saddlery (whose expertise may well need to be backed up by a physiotherapist or bodyworker). Although the saddle falls down the dip on the lower side, a computer analysis will show more pressure on the *higher* side. (Fig. 5.5d) Particularly worrying is the line of pressure which runs parallel to the spine. This becomes more intense towards the back of the saddle, which is pulled towards the spine as the saddle slips over.

'Pressure is not the only problem facing the horse, and the friction created by rubbing and the bruising that results from continual bouncing both add to his predicament.'

Unbeknownst to the riders who use them, the backs of many saddles move from side to side and bounce up and down as the horse trots, particularly when the rider is rising. This means that pressure (which is more often at the front of the saddle) is not the only problem facing the horse, and the *friction* created by rubbing and the *bruising* that results from continual bouncing both add to his predicament. Because of this, one cannot assess saddle fit without seeing the horse in motion. If the saddle moves, it does not match the shape of the horse – it may bridge the back, be banana-shaped, or be too wide, and having a panel which is too short increases its instability. On many better designed saddles (particularly dressage saddles) the back girth strap is attached further back than usual on the tree, which helps to distribute the rider's weight well, stabilising the back of the saddle and holding it down. If, from the ground, you can lift the back of the saddle up off the horse's back when it is girthed up tightly, you know that it will not stay down as you ride.

'The cumulative effect on the horse's tissues of nearly 150 steps, rubs or bumps per minute, or 9000 per hour can be devastating.'

The problem of friction, caused by movement of the back of the saddle, may only become obvious to the rider when the horse, especially when he is changing his coat, finally gets his hair rubbed so badly that a bald patch appears under the back of the saddle on each side of his spine. Saddlers can predict when the spring and autumn influx of calls from worried owners will begin; but there is no sure solution to this problem, although sheepskin (as long as it remains unmatted) is one of the best anti-friction surfaces. Neoprene-like pads are also useful because their bottom surface remains unmoveable on the horse, ensuring that any movement takes place between the top surface of the pad and the saddle. Those made of open-cell materials let the horse's skin breathe more than neoprene does. (An open-cell material absorbs water and would sink in the bath, whereas a closed-cell foam would not.) Hair loss which extends beyond the time of the moult is a very worrying sign, and whilst a new saddle may seem an extreme reaction to it, this is probably the only real answer to a problem which will not go away on its own. It may be tempting to just ignore it; but to do so is negligent, for in trot, the cumulative effect on the horse's tissues of nearly 150 steps, rubs or bumps per minute, or *9000* per hour can be devastating.

Another tempting solution is to use a pad which lifts the back of the saddle, fills in the gap under a rather short panel, and gives it (in theory at least) an immovable base to rest on. But the pad changes the *horizontal balance* of the saddle. Raising the cantle relative to the pommel rotates the

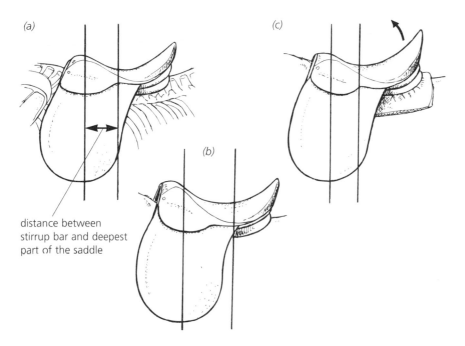

(a)

distance between
stirrup bar and deepest
part of the saddle

(c)

(b)

Fig. 5.9 The front to back balance of the saddle. (a) This sits level on the horse's back, and
the points of the tree lie behind the shoulder blade. (b) When the cantle is too low the rider
is tipped back, increasing the distance from the stirrup bar to the deepest part of the
saddle. In all probability this saddle is too narrow, and therefore the pressure under the
back of it is not as intense as one might expect. (c) Lifting the back of the saddle rotates it
forward, raising the cantle relative to the pommel and making it sit in the same way as a
saddle which is too wide. This shortens the distance from the stirrup bar to the deepest part
of the saddle, and increases pressure in the shoulder area.

saddle so that its deepest part lies further forwards, and the distance
between here and the stirrup bar is shortened (see Fig. 5.9c). As shown in
Fig. 5.3b, this tends to make the rider hollow backed. (So this distance,
which we discussed earlier, is not just dependent on the design of the
saddle; it depends as well on how it sits on the horse's back.) Lifting the
back of the saddle directs the rider's weight forward and down to land just
behind the horse's shoulder blades, and this rotation mirrors the balance
of the saddle which drops down in front because it is too wide.

Most riders, however, would rarely miss this problem, whilst the
opposite one of the high pommel and low cantle is very common indeed,
and it often goes unnoticed (Fig. 5.9b). This throws the rider's weight
backwards – which again makes it tempting to compensate by lifting the
back of the saddle. But this is the wrong solution, for it is highly likely that
the saddle is too *narrow*, and that it has tipped back because the front of it
cannot settle down around the horse as it should. The height at the front
rotates the saddle so that the deepest part of the seat is now further back,

increasing the distance between this and the stirrup bar, and tipping the rider back into an armchair seat. (See also Fig. 5.3c.)

So whenever you attempt to solve the problem of a low and/or moving cantle by lifting the back of the saddle, your 'correction' will almost certainly cause yet more damage. If you do this you have directed your weight forward and down onto the points of the tree, and it is highly likely that these were *already* digging into the horse. Interestingly, a computerised assessment of the saddle which tips back will not show as much pressure under the back of the saddle as one might intuitively expect. This confirms that its underlying problem is indeed its narrowness, and that the muscles each side of the wither are actually suffering the most.

'Whenever you attempt to solve the problem of a low and/or moving cantle by lifting the back of the saddle, your 'correction' will almost certainly cause yet more damage.'

Judging the horizontal balance of the saddle is surprisingly difficult. Many people say that the cantle should be $2^1/_2$ inches/60mm higher than the pommel, but to make this a golden rule is folly, since the cantle can be shaped in so many different ways, and tends to be higher in saddles which are designed to stop a passive rider from bumping backwards. The balance of the saddle is better judged by looking at the deepest part of the seat, which should be parallel to the ground – and it is important not to let the eye be deceived by the relationship of the pommel and the cantle. The issues involved in horizontal balance are very complex (and if saddle fitting is appearing to become more complicated by the instant, you can rest assured that the traditional manuals have lulled you into a false sense of security!).

....

Another major source of problems which many riders are unaware of is the gullet, which on many saddles is very narrow – often as little as 1 inch/25mm wide. (See Fig. 5.2.) This enables the saddle to clear the spinal processes of the horse's back, and it passes the traditional test of allowing one to see daylight all the way through from one end to the other. But there is so little room on *each side* of the processes that they could still be subject to bruising. To guarantee to clear them on all but the narrowest of Thoroughbreds requires a 2–$2^1/_2$ inch/50-60mm gullet which widens out towards the pommel; but many conventionally made trees are not wide enough to allow for both this and for a reasonably wide panel. So you are only likely to find this width on the new wave of well-designed saddles.

If you saddle up a horse, and ask someone to lead him in small circles within the confines of his stable, you will see that the back of the saddle actually crosses his spine. This is obviously one of the tightest turns you could possibly do – but it is not the sole province of dressage fanatics, since opening and closing gates could require equally tight turns. The horse's spine curves very little on a circle, especially in the thoracic area under the saddle, so the spinous processes remain in line whilst the rib cage bulges more to one side than the other. When the gullet of the saddle is narrow they are in danger of touching the edge of the panel.

Mounting from the ground may also affect the spinal processes: Lesley-Ann Taylor of the Balance team (of whom we will learn more about later) did an experiment in which she placed sticky coloured markers on the spinal processes of a horse, then saddled him and asked someone to mount from a block. Prior to this the markers were all in line: but after mounting they were seen to form a curve to the left. The saddle had a wide enough gullet to allow palpation, which showed that it was indeed the spinal processes which had been pulled to the left, and not just the horse's skin; so the horse had braced himself to be mounted. A group of students at Warwickshire College devised a simple experiment which showed that a group of unbroken two- and three-year-old horses had very symmetrical backs, whilst a group of older ridden horses had backs whose left side sloped away more than the right. We can only surmise that mounting from the left was the cause of this.

The way the saddle is placed on the horse's back is another common cause of problems, for it is very frequently put too far forward. This is the place where, to most of us, it 'looks right'. But when positioned here it is highly likely that the top of the shoulder blade will hit against the saddle during the phase of the stride when the forelimb is extended. (See Figs 5.9a and 5.4b.) At post-mortem examination, the vast majority of horses have a protective layer of fibrous tissue here, which is nature's response to continued bruising. Since the head of each shoulder blade moves back over 4000 times per hour when the horse is in trot, repeatedly hitting the saddle is not conducive to comfort! This effect can explain why many horses are restricted in the movement of their forelegs, either continually or as they begin work. They look 'stuffy', for they are trying desperately not to move from the shoulder. They are also extremely reluctant to extend, and do not like going down hill (since the forelimb must then move further forward in each step, bringing the shoulder blade further back). Their saving grace – as with all other saddle problems – is that after about fifteen minutes work they will probably become numbed to the pain.

The shoulder blade can pass easily under the soft knee roll of some forward-cut saddles. But if the saddle is too far forward, it hits the saddle so high up and so close to the point of the tree that there is not enough room for it to pass beneath the saddle. This is even more likely when the saddle is built on a tree whose points are directed forward rather than down (and since the horse's muscle development may well be uneven, one

'At post-mortem examination, the vast majority of horses have a protective layer of fibrous tissue here [at the top of the shoulder blade], which is nature's response to continued bruising.'

side is likely to be tighter than the other – a phenomenon which you can probably feel by slipping your hand beneath the saddle flap). I have, I must confess, ridden a large number of horses who were very restricted in their foreleg movement, and compelled them to extend so that their owners became aware of their movement potential. I now think twice about doing this and check the saddle first, for to be sure that you are not about to cause pain, you need to hold the forelimb extended and check that there is clearance between the shoulder blade and the saddle. (This is, ideally, a two-person job.) When you find that the saddle then 'looks wrong' to your eye, resist the temptation to move it forward again!

Unless the horse has particularly problematic conformation faults, each saddle will find its own right place to sit, settling there after a short time of work. Often, this is further back than the rider thinks it should be, so she uses a breast plate to keep the saddle forward, thus creating problems through her naive attempt to cure them. If the girth straps are angled correctly, the saddle will sit behind the shoulder blade, but the girth will still lie in the girth groove, and will not pull the saddle forward when tightened. Neither does it need to be tightened excessively. When using a girth with an elastic insert, it pays to keep the elastic on the offside of the horse; and to tighten the girth on the near side – or even to reverse this procedure each day. Then you are less likely to 'strangle' your horse as you tighten the girth. One of my old teachers used to boast about his ability to ride the horse on a very loose girth (or even no girth at all!) and whilst this is folly, many people winch the girth up so tight that their horse can barely breathe. This can also, as we said before, lead to dysfunction in the rib cage.

On some horses, an imaginary vertical line drawn up from the girth groove passes in front of where the saddle should sit – and this will inevitably cause the saddle to slip forward. Foregirths are a recent innovation, designed to be used in this situation and to keep the saddle back off the wither. To resort to a crupper may imply that your horse has the status of a rotund child's pony; but fashion has dictated that using a foregirth implies that you are a dressage rider to be reckoned with! They look rather like a roller, and ironically, they encircle the horse tightly just behind the wither, pressing on just the area of the back that the dressage rider in particular would like to lift and expand, yielding the carriage which earns her high marks. Whether they prohibit or merely discourage this is probably dependent on type, but I am convinced that the vast majority of horses would be far better off without one.

....

Mounting from the ground has absolutely nothing to recommend it. As we have seen, it pulls the horse's spinous processes to the left, and it may, over time, cause his back to fall away on the left. American vet Joyce Harman used a 'Saddletech' machine to perform a computer analysis of the pressures generated in mounting, and her results were reported in *Equus* magazine. Her experiment showed a concentration of pressure under the left point of the saddle tree, which is only slightly eased in mounting from a block. If you pull on the cantle as you mount you also create a pressure point under the back of the saddle on the right-hand side, and the best readings are obtained when somebody else gives you a leg up. Meanwhile, mounting from the ground probably does about as much good for your back as it does for your horse's. But it can also harm your saddle, for the repeated pull on it – especially if you grab hold of the cantle – can, over the years, cause the tree to twist.

If the saddle is to have an even bearing surface and not to pivot or rock, the symmetry of the tree is tremendously important. Yet one particularly astute saddler told me once how, out of a batch of one hundred trees which he had ordered from a reputable manufacturer, only *twelve* were truly symmetrical. The others were promptly dispatched back from whence they came; but he was sure that they would subsequently end up in the hands of another saddler, who would not notice or worry about their asymmetry. The saddles built on them would, inevitably, have been asymmetrical themselves, sitting on the horse's back in a way which generates a torque. Wooden trees are made by eye; many saddlers believe that they are badly engineered and too cheap, and that the traditions in tree making are holding the saddlery trade back more than any other facet of the industry. Considering that £35 ($55) buys an expensive tree, we would be better off paying more for a precision-made product.

Even if the tree is symmetrical, the stirrup bars can be riveted unevenly onto it (putting one of the rider's legs further forward than the other), and the girth straps can be set on asymmetrically. Unevenness in the stuffing of the panels can also create this effect, and cause the gullet to become

'Out of a batch of one hundred trees ordered from a reputable manufacturer, only twelve were truly symmetrical.'

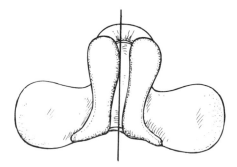
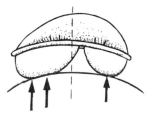

Fig. 5.10 An asymmetrical saddle.

displaced so that it does not run exactly straight down the middle of the saddle (see Fig. 5.10). To make a saddle with truly even panels is no mean achievement, for each piece of leather has its own characteristics, and even if completely symmetrical shapes are stitched in completely symmetrical ways, they will not 'give' in the same way. The leather ideally should be cut from the same side of the same piece of hide, or from pieces directly opposite each other on each side of the back bone. If a saddle is made from start to finish by one person this is easily achieved: but if one person cuts, another sews, and another stuffs, this may not happen – for no one person works with the leather long enough to appreciate its characteristics.

The panels are traditionally stuffed with white wool flock, and to do this evenly – with no lumps and bumps – is again extremely difficult. Since this is usually done by piece-workers who have to work fast, and who do not know the contours of the horse this saddle will fit, there is little incentive to take the care which is really needed. This is one good reason for suggesting that panels are better stuffed with felt, or with various synthetic foams. These have the disadvantage that they cannot be altered; and some have the advantage of *memory,* returning to the same shape if they are distorted. Also, they do not deteriorate as much as wool, nor do they belong in the food chain of the tiny animals who commonly invade the panels of older wool-stuffed saddles!

'At the very least, a flocked saddle should be completely restuffed every two years.'

Wool flocking changes shape over time, softening in some areas and compressing in others, and as these changes gather momentum the panels become lumpy, and can really change shape. Ideally a saddle fitter should look at a saddle after the panels have had a month or so to settle; for by then any necessary adjustments will be obvious. Follow-up care is still necessary every six months to one year, and this involves your saddler coming out to see your horse. (A good saddler will refuse to reflock a saddle without doing so.) At the very least, a flocked saddle should be completely restuffed every two years.

So, if you want to know the gruesome truth, especially about an old saddle (although new ones are clearly not immune), it is important that you can check it for yourself. Whilst standing with one foot out in front of you, rest the pommel of the saddle on that thigh, so that the cantle is closest to your chest, and the panels are away from you (see Fig. 5.11a.). Begin with the cantle tipped slightly away from your chest, and look straight down the gullet. Then gradually bring the cantle towards your chest until you see all the way down to the pommel. Are the edges of the panels even and symmetrical? Are they both exactly the same shape? Does the channel of the saddle run in a truly straight line? Do you see any lumps and bumps? Feel the panels too: are their edges even? Is there as much bulk of stuffing under one hand as there is under the other?

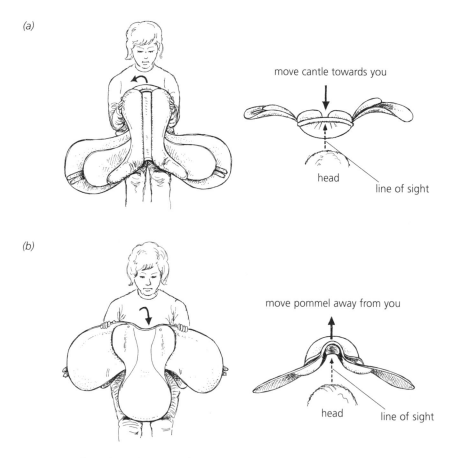

Fig. 5.11 Looking down the gullet of your saddle to check that the gullet itself is straight, and that the panels are evenly stuffed.

Next, turn the saddle the other way up, and rest the cantle on your thigh so that the panels are towards you. Begin with the pommel towards your chest and tip it gradually away from you as you look down the gullet, checking it as above (Fig. 5.11b). Bear in mind that any asymmetries you find may not be the fault of the saddle maker; for if you or your horse have a strong asymmetry, you may between you have deformed the saddle. One horse I know, with a rider who was relatively straight and extremely committed to becoming straighter, deformed the gullet of two saddles, as shown in Fig. 5.10, and the saddles always slipped to the right. Both of the horse's long back muscles appeared to be working well, and bodyworkers could find nothing wrong with him. Eventually, the uneven pattern of sweating between the horse's forelegs alerted the rider to the fact that the problem might lie in the abdominal muscles on one side. These were remaining flaccid instead of firming up to support his back, as they were on the other side. She eventually worked out how to ride the horse so that he engaged those muscles; the (remade) saddle now remains straight, and has not become deformed since.

Innovations in saddlery

Saddlers have recently responded to cries from women for a saddle which fits us comfortably, resulting in some changes to the dimensions of the seats. Saddle making, like riding, has traditionally been a male-dominated preserve, and this has given us a very one-sided view of the problems inherent in both arts, especially when put together. Back through time, however, many native Americans built different saddles for women and for men, reflecting both their different work duties and their differing anatomy. The majority of women have seat bones which are wider apart than men's, and the shape of the pelvis of both sexes is shown in Fig. 5.12, with Fig. 5.13 showing the underneath surface that rests on the saddle.

The rider sits on the bony rami, which join the seat bones to the pubic bone, and function like the rockers on a rocking chair or the runners on a sledge. They do, however, narrow in towards each other as they near the front of the body, since the pubic bone is shorter than the distance between the seat bones. The rami are more parallel to each other in men, whose seat bones are closer together than most women's. The horizontal axis of a male pelvis lies about half way along the rami, further back than it does in the female (see Fig. 5.13). This naturally rocks his pelvis back: so if he loses the ideal sitting position of 'neutral spine' (in which his pelvis and upper body are stacked up in the most efficient way) he will probably do so by 'sitting on his pockets' and *slouching*, with seat bones that point forward and a rounded lower back.

Since a woman has the horizontal axis of her pelvis further forward on the rami, she is more likely to lose her 'neutral spine' by tipping her pelvis *forward,* with her pubic bone pushed more firmly against the rise up towards the pommel, her seat bones pointing backwards, and her lower back more hollow. This predisposes her to the sudden excruciating encounters with the pommel which seem, surprisingly, to trouble women more than men. Deep-seated saddles with a steep slope up to the pommel can easily become a recipe for disaster, and the rami should – in theory – rest on the slope of the saddle as it rises up to the pommel. But if a flat seat gives way to a steep and sudden slope they cannot: the rider is destined to bash her crutch, especially at rising trot, and to save herself she has to sit so far back that she is then too close for comfort to the cantle.

Concurrently, the increased distance between the seat bones in women

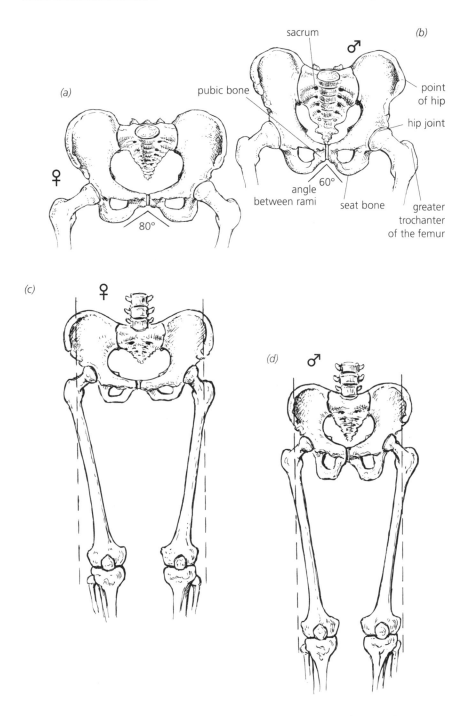

Fig. 5.12 (a) and (b) show the female (left) and male (right) pelvis seen from the front. Note the wider angle between the seat bones in the female pelvis, and the much bigger distance between the greater trochanters of the femur. (c) and (d) show how the thigh bones angle in towards the knee in the female, whilst going almost straight down in the male.

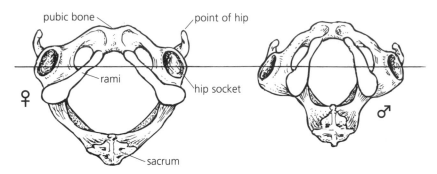

Fig. 5.13. The surface of the female (left) and male (right) pelvises as presented to the saddle. Women need a saddle wide enough to accommodate the width between their seat bones. The line of the pelvic axis is much more towards the pubic bone in the woman; in the man, the hip sockets lie further back on the line of the rami; this makes it easier for a man to sit in a way which makes his backside look square.

creates the need for a seat which is both wide and flat enough to accommodate them. Individual pelvic shapes vary, however, and some women have a more male-shaped pelvis. So to estimate the angles of the·rami in your own pelvis, stand in an 'on horse' position with your knees bent and your seat bones pointing down. Then slowly hollow your back to point them backwards, and imagine the lines which would be drawn on the floor if each one had a long pencil attached to it. Bring them forward until they point down, and repeat this movement several times. Then put your hands out in front of you (with your thumbs on the top and your palms vertical) to replicate those angles. Your hands may very nearly be parallel, but it is more likely that they will diverge significantly.

The extra width between the seat bones of most women means that if the saddle is narrow from side to side, with a seat which slopes away on each side of a central ridge, we can find ourselves in a position where if one seat bone is on the saddle, the other is floating off to the side of it; and if that seat bone is then placed on the saddle, its partner is left dangling in space. This is a 'no win' situation, for which the only solution is a saddle with a sufficiently broad and flat seat. The width of the saddle in the twist (the part of the saddle lying in front of the seat as it slopes towards the pommel) is also a critical measurement; for we need to be able to rest both rami on it, and if it is too narrow one of them will again keep falling off to the side. If a saddle is very narrow, with the width at the twist being less than the distance between your legs and the length of your pubic bone, it becomes virtually impossible to get both thighs snugly on it. This is extremely important since these, as well as the pelvic floor, need to be weight-bearing.

The width of the female pelvis, and the position of the hip sockets relative to the seat bones (see Figs 5.12 and 5.13), means that a woman's greater trochanters are much wider apart than a man's. Her thigh bones then have to slope inwards from here to her knees, leaving a large space on the inside of the bone which is filled in with muscle and fat. The man, with his narrower pelvis, has thigh bones that are almost vertical, and this gives him the flat inner thigh which most women wish they had too! So the shape of the inner thigh determines the ideal shape of the saddle in cross-section. Some saddles are concave each side of the pommel, creating an indentation beneath the top of your thigh on each side. If you have bulky inner thigh muscles you might be grateful for the extra space (see Fig. 5.14); but if you have a flat inner thigh, it is taken out of contact for several inches, and you can be left balancing on your crutch.

Although we commonly take wither tracings of horses, we do not often think to compare the upper surfaces of different saddles, selecting the one whose shape makes it easy to get both the rami and the inner thigh in contact by matching the shape of the saddle to our own contours. A twist which is too wide may well be uncomfortable; and women with a narrower pelvis prefer the traditionally shaped saddle – but the wide twist rarely has the same devastating effect as the narrow one. However, coupling either with a steep slope up to the pommel can turn riding into a very unpleasant experience! About 5 per cent of women have an extremely wide pelvis (the flat or platypelloid type) in which the rami do not follow a smooth, rounded curve up to the pubic bone; instead they are shaped almost like an S lain on its side, and the pubic bone protrudes beneath the rami making it very vulnerable to damage. I suspect that it is women with this pelvic type who suffer the most.

....

Saddle trees are traditionally made of laminated beech wood, but a variety of other materials has been used in recent years. Fibre-glass trees were

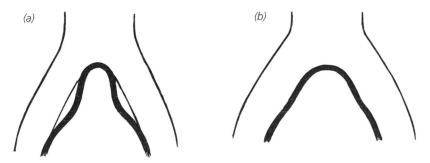

Fig. 5.14 A cross-section across the twist of the saddle: if it is concave as in (a), the woman with slender thighs will be left supporting weight on her pubic bone.

tried in the 1970s, and were found to break. Leather could not be tacked onto the tree and was stapled onto it instead, which was much less secure. Some modern trees are plastic (the majority of Stübben and Keiffer saddles are built on plastic trees), which does not break, and allows leather to be fixed with fine tacks or a staple gun. But unlike beech-wood trees, they have no possibility for slight adjustment.

The saddle needs to transmit the horse's impulse without adding or subtracting anything – which mirrors the texture of the body of the ideal rider. This suggests that the tree should perhaps be rigid, and whilst older spring-tree saddles might add their own 'bounce', I have sat on one (but only one) very old synthetic saddle which appeared to have gone 'soggy', and which added a very strange layer of interference between myself and the horse. Synthetic saddles are the cheaper end of the market, and as such, they have had their design faults; but over the years they have improved significantly, and if they bring a well-fitting, well-designed saddle within the budget of the average rider they have a very important role to play. They at least dissuade riders with limited funds from buying the cheapest leather saddles (which have only their price to commend them) or from buying secondhand 'bargains' at auctions. They can also allow a rider who could otherwise only afford one saddle to have two, and if she plans to jump and ride dressage to any level this can be a great help.

Few synthetic saddles are designed with really good, wide, weight-bearing panels, and the panels are notoriously difficult to reflock. (Some, indeed, cannot be reflocked.) Computer pressure analysis confirms that there is so much elasticity in the panels that the flocking can move, acting almost like a fluid medium. Commonly the panels become too long whilst sagging down the sides of the horse in the centre, and the saddle then bridges the horse's back. The saddler is easily tempted to over-stuff synthetic panels as he attempts to keep them firm, but the panels then become like rolling pins; so this is an inherent design problem which has not yet been completely solved. Only recently on the market are saddles whose panels are filled with gel, and time will tell how well they stand up to wear, and how effective they are at distributing pressure.

'Close-contact' saddles are currently very popular, especially for jumping. They were originally designed with no sweat flap, bringing the rider's leg closer to the horse. Over recent years, they have evolved to bring the rider's *seat* closer to the horse as well. They have thin, foam-filled panels whose biggest disadvantage is that they are not adjustable. This means that the saddles will not suit an asymmetrical horse; and they have such a flat tree that they are likely to make a four-point contact on some horses. Many close-contact saddles have very narrow gullets, but some are so well designed that they give good computer readings, and a good fit is much easier to achieve on a horse with a flat back and a low wither.

Adjustable trees are another modern innovation, which has not caught on like the synthetic saddle. These have a key which fits into a hole at the front of the pommel, and turns a screw thread to open or close the angle between the two sides of the saddle. I have heard a few stories of people who had difficulty operating the key; but this is, in theory, an eminently sensible idea, since horses change shape through the seasons and as they become more or less fit. However, it does not escape the generic problem of saddle fit, and imposing an inverted V on an inverted U is likely to create a pressure point which lies either close to, or further down from, the wither. (If someone could invent an adjustable tree in which one could widen out the top of an inverted U, adjustable saddles – and trees in general – might become much more horse-friendly.) It is also not possible to alter the position of the bars in the tree, which run parallel to the spine on each side and are wider apart in wider trees. Hence the adjustable saddle cannot fully mimic the change from a narrow to a broader tree.

The adjustment presupposes a knowledgable sophisticated user; but whether one would be astute enough to notice one's horse changing shape and to make the appropriate adjustment is another story. Undoubtedly, most people do *not* notice the changes in their saddle fit as their horse changes shape. It used to be commonplace for saddles to be checked by a saddler twice a year, but we modern-day horse owners may need some re-education if we are not to see this as an unnecessary expense (despite the fact that we pay happily our farriers and sometimes bodyworkers on an on-going basis as they attempt to undo the damage caused by our badly fitting saddles!). The adjustable saddle has, perhaps, not caught on because people do not trust themselves to adjust it, and I do not think I have met anyone who has used an adjustable saddle to its full advantage.

'Undoubtedly, most people do not notice the changes in their saddle fit as their horse changes shape.'

The American company 'Ortho-Flex' have probably developed the concept of the adjustable saddle more than anyone else. Their saddles were initially supplied to (and therefore tested by) endurance riders, but now they are made for and used by riders from all disciplines. Len Brown, who began the company in 1983, did so following his experiences on a 3000-mile trek through the western United States. Before he began this, he swore that his Western saddles would create no problem; but when they caused gruesome sores which no one seemed able to help him with, he set about designing a saddle which would keep his horses pain free. Having been an engineer, his thinking was guided by the principles of mechanics, and was probably far less constrained than it would have been if he had been a saddler.

The resulting saddles have two layers. The upper layer is the seat and flaps of a conventional saddle, which are built around a normal tree. The bottom layer replaces the panels on a conventional saddle, and is made of a sandwich of materials, including neoprene foam and more rigid plastic. The panels are then covered (and disguised) with a sheepskin 'bootie'. Each one has two attachment points to the tree, and these have a ball–and–socket effect, enabling the panels to flex and rotate about them. Thus they move with the horse, and work independently of each other. If necessary the front to back balance of the saddle can be adjusted using 'shim pads', and these help it to fit a variety of horses. They slip inside the 'booties' and are supplied with the saddle. The shims can also be used to build up the panel on one side, enabling the saddle to fit an asymmetrical horse – although inevitably, making an appropriate adjustment and monitoring it on a regular basis would test the skill of many riders.

The panels are much larger than a conventional panel, and a saddle with up to *four times* the normal bearing surface obviously creates a significant reduction in pressure – and in the inevitable damage which this causes. Furthermore, the panels are weight–bearing structures in their own right, and they absorb concussion in a way which a conventional saddle never can. They extend forward over the top of the horse's shoulder blades, which now move freely underneath them. In fact, horses become much more willing to lift their backs and reach into the rein, and the horse's entire back can move so much under the saddle that many riders get a shock when they first ride in one!

When the horse's movement shows this extra freedom, sitting becomes far more demanding. This only goes to show how much a conventional saddle can cramp a horse's style – but we have built this limitation into our traditional 'map', and it is often only *after* riding in one of these saddles that a rider appreciates how she did indeed have a saddling problem. Some riders also realise retrospectively that their saddle had disguised a *sitting* problem; although others (much to the consternation of these saddlers) decide to resort again to a saddle which provides them with a 'crutch'. The restriction in a horse's movement when he wears a traditional saddle implies that he soon learns how much his back can move before he is punished by it. For he is, in effect, held in a splint which cannot adjust as he lifts or dips his back, and as he moves around a circle. Advocates of the two-layer saddle suggest that saddling a horse conventionally is not unlike asking a human to run a marathon whilst wearing a pair of wooden clogs!

British saddler Barry Richardson has come up with another 'two-layer' design, and has created a saddle with 'reactor panels' (see Fig. 5.2d). The bottom layer is composed of acetyl glass acetate, and the two layers of the saddle are fixed together using a disc which is filled with sorbothane – a quasi-liquid material which also absorbs shock in the soles of a good pair of trainers. The disc is covered with aeroplane velcro – an extra strong type of velcro which needs a metal tool to prize its surfaces apart. This can be positioned differently for each horse, allowing the saddle to be personalised for him, and if necessary to take his asymmetry into account. But again, if the saddle is to be used on a variety of horses, it needs a sophisticated owner to make the appropriate adjustments. The panels of these saddles are also flexible enough to allow the horse's shoulder blade to move back underneath them, and at all times they maintain total contact with an undulating back.

On a 17-inch/43cm reactor panel saddle there are $350in^2/2.25m^2$ of panel in contact with the horse. Computer assessments of the pressures generated are extremely encouraging, and no conventional saddle registers pressures as low as $8oz/in^2$ ($0.032kg/cm^2$) under a 10 stone/140lb/63kg rider. The patterns of wear on the horse's shoes also often change significantly when he is worked in one of these saddles, especially behind. This suggests that his movement has altered substantially, and that the compensatory strategies which go from the feet to the back and the back to the feet make it unwise to view any one part of the horse in isolation.

The gap between the seat of the saddle and the horse's back appears, remarkably, not to affect the rider's ability to 'plug in', and to feel and influence the horse's carriage and movement – which is now much less constrained than it would ordinarily be. The 'two-layer' saddle is an innovation which holds tremendous potential for the comfort and free movement of the horse, and time will tell whether it ever becomes mainstream. For the horse world rarely embraces such a radical change without its effectiveness being proven over time – and the up-grade which is needed in the skill of the average rider may well prove a stumbling block to progress.

....

The need for panels with a large bearing surface, and for a wide gullet, is becoming acknowledged by more and more saddlers, who are righting the wrongs of the past in their newer designs. But one of the most radical changes which has recently been proposed has come from the Balance team, operating in Britain. Their story began when Carol Brett, a rider, trainer and dressage judge, became so frustrated with the way of going of a number of her own and her clients' horses that she took to removing all the tack and working them on the lunge. They then moved much more freely. So she put on the bridle, only to find that there was normally no change. It was when she put on the *saddle* that the restriction was both obvious and instantaneous.

This led her to think long and hard about why. One of the obvious possibilities was that the saddles were too narrow, and to test this she started putting narrow horses into medium-width saddles, and padding the front of the saddle so it was clear of the wither. The horses moved better, and over time, they filled out to fit the saddle so that the padding was no longer necessary. But over more time, their movement became restricted again, and the saddle dropped down on the wither, making it look like it needed restuffing. But Carol resisted the temptation to restuff it, or to put the horses back into narrow trees. Instead she began the process again; and when the horses appeared to fill out the medium-tree saddle she put them into a *wide* tree, padding that out as well. Again, the process repeated itself: the horses filled out to fit the saddle, making the padding unnecessary. But soon the saddles started to look too wide for them. As Carol began debating the extra-wide tree, her friends became incredulous. 'Can't you see', they said, 'it's obvious that the saddles are too wide. And you're trying to put them into even wider saddles. You need to go back to a medium tree.'

Undeterred, Carol did in fact try the extra-wide tree. Again, the horses filled out to fit it, they moved even more freely, and then – after more time had elapsed – the saddle began to look too wide for them. By now Carol had been joined in her experiments by Lesley-Ann Taylor and Maureen Bartlett, who together form the Balance team. They formulated a theory: that pressure from a narrow saddle causes muscle wastage each side of the wither, creating a concave shape and the very prominent bone structure which makes us define a horse as 'narrow'. But when that pressure was removed, the muscles regenerated, filling out the wider saddle, only to reach a stage where that too became too narrow, and there was again pressure… which caused the muscle wastage that then made the saddle look too wide.

Having reached the limit of available tree width, the team were now in trouble. But they finally persuaded a tree maker and a saddler to make an extra-extra-wide saddle. The process was repeated, and still the horses filled out the saddle only to waste away again. So they now needed an extra-extra-extra-wide tree, and so the process went on. At various stages, the different horses reached the tree width that really did fit them and did not finally lead to muscle wastage. This led to a range of saddles which now extend to seven 'extras' (or 7X), and a much more streamlined way of working, which rarely needs a horse to pass through more than one saddle on his way to his final width. Each saddle has an additional 2cm/0.78ins between the points of the tree, giving saddles up to *14cm/5.46ins* wider than we are used to seeing. If the Balance team's logic is correct, this turns our established map of saddlery on its head: for the horse who *appears* to have a saddle which needs restuffing may well have a saddle which is in fact too *narrow*. This has caused the muscle wastage which makes it appear too wide.

'Pressure from a narrow saddle causes muscle wastage each side of the wither, creating a concave shape and the very prominent bone structure which makes us define a horse as 'narrow'.'

If the logic of this is boggling your brains, take heart from the fact that it is a very new and very challenging way to think. If it is right, it means that the vast majority of horses in developed countries world-wide are being forced into saddles which are indeed too narrow for them. In fact, the horses (by wasting away) are adapting themselves to fit their saddles, instead of the saddles being adapted to fit the horses! During a saddle fitting with an incredulous client, Carol once made a wither trace of the client's whippet, and discovered that even the dog was wider than the saddle she had been using on her horse! So we are forced to ask ourselves (as we did when we considered the issues inherent in shoeing) whether a saddle should be fitted to the shape the horse actually *is*, or to the shape that he *ought to be*.

Carol believes that there is no such thing as a horse who is naturally narrow enough to fit a narrow saddle – that the contour shown by the narrowest horses is man-made – and even horses over twenty years of age have shown considerable regeneration of muscle when refitted using the Balance system. If you put a horse into a saddle which is too narrow you put him into a vice: with all our concerns about the saddle which is too *wide*, we have failed to appreciate that the 'safer' the clearance is above the wither, the more likely the saddle is to be doing damage of the opposite kind to the one we have all been trained to look for.

It is unfortunate that we cannot simply put a skewer through a horse and measure the distance between each side of his rib cage where the points of the tree would rest. If we could, I think we might be surprised by how wide horses actually are. At first sight, a Balance saddle looks so wide it appears ridiculous, but our judgments are coloured purely by the saddles we are used to seeing. Perhaps this will change over time – making the traditional saddle appear so narrow that we will one day marvel that we ever dared to put one on a horse. The Balance team's initiative has led to arguments about whether it is ever right to saddle a horse with a saddle whose tree is too wide for his present shape (so that the dressage whips in Fig. 5.7 are not parallel). The arguments will doubtless continue; but if a legitimate use could be found for all of those saddles which really should be consigned to the scrap heap, we could make a much easier transition towards the system (or systems) of saddling which eventually proves itself to be the best for the horse!

As with the 'two-layer' saddles, the difference in a horse's movement when he is first ridden in a Balance saddle can be phenomenal, giving riders the added challenge of stabilising themselves on a horse who bounces about underneath them much more. It is as if the horse were a Victorian lady, suddenly released from her corset and allowed to move freely. However, the change to almost *any* new saddle (even one which fits badly) can enable the horse to move better. For it takes pressure off the

'Horses (by wasting away) are adapting themselves to fit their saddles, instead of the saddles being adapted to fit the horses.'

points most badly affected by the old saddle – and the acid test comes in observing the horse's movement in three weeks' and three months' time. One authority on saddle fit has gone so far as to suggest that changing the horse's saddle every three to six months would circumvent many of the problems of long-term damage due to compression – even if the saddles themselves did not fit perfectly. For with or without the added consideration of muscle wastage and regeneration, horses change shape as they lose and gain weight through the seasons, suggesting that a winter and a summer saddle might be the ideal.

The process through which a horse who has suffered muscle wastage regains his natural shape has to be carefully orchestrated; it may need more than one saddle, along with complementary padding used over the wither. This keeps the saddle clear of it, and gives greater freedom of movement to the shoulder blade. It needs effective supervision and/or an extremely astute owner, and critics of the system have questioned the wisdom of leaving the rider to monitor this process. They also question how much the muscle system in general, and the trapezius muscle in particular, really can regenerate. For it is a very flat muscle – unlike the bulky biceps muscle in your upper arm, for instance, which will enlarge tremendously if you repeatedly lift weights.

Critics of the system argue that if the trapezius muscle were guaranteed to regenerate once it were no longer subject to the compression of a badly fitting saddle, then every horse left out to grass for over six months would show a much less prominent wither than many do. However, there usually is some regeneration in the resting horse, although there is inevitably not as much as there would be if he was worked, and had used his muscles gymnastically in an unrestricted way. If the trapezius muscle has been so badly damaged that parts of it have been replaced by scar tissue, that tissue cannot alter in bulk or revert to muscle. Arguments about whether and how much the muscle can regenerate will undoubtedly continue, with individual horses contributing their evidence; but whatever comes of the Balance initiative, it is clear that they have made both riders and saddlers question the wisdom of convention and fashion – a move which has to be for the best.

....

Balance use a variety of different pads, some filled with various high-tech materials, and some filled with polycotton wadding. The range of materials used in saddle pads has increased hugely in recent years, drawing on the technology involved in fields as apparently diverse as the space programme, and the care of the disabled. I for one have stacks of pads, each bought when it was the latest addition to the marketplace, claiming to be more effective than those which had gone before. From simple cotton cloths which essentially just keep the underneath of your saddle clean, you can branch out into numerous varieties of gel pads, open and closed cell foams, and moulded plastics. You can even buy pads containing the little wooden beads which are commonly used as covers for car seats.

Saddlers repeatedly tell us that a saddle which fits correctly should need no extra padding, but it seems that we take no notice. The panels of many saddles do indeed present the horse with a very hard surface, which does not claim to lessen the impact of (bad) riding. Since we now have materials which do, it seems short-sighted to ignore them – and the manufacturers of the various pads inevitably trade off the guilt felt by riders who *know* they bump, or who suspect that their mere presence on the horse's back is detrimental to his well-being! The gel pads, used by paraplegics and hospital patients to prevent pressure sores, were a revolution in pressure redistribution (and guilt reduction), especially since many of their predecessors were foam pads which actually *bounced,* adding yet another moving part to the rider-saddle-pad-horse system! To make it worse, they did not actually absorb any of the shock of the impact that can be generated when the horse's 'up' meets the rider's 'down'.

The most effective gel pads have within them a nylon mesh which stops the gel from moving – for computerised pressure readings show that the gels are very effective at the beginning of a ridden session, but that they 'bottom out', becoming less effective over a relatively short time. Another very successful pad is made from the open cell foam used in the seats of space rockets, which is designed to absorb the forces of landing and take-off. Its ability to redistribute pressure is such that you can put a dining fork on a chair, put this pad on top of it, sit on the pad, and feel nothing – but even this 'bottoms out' after a while. Polycotton pads do not have the same space-age properties, and are quite soft and compressible. As an unstable matrix, they only provide support in the areas of the pad which are compressed. In this respect they are rather like a feather pillow, and I suspect that soft pads appeal to riders partly because we imagine they would be just as comforting to the horse as they would to us.

'Soft pads appeal to riders partly because we imagine they would be just as comforting to the horse as they would to us.'

Unlike the panels in the 'two-layer' saddles, these pads have no inherent weight-bearing capacity, so they cannot dramatically reduce the pressure under a saddle. One very new possibility which does is an airtight pad filled with polystyrene beads. This too has been developed from products used in the medical field to alleviate pressure, particularly in the use of prosthetics. When air is introduced (through a small valve) the beads in the pad are free flowing, and as air is extracted they move less and less freely, or not at all. With a partial vacuum the pad moulds to both the underside of the saddle and the back of the horse, and a quiet hand-held pump allows air to be extracted each time the pad is used. With a little time and a little skill this creates the ideal interface between the horse's back and the saddle – regardless of any changes in his shape due to condition and fitness.

Irregularities in the profile of either the horse or the saddle are balanced out as the beads are dispersed from pressure points and packed into hollows. Peeling off the pad at the end of the session makes it abundantly clear that horses and saddles are not the same shape! The two panels make a distinct imprint on the top surface of the pad, whilst the bottom is the round, smooth shape of a horse. The pad has effectively given the saddle a larger bearing surface, as well as supporting weight in its own right. Computer scans have shown that the interface it creates between the horse and the saddle can reduce pressures enough to keep them within the range that minimises disruption to the circulation.

'All too frequently, pads merely change the pressure points under the saddle, offering temporary relief to the old problem whilst creating yet another.'

I have, at this point, to give the traditional warning that pads (however good) can only go so far in making the saddle which does not really fit into an acceptable 'pair of shoes' for the horse. Putting a pad under the saddle which is too narrow is actually *dangerous* – it is rather like wearing extra pairs of socks, and expecting to pad out a pair of shoes which are already too tight! This means that padding is only useful under the saddle which is slightly too wide. All too frequently, pads merely change the pressure points under the saddle, offering temporary relief to the old problem whilst creating yet another.

It is a strange paradox that although we want to spare our horses the discomfort felt by the princess whose sleep was so disturbed by the pea, we also need them to know where we are, and to feel the changes in our body position as we prepare for various movements. (That they do this so well through layers of pads and even the 'two-layer' saddles never ceases to amaze me.) On a computerised pressure measurement, the way the rider sits makes a significant difference. The 'sack of potatoes' rider hugely increases the pressures registered – especially in a moving reading – whilst the rider whose high muscle tone enables her to 'carry her own weight' will help to minimise pressure.

Rider asymmetries present a more complicated picture, for if the saddle sits square and the rider sits, say, to the right, more pressure will be registered under the right-hand side of the saddle. But if the saddle sits to the right, whilst the rider sits square to the horse, there will be more pressure under the *left*. When both are crooked, the complex picture created will be difficult to decipher; but I look forward to putting the pressure sensor directly under the rider's backside, and discovering if there is such a thing as a 'print-out' which accompanies good riding, and which is shared by riders whose work is biomechanically sound.

Modern technology has clearly only just begun to revolutionise the saddle industry, and when you consider how the technology of running shoes has developed in recent years, it becomes apparent that there may still be some way to go. (Also, comparing the price of a pair of running shoes with the price of a saddle suggests that even expensive saddles are quite a bargain!) Inevitably, it will take some time and some considerable wisdom to blend new discoveries with the methods and materials which are tried and tested. This, I think, is the challenge that faces us – although many traditionalists may not agree with me.

Our options are increasing all the time, and so are the numbers of innovative, intelligent, concerned people who are pitting their brains against the problems inherent in saddling. But for individual owners (as for saddlers) it is astute observation and the willingness to face up to our responsibilities which can make the most difference. Ignorance may be bliss for us, but the bliss is not shared by our horses. If we ignore them when they tell us of their discomfort – and we choose not to notice that our saddle is rubbing, bouncing or restricting our horse – then we force him to pay the price. How long will we do this for?

CHAPTER SIX

···

An Introduction to
Complementary Medicine

···

THE THERAPIES WHICH were once called 'alternative' have, over the last fifteen years, become much more accepted as additions to mainstream medicine; they have become 'complementary' to it. Many of the riders who turn to the various forms of complementary medicine for their horses do so because they themselves have benefited from treatment. In fact, vets who work with these modalities have described the owners of their equine patients as well educated, with some prior knowledge of the approaches they employ and also of the strengths and weaknesses of orthodox medicine. They are also primarily concerned with the long-term welfare of their horse, which makes them less likely than many to dose him with painkillers so they can ride in one more show. Most commonly, this profile fits dressage riders, although more and more people across the disciplines are exploring the alternatives which the veterinary profession has traditionally regarded with suspicion.

·····························

'Very few horses would not benefit from bodywork.'

·····························

Chiropractic treatment and various other forms of bodywork are probably the most widely available treatments, and are the cause of great controversy, for many vets (especially in the UK) do not believe that any kind of manipulation can possibly 'move bones' in the way that many chiropractors claim to. But despite scepticism from the veterinary profession, many riders have realised that bodywork can make a tremendous difference to their horses. Candidates for treatment include the many 'average' horses who are not actually *lame*, but who are not sound either – the 'walking wounded' who have a 'glitch' in their movement somewhere. At the other end of the spectrum are the high-powered equine athletes, who are demanding the utmost from their bodies, and who inevitably suffer as a consequence. They often receive routine treatment, largely as a preventative measure. Very few horses would *not* benefit from bodywork – for the musculo-skeletal system so easily becomes stressed through all the demands that we place on it.

Acupuncture is also an extremely helpful treatment for musculo-skeletal disorders, and is just one of the modalities which can be classed – along with homoeopathy, flower remedies, and radionics – as 'energy medicine'. So we can now return to a view of the body which extends beyond the confines of our everyday Newtonian map, and can view the body not as solid matter, but as an energy system. Physiotherapy, too, with its various machines delivers energy (in the form of electricity, magnetism, ultra sound, and laser light) to the body's tissues. It is the high-tech version of energy medicine, used mostly to speed the healing of injury, and to deal with its aftermath. For whilst the age-old cure of rest may ensure that we do not increase the damage, it often does not *decrease* it either. All too rarely, however, is physiotherapy part of an holistic approach to treatment, for instead of regarding the horse as a whole it often treats only the site of an injury.

A truly holistic approach takes into account any predisposing causes in the horse's working environment as well as his type and temperament. It looks at his nutrition, and may prescribe nutritional therapy in the form of herbs. It can even address his inherent *predisposition* to certain diseases, treating them before they materialise – and mirroring the way that skilful farriery is also good preventative medicine. Beyond the musculo-skeletal system, the ailments which can respond well to complementary medicine are wide ranging, varying from psychological problems to the many chronic diseases in which orthodox medicine and surgery do not meet with great success. They include equine influenza and other viruses, COPD (broken wind or heaves), sinusitis, laminitis, colic, skin diseases including sweet-itch, and metabolic complaints. Injuries ranging from infected wounds to sprains and fractures also respond well, as do spavin, arthritis, navicular and the other degenerative bone diseases. Reproductive problems can be helped, and even the treatment of allergies has met with significant success.

Horses with vague unexplainable symptoms – as well as those with the established symptoms of chronic disease – are presented every day for complementary treatment. It is often said that emergencies and acute injuries respond best to orthodox treatment, whilst chronic cases are better treated holistically. (Some practitioners would argue, however, that even emergencies can be dealt with equally well using the complementary techniques.) The upsurge in interest in these treatments demonstrates that many people welcome alternatives to bute, antibiotics, steroids and cortisone – especially when their long-term use has seemed inevitable. The 'energy medicines' also have the advantage of having no side-effects; furthermore, no residues are left in the body, so they can never be detected in dope tests.

The supporters of the complementary approaches rarely have the means or the desire to conduct statistical studies, and they are happy to rely on anecdotal evidence, of which there is plenty. However, this makes the detractors extremely hot under the collar, despite the fact that even

'The upsurge in interest in these treatments demonstrates that many people welcome alternatives to bute, antibiotics, steroids and cortisone.'

drugs intended for equine treatment undergo a testing which falls way short of the rigorous double-blind clinical studies used in the testing of human medicines. (In these, neither the prescribing doctor nor the patient know if they are testing the real drug or a dummy drug.) This is because large control groups of horses are expensive to maintain, the laws regarding animal treatment are less demanding, and the financial returns do not justify the enormous outlays which are justified in human medicine where such huge profits can be made.

Treatments like homoeopathy do not easily lend themselves to clinical studies, for different individuals with the same illness are often prescribed different remedies – the 'one disease, one drug' principle of orthodox medicine does not apply. Despite this, double-blind studies have shown homoeopathy to be more effective than placebos in treating some conditions in people (see Chapter 2). Acupuncture has also undergone a variety of trials, in both horses and people. Ironically, horses (as placebo-free guinea-pigs) were used in some early American studies into acupuncture. These were performed in the 1970s after President Nixon's visit to China; for the Food and Drug Administration has classed acupuncture needles as 'experimental devices', which severely limits the contexts in which they can legally be used on people. In Europe acupuncture has had a longer and less troubled history, for it was brought to France in the seventeenth century and has been in use ever since, with a great revival in the last twenty years.

'As the most field-tested technique known in medicine, it is debatable whether acupuncture really needs research.'

In 1980 the American Veterinary Medical Association stated that 'The AVMA has grave concern about acupuncture, regarding it as experimental. The public must be protected from those who make claims for acupuncture that are not based on adequate controlled experiments or documented research.' No other therapeutic options were mentioned in its statement. The American Association of Equine Practitioners took the same narrow view – ignoring all other complementary treatments, and also the fact that acupuncture is one of the oldest systems of treatment in the world. Western vets and medics have mistrusted it because of its philosophy and terminology, which seem strange to ears and minds trained in Newtonian logic. It does, however, seem reasonable to assume that over two thousand years of documented practice must surely count for something – and as the most field-tested technique known in medicine, it is debatable whether acupuncture really *needs* research!

However, despite the wariness of the AVMA, the history of acupuncture – along with the stories of its successes in the western world – piqued the interest of many veterinary surgeons. About four hundred of them worldwide have availed themselves of courses run or validated by the International Veterinary Acupuncture Society, which was founded in 1974. In the UK, the British Veterinary Acupuncture Association was founded in 1986, and since 1990, well over one hundred vets have done an introductory training in acupuncture. The IVAS will hold their training course in the UK in 1997.

In 1992, the National Institutes of Health Office for the Study of Unconventional Medical Practices was established in America. By then, the climate had changed. The AAEP took on a new official position, namely that 'Veterinary acupuncture and acutherapy are considered valid modalities…' The new AVMA guidelines published in 1996 go further, stating that 'veterinary acupuncture and acutherapy are now considered an integral part of veterinary medicine'. Both sets of guidelines also encompass chiropractic treatment, homoeopathy, herbalism and naturopathy, massage and physiotherapy. They require a licensed veterinarian to carry out diagnostic evaluations, and to perform or oversee treatments. Vets can take post-graduate training in acupuncture (which is more established in the USA), homoeopathy, (which is more established in the UK), and chiropractic (in the USA but not in the UK, where virtually all animal chiropractors have originally trained in human practice). Equine massage is usually performed by people who trained initially in human massage, and then took a short training course (some say too short) in equine massage. Neither country yet has courses in veterinary herbalism.

In Britain, the Veterinary Surgeons Act of 1966 stipulates that manipulative therapy alone may be done by a non-veterinarian, provided that the animal has been referred to the practitioner by a vet. In some US states only a licensed veterinarian who has received post-graduate training can perform chiropractic treatments; in others a licensed chiropractor who has completed further training in animal treatment may practise under the sanction of a vet. Physiotherapists may practise in both countries under the auspices of a veterinarian, and there is – as yet – no post-graduate training in animal practice. British physiotherapists, however, can become registered for animal practice once they have completed two years of human practice, and have worked for two years under veterinary supervision, so that two vets are willing to certify that they are competent. The aim of the law in both countries is to protect the public (whether they be believers or sceptics) from incompetence and 'quackery'.

The demand for qualified, skilled practitioners who are insured to work with animals far exceeds the supply, which means that there are indeed some unqualified and unscrupulous people trying to get in on the act. (There are also many others who are extremely well qualified and experienced whose work is, strictly speaking, illegal.) The most outrageous story I have heard of this concerned a travelling 'salesman' who arrived in a friend's town selling a remedy in paste form which supposedly helped a horse to relax: one squirt relaxed his neck, two squirts relaxed his back, and three relaxed his whole body. You need to understand very little about physiology to know that this is nonsense, for the bloodstream would have carried his paste to all parts of the horse's body. There is also a danger (especially in the USA, where there is less regard for training and for the integrity of different disciplines than there is in the UK) of, say a massage therapist beginning to suggest a few homoeopathic remedies, and then a few herbal remedies, until she becomes a self-professed treater of all conditions using all modalities.

The law regarding animal treatment is far more restrictive than the law relating to humans, since horses and other animals cannot make informed choices about their treatment. It also contains some grey areas, especially around herbalism, and in the UK even the horse owner herself can be liable to prosecution if she causes suffering to a horse by not calling in a veterinary surgeon. If we choose to look beyond the orthodox veterinary map, we find that we are living in times which are very confusing, and are not dissimilar to the days before legislation regulated the medical professions, and anyone could call himself a doctor or vet. All of us – horse owners, vets, and the practitioners of the complementary treatments – must find our way through this time. There are many conflicting interests at play (within each group as well as between each group), creating huge potential for 'map battles'. My hope is that the new associations being formed by the complementary practitioners will encourage and endorse the best possible standards of practice, and will speak loudly enough that they – along with public opinion – will become a force to be reckoned with.

There is indeed good reason for caution in the use of complementary medicine, and one of my friends, for instance, is lucky to be alive today. For many years ago, he broke out in terrible eczema, and was being treated by a homoeopath for this condition. As it worsened, he maintained a foolish determination not to go to his doctor, but was eventually persuaded to see an Indian acupuncturist who was also medically trained. He diagnosed an underlying liver condition, which over time was successfully treated with acupuncture. But the doctor believed that the level of toxicity in my friend's body could have cost him his life if he had not received effective treatment within a couple of weeks.

I have not come so close to death; but the tunnel vision of orthodox medicine meant that it took over nine months from an initial visit to my doctor for me to see the right specialist, and be treated for a (by this time rampant) infection in a *different* system of the body to the one which had already been intensively investigated. The strong antibiotics I subsequently took had devastating effects on me as well as the infection – and I cannot say whether any form of complementary treatment could have been successful at this or any other stage of the saga. But as this story shows, neither approach is fool-proof, and although safeguards are definitely needed, the holier-than-thou attitude of some vets and medics is definitely open to question.

CHAPTER SEVEN

Equine Bodywork

Manipulative treatments

As I have travelled the world, it has become abundantly clear to me that within each of the bodywork disciplines originally developed for working with people, there is bound to be someone, somewhere, who has been motivated by an insatiable curiosity and their love of horses to put their hands on horses too, and to discover the added nuances of equine treatment. This has resulted in a number of training courses in equine bodywork, and we commonly hear about equine chiropractors, about massage therapists, and about TTEAM practitioners who are using the Tellington Touch, devised by Linda Tellington-Jones and based on Feldenkrais bodywork. Then there are the practitioners of the oriental arts of shiatsu and acupressure, who may not have done a formal equine training, but who nonetheless have a lot to offer. But you will also find a few innovative people treating horses using some weird and wonderful techniques which you have probably never even heard of, like cranial osteopathy, zero balancing, and kinesiological manipulation – strange names which cannot, of themselves, demonstrate the power of these techniques to transform the body's functioning.

Since many of these techniques may be as beneficial to you as they are to your horse, and since the field of animal treatment mirrors that of human treatment, I will refer to both throughout. (I will, however, consider only those disciplines in which you are a *patient* and not a *pupil*; for the re-education approaches to bodywork – the Alexander and Feldenkrais systems – will be discussed in my next book.) Doctors have, over the years, gradually come to terms with physiotherapists and with bodyworkers – primarily osteopaths, chiropractors, Alexander teachers, Feldenkrais teachers, and massage therapists. Many doctors recognise that very often, all they can do for the person with back pain is to prescribe rest, painkillers, and ultimately surgery. Even they are beginning to realise that this is not enough.

Doctors, like vets, tend to look at the 'small picture' of an injury, focusing only on the symptoms present in just one part of the body. This often prevents them from appreciating that the presenting problem is not one of *structure* – which could indeed necessitate chemical or surgical intervention – but one of *function*. So the symptoms visible in one small part of the body commonly disappear when a bodyworker reduces the stress on it by addressing the balance of the body *as a whole*. In treating horses this can even take us beyond the confines of bodywork, also involving the farrier, saddler and dental specialist in the attempt to solve an extremely complex puzzle.

In human medicine, the structural approach drives many people to such desperation that they vote with their feet and seek out the bodyworkers. The vast majority testify to the effectiveness of the complementary treatment they have received; and those who have used it to spare themselves from continual pain or the surgeon's knife become positively eulogistic about its benefits. There are many typical patterns of damage to the human body: for instance, the car driver who is stationary when hit from behind often has her right foot pressing on the brake pedal whilst her left rests on the floor. So the impact causes both a whiplash injury to her neck and an 'upslip' in the right side of her pelvis. For unlike the left side of her body, the right is trapped between two opposing forces. Less traumatic injuries will often go unnoticed: one side of your pelvis, for instance, can become rotated relative to the other on those occasions when you *expect* to take your next step on level ground, only to discover (as your foot hits the ground with an unexpected jar) that there was indeed a step down. Since this is an experience which is all but universal there must be very few of us with unscathed bodies.

Historically, most of the arguments between medical doctors and the manipulative therapists have centred around whether certain joints are fixed, or capable of movement. The sacroiliac joints in the pelvis, and also the joints in the skull, for instance, are suture joints which, according to the traditional medical map, allow no movement (a fact contested by the osteopaths and chiropractors who claim to have been moving them for years). However, recent research at Michigan State University has shown that movement of the bones in the skull is indeed possible, and this finding could – in theory – pave the way to a melding of maps.

Many veterinarians are less convinced by manipulative treatment than doctors, and since everyone who treats animals earns their living in private practice, the conflict of interests is greater. So arguments about 'the back man' abound. They are fuelled at least partially by Newtonian logic, vested interest, and research performed on *dead* horses – as well as by a small number of poorly trained and unethical practitioners. The arguments centre mostly on the massiveness of the horse's spine and the impossibility

'Many veterinarians are less convinced by manipulative treatment than doctors.'

of moving it, for it is surrounded by muscles which are relatively larger than our own, and which have much less flexibility.

As far as most veterinarians are concerned, any changes to the alignment of the vertebrae which cannot be seen on an X-ray do not exist. But chiropractors claim that 'invisible' changes do indeed exist, and that these 'subluxations' (which are far smaller than a dislocation) are actually palpable. They are the subject of much controversy, for veterinarians counter the argument by saying that if a vertebra were sufficiently out of place for this to be felt by palpation, the spinal cord which passes along a canal within the bodies of the vertebra would have been so damaged that the horse would be incapable of movement. So vets question whether the vertebrae are capable of going 'out' (of alignment) at all, and if they cannot, it follows that they cannot possibly be put back 'in' again. But many vets (like doctors) have been forced to admit that chiropractors can indeed make a difference – so they have unhappily concluded that they must in reality be doing 'something else'.

It is perhaps unfortunate that the ideas of 'in' and 'out' have become part of our colloquial language – and they probably express well how it feels to the person (and perhaps the horse) who has the problem. Commonly, we respond to them by visualising a line of bones in which one is out of place, rather as if one brick in a brick pillar were off to the side. This is clearly a very crude – if instinctive – interpretation of the facts; yet I suspect that this obviously simplistic 'map' drives the arguments between vets and chiropractors (and it probably leads to more bad feeling than any of the 'map battles' within veterinary medicine). Most research into chiropractics is taking place in the USA, but the foremost workers in the field do not – as yet – have an explanation for the mechanism of their work which is convincing both to them and to medical science. When they do, it is guaranteed to be far more sophisticated than our home-spun version, and to focus much more on the subtleties of *function* than on the gross level of *structure*.

The concepts of 'in' and 'out' (as well as our ways of visualising them) suggest large-scale structural change. Whilst some chiropractors may indeed claim to 'move bones', present-day students are taught that it is the *soft tissue* in the area of a joint which is the focus of their adjustment, and that the bones concerned may or may not have 'moved'. Prolonged muscle spasm near a joint (whether human or equine) will eventually cause tightening of the ligaments which stabilise it, and also of the joint capsule itself. This could eventually lead to the formation of bony growth within the joint, and any organic tissue change would indeed take the condition beyond the scope of the bodyworkers, requiring the intervention of orthodox medicine. But this is extremely rare; more often, the spasm restricts the possible movement of the joint so that there might be – for instance – only a small amount of movement at one end of its range of motion.

The restriction of the joint effectively creates a strong cohesive force within it – making it function rather like two panes of wet glass which cannot be pulled apart. Equine chiropractors argue that the cumulative effect of this decreased mechanical efficiency through many joints creates the 'stiff' and ultimately the 'unlevel' horse. However, in the human body it can take only the smallest restriction in the possible movement of *one* joint to cause us discomfort. If nerves are pinched or trapped the consequences of an injury will be much greater, making it extremely traumatic and painful. The minutest amount of pressure affects nerve functioning; and nerve pain may be felt (as in the case of sciatic pain) far from the site of the original injury.

Thus the 'subluxation complex' involves ligaments, nerves, blood vessels and muscles as well as bones, and many chiropractors, osteopaths and physiotherapists work from a 'map' which is much more subtle than 'in' or 'out'. But they are still operating within a Newtonian mechanistic view of the body, viewing it as a system of levers and pulleys controlled by the smart technician who lives in the brain. We move to a much more subtle level if we consider the role of the nervous system; this brings *live intelligence* into the equation, and makes it far harder for us to 'stop the game' and make our maps. The effects of the nervous system on functioning are infinitely harder to pin down than the various parameters affecting levers and pulleys – and they cannot be assessed in the dead horse.

Most of the foremost thinkers in the chiropractic field believe that their adjustments work on a *neurophysiological* level, and that a subluxation is best thought of as *a functional disturbance of the nervous system*. Thus it affects the nerves which exit the spinal cord between the vertebrae, and also affects the neurological messages sent between the brain and the muscles and organs. This disturbance can limit a muscle's ability to contract and relax – since its *neurological control mechanism* is either under- or over-active, the resting muscle has a tension which is lower or higher than it should be. Changing the neurological message given to the muscle changes its tension – and this is turn affects the forces acting on a nearby joint. In effect, the short sharp stretch created by a chiropractic thrust *feeds new information into the nervous system*, as does the longer slower stretch of other bodywork approaches; alternatively, the messages delivered by the spinal cord itself can be influenced by adjusting the pulsations of the fluid which surrounds it. This is part of the delicate task of the cranial osteopath, who also addresses the inherent motion of each and every tissue..

The nerves of the sympathetic and parasympathetic nervous systems (which rev. us up or calm us down) also leave the spinal cord between each vertebra, so they too are involved in the 'subluxation complex'. This

'The short sharp stretch created by a chiropractic thrust feeds new information into the nervous system.'

is why osteopathic and chiropractic treatments (in humans and perhaps horses) can be effective with asthma, irritable bowel syndrome, and many other conditions. However, our conventional medical map puts them in such a different compartment to 'bones' that it cannot conceive of a link (albeit anecdotal rather than scientifically proven) between them and manipulative treatment. Despite this, my hunch is that only the *neurophysiological* viewpoint will eventually end the 'map battles'; for when we attempt to confine our thinking and our maps to a crude Newtonian view of the body, there will inevitably be falsifications and incongruities which stretch the limits of credibility.

....

American chiropractors have put forward the following model to explain how joints move, and how chiropractors work (see Fig. 7.1). The range through which you can move, say your arm, is known as the active range of movement. Beyond this is the passive range of movement. This is the extra distance through which I could move your arm, and it extends to the *physiological barrier*. The mobilisations done by physiotherapists would move a joint to this point, but this is not the *anatomical barrier* where something would tear, break or dislocate under further pressure. Between

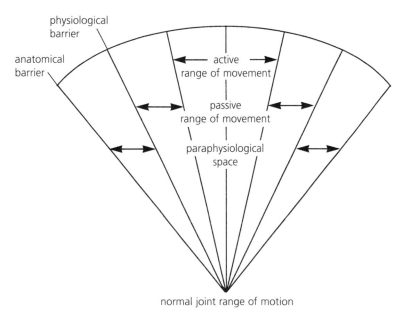

Fig. 7.1 A diagrammatic explanation of the relationship between the active and passive range of movement of a joint; also showing the paraphysiological space, within which chiropractors make their adjustments.

the physiological barrier and the anatomical barrier lies the *paraphysiological space*: this is the area where osteopaths and chiropractors make their adjustments.★

When your joints crack you are moving them within the paraphysiological space, and if you can do this you have a joint which (instead of being held tightly by cohesion like the two panes of wet glass) is healthy, with plenty of 'joint play'. As children, we used to pull on our fingers hoping that the joint in the knuckle would crack (in fact, we much preferred pulling on someone else's fingers!). If you make a habit of this, a joint can become hypermobile, and so loosely bound that this too invites injury. The crack signifies that the joint capsule has been extended to the point where the pressure in it decreases enough for some of the fluid to become gaseous. It is the formation of *gas* which causes the crack, so this has nothing to do with the bones themselves. Any restriction in the paraphysiological space will lessen the 'joint play' and affect the joint throughout its whole range of motion. Even this limitation causes sufficient discomfort to bring people in for treatment.

A chiropractic adjustment is often thought of as a short, sharp stretch of the ligaments surrounding a joint. Those who use a thrusting technique to create this stretch are at pains to point out that it is *speed* and not *force* which makes their adjustments effective. Different chiropractors, however, use different techniques, and the field of equine practice has progressed enormously from the days when it was acceptable practice to hang from the rafters of a stable and kick a horse in the back! Some practitioners prefer not to use a thrust, but to put the body into a position from which it will – instinctively and of itself – make that last final stretch through which the correction occurs. The most important factor, however, in the success of a treatment is probably not the technique itself, but *the skill of the person who uses it.*

> 'The most important factor in the success of a treatment is probably not the technique itself, but the skill of the person who uses it.'

Different parts of the body require an approach suited to both their structure and their function, so we cannot view the hinge of the jaw, the relatively mobile vertebrae of the neck, and the much more fixed vertebrae of the spine all in the same way. Then there are the four corners of the horse where his limbs attach, which we can usefully think of as his 'chassis'. Any problem here (or in the limbs themselves) will put uneven stresses on the back, as will unequal muscle development within the two long back muscles. So problems which manifest between the withers and the croup may well be the inevitable result of limb and muscle imbalance.

★ *I am using the term chiropractic treatment to include all manipulative techniques, also performed by osteopaths and physiotherapists. In the UK and Australia, the osteopathic and chiropractic schools of thought are becoming closer over time, and I hope we can look forward to more open discussion and a freer sharing of maps between these practitioners.*

Some chiropractors never touch this area at all, believing that it will right itself when the stresses on it are evened out.

The McTimoney chiropractors (trained in England) liken some of the corrections which they use on the vertebrae of the back to a 'flick' on the top of the spinal process (see Fig. 5.4, page 124). We can feel the tips of these running along the centre line of the horse's back, and they act like a long lever arm, connecting to the vertebrae which lie too deep to see or touch. In the horse's neck it is the transverse processes of the vertebrae which are palpable, and used in treatment. To mimic the vertebrae of the horse's back and the 'toggle recoil' technique used by the McTimoney practitioners, make a fist of your hand and point your forefinger upwards. Your finger represents the spinal process whilst your fist represents the vertebra itself. If you then flick the end of your finger with the second finger of your other hand you can feel a vibration go right down into the fist you have made. We could say that you have sent an 'energy force' down your finger, and in the case of the horse, this has been sent into the vertebra itself. The McTimoney chiropractors argue that they can palpate a deviation of two degrees in the line up of the spinal processes, and that this represents a minute twist of the vertebra itself, which can be righted through their technique.

....

Chiropractic treatment often gives instant relief of pain. Whilst you might sigh with relief when it is over, horses often indicate their relief by licking their lips, making chewing motions, and also by sighing or yawning. These are responses of the parasympathetic nervous system – which counteracts the effects of 'fight or flight', slowing heart rate and returning blood to the skin and internal organs. Practitioners look for this response and take it very seriously; if they do not get it, it is questionable whether their correction really made the mark. Horses (unless they have previously received treatment of very dubious quality) are much less wary of their touch than people usually are, and they will stand quietly and untied for treatment. In contrast, one of my friends – a farrier who has spent a lifetime developing the quick reactions which allow him to avoid being kicked – finds that he can only go to one of the chiropractors in his area. For only this one is quick and clever enough to perform his adjustments before my friend leaps up off his table!

Most practitioners working with humans will follow up their treatment by recommending both active and passive stretches. (In the latter, someone moves your body for you.) But to really get to the root of the problem they may ask you to pay attention to your posture. If necessary they will show you ways of protecting and strengthening your back, especially when you lift heavy weights. The traumatic event which so often causes back injury is usually the straw which breaks the camel's back – the final event which causes the breakdown of a system already made vulnerable by less-than-ideal patterns of muscle development, tension and use. When muscle imbalance is pulling on your spine, you are an accident waiting to happen; and a healthy human – like a healthy horse – will withstand trauma far better than his counterpart whose functioning is already compromised.

It is not so easy, of course, to ask the horse to pay attention to *his* posture as part of his ongoing treatment, and that is where you, as a rider, become involved in a horse's rehabilitation. When a chiropractor has treated your horse, she may prescribe several days of rest or light work, using only straight lines. She may also suggest that you work the horse 'forward and down' in a long, low outline. In my opinion, many chiropractors overestimate the skill of the average rider, for only a small proportion of riders have the expertise to do this well. Many will continue to ride using a saddle which is less than ideal. They will fall down the 'man-trap' (the name I use for the hollow in the horse's back), ride with their usual asymmetry, and twiddle on the reins to bring the horse's head down. Both the rider, the state of the horse's feet, and even the state of his teeth, can combine to recreate the problems which the chiropractor has just attempted to cure. A physiotherapist who uses adjustment techniques recognised the enormity of the problem when she recently said to me, 'I used to think that I could cure every horse. But now I realise that my work is just one piece in a huge interacting puzzle.'

As with people, it is accidents and poor patterns of use (this usually means poor riding and/or poor shoeing or saddling) which lead horses to need treatment. One horse I know somehow landed upside down in a ditch when only a few months old. His wither always looked very ill-defined, and when he saw a chiropractor as a four-year-old (by which time he was working under saddle), both his wither profile and his personality underwent a dramatic transformation. Falls when jumping are renowned for causing problems, as is leaping about and/or rearing – perhaps during a traumatic experience with trailer loading. One of my chiropractor friends once treated a number of foals who had all travelled over from Ireland as weanlings. Horse after horse showed the same pattern (a very rare phenomenon), which set her thinking. It was consistent with being loaded into a lorry by someone who had taken hold of the headcollar and then taken hold of the tail, pulling it around to the left and hauling the foal up the ramp.

A chiropractic problem can even be caused by lungeing a fresh horse and pulling sharply on the lunge line as he cavorts about. Pulling back when tied can be equally destructive, as can sudden stops in a trailer,

'When muscle imbalance is pulling on your spine, you are an accident waiting to happen.'

covering for a mare, and perhaps even a difficult birth (for both mare and foal). Then there are the slips, stumbles and mis-steps which you might never think about twice. Horses whose behaviour is 'quirky' – one day good and the next day difficult – are highly likely to be in intermittent pain. The 'crazy' horse, too, is often running away from discomfort. The grumpy or listless horse, or the horse who is desperate to rub his head against you, may well have a headache – a concept which had never entered my perception until put there by a chiropractor. One of my friends has a horse who, on some days, virtually climbs the walls of the stable when she shakes out clean straw – desperate behaviour which you also might indulge in if you felt you had a hang-over!

When you purchase a horse you have, in all probability, no knowledge of many of the events which have had an impact on his body, for most of these traumas do not leave scars. But astute observation can tell you a lot, and of the horses I see in my clinics, over 70 per cent look to me as if they have problems. The horses concerned are probably not actually lame, but they lack the free and easy movement which leads me to believe that they are comfortable in their bodies. Nine times out of ten, their owners just thought that they had a very average horse – which may only go to prove how 'average' it is for us to be riding horses who are restricting and contorting their movement as they work around their aches and pains.

More sophisticated riders can usually identify factors in their ridden work which might make them suspect a problem – although it can be difficult to know which of the partners in the rider/horse combination is the chicken, and which is the egg. When the horse's pelvis is dropped on one side (as in Fig. 4.13, page 92) he can feel, when you are riding, as if he has 'a flat tyre', with that corner of his body dropping away from beneath your seat. If you have difficulty striking off on one canter lead, the problem may again be that his pelvis is crooked, or that you are. Horses who jump to one side are usually doing so to avoid pain; but again, it may be you who is the precursor of the problem. The horse who is extremely hollow and very difficult to persuade to reach into the rein may again be suffering from your bad riding, from bad saddle fit, or from his own problems with his body, which could include his teeth or his feet. If you find that you have a constant, very strong contact on one rein, and that the horse is extremely hard to turn that way, you either have a very marked asymmetry yourself, or your horse has his own difficulties.

There is always a reason for evasions as strong as these, for horses do not pull on one rein, go hollow, or crab sideways just for fun or just to get at you. In addressing all of these issues it can be very helpful to have a better rider work the horse, and unscramble the 'chicken and egg' phenomenon by assessing how easy she finds it to ride through the evasion. My ridden assessments are usually proved quite accurate; but there are some interesting cases where I have been proved wrong (like the young horse I wrote about on page 65, in the chapter dealing with equine dentistry) Another young horse looked, when ridden by his rather crooked rider, as if he had a chiropractic problem, but he was surprisingly easy to ride straight. When the saddler, dentist and chiropractor all found no major problems we were left concluding that the rider needed to straighten up fast – and this implied that she herself might well benefit from bodywork.

One pupil of mine arrived on a course with a horse who looked unwell, felt dreadful on the left rein, and was well nigh impossible to turn to the left. The difficulty that I had in riding him told me that the problem was primarily his. But whilst watching the horse in his stable, it became apparent just how acute it was. For he would move happily from the door to the haynet, which entailed about a 30° turn to the right. Then, to look out of the door again he would complete the circle, preferring a 330° turn to the right to a 30° turn to the left! The owner had been blaming herself for the problem on the left rein (no historical cause was apparent to her) and had simply been aware that her horse was extremely dirty in his stable, without realising that all of this circling was the cause of the mess. More astute observation was needed.

I have met many riders with an equivalent tendency to turn only one way – and some have admitted to me that when riding out on the English country lanes they look over their *left* shoulder to assess whether any traffic is coming up behind them on their *right*! So I refer a rider to an osteopath or chiropractor when I see that she has a pronounced twist, and/or that her spine is unusually out of true. During a first lesson, I invite her to sit on my hands. Sometimes one seat bone is easy to feel whilst the other is nowhere to be found, and if she cannot easily remedy the situation, I ask if she has ever had back pain or if she has had an accident. Often her pelvis is twisted and permanently raised on one side. This will inevitably cause her to collapse one way, with its inevitable repercussions for her horse.

The effects of bad riding are so enormous that one of my farrier friends has even coined the term '*rider induced lameness*'. His long-term suspicions about this were reinforced after watching two riders exchange horses. One horse had been at grass following lameness; but with his new rider he stayed sound. *Her* horse, however, went lame with his new rider, showing the same type of lameness as her original horse.

When a rider has a crooked pelvis, this is likely to be associated with a functionally short leg, for we can contort ourselves enough to create an apparent difference of up to a quarter of an inch (6mm), in legs which are

'Horses do not pull on one rein, go hollow, or crab sideways just for fun or just to get at you.'

actually the same length. We do this by ramming the thigh bone into the hip socket, and reducing the space in the joint. A difference in leg length can also be caused by an anatomically short leg (which is usually the result of a fracture), or it may be the symptom of a scoliosis which curves the spine in the area between the shoulder blades. The issue of leg length raises the question of whether the rider should ever ride with one stirrup shorter – and if the difference is functional my answer is no; for this compensation addresses the *symptom* and not the cause. It holds the discrepancy in place, and prohibits us from finding a way to even out the spaces in the rider's joints. We are now entering extremely controversial ground, for the same argument might discourage us from putting a wedge beneath the foot of the human (or the horse) who has a functionally short leg. The equivalent is done by some farriers (see page 93), and is the basis of orthotic treatment in humans.

About 95 per cent of horses who are grade 'O' sound (classed as completely sound) weight their forelegs differently, and the difference in weight-bearing between the hind legs can be significantly *greater* than in front, even though the horse appears completely sound. Assuming that each foot has been correctly balanced to its limb in shoeing, bodywork is probably the best way to address this imbalance. Time, along with the high-tech gait analyses given by tread mills and force plates, will give us scientific data about the effectiveness of both chiropractic manipulations and sports massage. It will also tell us whether there are indeed cases where it is best to let the body have its own inherent compensations, and to leave well alone.

....

Whether or not you have your suspicions about the state of your horse's body, there are a number of (extremely low-tech) tests you can do which may confirm or allay your concerns. These should follow a very careful observation of his muscle asymmetries (see Chapter 4) and his walk, for these give many clues about how comfortable he is likely to be. If the horse's shoulders are unevenly developed, or if the pelvis is asymmetrical, you can expect to have a problem. (See Figs 4.11–4.13, pages 91–92.) You may find that the points of his hips (the tuber coxae) are at different heights. You may also find that one of the tuber ischia – the horse's seat bones, which you can feel within the hamstring muscle on each side of his tail – is higher or further back than the other. The tuber sacrale or points of the croup can also be at different heights. Remember, though, that the horse *must* be standing square as you check him – which is often easier said than done, especially if he is not comfortable in his body.

If you pick up the horse's front foot and bring the lower part of the limb right up against the upper limb, the hoof should touch the elbow. If it lies to the *inside* of the elbow (which happens usually only on one side) the horse has a restriction in that diagonal, which will need to be released both within that forelimb, and in the opposite side of the pelvis. (He could, however, have a very badly conformed knee or lower leg, so check for this too.) If you run the pads of your fingers quite quickly across his quarters, through the belly of the muscle which lies between the croup and the point of the hip, the horse should not flinch. If he does (again, usually on one side), he is showing a pain response.

It is normal for the horse's back to dip if you run your fingernails or a ball point pen very close to the spine on each side, so this is not a reliable diagnosis of pain. You will learn more from slowly running the pads of your fingers along the belly of the longissimus muscle, about 2 inches/50mm away from the horse's spine. The horse should not dip his back away, flinch, quiver, tighten the muscle into a protective splint, or want to move away from you. Many horses show tenderness in the loin area, and this is often said to be indicative of a sacroiliac problem – although it is folly to make such a precise diagnosis. (As we shall see later, some horses block pain so effectively that even though they are all but crippled, they do not respond to these tests.) Using the pads of your fingers to palpate the muscle on each side of the wither should not provoke any twitching, and neither should touching the horse in the girth area behind the elbow, where 'ticklishness' is really muscle soreness. (Linda Tellington-Jones, however, believes that many horses are *born* ticklish in this region.) 'Reflex points', which *should* provoke a response, lie on each side of the spine in the loin area, and when you press in deeply with your thumb and first finger, it is normal for the horse to suddenly drop his back. If you place them just above the top of the tail on each side and press in, the horse should tuck his pelvis under him and lift his back. If you can safely stand behind him as you do this, you can observe whether the two sides come up evenly; if they do not, he has a problem.

If you place the tips of your fingers along the centre line of the horse's belly, just where the girth would cross it, and you tickle him gently, his whole back should rise; if it does not, if you feel as if you are trying to move concrete, and/or you are met with a resentful response, he has lost flexibility. Doing this daily constitutes a very therapeutic back stretch, as does stretching to reach a carrot held between and behind the horse's knees. As he does his, the horse should be encouraged to nibble a bit, breathe a bit, and then nibble a bit – and not to grab for the carrot and then fling his head back up again! Any horse should be able to reach a carrot placed at his side by the girth: if he cannot (again, usually on one side), you know that the other side of his body is restricted. To motivate him to move his neck rather than his feet, however, you may have to place his *body* parallel to a wall.

Doing these stretches every day can make a remarkable difference, although stretching the limbs safely and effectively is a more difficult job which many horse owners do not do well. Here, we are primarily using the stretches *diagnostically*, and the stretches which your horse is not happy to sustain tell you about possible restrictions in his body. The *therapeutic* use of the stretches – which have to be done daily to be effective preventative medicine – is described in several of the books in the bibliography. You would be best advised, however, to ask a skilled practitioner to teach you how to do them, for they are not easy to do well.

It takes significant trust for a flight animal to stand quietly on three legs for the thirty seconds which are required for the stretch to be really effective. It also takes significant sensitivity for the handler not to get carried away, and to pull so hard that she creates more problems than she cures! The skill lies in noticing the point in the stretch at which the horse backs off; so this is the time when you too back off, before bringing him gently back to his 'edge'. If you are doing the stretches well *you* are supporting the weight of the horse's limb (for if he is holding it, he is contracting his muscles to do so); this means that the stretches are taxing to do, and you have to take good care of your own back in the process.

....

'An educated touch will easily differentiate between spasm and bruising within a muscle, for they feel very different.'

When you are buying a horse, these few tests may help you to appreciate that unless you are happy to ride about the countryside in straight lines and a very hollow outline, the horse will become a rehabilitation project. Professional bodyworkers, however, will base their assessments on much more sophisticated methods of palpation. For they have learned how to 'read' the body through touch, in ways that you or I cannot hope to do without training. It entails putting your hands on so many different horses that you discover what 'normal' and the various forms of 'abnormal' feel like. It is the *comparisons* you can make which determine your level of skill, and – as with riding – years of practice go into developing a sophisticated sense of feel. An educated touch, for instance, will easily differentiate between *spasm* and *bruising* within a muscle, for they feel very different.

Practitioners also call on other methods of discovery: two of the most obvious are observation of the horse both standing and in movement, and questioning the owner about his history and behaviour. But other more unusual options include the use of acupressure and 'muscle testing'. Diagnosis using acupressure is the forte of a chiropractor who was a member of the British Army Veterinary Corps stationed in Hong Kong, where he learned this technique from a Chinese vet. He uses the lightest touch on points along the edges of the spinal processes, and this makes horses do the 'hoola', moving their backs in ways I had not thought possible (and challenging the accepted idea of their rigidity). It is the *restrictions* in this movement which give him his clues about how to proceed.

One inventive physiotherapist I know has borrowed the muscle testing technique used in Applied Kinesiology and Touch for Health. The horse's owner acts as a 'surrogate', positioned with one hand on the horse's rib cage and the other arm raised. The practitioner firstly touches the relevant joint on the horse's body, and then she pushes down on the surrogate's wrist. This will withstand a gentle downward pressure as long as all is well. But if there is a restriction in the flow of energy through the horse's joint, the surrogate's arm will drop. For in effect she forms a circuit with the horse, and this reduced energy flow leaves her body unable to sustain its normal reactions. This is a very strange feeling, and an interesting experience for the sceptic!

....

I have learned a tremendous amount through riding the horses who come on my courses, making my own assessment, and then having them treated, often by both a chiropractor and a sports massage therapist. I then compare their diagnoses with my own, and the opportunity to ride the horses again later (which, given my particular expertise, tells me much more than just watching them) shows me how much effect the treatment has had. The difference is very often dramatic. Sadly, it is normal for us to be riding horses who have aches and pains not so dissimilar to our own. Sometimes pain stops us or them from functioning; but more often we all work around it, using our bodies rather badly as a result of (or perhaps as a precursor of) our limitations.

If the ligaments surrounding a joint have become shortened, several treatments may be needed to release them. Necks seem to respond very well to treatment, and it is pelvises which repeatedly go 'out' – although these are such massive and complicated structures, and are subject to such huge mechanical forces, that it is perhaps not surprising (especially given the contributing influences of bad riding and saddling). One practitioner I know expects to need two treatments to do a good job with a horse. When she finds herself making a pelvic correction for a third time she begins to look for other mitigating factors – and the fourth time convinces her that no one has yet reached the nub of the problem.

Bodyworkers from other disciplines who regard chiropractic treatment with some scepticism argue that it has an in-built limitation, and that instead of giving the body an *invitation* to change, the chiropractor gives it an *ultimatum*. This is like saying 'You *will* change'; so when the body cannot take the change it reverts to its original state – instantly, or within hours or days of the treatment. Chiropractors themselves refute this argument, believing that they offer very subtle invitations; but even they admit that the techniques they use are easy to do wrong.

Whilst I am a great fan of good chiropractic treatment, it has to be said that it is probably more open to abuse than any other bodywork system. Some equine practitioners have adapted human techniques to animals without further training, and between different schools and different practitioners there is a huge variation in the techniques used. However, the skill of the person who uses the technique is probably much more important than the technique itself, and at their best, chiropractic adjustments are very respectful and harmonious. At their worst, they have the power to create some of the conditions they propose to cure – which is why you must choose your practitioner with extreme care, and be sure that you have confidence in her skills. Beware of anyone who uses mallets, or any other device which increases the force exerted by her adjustments, and ask around, about a practitioner's qualifications, and about her track record. Whilst most other 'alternative' approaches simply do not work when badly applied, heavy-handed adjustments have the capacity to do harm.

'The skill of the person who uses the technique is probably much more important than the technique itself.'

Soft tissue work

Whilst chiropractic treatment is probably the best known form of bodywork, other options encompass massage and sports massage, kinesiological manipulation, the Tellington TTouch, shiatsu and acupressure – to name but a few. The approach you choose in treating your horse will probably depend primarily on who is practising in your area, or on how willing and able you are to learn some simple techniques from books and video tapes. The part of the world you live in makes a huge difference to the availability and type of practitioners – massage, for instance, is much more widely practised in the USA than it is in the UK, although the UK has many more chiropractors. But if you wish to make a *theoretical* choice about which approach to follow, you will almost certainly base that choice on your preferred map; for every discipline is built on a map of the body, which in turn is based on a philosophy, which will – broadly speaking – be either Eastern or Western in its origins.

For many, the most easy bodywork approaches to accept and understand are the massage techniques, for they mesh with a mechanistic understanding of the body. However, massage, in its most common form of 'Swedish massage' is named after a Swede who brought it to the West from China! There, massage has been a cornerstone of treatment for thousands of years; hence our modern Westernised version of it shares many techniques with the ancient arts of shiatsu and acupressure. Massage can be a generalised way of relaxing the patient whilst stimulating the circulation and removing waste products from the muscles; or it can pin-point and release specific areas of tension within certain muscles – in which case it classes as *sports* massage. Both approaches remove toxins from the muscles and leave them circulating in the bloodstream, so after treatment people are often advised to drink a lot of water, and horses should ideally be worked – so that sweat as well as urine can help to eliminate the toxins and cleanse the body.

As we saw in Chapter 2, muscles are like fluid-filled balloons, and the free passage of fluids is needed to keep the body working well. The heart is a pump which forces blood through the arteries, and ultimately into the muscles. But the venous system and the lymphatic system, which between them form the return circulation, do not have a pump. The veins, however, are aided by one-way valves which stop fluid from draining back down into the legs. Movement naturally brings with it the muscle contractions which squeeze the veins and lymph vessels, encouraging the passage of fluid towards the heart; hence prolonged inactivity can cause both your legs and your horse's legs to swell up. As far as possible, massage strokes are done *towards* the heart, aiding this part of the circulation – although on a horse the direction of the hair is another important consideration. Massage therapists need a good understanding of anatomy, for the bony prominences of the body should not be subjected to pressure, and firm or more gentle strokes are appropriate for different parts of the body, depending on how massive or how sensitive the muscles are.

Muscle fibres (as we saw in Fig. 2.3, page 39) all run in parallel, and are like fine insulated wires bundled together and then enclosed in more insulation. This is known as fascia, and the layer which surrounds the muscle is in effect a skin, which can become very tight – thus limiting the freedom of the muscle to contract and relax. The layers of fascia which enclose adjacent muscles can become glued together, and since they no longer move separately, the muscles cannot glide over each other as they should. This compromises the movement possibilities of the horse or human involved, and some bodywork systems – notably Rolfing, which is done much more commonly in humans than horses – directly manipulate fascia. *Muscle spasm*, which is a permanent state of muscle contraction, also restricts movement. When a muscle contracts, its individual fibres shorten, for each is made up of filaments which can interlock. To illustrate their resting state, put your hands in front of you with your palms facing your body and your fingertips lying between each other. Then interlock your fingers: on contraction, filaments within the muscle fibres interlock in a similar way, and all remains well in the muscle as long as the fibres *completely release again afterwards*, but often they do not.

Thus any repetitive activity will tend to cause a shortening in the muscles used (and also in the nerves and fascia), and stretching – which is done most safely and effectively when the body is already warm – is one way to counteract this. Spasm also commonly occurs as a reflex response to injury, for the hardened muscle effectively makes a protective splint around the injured area. Pain causes spasm, which in turn causes more pain, which then causes more spasm. Thus more and more muscle fibres are added to the original knot, which cannot undo itself. When you are caught in this spiral after injury, you become all too aware of the anguish it causes; but the most insidious cause of muscle spasm in both horses and humans is *habit* – ways of moving and holding the body which are intensified by athletic endeavour, but whose roots lie in normal everyday movement. Until they produce pain, they usually go unnoticed.

The patterns of tension found in horses and humans are remarkably similar, and since the major muscle groups correlate with each other, equine practitioners must first learn human anatomy and massage. Think again of the startle reflex, which leaves people permanently holding their shoulders up around their ears, and horses permanently shortening their top lines, dropping their backs and tensing all the way to their tails. In people, the muscles around the base of the skull, and around the collar bones and shoulder blades are almost bound to have areas of spasm. The middle of the back between the shoulder blades is a place where these can often lead to pain.

In the horse, tension around the shoulder blade has the knock-on effect of restricting the movement of the foreleg. In both species the buttock muscles and the hamstring muscles can become extremely tight. (These latter run down the back of the thigh in humans, and each side of the tail in horses.) This then puts more stress on the lumbar spine and can lead to back pain, including (in horses) the notorious 'cold back'. The affected horse can lose the side-to-side swing of the croup in each step, and his hind leg movement becomes restricted. This can make him look as if he is trying to avoid the consequences of wearing a nappy or diaper with something very nasty inside it!

Normal muscle tissue (in horses as well as humans) feels soft and pliable, and even the well-developed muscles of a body builder should be soft when relaxed. A spasm is a hard lump of tissue, ranging in size from a pea to a golf ball. In the case of the hamstring muscles or the long back muscles running each side of the spine, a spasm could feel like a long roll of hard rubber. The major muscle groups in the horse's body – including the long back muscles, buttocks and hamstrings, as well as the muscles of the neck and shoulder – should be *soft* to the touch. This means that many

'The horse who has thrilled us by developing hard muscles as he fittens up is in fact seizing up before our very eyes, with his muscles going into spasm.'

of us have misunderstood the basics of muscle functioning, for the horse who has thrilled us by developing hard muscles as he fittens up is in fact *seizing up* before our very eyes, with his muscles going into spasm.

Even as an untrained palpator, you can probably detect a hardness in the horse's muscles which you may never have recognised as abnormal. (In fact, it is probably *not* abnormal, given the stresses placed on the athletic horse.) But it is important for you to appreciate that it creates a restriction in movement and a loss of elasticity which has important ramifications. The person who is seizing up will complain of her aches and pains; the horse who is in a similar state will not speak of his discomfort, but a trained observer will spot its effects on function (whether as a rider, an observer, or a bodyworker) long before the knock-on effects finally lead to lameness.

....

Muscle spasm usually begins at the point where the muscle fibres form the tendon which then inserts the muscle into bone, for this part of the muscle is least elastic and has the lowest blood supply. As a muscle group loses its elasticity, extra stress is passed onto a neighbouring group, which tightens as a result, and as this goes into spasm the stress is eventually passed on to the next group. Ninety per cent of the elasticity in the body lies in the muscles, but this is now being significantly reduced. Only *10 per cent* of the elasticity lies in the tendons, which lie at the end of the line. So, as most of us learned in Pony Club, it is when muscles fatigue and lose their flexibility and perfect timing that the tendons become vulnerable to damage.

The capacity for damage in athletic endeavour is recognised by athletes in virtually every discipline, who are accompanied by a team of physiotherapists and massage therapists who stop their bodies from seizing up. Jack Meagher, one of the founders of sports massage in people, popularised equine massage in America through his work on the horses in their international teams. Although this began in the 1976 Olympics in Montreal, it has taken a long time for its benefits to become more widely recognised. In the 1996 Atlanta Olympics, physiotherapists using massage and other techniques with both horses and riders, were present with a number of the international teams.

In a healthy muscle, the feeling of even a very firm massage would be extremely pleasant; but the presence of a spasm will give both you or your horse a disconcerting sensation which could lie anywhere between outright pain and the feeling you would get if you were being tickled. Thus any massage treatment must begin gently, with a reassuring touch, so that the patient is responding to that touch and not either to pain or (more insidiously) to the *fear of pain*. It is usual to begin and end a massage with long sweeping strokes which cover the whole body and give a feeling of wholeness. When it comes to the nitty-gritty of undoing spasm, any massage practitioner should work only within the limits of her client's pain tolerance (it is not good for business to do otherwise!). If she is working with *you*, she can at least remind you to keep breathing deeply when it begins to hurt. But it is not so easy to convince horses that it 'hurts good'.

> 'Horses soon realise when someone is out to help them (even if this involves discomfort) and often they become actively involved in their treatment.'

Some practitioners work with a horse untied, so that the animal can move away if it wishes, and can and make his responses clear. The negative reactions are a sign to back off, to work less deeply, or to go to a less sensitive place. But horses soon realise when someone is out to help them (even if this involves discomfort) and often they become actively involved in their treatment. Positive responses include activity of the parasympathetic nervous system – licking and chewing, yawning and sighing. Some point with their nose to the spot which they think the masseuse *ought* to be treating, and they move around to present her with the place they want worked on next. Or they may press back against the practitioner who is not using enough pressure for their liking. I once watched my horse, whose face was contorted with pleasure, virtually *sit* on a (rather small) practitioner who was working around the point of her buttock! Horses, like people, can get 'zoned out' by a good massage, and can begin to look as if they have seen Nirvana. Their gratitude is often as obvious as the increase in the freedom of their movement.

The ability of a massage practitioner to locate spasm depends hugely on her experience and training. Those who have not learned sports massage tend to use a lighter touch, which, although it does not address deep-seated tensions, benefits the circulation and can be extremely soothing. This is usually a stroking, known as effleurage, which follows the line of the muscle fibres, encouraging them to return to their true resting length. Other options are kneading, wringing, and percussion, which – although you need tuition to learn to do them safely – are well described by these words.

Sports massage practitioners use 'cross-fibre friction' to release muscles in spasm, for this rubbing *across* the fibres helps them to 'unglue'. On the horse this takes 10–15lb (4.5-6.75kg) of pressure to be effective (try pressing this hard on your bathroom scales) so practitioners often resort to using their knuckles, or their elbows (even on humans!). If you have a basic understanding of massage and want to become more specific as you work with spasm, Jack Meagher's book, *Beating Muscle Injuries for Horses,* is an invaluable guide which explains the process and the effects of spasm very well, showing you the most vulnerable areas in the body of the athletic horse. It is not, however, for the beginner, who needs a more general understanding of the muscular system before embarking on such specialised treatment.

Myotherapy, another variation on the theme, focuses solely on the painful areas within a muscle, which myotherapists call 'trigger points'. A gentle three-second pressure of the three middle fingers is used to diagnose if an area is painful and in spasm. If the horse's response confirms that it is, myotherapists use a further seven seconds of pressure which is then released slowly. If the initial pressure reveals a particularly tender spot, the practitioner reduces its sensitivity by starting about 10 inches/25cm away from it, and spiralling in towards it, using pressure at ½-inch/12mm intervals. A trained myotherapist will know where to expect trigger points, and will find them more easily than you will, but you can work systematically over your horse's neck, chest, back and quarters, pressing in about every 2 inches/50mm along lines about 2 inches/50mm apart. No other form of hand movement or pressure is used in myotherapy, although stretches done with the horse every day after work are needed to maintain the improvement and stop the shortening of muscle which spasm indicates.

If a muscle spasm has developed in response to repetitive activity and/or poor use of the body, it will tend to reform after treatment. The body will work optimally for about four days after a massage, and then the old patterns will begin to reinstate themselves – which is why stretching is good preventative medicine. But once you have experienced what freedom of movement really means, you (and your horse) are likely to want it again; so many people and horses receive treatment every few weeks. When performed well, massage does more than just treat the symptoms: for some people it has been the only technique to reach the root of an old injury, breaking down the muscular protection which surrounded it and prevented full healing. Deep massage has been some of the most effective (if painful) bodywork that I have ever received, and realising how 'gummed up' my body can become has motivated me to keep stretching and to take better care of myself – and of my horse.

Whilst grooming is indeed a very general massage, it is usually done without the sensitivity which could make it a much more useful tool. Any massage therapist who treats your horse will probably be happy to show you some strokes and stretches which you can do in between treatments, and I would advise every horse owner to spend *less* time simply brushing her horse and *more* time learning to 'read' his body through touch. A number of basic texts and video tapes give a good introduction to massage (there are details in the bibliography), and enough information to enable you to have a go on your horse. Safety, though, is an issue not only for *you*, but also for your horse, as incorrect techniques can actually damage muscles. To become really skilled at equine massage takes training and

'The body will work optimally for about four days after a massage, and then the old patterns will begin to reinstate themselves.'

practice, and only very recently has specialised training become available in the UK. In America there are a number of short training courses.

Take care when choosing a massage therapist, as many people who proffer their skills in the marketplace are not as skilled as they should be. Between one and four treatments should be enough to improve a horse's performance and/or comfort – and if you are not seeing this difference, you may want to think again about how you spend your money. It is also important to realise that muscle spasm can be part of a defence mechanism which protects your horse from the effects of bad riding. So if you are going to take this defence away, you owe it to him to hone your riding skills, so that you control your centre of gravity and minimise the damage you inflict.

....

Some soft tissue workers utilise the premise that muscles can only do what they are told to do by the brain, and they opt for approaches which primarily consider the functioning of the neurological system. Disruptions in the neurological communication to a muscle have consequences which massage itself cannot address, and a muscle which receives the signal to tighten has no option but to obey that command. Injury creates pain, and pain creates spasm (which in turn creates more pain), so in many cases the brain responds to this spiral by creating a block somewhere along the neurological pathways between the brain and the injury. This ensures that the message of pain *does not reach the brain.*

'As a result of impaired communication between the brain and the muscles, some horses have difficulty sensing their bodies.'

With this loss of sensitivity the injured area cannot cry for help, and there is a concurrent loss of the ability to heal, for blood and nutrients which should reach the site of the injury are never sent there. The horse (or human) concerned now has a strategy for coping, and a protective pattern which becomes imprinted in the nervous system – a habit which is followed until the body is shown another, more efficient way to move. Some bodyworkers believe that horses are *as* able – and perhaps even *more* able – to block out pain than we are. As a result of this impaired communication between the brain and the muscles, some horses (like some humans) have difficulty sensing their bodies.

Michel Kaplan, who works on both horses and people, uses a system which he calls 'kinesiological manipulation', to find and release the block which lies between the pain and the brain. He initially trained as a massage therapist, after he finally discovered that massage gave him relief from the terrible pain which he suffered following a severe back injury. He then studied kinesiology (the science of motion, not to be confused with Applied Kinesiology, the diagnostic technique discussed earlier), and delved into many other bodywork techniques before synthesising his system. His training has made him an extremely astute observer of the body and of movement, and he always watches a horse standing and in walk before he uses a hands-on exploration to give him yet more information.

So, when Michel finds that a spasm does not release as a result of his touch, he presumes that the horse is unable to send the neurological signal which will relax that muscle. The flexor, extensor, adductor and abductor muscles of the limbs are each part of a *tract* of muscles, which work together to create movement. So, if a horse drags a hind leg and wears the toe of the hind shoe, Michel knows that the chain of the flexor muscles is not working well, and he can follow that chain all the way from the hind limb, over the croup and back, and up the neck to the ear and above the eye. He follows that tract of muscle until he finds a muscle which *does* respond to his touch. Then he knows that the neurological block lies further back, between those two muscles. But if the muscle he is working on *still* does not release, he follows the muscle tract on up towards the brain, searching for the place where the nervous system is blocking sensation.

With a hind leg problem, there is usually a block in the back – so if your horse is completely non-responsive when you touch his back he may have *no* pain, or have *so much pain* that he is continually blocking it. There may also be a block in the neck, and if so, both will need to be released before the symptoms permanently disappear. A block in the neck will also accompany a foreleg problem or a more overall difficulty. At each stage in his treatment, Michel can check the effectiveness of his work by testing the responses he gets at various points along the different muscle tracts. So he can track down the root cause of problems with an accuracy which defies many bodyworkers. He also uses some chiropractic manipulations, and draws upon the many disciplines he has studied whenever the need arises.

Much of the inspiration for Michel's system came from studying the work of Moshe Feldenkrais, the Israeli physicist who developed the Feldenkrais Method. This focuses on refining movement by opening up new communication channels between the brain and the body. Feldenkrais discovered that old habit patterns will easily drop away when the body is given a better choice, and he fed this choice into the system by using non-habitual movements. So, as you may have realised, there are similarities between the map which guides Michel, and that used by Linda Tellington-Jones, who actually trained with Moshe before she developed her TTEAM approach. But whilst Michel does indeed teach small groups of students, becoming proficient in such a precise system obviously necessitates astute observation, a specialised knowledge of the functions of the body, and supervised clinical practice. One of the strengths of Linda's

'If your horse is completely non-responsive when you touch his back he may have no pain, or have so much pain that he is continually blocking it.'

much simpler approach is its availability to everyone, both through her books and video tapes, and via the short and longer courses through which you can learn the Tellington TTouch.

Her ways of reprogramming the nervous system are much less specific, centring around non-habitual movements (i.e. movements that the horse would not do for himself), and the 'TTouch' – small circles, made on the horse's skin with the fingertips or the whole of the hand. She takes care to differentiate those circles from massage strokes, which move the practitioner's hands *over* the horse's skin. In Linda's circles, the fingertips maintain contact with the same piece of skin, moving it over the underlying muscle.

The circles begin at six o'clock, and the fingertips perform one and a quarter rotations, moving (usually) clockwise to finish the circle at nine o'clock. Linda grades the pressure used from a one, which you could comfortably tolerate on your eyelid, to a ten. So on this scale a three would be three times the pressure used on your eye, and a nine would be three times the pressure of a three. Linda positions each new circle in a different place, whilst keeping the other hand in contact with the horse's body just to give him a sense of continuity. Linda does not directly address the issue of muscle spasm; her premise is that the TTouch 'awakens cellular memory', releasing the body from its habit pattern, and reminding it of a more integrated way to be. The circles are an extremely pleasant sensation (workshop participants learn to do them on each other before they begin to do them on horses), and they can change the hang of an arm, the look of the face, or the colour of the skin.

'Some extremely difficult horses have often spent their lives trapped between fear (most probably of the stick) and pain (which accompanies movement).'

Linda deals with some extremely difficult horses in her courses and public demonstrations – horses who have often spent their lives trapped between fear (most probably of the stick) and pain (which accompanies movement). Fractious horses are quietened by the circles, beginning to breathe more deeply and to relax. If Linda cannot get close enough to actually touch them she begins by using the 'wand', a 4-foot/1.2m dressage whip that has very little flexibility, and is used to stroke the horse until he accepts the touch of her hand. She also uses a heated pad, or a warm damp cloth to touch difficult horses.

As well as the circles, Linda uses many other forms of touch, and she also works the horses in hand, using obstacles created by placing poles on the ground. This forces the horse to slow down and *think* about where he is putting his feet. Negotiating some of the obstacles requires non-habitual movements – requiring the legs on one side of the body, for instance, to be lifted higher than those on the other. She draws on such an array of techniques that she is never left feeling stumped, even by the most (apparently) uncooperative animals.

She too believes that many horses do not perceive their bodies clearly, and that this leads to all manner of evasions. For no self-respecting horse will load happily into a trailer when he cannot tell how wide he is and whether he will fit in. The horse who cannot feel his feet is highly likely to stumble over trotting poles, and really cannot be blamed for his 'carelessness'. So stroking the horse with the wand, or tapping his feet with it, gives him information about where his body ends, filling out his 'body image' and making him a far more confident, competent horse. Linda also teaches horses to control their fear. This means that one of her first aims must be to lower the horse's head, for when his head is raised his adrenal glands are stimulated to produce the hormones which fuel 'fight or flight'. The lowered head allows full blood flow to the brain, and only then can the horse begin to think.

Linda particularly advocates 'ear work', and the tradition of rubbing the ears of the stressed horse who has broken out into a sweat has a sound basis. The ears contain many acupuncture points, and in particular there is a point on *the inside of the ear near its tip* which can bring the body out of shock, or stop the shock reaction from occurring. So if you ever have some horrible mishap – or you suspect that your horse has colic – rub his ears until your vet arrives. The area of the muzzle, lips, and gums is also one she concentrates on particularly, for the upper lip (remember the expression 'stiff upper lip') has a specific connection to the limbic system, which is the seat of the emotions. Horses who are 'uptight' about their work often hold tension in the muzzle as you ride them, and even extremely good riding may not change this. Massaging the muzzle until it softens can make the emotional horse much more tractable and can create a lasting change in behaviour, as can rubbing your hand (which you may have to wet) backwards and forwards across the gums above the front teeth.

One of the other non-habitual movements which Linda uses is circling of the feet and lower limbs. Holding the foot up as if you were going to pick it out, the hoof capsule can be circled around the pastern bones. Or by allowing the whole leg to move, the hoof can be made to trace horizontal circles in both directions. Another of Linda's favourites is 'tail work'. She holds the dock with both hands so that the tail is lifted into the shape of a question mark, and maintaining this shape, she rotates the tail in circles. This is another non-habitual movement, which the horse would not do for himself, and it offers his system an alternative to its habitual holding pattern. Horses who clamp their tail hold an enormous amount of tension in their back and hindquarters, and in all animals, clamping of the tail and tension in the buttocks are associated with fear. This technique may also stop swishing or wringing of the tail. To stretch the whole of the horse's spine, she stands behind the horse, holding onto the bones in the tail, and aligning it with his spine. Then she pulls on it

'No self-respecting horse will load happily into a trailer when he cannot tell how wide he is and whether he will fit in.'

'In all animals, clamping of the tail and tension in the buttocks are associated with fear.'

for six seconds, releasing that pull *slowly*. This is a stretch which many horses really appreciate, pulling back against you, and breathing deeply as you let go.

....

As her work was developing, Linda began to realise that she was unknowingly using techniques which others recognised as acupressure or shiatsu, and this encouraged her to study those systems, and to blend their wisdom with her own. But whilst there are tremendous similarities between techniques used in TTEAM, and those of Oriental bodywork, their philosophies, and their maps of body functioning differ greatly. For the Eastern traditions seek to maintain a continuous and balanced flow of Qi, the essential life force which flows through the meridians of the body. A shiatsu massage does not specifically address the muscular system or the nervous system; instead it works on a more subtle plane, seeking to balance out any energetic disturbances before they eventually manifest in the body as disease.

The skilled practitioner can detect areas of too much energy (which may feel tight, hard, hot, pulsating, or even vibrating) of too little energy (which may be cool, cold and hollow looking). Then they can balance them out through a touch which can be either tonifying or sedating. Energy is moved through pressure – of a palm, the fingertips, the thumb, the side of the hand or the elbow – always with the other hand making a quiet still contact with the horse, and completing the circle of energy between horse and human. Energy is also moved by stretching and by rotations of joints, or by 'jiggling' the neck or the limbs, creating rippling waves that move through the muscles and show how fluid they are.

Percussion (a technique which is also used in Swedish massage) is another way to move energy, as is a kneading action done across the muscles. Movement of energy will release tightened muscles, and can even cause vertebrae to become realigned. But whilst this may require a very skilful touch, Marion Kaselle and Pamela Hannay insist, in their beautiful book *Touching Horses,* that even a novice can make a difference to her horse by applying the shiatsu techniques they describe, and I have proved this to be true. Their explanations are very clear (although they may, at times, be slightly lax about safety), and the book is an inspiring tribute to bodywork.

A shiatsu treatment rarely addresses specific acupuncture points, considering instead the energy flow within the meridians. But whenever you use thumb or elbow pressure on a specific point, you are effectively doing acupressure, even if your choice of points is based on guesswork! Acupressure and myotherapy suddenly look very similar – even though they are based on such different maps of the body — and the various schools of bodywork involve a fair amount of 'reinventing the wheel'. The book *Equine Acupressure, a Treatment Workbook,* by Nancy A. Zidonis and Marie K. Soderberg, gives some guidelines for simple acupressure treatments, along with some specific points for colic, laminitis, and various forms of lameness. A veterinary acupuncturist, however, would be much more specific in his treatment. Shiatsu and acupressure can interfere with other energetically based treatments, so you should always tell your vet if you are using them. He may be willing to show you some more precise techniques which will back up his work with needles.

....

Amongst my personal friends are a large number of bodyworkers from many different disciplines, some of whom work with people, and some with horses. A few of them faithfully practise the technique they were taught in the way they were taught it, whilst others are more eclectic, and more intent on learning through discovery. Their skill in bodywork evolves over time in much the same way that a good rider's skill evolves — by going on a journey through which they test and refine their perceptions, learn from the great masters, increase their subtlety, and gradually change their ideas about what works best. As bodyworkers learn to evoke 'the wisdom of the body' they discover through their practice that 'less is more'. Often, they tread a fine line between the dictates of logic and of 'feel'; and ultimately, the good ones learn to 'let their hands do the talking'.

Watching these friends develop over years, I have seen a number of them move from the more invasive techniques to *less* invasive — and often lesser known — ones (and apart from the massage practitioners who gradually learn how to work more deeply, I have never seen anyone graduate from a *less* invasive approach to a *more* invasive one). Cranial osteopathy, zero balancing, orthobionomy, body harmony, and deep lymphatic drainage, for instance, must be some of the least invasive and yet most potent of all the bodywork approaches. So little appears to happen during a treatment that the observer can easily be left wondering whether she has just witnessed 'the laying on of hands' — and perhaps some healers unknowingly utilise their principles.

For an intriguing perspective on how a treatment might feel to your horse take a turn on the bodyworker's table. For being the client on the receiving end of these treatments can be a very strange sensation — never unpleasant or painful, just disconcerting. For whilst lying on the practitioner's table, I have suddenly become aware that some part of my body was moving itself, completely without 'my' involvement. When the process of change proceeds unhindered it is surprisingly fast, effective, and pain free; although bodyworkers who love to work with horses insist that without the shackles of logic and reason (and without the hidden benefits of sickness which can sometimes prevent us from recovering), horses move through the process of change much more gracefully and easily than we do.

Good riding can also become bodywork. This requires great finesse – but whilst skilful work can change a horse enormously, it can never be all that is needed. It is paradoxical that riding can simultaneously improve the alignment, the centredness and the balance of both partners; but alongside this, the 'micro-trauma' of repetitive activity will inevitably take its toll on the body. So to mitigate this you may choose to have bodywork yourself, to call in an equine bodyworker, or to learn some simple techniques and to work on your horse yourself. If you do, bear in mind that skill in this field is partly a matter of *what you do*, but even more a matter of *the way in which you do it*. When I trained in human massage, we all learned on each other by exchanging massages, and it became abundantly clear that the wholesome, reassuring touch of a good professional cannot be taken for granted. For (as in riding) tension in the bodyworker is communicated to her client in ways which can make her touch not just unpleasant, but extremely nerve-racking.

In converse, the riding pupils who stand out to me over the years as being the most sensitive and aware of their bodies, and the most quick and able to learn, have all been bodyworkers. It is as if they had already learned what they needed to know, and they just needed guidance as they applied their skills in a different context. In both riding and bodywork, full deep breathing is a must, tension in the arm and hand has terrible consequences, and stance, the use of weight, and the overall organisation of the body are paramount. Without this, a practitioner will inevitably communicate her own out-of-synchness to her human or equine client.

Thus the approach to yourself and to learning which will make you a good rider will also make you a good bodyworker; being hurried, being distracted, or hopefully trying a bit-of-this and a bit-of-that will not. Both skills are primarily about paying attention to what you are feeling, and noticing how it changes. It takes experience – and tuition – to know what those feelings and changes mean, and to discover how best to respond. However, the 'master skills' lie in holding your attention 'in the moment', and in organising movement from your centre. It is these which open the door to profound change.

CHAPTER EIGHT

....

High- and Low-Tech Approaches
to Injury

....

WHETHER YOU OWN a high-performance horse or a back-yard chum, the prospect of him becoming injured probably fills you with dread. Yet few of us are as clued-up as we should be about the best immediate action, and many injuries fall in that in-between area which leaves us 'umming and aarhing' about whether to call the vet. Yet his fee is the price of our peace of mind, and home-spun first-aid can leave so much to be desired that when the vet finally *is* called in, he cannot pursue what would have been the ideal course of action.

Even more likely to be mishandled are those injuries which do not leave scars. Often they receive no specific attention at the time, and the traditional cure of rest may well allow only partial healing. This results in a horse who contrives to minimise pain, moving in a way which spares the damaged muscle groups through over-working healthy ones. Thus he develops unusually large asymmetries (see Figs 4.11-4.13, pages 91-92). Many of us unknowingly purchase a horse whose performance is marred by muscle damage; and as prospective purchasers we may well not think to look for these – just as the previous owners did not think to prevent them.

Human patients (whether or not they are athletes) are never kept on the human equivalent of box rest, and left to wait while their injuries heal. If you are hospitalised and confined to bed, the resident physiotherapist will do passive stretches with you, and will get you pulling weights with the parts of your body that you *can* move. For unused muscle soon loses its tone, becoming flaccid and weak. Even bone which is not subjected to the stresses of daily living will soon lose its density. To emerge from bed looking and feeling like a soggy, weak blob is not conducive to recovery, so even a recumbent body is put to work.

The ultimate in treatment for injured athletes is often provided by the athletic trainer (a familiar figure in television sport) who rushes onto the scene as soon as the injury takes place. She concerns herself with its immediate aftermath, with its ongoing treatment, and with the prevention of a recurrence. Her work is similar to that of the equine physiotherapist (who cannot rush onto the scene because she works only on veterinary referral). The tools of their trade are their hands and various machines – in the form of ultrasound, magnetic fields, electrical stimulation, and light from low-level lasers. These all facilitate healing, primarily by increasing the blood supply. They are combined with exercises and the more conventional treatments using massage, lotions, and hot and cold applications and so on.

Over the last twenty or so years, swimming horses and working them on treadmills (often with an uphill slope, designed to keep weight off previously injured forelimbs) have become accepted practices for injured horses coming back into work. But since physiotherapy itself is not included in the veterinary curriculum, vets (like the public) knew little about it. So it has taken somewhat longer for the machines which form the physiotherapist's arsenal to become more widely used in the care of equine injuries. Over recent years they have proved their worth in the treatment of wounds and damaged tendons, and in mitigating the long-term effects of muscle damage.

In both Britain and America, a few physiotherapists who originally trained to work with people have turned their hand to horses and become pioneers in the field. Their hard work has opened it up for others to follow. In the UK, the Association for Chartered Physiotherapists in Animal Practice (ACPAC) was founded in 1985, and now has 54 practising members. The National Association of Animal Therapists (NAAT) was founded in 1990, for practitioners who are not chartered physiotherapists, and who (unlike most of them) work full time in animal practice. Their American equivalent, the National Equine Therapists Association (NETA) was founded in 1983 to cater for physiotherapists and others who have entered the field via a training in sports medicine. It has, however, been inactive for several years, although there are hopes to revitalise it soon.

There is no officially recognised training in animal physiotherapy in either country, and British physiotherapists have to spend an initial two years in human practice, before undergoing a two-year apprenticeship. In this they see practice with both vets and equine physiotherapists. Many of the members of NAAT began from a degree in animal science, obtaining qualifications in veterinary nursing before serving their apprenticeship.

Equine physiotherapists adhere very strictly to a code of ethics which does not allow them to see a case without being referred by a vet. (In fact, the new liaison between vets and physiotherapists was prompted by concerns from both parties about unqualified, inexperienced people buying the machines and using them incorrectly.) The law prohibits physiotherapists from diagnosing any presenting problem, so they have to tread a very fine line with respect to it, and stay in touch with the vet throughout treatment. Bodyworkers most often deal with chronic problems, and are called in when owners finally recognise that something is not quite right with their horse. Physiotherapists are most often called in to treat acute injuries – although they can also use their equipment to reduce chronic pain and muscle spasm, and to build up damaged muscles which have atrophied over time.

....

Animal physiotherapists and veterinary surgeons both provide *second* aid – *first* aid is the job of whoever first arrives at the scene of an injury. The machines used in physiotherapy stimulate the body's healing mechanisms in much the same way as good first-aid; however, they have greater impact. (Few people are aware, for instance, that early treatment with magnetic fields can stop a wound from swelling, and that laser treatment can speed its healing dramatically.) But since immediate action pays immense dividends, first-aid must be our beginning point. The age-old remedies are the application of either heat or cold – but many people are confused about when each one works best. I shall never forget the day, many years ago, when a horse came back from hunting with an obvious bowed tendon, and I stood with my boss, watching the horse's leg blow up before our very eyes as we argued about which would be the better procedure. With human injuries the recipe is RICE – Rest, Ice, Compression, and Elevation. It is not feasible to elevate a horse's limb, but in cases of acute injury the rest of the recipe still applies.

Injury causes chaos within the tissues. British physiotherapist Mary Bromiley likens it to someone dropping a bomb on a city, disrupting its communication system, and making it very difficult to get both help in and the casualties out. The body immediately sends more blood to the site, which brings with it the healing agents needed, including cells which digest and clear the debris. Blood flows from the damaged capillaries into the tissues, and if the wound is open much of that blood may be lost. Arterial bleeding represents a huge danger, and if bright red blood is being lost in spurts, you know that your horse could conceivably bleed to death. He obviously requires immediate veterinary help. But in general, bleeding helps to cleanse a wound, and there is no hurry to stop it unless the flow is heavy. In this case, pressure (or compression) is particularly important, and if you do not have access to a sterile dressing, use anything which comes to hand. When blood oozes through the pad or bandage which covers the wound, add more layers: this stops you from disturbing the process of clotting as you remove the soiled dressings and begin again. When a wound is not bleeding so profusely, it should be washed with

'The machines used in physiotherapy stimulate the body's healing mechanisms in much the same way as good first-aid.'

copious amounts of water. The solution to pollution is dilution, and pressure helps to remove both bacteria and foreign bodies, which are forced out of the tissues along with the rebounding liquid. A plastic spray bottle, adjusted to produce a stream rather than a spray of water, works well. If it looks likely that a wound will need stitching, water should be used sparingly, if at all, as it can shrink the skin so much that its edges cannot be joined together. In fact, many vets would rather you did not touch a wound which will need their attention. If the wound involves a joint, ligament, tendon sheath, or organ you *definitely* should not touch it, nor should you move the horse. If he is losing not only blood but also the yellow synovial fluid which fills joint capsules and lubricates tendons, be extremely careful.

'Although our horses usually survive, trained human first-aiders would be appalled at our antics.'

Many people's attempts to 'cleanse' a wound are extremely dubious, for rarely do we use a truly sterile pad and boiled water. Dabbing at a wound with a previously opened roll of cotton wool is asking for trouble (especially if you use each piece more than once), and although our horses usually survive, trained human first-aiders would be appalled at our antics. They would undoubtedly counsel us to clean up our act or leave the job to a professional.

We have traditionally been taught to wash a wound using salt solution – a teaspoon of salt added to a pint of previously boiled water forms a simple antiseptic, which many vets swear by, despite its simplicity. Other options are various antibacterial and antiseptic washes, and the herbal alternative of distilled witch hazel, or the homoeopathic wash made by adding a few drops of hypericum tincture to water. The herbal and homoeopathic first-aid treatments for wounds are extremely effective, and worth knowing about. Your best source of information, of course, will be a homoeopathic vet, and most of these are very happy to give talks to riding clubs and interested groups.

As the bleeding slows, a blood clot begins to form, bridging the gap between the damaged fibres (which will not regrow for about a week). As long as the wound is clean, pressure – using a fibrous substance like gamgee or sheet cotton – will help this process along. Continued washing, however, would disrupt it, as would poulticing, which slows wound healing by making the edges of the wound waterlogged -- as evidenced by a whitening of the tissues. The advantages of poulticing as a means of drawing out infection or foreign bodies must be balanced against this disadvantage. This makes poultices most appropriate for puncture wounds.

A wound should never be poulticed for more than 48 hours without seeking veterinary advice, and a poultice should be renewed three times a day. It must be cool enough that you can bear its heat on the back of your hand, but not so cool that it will be ineffective. A layer of plastic over the poultice stops it from interacting with the air around it and ensures that the salts in the poultice attract fluids only from the wound. A layer of tin foil over the poultice keeps it warmer for longer, thus making it more effective – and an old pair of tights can be very helpful in keeping it and other dressings in place over areas of the body which are difficult to bandage.

As a wound stops bleeding, we then face the question of what (if anything) to leave on it, and the huge number of sprays, creams and powders that are available on the market (and which include both herbal and homoeopathic applications) gives us tremendous choice. In horses, the skin tends to dry out more quickly than it does with other animals, making creams a more appropriate choice than powders or sprays. Powders will help to dry up a moist wound, but often they clog up the wound site. To leave the wound covered and bandaged maintains *compression*, and using a Gelonet dressing stops the bandage from sticking. However, the latest generation of dressings and self-adhesive bandages to come on the market (some of which use herbal preparations) do not stick and allow a wound to breathe. If a wound is to be left uncovered in summer, it should be dressed with a product that will repel flies; and a wound which has stopped bleeding is best exposed to air. A good rule of thumb is that if you think a wound is bad enough to be covered, then it is also bad enough to need veterinary attention.

Once the clot has formed – or if instead the area is bruised, and/or grazed – blood and plasma (the clear fluid found within the tissues themselves) will clog the whole area. The damaged venous return cannot take away all of this fluid, and the inevitable result is swelling. Tearing of the fibres of muscles (known as a strain) or of tendons or ligaments (known as a sprain) also leads to swelling. Engorgement with fluid increases the temperature of the area, creating the heat we expect to feel. If fluid remains in the tissues for any length of time it becomes more likely that there will be greater long-term damage, for layers of tissues can adhere to each other creating scar tissue. These stop the layers from moving easily over each other; and when exercise is finally resumed, there is an increased likelihood that the adhesions will tear. This starts the inflammatory process all over again, creating a vicious circle. So it is important to take immediate action which limits the degree of swelling, and later (under veterinary advice) to use very controlled, gentle exercise when possible. This breaks adhesions as they form.

In effect, nature is over-enthusiastic in her response to injury, but by initially slowing this down we can reduce the effects of the chaos. As healing progresses, the most obvious sign of this is the development of 'proud flesh', which occurs most commonly in wounds of the extremities, especially if they are near a joint. Horses in particular are prone to proud

'Nature is over-enthusiastic in her response to injury, but by initially slowing this down we can reduce the effects of the chaos.'

flesh, some (especially older horses and those whose skin and hair are in poor condition) being more susceptible than others. In people, dead cells continually slough away from the skin, but proud flesh is a proliferation of cells which have not sloughed off. They have no nerve supply and therefore no feeling. The skin cannot grow over them, and even if a vet slices the growth off, it is likely to reform. One physiotherapist I know repeatedly scrubs the wound site to remove the cells as they form, and various preparations can be used to discourage their growth.

....

Cold applications reduce both swelling and heat, constricting the blood vessels so that the inflammatory reaction is lessened. Although heat is usually thought of as being more soothing, the application of cold also reduces pain, numbing the area since colder nerves cannot send or receive their messages so easily. This in turn helps to prevent muscle spasm, stopping the pain/spasm/pain cycle from taking hold. Cells in the injured area cannot get enough oxygen, so even cells which have *not* been damaged can suffer as a result of the injury, and lowering their temperature slows their metabolic rate. This helps them to survive and thus it lessens the final death toll. Cold applications should be used within the first hour of an injury: so if you are on an outing when you have a mishap, and you trail the horse home rather than treating him in situ, you may well do him no favours.

The traditional method of cold hosing cools the skin surface, as does standing the horse in a stream, or in its high-tech equivalents − the whirlpool tub, and the 'jacuzzi wellie'. The massaging effect of moving water helps to limit or disperse swelling; but to also cool the deeper structures, *ice* is needed. When the limb is in a tub, wellie or bucket, ice can be used to lower the temperature of the water which surrounds it, but even more cooling can be obtained by applying ice to the covered limb. A plastic bag filled with crushed ice cubes, or a packet of frozen peas, can be placed over a cloth or bandage and secured in place with another bandage. Alternatively, a frozen styrofoam cup of water can be used to massage the area. This has an advantage over hand–held ice cubes, because you can peel back its edges as the ice melts, protecting your hands as you massage the horse.

To lower the temperature of the deeper structures, an ice–cup massage should be used for at least five minutes over each $5cm^2/0.77in^2$. Maximum cooling is achieved after about eight to ten minutes, and ice should never be used for more than fifteen minutes − for freezing the tissues involved would have terrible consequences. (In fact, grey and chestnut horses are particularly prone to ice burns, and so need extra care.

Applying a light layer of baby oil to the skin helps to protect it.) Bandaging with crushed ice or frozen peas gives you about fifteen minutes off from your role as full-time carer, and adds *compression*. So do Bonner bandages, which, when dampened and placed in the deep freeze, cool quickly, and remain cold in a freezer bag for many hours. (This makes them a useful travelling companion.) A less immediate, home-made alternative is frozen gamgee, sheet cotton or cotton wool, which can be dampened and moulded onto the limb before being frozen in its shape, and then bandaged on over a towel. Compression limits the space within the tissues into which blood can flow, and thus it reinforces the effects of ice. Studies have shown ice to provide much more effective cooling than frozen gels, and cold water bandages become hot-water bandages so quickly that they are next to useless.

Initially cold constricts the blood vessels. But if its use is continued they dilate, or expand again, bringing in more blood as the body attempts to raise the tissue temperature. At the same time, however, this response opens connections between the arteries and veins which by-pass the smaller capillaries, keeping blood away from the damaged areas so that they still remain cool. The effects of applying cold last from sixty to ninety minutes – longer than the effects of applying heat, which will not persist beyond thirty to forty-five minutes. This is because the constriction of blood vessels created by lowering their temperature prevents an area from warming up again. Heat, however, is carried away relatively quickly when the blood vessels have already been dilated.

Using cold applications is an exercise in damage limitation during the acute stages of injury. But internal bleeding will stop from one to three days after an injury has occurred, and once the swelling has not increased over a twenty-four hour period, it is time to use heat, or the alternate application of hot and cold. Heat dilates the capillaries, and the increased blood flow – which would have *increased* the swelling in the early stages – can now assist in removing all the accumulated waste products. (It is hoped that there are less of these than would have been the case if cold had not been applied initially.) Heat is also soothing: warmer nerves have an enhanced ability to send and receive messages – including the messages of pain; but when heat is applied the brain is bombarded with so much sensory input that its perception of pain is reduced.

Hot applications should last for ten to fifteen minutes, and should be repeated three times a day. Bathing with warm water is a very labour-intensive way of applying heat, and a hot wet towel which has been wrung out within a dry towel will remain warm for about ten minutes if held or bandaged in place. The manufactured gel packs which can be heated in boiling water are much more efficient, retaining their heat for about twenty minutes. Hot-water bottles and electrically heated pads do not lend themselves to use on horses, and they are potentially dangerous, even when the horse is constantly supervised. The advantage of using hot and cold applications *alternately* is that by dilating and then constricting the blood vessels, blood is brought into the area and then forced out of it. Changing from hot to cold every three to five minutes has the optimum effect.

Like cold, heat reduces muscle spasm, this time by relaxing muscle fibres. The application of heat makes all of the tissues more extensible, and the end result of warming muscles, tendons, ligaments and the joint capsule itself, is an increase in the range of movement of the joint. (In contrast, cold reduces the tissue's extensibility, and thus it increases rather than reduces stiffness.) A rise of 5°C (9°F) is needed within the tissues to achieve these effects, but it is difficult to warm up the deeper structures of the body without overheating the skin. The dangers of this – which occurs after a 10°C (18°F) increase – are obvious, and scalding or burning a horse leaves you treating *two* injuries rather than one.

The most common high-tech ways of providing heat are whirlpools and heat lamps. Some whirlpools can be used with hot water, and a few are even big enough to treat the whole of the horse's body! Infra-red lamps and lamps which mimic sunlight are more commonly used, usually to warm the horse's back after work. But all of these heat sources (whether high- or low-tech) have only superficial effects, heating the skin and perhaps the underlying connective tissue. Warming the nerve endings within the skin can reduce sensations of pain; but in the large majority of cases, *heat from these sources will not penetrate deeply enough to reach damaged tissues.* This requires the use of more sophisticated machines.

....

We are now entering the realm of physiotherapy, and considering the use of potentially dangerous equipment which should only be handled by skilled personnel. But it may one day be useful for you to know what therapeutic options exist in the physiotherapist's arsenal, and when their use might be appropriate. In practice, the physiotherapist's approach overlaps with that of bodyworkers, and may include massage and manipulative treatment. But only physiotherapists are trained to use the machines, and the treatment given by a particular physiotherapist will be determined by the equipment to which she has access. Often there are several options, with overlaps between the various machines. So she may begin by using laser, then treat with ultrasound, and leave you to do ongoing treatment which uses pulsed electromagnetic fields.

Ultrasound is probably best known for its use in scanning – it is commonly used during the pregnancies of both people and horses, and is also used to assess the extent of the damage, or the success of treatment, after a horse has sustained a tendon injury. The pictures are produced as a result of sound waves echoing off the tissues (this is similar to the way in which bats use echoes to navigate) and since soft tissues as well as bones show up in the pictures, they provide a tremendous advance on X-rays.

Therapeutic (as opposed to diagnostic) ultrasound has two uses. At low settings it helps to organise the tissues, so that tendon fibres, for instance, are laid down parallel. At high settings it warms up the tissues, and different transducer heads result in different levels of penetration. So *without warming the skin* a deep head can cause a temperature rise of 5°C (9°F) or over to a depth of 2 inches/5cm. Herein lies its danger, for the operator could overheat those tissues *before* the horse responds to the pain involved, and without there being any external symptoms. The periosteum (the connective tissue which surrounds bone) is most vulnerable to damage, since bone reflects a large proportion of the waves, and the reflected wave can interfere with the incoming wave to produce a 'hot spot'. So the deep head must never be used on legs.

Ultrasound affects the deeper tissues in the same way that the external application of heat affects the more superficial tissues: pain is reduced, there is relaxation of muscle spasm, and with increased blood flow there is increased removal of the debris left from injury, along with enhanced tissue repair. This reduces swelling, filling and haematoma (which is a blood blister). The tissues become more extensible, especially those which are high in collagen, as this becomes more elastic at higher temperatures. The structures around joints are particularly collagen rich, so using ultrasound treatment on an injured joint before doing passive stretches can be extremely helpful in the attempt to regain joint mobility. Tendons can contract when there is injury to an associated muscle or joint, and again ultrasound treatment followed by stretching and controlled exercise can help to re-establish the correct length. Scar tissue can be softened and wound healing hastened, taking extra care when bone lies close to the skin within the treatment area.

Ultrasound waves cannot pass through even the tiniest thickness of air; so a gel is used between the head of the machine and the horse's skin. Clipping the area helps to reduce the number of air bubbles in the hair, which reduce the effectiveness of the treatment. When the lower part of a limb is treated, water can be used as the conducting medium, with the limb immersed in a bucket or 'wellie'. The skill in using ultrasound lies in selecting the most appropriate time in the healing process to begin its use, and the most appropriate intensity for the treatments, as well as for their frequency and duration. Different heads, different settings, and a beam which is either pulsed or continuous, all serve to modify its effects. If a large area is to be treated, it is divided up into small areas, and each one treated for a few minutes. The sound head is always kept moving, or it will generate a dangerous amount of heat within the tissues. Ultrasound should never be aimed at the eyes, and should not be used over the growth plates of the bone until growth is complete, or near developing splints or a healing fracture. It should not be used on a horse who is receiving steroids, and there are other contra-indications too. Skilled operators are all too aware that although ultrasound is a tremendously powerful healing modality, more is not better – it is dangerous.

....

The word 'laser' (which stands for Light Amplification by the Stimulated Emission of Radiation) conjures up images of sci-fi weapons and victims who are frazzled into nothing; but in contrast to the hot lasers which are used in surgery, the cold or low-temperature lasers used by physiotherapists do not burn, and do not even raise the temperature of the tissues. The light produced by lasers is all of the same frequency (unlike white light, which can be split into all the colours of the rainbow, each one representing a different frequency). It is also *coherent,* with all of its waves in phase, like a platoon of soldiers who march in step. This gives it much more power than ordinary light.

How lasers affect the tissues remains something of a mystery, but when energy is supplied by laser it influences cell functions, changing their metabolism. One theory (which sounds highly reminiscent of our discussion in Chapter 2) is that the energy field of individual cells should resonate with the energy field of the organ they are part of; but if the resonant frequencies of the cells are out of phase with the organ's frequency, then energy supplied by the laser can bring them back into phase again.

There are two major types of lasers. One, the helium neon (HeNe) laser, uses visible red light, which penetrates the body to a depth of just under half an inch (i.e. just over a centimetre). The Gallium arsenide (GaAs) laser uses invisible infra-red light, which penetrates for over 2 inches/5cm. One of the primary uses of lasers is in pain relief, and lasers are believed to stimulate the release of endorphins – which are the body's own painkillers. The mechanism of this has not been completely explained, however, and this lack of scientific reasoning makes some people sceptical. In practice it is extremely convincing to watch a fractious horse (whose behaviour is driven by pain) calm down and become quite soporific when his long back muscles are given laser treatment. The more ill at ease the horse, the more his behaviour is changed by treatment, and laser is often the physiotherapist's first port of call. It can allow her, for instance, to follow lasering with the kind of deep massage which would otherwise be too painful for the horse to tolerate, but which is an extremely effective way of releasing his back muscles from spasm.

This treatment requires a laser with a large 'cluster head'. The probe is held close to the skin, and each area is lasered for about thirty seconds – the exact time depending on the strength of the beam, how warm the horse is, how thick his coat is, and what colour he is. Some practitioners use a laser with a very small probe, and laser only specific acupuncture points, as well as 'trigger points'. These are points of increased muscle spasm which are painful to the touch and which, like acupuncture points, have lowered skin resistance to electricity. (It is a strange anomaly in UK law that physiotherapists can legally lase acupuncture points but cannot insert needles into them!) The probe is held right against the skin, and each point is treated for about thirty seconds. This has been shown to increase the skin resistance of the points, and to make them less tender.

Lasers, especially the helium-neon type, are also tremendously effective in healing wounds, and can *halve* the time needed for healing. They are particularly useful when a large open wound cannot be covered or stitched. Lasering the periphery of the wound helps the cells to synthesise the proteins needed to repair the damage, and more collagen is also produced. If treatment is begun within the first twenty-four hours, infection is controlled and proud flesh is much less likely to develop. This allows healing to occur at an accelerated rate, with minimal scarring and normal hair growth. Wounds which have already developed 'proud flesh' and which are not healing well can also benefit enormously from laser treatment. The laser head is held 1 or 2 millimetres from the skin, and each square centimetre is lased for about ninety seconds, depending on the strength of the beam.

The calming effects of laser treatment, and the fact that no gel or water is needed in its use, make it easier to apply than ultrasound or electrical stimulation. Lasers do not have the inherent dangers of ultrasound, and the newer machines are much less likely to 'cook' horses and cause cellular damage than the older, more highly powered lasers. However, it is still important for the operator to know the most effective frequency and duration for treatments. Over-treatment on wounds can lead to development of collagen with low tensile strength, which means that the wound could break open if stressed too early. Lasers should never be aimed at the eyes, and should not be used on horses receiving cortisone, which is a light-sensitive drug. If an iodine preparation has been used on a wound, it should always be washed off before treatment, as it blocks the transmission of laser light. Perhaps the biggest danger of lasers is that they could be used to relieve pain in conditions which actually need further treatment, and which become more difficult to treat if they are left to develop.

....

Electricity was used in medicine in the 1600s, albeit in a rather crude way: torpedo fish, which generate over 100 volts, were put on a patient's head, or he was made to stand in the ocean until they made contact! This treatment was used for headaches, arthritis, gout and haemorrhoids. Even relatively recently, improvements in the equipment used have made treatment with electric currents a much more pleasant experience than it was some years ago. The electrodes of the old faradic machines – which were used, like the newer designs, to speed healing of injuries and to rebuild damaged muscles – used to have to be placed *exactly* on the motor point of a horse's muscle. This is where the nerve enters it, and where the minimum amount of stimulation will produce the maximum response in terms of visible contraction. One physiotherapist I know recalled with great feeling how a slight misplacement was likely to result in the operator making a hasty exit from the horse's stable!

So these older machines have been superseded by newer machines known as neurostimulators, in which the sensation of the current has become quite soothing, and eminently suitable for treating horses. However, skilled operators still need a knowledge of anatomy and functioning which is extremely precise, and their treatment makes use of trigger points, acupuncture points and motor points. Neurostimulators can be made to stimulate muscle contraction and to keep a muscle working when the nerve which serves it is not intact. They can also be used to block pain. H-wave machines, interferential machines, Electrovet machines (designed especially for use on animals), and a host of other variations on the theme are used by different practitioners. The different machines vary in how specifically they can target a muscle; some even mimic the way in which the nerves 'fire', giving a muscle the most precise form of stimulation possible.

The tone, strength or endurance of a muscle can be specifically targeted by the use of different settings and different machines, each one producing a current with a slightly different wave form. Commonly, a muscle is made to contract and relax repeatedly, pumping blood and lymph through the circulatory system, and speeding up healing once the acute stage of an injury has passed. A different setting will be used when there has already been severe muscle wastage, or to prevent muscle wastage from occurring as a result of either injury or surgery. Contractions can be made more or less long, more or less frequent, and more or less intense. They can be sudden or gradual – and all of these variables, along with the positioning of the electrodes, have an enormous bearing on the results achieved.

It takes about 70 volts of electricity to make the skeletal muscles contract in humans, and a much lower stimulation will work on horses. With a higher voltage, the current penetrates the tissues more deeply, and it feels more uncomfortable. Very small electrical currents of only a few thousandths of an amp are enough to give the body a shock, so the machines avoid this danger by producing current in very brief pulses. If you think of the *voltage* as being like the pressure in a water hose, then the *current* is analogous to the amount of water coming out of the hose. If a machine was not registering the expected level of current (water) it could become tempting to turn up the voltage (tap): but the danger is that the current is not getting through due to a poor electrical connection (the equivalent of a kink in the hose).

The most likely source of this is the electrodes which contact the horse, and to ensure good contact either the horse's coat must be well wetted underneath them, or they must be used with a conducting gel. As with ultrasound it can be helpful to clip the coat in the area of treatment. Placing an electrode precisely on the muscle's motor point also improves its functioning, and turning up the voltage in response to any problem obviously creates the risk of shocking the horse by mistake. So before working on a horse, conscientious operators usually take the precaution of testing their machines on themselves!

The electrical stimulators are often used to locate exactly where a horse is sore. Usually one electrode, known as the dispersive electrode, is placed at the wither. This is a large pad attached to a wet sponge, and held in place with a surcingle. Its large size reduces the amount of current per unit area so that there is virtually no sensation. The second electrode is much smaller, so its current is more easily felt. By wetting areas of the horse's body in turn, and slowly moving the electrode over them, the operator can detect if the muscle contractions generated make the horse sore – for if they do he will make his discomfort obvious. This same set-up is often used during treatment, especially when the deeper muscles are being targeted. But with other types of machine, both electrodes are placed over one particular muscle, sending the current along (rather than across) its fibres. Treatment times are longer than they are in the other modalities, and often two fifteen-minute treatments, or one twenty- to thirty-minute treatment, are given per day.

Many of the horses referred to physiotherapists for electrical treatment have had road accidents, or falls in which muscles were bruised and torn, making wastage and the formation of scar tissue highly likely unless preventative measures are taken. Commonly, horses come for treatment some while *after* the accident, when muscle damage has become chronic. However, if used in the early stages of healing, electrical treatment can stimulate the circulation, reducing inflammation and aiding recovery. The treatment also offers pain relief, helping the horse to use a damaged limb in a more normal way, re-establishing a full range of motion and normal weight-bearing. This makes a combination of electrical stimulation, controlled exercise and stretches a much better alternative than just leaving the horse in his box.

Weakened muscles will not recover fully unless they are given specific exercise, but the *illusion* of recovery may well be created as other muscles take over their work. This can happen in ways which are virtually imperceptible, but which can still create secondary problems as other parts of the body are stressed. The injured muscle is worked by making it repeatedly contract and relax, and it can be rebuilt even if its nerve supply has been damaged. Since this damage leads to a reduction in the muscle's elasticity, and in the number of capillaries which supply it with blood, its functioning can otherwise decrease until a stage is reached where the muscle cannot recover fully, even with treatment.

'Weakened muscles will not recover fully unless they are given specific exercise, but the illusion of recovery may well be created as other muscles take over their work.'

....

Pulsed electromagnetic fields have been used extensively in the healing of fractures and other conditions involving bone. Their value in soft tissue injuries has been less well researched, although they are helpful in breaking up oedema, in healing tendon injuries, and in injuries involving the muscles of the back and quarters. Large areas of the back can be treated at one time, making the treatment extremely practical. Magnetic fields affect the positive and negative ions within the area of damage, attracting each type towards one magnetic pole. This movement increases blood supply, bringing in oxygen and removing waste products – with much deeper penetration than the other therapies.

The most sophisticated equipment uses pulsed magnetic fields which are generated by electrical coils. Other devices use rechargeable batteries to activate magnets which can be strapped to a limb or mounted on a rug. Varying the intensity of the magnetic field and the frequency of its pulsations influences the effects of treatment, whose frequency of repetition and duration must be monitored with care. The equipment, however, is one of the safer modalities, and having performed laser or ultrasound treatment themselves, physiotherapists will often leave an owner to administer follow-up treatment with pulsed electromagnetic fields. Yet accidents do happen: one physiotherapist I know always warns her clients that their horse is 'plugged into the mains, so *please* be careful' – and she recalls one case where clients left their horse plugged in and unsupervised in the wash box (of all places), causing a rather devastating accident.

Even more useful for the layman are magnetic shapes contained within flexible pads which can be bandaged on over an injury. Also available are rugs and boots which contain magnetic shapes, and which have proved their worth in pain reduction, keeping both high performance horses and old campaigners sound enough to continue work.

Whilst magnetic treatment has become extremely high tech, magnetic materials themselves are an ancient remedy. Another folklore tradition is the use of copper bracelets for arthritis. The way in which they work is unknown, but many people swear by them, and they have been used to good effect on horses.

....

We, the horse-owning public, have remained amazingly ill-informed about the benefits of physiotherapy for horses, and only recently has it become a more accepted part of veterinary treatment. There are many cases where the machines are an extremely useful alternative to bute and rest, speeding the healing process and even having a beneficial effect on chronic injuries. Any machine, however, can only ever be as good as the person who operates it – and since each machine has various settings which have a huge influence on the precise way in which it affects the tissues, a little knowledge is a dangerous thing. The duration and frequency of their use is also vital, and damage can be done if the equation is set up wrongly.

The machines can be bought by the general public, although it is probably only racehorse trainers or highly competitive riders with financial backing who would contemplate making the considerable investment which they represent. One hopes – for their horses' sakes – that new owners will read the instructions, and invest in the training needed to use the equipment wisely! But even then, there is the issue of correct diagnosis, and of allowing complete healing to occur rather than masking the symptoms of an injury and returning a horse to work too soon.

Insurance companies now often include physiotherapy amongst the treatments they will finance, and although it may represent a large financial outlay for the uninsured owner, the pay-offs could make it worth considering. From the roving physiotherapist with a few 'gadgets' to the fully equipped equine rehabilitation centre, skills and facilities are on the increase – and physiotherapists will now hire out some of the simpler, safer machines to the horse owner. Vets are far better informed about the treatments than they used to be, and most will willingly make the appropriate referrals. Physiotherapy is all too rarely used as preventative medicine, however (and at the opposite end of the spectrum, physiotherapists tell me that the bane of their lives are the riders who are

'The application of energy to the tissues reminds us that the body itself is an energy system.'

convinced that they can 'ride through' any problem!) Since physiotherapy considers only the area of injury it has rarely been part of an holistic approach to treatment; but used wisely, it has tremendous potential here, and more and more physiotherapists like to work preventatively with the athletic horse. The application of energy to the tissues reminds us that the body itself is an energy system, and in treating this, we have many more healing options than drugs alone.

CHAPTER NINE

'Let Food Be Thy Medicine'

Food and drugs

Of all the complementary treatments, herbalism is the most akin to our traditional Western medication. However, its guiding ethos – as with other complementary treatments – is to strengthen the body and to treat it as a whole, rather than to attack the symptoms of disease. About 25 per cent of the drugs in common use today are either derived from, or are the synthetically made equivalents of, the 'active ingredients' of plants which have traditionally been used medicinally. Aspirin, for instance, is a chemical transformation of salicin, which is a component of the bark of the willow tree, and is also present in meadowsweet. The painkiller morphine comes from the opium poppy. Witch hazel, which is a sacred herb of the Native American Indians, is one of the few herbs which has survived mimicry by the chemist, and extract of witch hazel mixed with alcohol is sold in pharmacies as well as by herbalists. It is used by many people as a first-aid treatment for wounds and bruises, for it is both antiseptic and a powerful astringent which helps to stop bleeding and reduce bruising.

Herbs used medicinally vary from those which provide gentle nutritional therapy (of which garlic is a good example) to those which are very toxic, causing violent reactions in the body. As children, we all learned to steer clear of deadly nightshade, which depresses the central nervous system and can be used to treat spasm in the gut, gall bladder, and urinary tract; but it can also prove fatal if eaten. Digoxin, a drug used in the treatment of heart conditions, was originally derived from digitalis found in foxglove, which is also highly dangerous. In small doses digitalis increases the force of the heart beat whilst lessening the frequency of beats. In large doses, it causes the heart muscle to go into spasm, ultimately causing death by cardiac paralysis.

These examples are intended to show that even though the medical profession has succeeded in convincing us that herbal treatments are only useful in treating minor problems, herbs are not necessarily mild or safe. (Their homoeopathic equivalents, however, do not carry such dangers). Modern drugs have the advantage that their dosage and potency can be

'Even though the medical profession has succeeded in convincing us that herbal treatments are only useful in treating minor problems, herbs are not necessarily mild or safe.'

determined much more precisely than they can in herbal treatments, and their action is often quicker. But modern drugs are in some ways more dangerous, for when the active ingredient in the plant is isolated, the secondary agents are removed. These almost always moderate its effects, and ensure that the body is receptive to it; so some synthetic drugs have many more side-effects than their herbal equivalents. (One could easily argue that we have been conditioned by the drug companies to expect both immediate results and side-effects.) Ephedrine, for instance, is used in orthodox medicine to treat nasal congestion, but as a side-effect it raises blood pressure. The herb Ephedra, however, contains another alkaloid which prevents this in many people. Synthetic diuretics (which increase the flow of urine) seriously reduce the levels of potassium in the body. But dandelion leaves − a potent natural diuretic − contain potassium which naturally replaces whatever is lost.

Whilst herbalists train in schools across the world, there is, as yet, no official post-graduate training for veterinary herbalists (as there is for veterinary homoeopaths and acupuncturists). In the UK, however, there is a BSc degree course in phytotherapy (*phyto* = herbal) which would allow a veterinary surgeon to call himself a veterinary herbalist − and to my knowledge only one vet has so far completed the course. This lack of training, along with the dubious quality of some of the herbal supplements offered by the feed companies, makes herbalism a more difficult field than most in which to find a practitioner whom you can trust. This is even more true because the effects of herbs can be very different in animals with different digestive systems − so the study of herbs for human use does not imply an understanding of their use in treating animals. Clover, for instance, is recommended for treating human skin conditions like eczema. However, in light-skinned horses some clovers can cause liver damage and photosensitivity − which leads to painful sunburn. Different animal species also differ in their response to various plants, with pigs thriving on the quantities of acorns which would cause poisoning in cattle and horses.

Historically, gypsies, farmers, and other native people have been the carriers of knowledge about herbal remedies for animals as well as people, following traditional recipes which have been handed down through generations. Different parts of the world, with their different native plants, have each developed their own practices, offering many varying approaches to the same problems. Many traditional treatments have undoubtedly been lost − both by not being written down, and through the wars and clashes of cultures in which written records were destroyed. But recently, as worldwide travel has led to an intermingling of cultures, different treatments from across the world have become more widely available, with Chinese and Ayurvedic (Indian) doctors coming to the

West. I for one am extremely grateful for this, for I feel that I owe much of my present strength to a Chinese herbal doctor who recently arrived in my home town. Several British vets are using Ayurvedic herbs in treating horses, and in the USA there is now a training course for vets in the use of Chinese herbs.

The Chinese tradition is the oldest of all, for the Chinese Emperor Shennung studied herbs nearly five thousand years ago, leaving us the Shennung herbal. This lists about three hundred and sixty-five substances, some of which are the basis of modern medicines. The Egyptian tradition dates back to at least 1500BC, and over eight hundred remedies are listed in the Elbers papyrus, which is believed to have been found between the knees of one of the mummies at Thebes. The Romans introduced about four hundred herb species to northern Europe, and the ancient Greek physician Hippocrates described the beneficial and harmful effects of many plants. Like the Egyptians, he appreciated the importance of diet, stating 'let food be thy medicine, and medicine thy food'.

In the Western world one of the ancient rationales for herbal medicine was *The Doctrine of Signatures.* According to this, the possible medical uses of a plant were suggested by its appearance, and its habitat. The greater celandine, for instance, has bright yellow sap, which turns the skin an orangey-yellow on contact – exactly the colour of jaundice, for which it is an extremely effective remedy. As the age of technology advances, and the drug companies constantly attempt to better nature, this idea seems too simple to be true – and it is all too easy to forget that we live on a planet which has been abundantly stocked to supply all of our needs.

'It is all too easy to forget that we live on a planet which has been abundantly stocked to supply all of our needs.'

....

Until the beginning of this century, Hippocrates' philosophy about food and medicine was indeed true for the horse, who had access to a large variety of herbs and grasses, even when grazing on farm land. But pastures have declined since then: a modern meadow contains about seven species of grasses, whereas a traditional one at the turn of the century would have contained over *sixty,* with about four times the number of herbs that one would find today. (Although we still enthuse about 'Dr Green', his medicine is much less varied and potent now than it would have been then!) At one extreme of modern methods, fertilising pasture hugely changes its growth rate and its nutritional profile, making it dangerously rich in nitrogen. Weed-killers then add their poisons. At the other end of the spectrum, neglected, horse-sick and weed-infested pastures are not just un-nutritious, they are actually dangerous – especially when pollution increases their toxicity.

Horses have a reputation for never poisoning themselves in the wild state, and for choosing well what they most need to eat, using their instincts to balance their diet and keep themselves healthy. 'Bleeders', for instance (horses who bleed from the nose during or after exertion) will eat plantains if they are available. These are used in human herbal remedies to control bleeding. It is when a horse's choice of herbage is restricted that he does not fare so well or choose so wisely. Many horses are thought to suffer from the effects of mild toxicity (the result of grazing in less than ideal conditions, and even of eating processed feeds), and this may be the cause of some allergies, and of mild digestive problems or weight loss. Fatal or serious poisoning in horses is most commonly caused by ragwort, yew, laburnum and bracken, with yew being immediate in its effects. Next to this in toxicity is laburnum, which affects the nervous system. Bracken and ragwort both damage the body over time, with ragwort causing liver damage and bracken destroying vitamin B_1, so that weight loss and mis-coordination result.

Before the Second World War, chemists and medical students studied the ways in which drugs were derived from plants, and herbal medications were listed alongside chemical drugs in the pharmacopoeia. But as science promised to produce the answers to all of our ills, this was stopped, and the developing pharmaceutical industry made us believe that herbal medicine was obsolete – or at best, secondary to the real thing. This was greatly to the industry's benefit, for molecules created in the chemist's test tube can be patented whereas plants cannot. Now, with medicine's 'magic bullets' widely criticised for their side-effects, the renewed demand for herbs and natural remedies is evidenced by the products which fill the shelves of health food shops and pharmacies. (How you choose the most appropriate remedy, however, and wade your way through the mass of confusing and conflicting information on health and nutrition is another question – as it is with horses.) In America, the use of herbs and supplements is more restricted than it is in Europe, where Germany leads the revival, and since 1993 German doctors have had to take an examination in herbal medicines before becoming licensed.

Changing trends in feeding

The companies producing horse feeds have followed the trends which influence how we both feed and medicate ourselves. In this, they have catered for the burgeoning numbers of horse owners who do not have the knowledge of the traditional horseman – flawed though this may have been – and who do not trust their own judgment. As crops were analysed, their nutrient values were shown both to differ widely, and to differ from the ideal balance, and we were advised to mistrust traditional feeding methods. The newer thinking behind equine nutrition could itself be flawed, however, for little experimental work has actually been done with horses to determine what their ideal nutritional requirements are! A few of the US feed companies keep a herd of horses for study purposes; but research using horses is always a long, drawn-out and expensive process. Since research using cattle is much more financially viable, cattle science is more often used as the basis for feeding horses.

In the USA, the National Research Council (NRC) draws up nutritional guidelines for horses which are followed by the feed companies both there and in the UK. However, basing these on interpolation from data on cattle brings with it unanswered questions, for the cow is a ruminant with a very different digestive system. Furthermore, it is intended to convert food into meat or milk, and not into work – and it does not live to the same ripe old age which allows potential problems much more time to develop.

Following these guidelines, concentrate feeds (known as sweet feed in the USA) are formulated to be fed with grass hay (which will have a very variable protein content, and a mineral and vitamin content very much influenced by its quality and the soil and conditions in which it was grown). Because of the lack of research on horses, many of the conventions which are followed in the feed industry are actually *suggestions* rather than proven fact – although we as consumers have little choice but to trust them. We can no longer leave the horse to graze a large area of natural herbage, and even if we could, this would not provide the extra nutrients needed to fuel high performance. Neither can we bury our heads in the sand and gaily assume that traditional feeding methods must be the best; so we have to either rely on 'straights' – the concentrate feeds of oats, barley and maize (known as corn in the USA), fed either singly or together – whilst supplementing their deficiencies as best we can; or we have to put our faith in the feed companies, and rely on them to do it for us.

Before you get too concerned about the intricacies of feeding, and the various vitamins and minerals which constitute the micronutrients of a feed, it is important to appreciate that most nutritional imbalances actually occur at the level of the *macronutrients* of protein, carbohydrate and fibre. Watching riders on my courses as they make up their horse's feeds makes it abundantly clear that there are huge variations in the quantities – as well as the substances – that riders feed to similar horses doing similar work. (This has been a real eye-opener, and I would not have believed the differences without seeing them!) When questioned, few people have a convincing rationale: many are loyal to a particular feed company or a particular product which they feed out of habit. Very few have done much research, and those who have, have often been daunted. Friends, magazine articles, hearsay, half-truths and guesswork are often their guiding principles.

'Little experimental work has actually been done with horses to determine what their ideal nutritional requirements are.'

'Most nutritional imbalances actually occur at the level of the macronutrients of protein, carbohydrate and fibre.'

Very few riders know the weight of their horse, the weight of the concentrate feed they are using, and its proportion in the total ration. Many over-estimate the work their horse is doing, and feed for hard work (i.e. high intensity work for short periods of time, or lower intensity work for long periods) when they are only doing light or medium work. – which involves low intensity work for only short time periods. Interestingly, recent research has shown that the intense bursts of energy needed by the flat-racing horse require less than *half* of the additional digestible energy needed by an event horse, who needs *half* of the extra energy needed by an endurance horse over the course of the day – so our traditional definitions of 'hard work' are changing.

Adequate nutrition for adult horses will usually be supplied by feeding a total of between 2 and 2.5% of their body weight, with ponies and warmbloods being on the lower end of this scale. A 500kg/1100lb horse – which is a fairly lightweight 16hh Thoroughbred type – then needs a total of 10-12.5kg/22-27.5lb of feed. Only if he were in extremely hard work would that ever be divided 50/50 between hay and concentrates. More commonly an 80/20 or 70/30 split will satisfy the horse in light or medium work, providing the higher fibre levels which are much more natural to a 'trickle feeder' who – given the choice – would eat for over sixteen hours a day. The concentrate feed would normally provide 10% protein for horses in light or medium work, and possibly up to 14% protein for horses in heavy work, although some people dispute the necessity for this increase. Protein is not an efficient source of energy: its utilisation releases six times more heat than the use of carbohydrates or fats, and the process releases nitrogen, which is excreted through urine – so increasing the loss of water and electrolytes. Thus protein levels higher than 14% are only ever suitable for lactating and growing animals.

In devising a ration for your horse, your first port of call should be a 'weight tape'. These are manufactured by some of the feed companies, and give a useful guide. Measuring the horse around his barrel allows you to read off an estimate of his weight and an appropriate total daily feed intake for light, medium and heavy work. Along with this, the tape shows the proportion of fibre and concentrates needed for different work regimes, and this provides a good beginning point in devising the equine diet.

The most knowledgeable stable managers treat each horse as an individual, recognising that some 'good doers' might need much less feed than expected. They know the importance of insulating their horses well in winter, and realise that not doing so could force the horses to use up to 80% of their ration to keep themselves warm – leaving very little to fuel their work and keep them looking well. Good stable managers also question the many factors which might cause a horse to fare much less well on a certain diet than they had hoped. (These could range from the state of his teeth to pain and emotional distress, as well as intestinal worms, subclinical illness, or the inappropriateness of the feed.) They evolve their feeding programmes through astute observation coupled with trial and error. The feed companies, however, cannot treat each horse as an individual; they must divide horses into categories – like the performance horse with a high energy requirement, the horse who puts out just a small amount of energy, and the horse who is growing, pregnant, or lactating. Then they must provide a food which is safe for the horses within that group – doing so in a way which is economical for them, and affordable for us.

This is often called 'lifestyle feeding'. Another possibility is 'stages feeding', in which a 'base feed' provides all of the maintenance ration, including the necessary vitamins and minerals. According to the horse's work, various 'stages' are then added: light and medium work can be fuelled by a feed which provides energy basically in the form of vegetable (corn, soya bean or canola) oil. Horses can utilise this very well: it presents them with fewer digestive problems than cereals do, and some evidence suggests that horses prone to tying-up fare much better on a diet which has 10% added fat by weight. Fat burns slowly and cleanly, and whilst it used to be used only for endurance horses, it is now believed that even sprinters benefit once the body has adapted to it, with more power being generated during fast work. (Before you rush to pour corn oil all over your horse's feed, however, please seek further advice, and work out how much oil that feed already contains. Do not feed more than two cups per day; introduce it gradually, and make all the appropriate adjustments to the feed as a whole.) Hard work also needs the added starch from cereals, and the various 'stages' add those vitamins and minerals whose requirements increase with work. However, in 'lifestyle feeding' many of us feed *less* of a concentrate feed than the manufacturers recommend, so we are not actually providing all the vitamins and minerals which they have deemed necessary. So many of them suggest that if we feed beneath a certain 'threshold level' of their feed, then we should use a supplement. The unfortunate truth is that few of us obey instructions well enough to completely fulfil the manufacturer's expectations.

The ethos of the feed companies is very different to that of holistic thinkers (as we shall see further on), and their high-tech approach focuses much more on *nutrients* and chemical formulas than it does on *ingredients.* If you accept that this way of thinking is suitable for horses, then it has to be said that the feed companies do a very good job. But along the way, we – the consumers – are blinded with science, and so many different claims are made for so many different horse feeds that it can be hard to know where to turn.

In the old days when ignorance was bliss, we had little more to worry about than protein, carbohydrate, and fibre. Now we have to deal as well with *micronutrients,* and there has been such an explosion in our knowledge that more has been written about the roles of vitamins and minerals in disease during the last five years than was written in the previous two hundred! Micronutrients are needed in only the tiniest quantities, yet they play vital roles in the maintenance of strong bones and teeth, normal nerve conductivity, muscle contraction, vision, and so much more. Within the complex processes of metabolic activity, a whole chain of interactions can be stopped in the absence of *one* vitamin or mineral.

'The role of micronutrients within the equine (as well as the human) diet is an exceedingly complex subject which only a biochemist could expect to understand.'

The explosion in scientific knowledge makes it apparent that the role of micronutrients within the equine (as well as the human) diet is an exceedingly complex subject which only a biochemist could expect to understand! Yet the truth is that horses are more than test-tube processes; they have evolved to eat grass throughout the seasons, and to deal with fluctuating mineral and vitamin levels. (In contrast, the vast majority of feeding regimes must make it seem like spring every day!) Their ability to store, conserve and manufacture micronutrients is almost without parallel, and it is a godsend to us that they are so adaptable.

I consider it extremely important that we, as consumers with a responsibility for our horses, know more than most of us have traditionally done about the principles of saddlery and farriery (and I know that I have probably stressed your brain cells in presenting these through much more detailed 'maps'). I have argued that these first two arts both need a more rigorous and scientific basis, and that their practitioners are not always sufficiently thorough. The explosion of knowledge which has already transformed the feed industry is only just beginning in those two fields, and since they can never be reduced to test-tube processes, they will probably never be as clear-cut.

In the case of feeding, there is no third party in between us and the producers – no equivalent of saddlers and farriers – whom we can easily blame for our problems. The feed companies do what they do extremely well, and their technical know-how is not in question. So as we work our way through the jungle of information about feeding, how much do *we* need to know? The nutritionists in the feed industry (who really are an elite few) want us to defer to them, and to question the accumulated wisdom of our forefathers. They want to convince us that common sense, a keen eye, and the traditional 'rules of good feeding' are no longer enough. Unfortunately, in view of the complicated choices we now face about the contents of our feeds, it is all too easy to become so blinded by science that we forget this simple wisdom.

Today's good feeder (so the feed companies want us to believe) relies not just on the traditional rules but also on the latest in biochemistry. Although the feed companies stop short of blinding us with the chemical formulas which guide and fascinate them, the basic premise of their advertising is that 'the more scientific it is, the better it must be'. Once we accept that, it follows that we should indeed leave them to formulate our horses' rations. This allows us to remain relatively ignorant, and simply to follow instructions. However, in deciding who we are going to defer to what we *really* need (but are not so readily offered by most feed companies) is a more practical map, which tells us how they make their feeds, what goes into them, and how compatible they are with the digestive system of the horse.

Macro- and Micronutrients

In the face of all of the new information about macro- and micronutrients, one can easily be left wondering how the poor deprived horses of old ever managed to survive. It may be a surprise to discover that some did not: one hundred years ago 'big head disease' (nutritional secondary hyperparathyroidism) was also known as 'miller's disease' because it occurred so commonly amongst wheat millers' horses, who were fed a high proportion of bran – a by-product of the milling. Their bone was gradually replaced by fibrous connective tissue, which gave a puffed out appearance to the upper and lower jaws. The weakness of their diet was its mineral imbalance, and in particular its calcium to phosphorus ratio. This – and miller's disease – is still a common problem in parts of Australia and other subtropical areas, where some of the native grasses are extremely high in phosphorus.

Ninety-nine per cent of the calcium in the horse's body is located in his bones and teeth, as is 80 per cent of the phosphorus. Together they form most of the mineral matter in his body, and this can only develop correctly and then remain strong and healthy if calcium and phosphorus are present in the diet in the right quantities and the right proportions. Horses require at least one part of calcium to one of phosphorus, and when they are growing, pregnant, lactating, or working hard, the proportion of calcium must be higher. Even a proportion of six to one will not harm the adult horse (as long as there is sufficient phosphorus).

As soon as the proportion of phosphorus *exceeds* that of calcium, it interferes with the absorption of the calcium, and it is this which leads to bone disease. Both minerals need to be made available in a form from which the horse can readily assimilate them, and vitamin D is also needed for this process of turning food into bone. Where there is an imbalance, young horses could be prone to rickets, and older horses to osteoporosis – and since all horses are constantly remodelling their bones, calcium and phosphorus are needed throughout life.

It is the *cereal grains* which are higher in phosphorus than calcium – and when the grains form more than 50 per cent of a ration of hay and grain, the hay can no longer compensate for the imbalanced ratio in the grain. The picture is complicated by the fact that horses cannot readily assimilate the phosphorus in grains, although it is more readily available in hay. It is ideally given to horses as a supplement derived from an inorganic source, like dicalcium phosphate. This adds both calcium and phosphorus in a suitable ratio; but more often limestone flour is added, for this is a cheaper source of calcium – which all of us know is needed. (We have a conditioned expectation about how much we are willing to pay for a bag of feed, and this ties the hands of producers who would like to use better and more expensive ingredients.) Nature, however, has catered well for the foal, for milk is the perfect bone-growing food. Legumes like clover and alfalfa (known in Australia as lucerne) are exceptionally rich in calcium, and Timothy grass contains twice as much calcium as it does phosphorus – so the danger only arises when a high grain ration is fed.

The scientific revolution in feeding really began as it became clear that many horses fed on the traditional diet of oats, bran and hay, suffered from calcium deficiency. So the feed companies assured us that 'straights' (usually oats) could no longer be considered an adequate diet for today's working horse. Instead, they offered us 'convenience', 'balanced' feeds, and included within these the additives which would supposedly produce a balanced diet. But alongside the 'balanced' rations we could also buy the supplements which would balance a diet which was *not* already balanced, tempting us to do the job twice! As the supplements have become more popular and more sophisticated, advertising – with its promise of better performance, improved condition, a shinier coat, or stronger hooves – only increases the temptation. But since many supplements have similar ingredients (and similar ingredients to the additives already present in prepared feeds), it is all too easy to double or even *treble* the horse's necessary requirements. Fortunately, the margins for error in regard to each individual nutrient are wide; but it is when one mineral interferes with the absorption of another that damage is done.

Furthermore, both the macronutrient and the micronutrient balance of the 'balanced' feeds are disturbed by adding any other ingredient of our own choosing. Chaff and sugar beet do not affect this too much; but bran and/or cereals do, and adding oats to a high-performance feed can even *reduce* its energy value. It seems that we cannot wholeheartedly trust the feed companies to make up our horse's ration for us (or perhaps we just want to 'cook' for our horses, unable to resist the satisfaction of mixing things together in a bucket!). Yet few of us decide to start from scratch and feed 'straights'. We fall between the two systems, and instead of making a clear choice between them we muddle along. If we do not believe that we can beat the feed companies, we would be better to join them wholeheartedly.

The complexity of the situation, and the dangers of over-supplementation become clear when you appreciate how a surplus of one mineral can deny the body access to another, as with calcium and phosphorus. Excessive calcium interferes with the absorption of trace minerals, like zinc. Excessive zinc, iron, and/or manganese can disrupt the absorption of calcium and phosphorus...and so the story goes on, yielding complex inter-relationships which begin to sound like a brain-teaser set by MENSA. Both excessive and inadequate levels of selenium and iodine are damaging to the body, and since selenium deficiency is common in some areas of both the UK and USA, it is commonly added to feedstuffs. Intentionally or not, all of this science baffles the poor horse owner and can undermine her confidence. She is easily made to feel guilty that she is not doing the best for her horse: worried about mineral imbalance she feeds not fewer supplements but *more* – creating the imbalances which result from over-supplementation.

However, the feed companies – who are operating in a highly competitive market – can hardly be blamed for trying to out-do each other. Neither can they be blamed for our folly if we insist on spending far more money than we need to, and on producing a horse who suffers from over-supplementation. In truth, anyone who no longer feeds 'straights' should be just as scared of the dangers of *over-supplementation* as of the dangers of inadequate mineral levels. Probably the least harmful effect of over-dosing (for the horse, if not for your pocket book) is his inevitable tendency to convert our hard-earned cash into vitamin and mineral enriched urine! In our blissful ignorance, we gaily pour money into one end of our horse and watch it come out of the other.

'In our blissful ignorance, we gaily pour money into one end of our horse and watch it come out of the other.'

The over-supplementation of vitamins is probably more common than that of minerals, but fortunately it does not carry the dangers associated with excesses of phosphorus and selenium. Many horses do not need supplementary vitamins, since forages are a good source of the fat-soluble vitamins (A, D, E, and K) as well as the water-soluble ones (the B complex, C, H, and P). Furthermore, the horse can synthesise a significant quantity of these latter through microbial fermentation in the hind gut. (Only man and a few other animals cannot synthesise vitamin C.) However, high performance horses – along with pregnant and lactating mares – benefit from some extra help.

Vitamins, especially natural ones, do not store well and this plays a part in what deficiencies there are. Vitamin A, for instance, which (as beta-carotene) is common in fresh forage and well-made hay, is lost through the oxidisation which occurs if hay becomes bleached by sunlight and/or is stored for a long time. The new vacuum packed types of haylage escape degradation until the seal on the bag is broken: then its contents also start to oxidise. So vitamin A is commonly added to feeds, as is vitamin D_3 and vitamin E.

In the UK and USA any bag of prepared feed which you purchase will state minimum levels of these three vitamins, as well as of selenium, copper and molybdenum. But since the vitamin content will decline through storage, *more* must be present when the bag leaves the factory, for only this can guarantee that those minimum levels are still there by the time it reaches its 'use by' date. So if you thought it was necessary to know exactly the vitamin and mineral content of your feed, you could not in fact do so! Given that completely defining both the macro- and the micronutrients of your horse's diet would also require you to have your hay and your soil analysed, the majority of small-time owners are probably defeated before they begin; so it is as well that the margins for tolerance are as high as they are.

Exposure to natural sunlight provides vitamin D, which is needed in the metabolism of calcium; so stabled horses can be indeed be deficient, especially given that it is found in very few forages. Vitamin D_3 is commonly added to feeds at about 10% of the level of added vitamin A. Turn your horse out, however, and you can have it in the way that nature intended – as a free additive. Biotin, which has recently become known for its benefits in hoof growth, is actually one of the B-complex vitamins; it is synthesised in the gut, and is available from many natural herb sources.

The B-complex vitamins are not normally added to prepared feeds, and a horse receiving large quantities of grain could benefit from supplementation with the B-complex, as can horses who are growing, or are significantly stressed – particularly by travelling and competition. With stress comes an increase in adrenalin. This alters the acidity in the hind gut, causing a disturbance to the balance of the intestinal flora, and resulting in the frequent loose droppings which tell us that our horse is nervous. Increased numbers of harmful micro-organisms crowd out beneficial bacteria, which – as well as digesting fibre – have the ability to manufacture vitamins B and K as well as some animo acids. So it is not surprising that anxiety and nervousness are associated with the lack of the B vitamins. Digestion becomes less efficient; recovery from a period of stress or excitement is slowed, there can be a loss of appetite and vitality, and various metabolic disorders become more likely.

The most recent answer to this is *probiotics* which are live, equine bacteria that can be used, in effect, to seed the gut. (This is the horse's equivalent of eating live yogurt, which many people eat after a course of antibiotics has killed off the flora in their gut. However, yogurt is not a good choice for your horse.) In Europe EEC rulings are about to impact on the makers of probiotics, and licences will be issued for their production. Instead of being fed as a powder in the feed, many will now be designed for direct feeding. A good-quality probiotic will rarely have enzymes and B vitamins added, for it will enable the horse to produce his own. The better products contain a broad spectrum of appropriate micro-organisms which are present in high concentrations. The poorer (and often cheaper) products contain a much lower concentration of organisms, and are unlikely to achieve the beneficial effect required. Whilst some manufacturers of probiotics recommend their use on a daily basis, others believe that this makes the gut 'lazy'. Their recommendation is that probiotics should only be fed a few days before and after a big event which might stress the horse. Probiotics also have a use with newly born foals, and with brood mares and stallions.

The feeding of yeast provides another approach to the regulation of the acidity in the hind gut, and thus of the bacteria which inhabit it. Yeast is included in some feeds and supplements, and it has to be fed daily. It helps to create an environment in which micro-organisms can thrive – but it cannot distinguish between different strains. Its use, therefore, is controversial, with many nutritionists believing that a healthy gut should not need it, and that an unhealthy gut is better treated by seeding it directly with the most horse-friendly equine bacteria. One thing you can be sure of, however, is that the thrifty horse has his hind gut working well – and that the horse who fails to thrive would benefit from having this issue addressed.

Another time when it pays to quickly replace what work has removed is during and after the profound effort which leaves the horse sweating profusely. Sweat is derived from blood plasma, and dissolved in it are blood salts. These are the trace elements sodium, potassium, calcium, magnesium, phosphorus, and chloride. When in solution they have an electrical charge and are known as electrolytes or ions. Sweat is a cooling mechanism for the body: as muscle cells burn the fuel which makes them contract, a chemical reaction takes place in which excess heat is produced. Even during gentle exercise, heat production within the body is ten to twenty times that at rest, and to stabilise the body's temperature this heat must be lost. Sweating lowers body temperature through evaporation: but inevitably its efficiency is affected by the temperature and humidity of the surrounding air.

Horses sweat more than any other species, and their sweat contains a greater proportion of minerals. In one hour of hard work when conditions are hot and humid they can lose about 5 gallons/23 litres of sweat, and can easily become dehydrated. The easiest way to test for this is to pick up a piece of skin, pinch it and then let it go. If it does not immediately flatten down against the horse's body he is in danger from dehydration, and the lost fluid and minerals should ideally be replaced. If

'Horses sweat more than any other species.'

they are not, the consequences could become catastrophic, and the most dangerous scenario is prolonged hard work in hot humid conditions in which the horse's sweat never evaporates. Thus it cannot serve its function of cooling the body; so the horse keeps sweating, and will eventually dehydrate. Research prior to the Atlanta Olympics suggested that the best way to cool a hot horse is to apply cold water liberally to the large muscle groups of the neck and quarters, interspersing 20 to 30 seconds of spongeing with 20 to 30 seconds of walking (staying in the shade if possible). This is far more efficient than the use of ice-packs, sweat-scraping, wet towels, and/or keeping the horse still, and there is no evidence that it leads to tying-up.

The diet of a horse in such hard work will not provide enough sodium and potassium to replace the losses. It is worthwhile giving even resting horses free access to salt, and the feed companies presuppose that we will do so. Other than this, one cannot supplement pre-exercise – for the body always maintains a balance appropriate to its immediate situation, and will excrete any excess minerals via the urine. So electrolytes are commonly given to endurance and event horses during and after competition. This is usually in a more sophisticated form than common salt, although this – mixed with sugar – is better than nothing, and the most effective products on the market have the most appropriate balance of trace elements.

Rather cleverly, some old stud grooms used to sweat-scrape a horse, collect the liquid sweat, dilute it with water, and give it to the horse to drink. This, and our modern-day electrolytes, utilise the same principle as the saline drip used in cases of extreme exhaustion – but, of course, one never wants to reach this stage. If you have ever taken electrolytes yourself (they are commonly used both after heat exhaustion and after a bout of diarrhoea, which also causes the loss of trace elements) you will know that even when their taste is disguised, they are not very pleasant; so horses should be accustomed to drinking them before their use becomes critical, and if they consistently refuse them they can be given in paste form or as a powder in the feed.

The high-tech revolution

'Arguments abound about whether synthetic vitamins are absorbed by the body in the same way as natural ones.'

Another dimension to the scientific revolution in feeding concerns the way in which horse feeds have progressively become further removed from nature. In general, the micronutrients in both the 'balanced feeds' and the supplements are synthetically produced, and arguments abound about whether synthetic vitamins are absorbed by the body in the same way as natural ones. Little is actually known about the effects of the long-term use of synthetic vitamins in horses, and mostly both we and the feed companies gaily presume that they will not turn out to be harmful.

Many feeds contain raw materials which are by-products of other industries, and one could even argue that the horse-feed industry has evolved as a way to utilise those products. Sugar-beet pulp, for instance, has always been molassed because this suited the sugar industry, and only recently has unmolassed beet pulp – which is really much more suitable for horses – become available on the market. The baking industry is another source of by-products, and stale bread (along with sweeter goodies) is used in a number of horse feeds. In the USA, protein additives could legally include pig hair and hydrolysed chicken feathers – and historically, some extremely dubious ingredients have been included in a few of the cheaper horse feeds both there and in the UK. I am sure you do not need me to tell you that animal products should never make their way into the digestive system of the horse – and in the UK, we have already learned the hard way about the dangers of messing with nature. Yet many of us have given cod liver oil to our horses. So where does one draw the line?

Interestingly, very few cattle farmers were aware that they were routinely feeding processed sheep's brains to their cows until the scare over BSE ('mad cow disease') in 1989 led to a ban on animal products in cattle feeds. Following the European ban on British beef in 1996, many of the UK feed companies issued public statements which assured us that their horse feeds were free of any animal products. The irony is that these products normally have a very good chemical analysis on paper; but this says nothing about whether they are absorbable and usable by the body – and even if they were, they are *not* feeds which the horse evolved to eat. It is an undeniable fact that basing the science of feeding on *nutrients* instead of *ingredients* makes it remarkably easy to contravene nature.

The feed mills do far more than just mix ingredients – they use extremely high-tech processes to produce a feed with a specific nutritional profile. Grains and forages are first inspected for moulds, and specimens are tested in a laboratory to determine their nutrient content. Grains are prepared for inclusion in pellets or mixes through being cracked, flaked, or rolled, and computers measure and weigh the main ingredients for each recipe. These pass through blenders for the addition of other ingredients, like molasses, fats (probably vegetable oil), supplemental protein (which could be soya-bean meal, or brewer's yeast), vitamins, minerals and preservatives. Unfortunately, the antioxidant chemicals which prevent bacterial degradation during storage also affect the bacteria in the horse's gut which – as we have seen – are a vital part of his digestive system; some would say that they are toxic, and can cause allergic reactions. The added vitamins have been manufactured in the laboratory, for natural vitamins are largely destroyed by the heat processing which will follow, and without supplementation this would render the grains much less vitamin rich than their untreated counterparts.

Some ingredients are individually heat processed – and micronised barley has, in effect, been microwaved. Pelleting, which may produce either the small pellets used in coarse mixes, or the pellets of a complete feed, involves heating a moistened mix of ingredients to between 140°F/60°C and 230°F/110°C, and forcing it through dies which create the pellet shape. Extrusion is used to increase digestibility, for in effect cooking pre-digests the foods. The process places the mix under high pressure and forces it through a cooker which bathes it in steam and heats it to between 240°F/115°C and 330°F/165°C. It is then passed through a die, compressed into long 'sausages' of the desired shape, and shot into colder air which makes it puff out. It is then chopped with rotating knives, dried with heaters, and cooled. Further samples of the feed are often taken and tested before bagging, labelling, and shipping to the wholesaler, who sells it to the retailer, who sells it to the consumer. It is a very sterile process; but the finished version may bear little relation to the natural ingredients one could find in a field.

Horse and pony cubes or pellets were the original high-tech feed, designed for 'idiot-proof' feeding. In the UK coarse mixes, and in the USA 'sweet feeds', now sell more than pelleted feeds, and extruded feeds account for a very small share of the market. We like products which *look nice,* and the feed companies want us to open a bag of their feed and think, 'Ummm… that looks so good I could eat it myself!' Micronised barley, for instance, is bigger and chunkier than untreated barley – but its vitamins (which do not withstand heat processing) have been replaced by synthetic ones which do. A mix must look open, colourful and shiny, not tired, sad and dusty – hence the addition of molasses, which lays the dust in coarse mixes. It used less than it used to be, but high concentrations are used for hotter climates where the feed dries out faster in storage.

Molasses is also used to bind together the different ingredients which form cubes, albeit in smaller quantities than in the mixes, but in each case it gives the feed a very high sugar content. The more complex and indigestible carbohydrates contained in fibrous foods are not broken down and then absorbed until they reach the hind gut; but molasses is absorbed from the small intestine. The feed companies mostly defend the use of molasses in feeds, saying that the sugar content of spring grass is far higher. But it is conceivable that a large feed (especially if you are unwittingly feeding a molassed mix, along with molassed chaff, and molassed beet pulp) could lead to a sudden surge in blood-sugar levels – some badly behaved horses may well be on a sugar 'high' just when their owners choose to exercise them! Horses with behavioural problems who look puffy in the kidney area could well have a food allergy, and you can test for this with radionics (see page 243) or by using the muscle-testing method of Applied Kinesiology (see page 175). This latter is a two-man

'The feed companies want us to open a bag of their feed and think, "Ummm… that looks so good I could eat it myself!" '

'Some badly behaved horses may well be on a sugar 'high' just when their owners choose to exercise them.'

job: the surrogate puts one hand on the horse's rib cage and raises the other, and then you test for a strong arm which withstands a gentle but firm downward pressure. Then separate the horse's feed into its component parts, and let him chew on a mouthful of each as you touch his mouth, and then test again. If you find that the surrogate's arm cannot withstand the test when the horse is eating a particular component, you know that this is the culprit.

Molasses could also be used to mask the taste of raw materials which do not taste good to the horse. Fragrant herbs can also serve this purpose – and convince the owner that she is buying something natural and good. Some people worry that using herbs constantly like this renders them less potent should you want to use them in treating a specific condition, but such tiny quantities are added that this is, in fact, highly unlikely. The chemical analysis on the label of your feed bag will undoubtedly be a specifically designed formulation which follows the latest scientific principles; but be aware that you are being told about *nutrients,* not *ingredients.* So the actual *contents* may not be ones your horse would choose: the molasses, for instance, could come not from sugar beet but from *citrus* sources, which would never be eaten by the horse in his natural state. A wide range of ingredients can produce the same package of nutrients, and through buying on the world markets, the feed companies can compensate for the varying nutritional contents of the raw grains and forage, and can maximise their profits.

In the final analysis, however, the feeds must be acceptable to horses, and fortunately they are such fussy eaters that they themselves place limits on acceptable ingredients. Cows, in contrast, will accept any old rubbish. Fish meal is commonly included in cattle feeds, but horses do not like the smell of it, and it is perhaps fortunate for us that they are so discerning. In one case, a large feed company found that their stud cubes were suddenly and consistently refused by horses, and it took quite some investigation to discover that the problem lay with the locust beans contained in them, for these had been purchased from a different country of origin to the one used previously.

The animal feed industry actually evolved by making feeds (and more recently supplements) from the by-products of other industries. It does not think about nutrition in the same way as the herbalists and horse keepers of old. Food is no longer medicine: formulas are based on chemical reactions and the smart buying of ingredients. *Holistic thinking* is an alien concept in this high-tech world, and holistic thinkers talk of 'inverted nutrition' – the philosophy which allows one to add this vitamin or that mineral, instead of considering that an appropriate micronutrient profile requires a *balance* of micronutrients, which come from a variety of different sources. If you put a group of holistic thinkers in with a group of academically trained nutritionists, you could sit back and watch the 'map battles', for neither would speak each other's language.

It is inevitable that the feed companies want to keep their secrets from competitors, but as a result we – the consumers – are often faced with a dearth of information about the contents of a feed. Legally, the label must tell us the percentages of oil, protein, fibre and ash, as well as the quantities of certain vitamins and minerals. (Ash is what would remain if you burnt the feed, so it includes its mineral content; a high percentage could indicate, however, that the feed was full of stones - so stating the ash content helps to protect the consumer.) The labelling protocol differs somewhat in the USA, and there the ingredients do not have to be listed in descending order of inclusion, as they do in the UK. In both countries the label states generic terms which do not say much. 'Products and by-products of sugar production' implies a high molasses content, although 'High fibre materials' still leaves us guessing! 'Products of tubers and roots' is certainly vague, and 'By-products of cereal production', could mean almost anything. It could be chopped straw (which has its value as a high fibre feed), bran, or waste cereal – like 'oat feed', the hulls and husks of oats which remain after the muesli manufacturers have created your breakfast cereal. Although by law these generic terms have only certain allowed interpretations, some would argue that not all companies interpret the law that rigidly (and one nutritionist even suggested to me that wood shavings – which would certainly qualify as 'high fibre materials' – have been used in cheaper horse feeds). Whatever the truth of this, you can be assured of one thing: the law has not been set up for our benefit.

If you attempt to find out what the contents of a feed really are you may in some cases have a great deal of difficulty, and personally, I would take this as a warning signal. Since most feed manufacturers have telephone 'help lines', they should not be difficult to contact – and they should be held accountable. Telephoning their advisers, and comparing their explanations and suggestions is probably the most appropriate way to make the decision about what you will feed your horse. It should also prove an interesting learning experience, and by inference at least, you will discover the ethos of the companies you talk to. Most people phone the 'help lines' only when they have a problem, so calls become seasonal, from 'My horse is losing weight. What do I do?' in the autumn, to 'My horse has azoturia,' in the cold spells of winter, and 'My horse has laminitis,' in the spring. But we could do much better than this: one nutritionist I spoke to suggested that we should treat the 'help lines' like we would treat car dealers, going to them for advice about buying (or in our case feeding) a high-performance model or a family run-about. But when we decide whose advice we like best we should not tamper with it – just as we would not tamper with the car – because if the wheels fall off it then becomes entirely our own fault!

The fundamental dilemma which faces all of us in feeding is this: we can either know the *nutritional profile* of a food, and have very limited knowledge about its ingredients; or we can opt to feed 'straights' so that we know the *ingredients* but have a very limited knowledge about their nutritional profile (given the variability between samples). To know *both* would take a tremendous amount of research, and I know of only one person who has fully undertaken this task. Following long-term sub-clinical illness in her horses she had her soil analysed, revealing a copper deficiency. She now has her oats analysed before purchasing a year's supply. A well-known feed company produces an 'oat-balancer' pellet to her specification, which balances out any micronutrient deficiencies. She bruises her own oats every other day, and feeds them with alfalfa. Her horses look a picture of health.

....

Following on from the balanced and processed feeds, we now have the next generation of products which are aimed at the 'green consumer'. Firstly, herbal supplements have come onto the market, and (although they cannot legally be classed as medicines) are purchased for their medicinal qualities. Herbs are now added to many horse feeds (albeit at levels which probably do more for the owner than for the horse). Also lying in that grey area between food and drug are the 'nutraceuticals' – feed additives which usually contain naturally occurring ingredients, and which are used to combat various forms of soreness and to enhance tissue repair. Since they are not approved drugs, no medicinal claims can be made for them; but this (and the lack of research into their benefits) cannot stop anecdotal success stories from being their greatest sales pitch. One groupd of nutraceuticals are the antioxidants, which clean up free radicals – the oxides which are by-products of normal metabolism as well as of injury repair. There is conflicting evidence about how damaging free radicals are to the cells of the body, but as a crude analogy, you can think of us all rusting as the years go by. So their presence accelerates ageing, and is thought by some to contribute to cancer and heart disease.

Dietary antioxidants like MSM (methylsulfonylmethane) have helped many sore horses, and a number of vitamins are antioxidants, including vitamin E: hence its value – along with selenium – in the prevention of tying-up. Antioxidants can also enhance the health of cartilage, and as well as the regulated drugs available from your veterinarian, there is an increasingly large range of over-the-counter feed additives based on animal-derived proteins. These are identical to components of the horse's cartilage and joint fluid, and they migrate through the body into the joints, where they encourage the cartilage to produce healthy synovial fluid. This stops any further degeneration of the joint. Thus anyone facing the alternatives of a lame horse, a drugged horse, or a horse consuming animal proteins, may well find that their scruples about feeding animal products are put to the test. (There are, however, herbal and homoeopathic alternatives, as we will discover later.)

However, for the ultimate 'green consumer', the most recent addition to the market place are the 'natural horse feeds', containing only foods which the horse has evolved to eat. The feed companies involved, however, all set slightly different parameters in deciding what the horse 'evolved to eat': some will not use yeasts, but do use synthetic vitamins. Or they do use vegetable oils, but do not use molasses. There is a geographical issue involved in this, and whilst soya-bean hulls and rice bran might seem very strange feeds to us, one could probably argue that working horses native to China have traditionally been fed on them, just as ours have been fed on oats and wheat bran. This makes a number of apparently strange ingredients suitable for inclusion, and some would maintain that British attitudes to feeding are extremely parochial (especially if we reject on principle any foods which could not be grown in rural England!). Arguments about the suitability of (seemingly) exotic feeds from other countries divide the industry – largely into the large multi-national companies and the smaller manufacturers. So for high-performance or growing horses, for whom nutrition is critical, it may well be worth paying more for a feed with known (and perhaps local) ingredients and a locked-in formula.

In the UK, the British Association of Holistic Nutrition and Medicine (BAHNM) licenses one such 'natural' feed, but others which are not licensed by BAHNM utilise similar principles. The feeds contain many more raw materials than other compound feeds, but the licensed feed is guaranteed to contain no artificial products, molasses and syrups, or animal and fish products. All of the raw materials included are stated on the bag, and high standards are adhered to in all stages of production, so you know exactly what you are getting. BAHNM hope that they will soon be able to endorse feeds whose ingredients are organically grown – but these are hard to find in sufficient quantity. The only disadvantage of these feeds is price; for with less flexibility in ingredients, they cannot be so cheaply produced. So if you want to feed your horse according to holistic principles, using naturally occurring ingredients which are in balance with each other, you will have to 'put your money where your mouth is'. You will, however, recoup at least some of your losses through feeding *less* of the product than you would of a feed in which 'fillers' play an important role.

Herbs

With herbs, be they proprietary mixtures or single herbs bought from mail order companies, your guarantees of quality are not so stringent. Many herbs are imported, and inevitably their quality varies – yet any literature on the beneficial qualities of a herb will always assume that the herb was grown under ideal conditions. Common sense, however, is often enough to tell you if you have bought wisely: if a mixture looks as if small quantities of herbs have been blended with a filler like chaff, or if the herbs are a dusty powder which does not smell like the original, you should be very wary.

You can feel confident if the look and the smell of the product you have bought matches listed names which you recognise; but if the contents are *not* listed on the product (and the company will not tell you them over the telephone) stay away. If extreme claims are made for a product, be wary. From time to time a 'wonder herb' appears on the market (aloe vera, though not a herb, is one of the current 'wonder cures') – and although it may be extremely beneficial, it is unlikely that it cures quite so many conditions as its advocates suggest. The gap between sales talk and common sense is sometimes fuelled by network marketing methods – which also fuel the divide between the people who swear by a product and those who reject it on principle. Traditional herbalists, in fact, become extremely angry when the outrageous sales pitch brings the whole of herbalism into disrepute.

Old established companies are usually the safest source of herbs, for they have access to traditional knowledge. (As one herbalist said to me, 'I'm a herbalist who's pretending to be a commercial company; and that's very different to being a commercial company that's pretending to be a herbalist.') Do seek their advice, for working directly with a herbalist gives you much more chance of finding a remedy which is specifically tailored to your horse, and not an 'umbrella' mixture which is a 'cure-all' for the general market. A horse might be stiff, for instance, because of navicular disease, because of arthritis, or because he has just been round a gruelling cross-country course – three different cases in need of three different treatments. The best herbalists work very precisely, and some like to see the results of a blood test before offering their advice.

Having said that, there are some excellent products on the market, mostly intended to keep the horse calm – using herbs with a known sedative effect, such as valerian, hops, and camomile. It has to be said, however, that many horses being fed calming herbs are actually the victims of bad riding and/or saddling, and that eliminating the tension and misunderstanding which causes their behavioural problems would be a much better way to alleviate their suffering. Calming herbs can only address the *symptoms* of the problem, and are highly likely to lose their

'Many horses being fed calming herbs are actually the victims of bad riding and/or saddling.'

effectiveness if fed all the time.

Other herbal products are formulated to keep the horse out of pain, using herbs which are anti-inflammatory and analgesic (pain-killing) in their action. Yet others enhance digestion and the body's ability to utilise existing nutrients; or they boost the immune system, and help in the elimination of toxins from the body. It is questionable whether these products should be used on a regular basis without veterinary advice, but many satisfied owners swear by them, telling anecdotal stories about their effectiveness, and feeling a great sense of relief that they have been able to keep their horse in work without having to resort to drugs. Indeed it is the desperate need for alternatives to bute and other drugs which has spawned a rapidly growing market, with more and more companies who do *not* have traditional knowledge getting in on the act.

In her book *Veterinary Aromatherapy,* Nelly Grosjean gives wonderful examples of herbal folklore, quoting from *L'Ecole de Cavalerie* by Monsieur de la Guerinière of the Royal Stables, which was published in Paris in 1769. Although Guerinière is remembered as a rider and not as a herbalist, his recipes give an interesting insight into historical remedies. One for stimulating the appetite requires 2 ounces each of 'fenugreek, common salt, linseed, fennel seeds, anise seeds and bay seeds, sulphur flowers, liquorice, birthwort, agaric, myrrh, Socotrine aloes, and roots of the knapweed thistle, and 1 ounce each of clove, nutmeg, cinnamon and ginger'. This was to be ground to a fine powder before use and two ounces of it fed morning and evening with bran boiled in water and 'half a peck of wheat'!

If you wish to make home brews, the descriptions of herbs and the herbal remedies in Juliette de Baïracli Levy's book, *A Herbal Handbook for Farm and Stable,* make fascinating reading; but although she guaranteed them to be safe, I would be very cautious about using them! *A Guide to Herbs For Horses* by Keith Allison is also a useful resource book, as is *A Modern Horse Herbal* by Hilary Page Self. But very few modern-day horse owners − even the great enthusiasts for herbal medicine − are likely to start searching in hedgerows for herbs, as a prelude to drying them and creating their own infusions or inhalations. (And if you did so in the UK, you would run the risk of contravening the Wildlife and Countryside Act of 1981 and its Variation of Schedule Order of 1988, which makes it an offence to pick, uproot, destroy, or sell over one hundred wild plants.)

You would also run the risk of identifying a herb wrongly, and of picking herbage that has been subjected to pesticides, weed-killers, or exhaust fumes and other toxic substances. One thing you *can* easily do, however, is to enrich your horse's diet by scattering herb seeds in your fields, or even in the fields of the establishment where you keep him. (BAHNM, whose address is given at the end of the book, can advise on mixes.) Failing this, you will have to rely on prepared products, and on the advice of the companies or herbalists who sell them.

Traditional herbalists have rarely bothered to find out the active ingredients of their treatments, but (despite the enormous costs involved) more and more of them are being chemically analysed. This allows them to be selected not just according to folklore, but according to the actions of their known ingredients. EEC and FDA regulations may make it imperative to discover these, and herbalists of all kinds are fighting an ongoing battle with bureaucracy. The American Horse Shows Association (fairly or otherwise) tests horses for all foreign substances including the various herbs and nutritional supplements which have a calming effect similar to that of banned substances. It is important to be aware that there are some herbal products which would presently not pass the drug tests administered in competition, and not all herbs are safe, especially for long-term use and in the treatment of pregnant mares. Fortunately, research into herbal treatments is being done on horses in the UK and Germany, and this can only add credibility to the whole field.

Probably the best known of all herbs is garlic, which is used medicinally all over the world. In the last twenty-five years over one thousand research papers have been published about its effects on humans, and these have shown raw garlic, dried garlic, garlic oil and various garlic preparations to have significant effects as antibiotic, antiviral, and antifungal agents. They help to prevent (but not to cure) colds, 'flu, and sinus congestion. Their use discourages intestinal worms, and they also thin and cleanse the blood. This suggests that garlic in various forms may well help horses in all of the above ways, as well as those with navicular disease or laminitis. Its odour makes it a good fly repellent, and it has been shown to be effective in the treatment of sweet itch/allergic dermatitis.

Judging by the smell in the feed room when groups of riders convene for my courses, many people are aware of the beneficial effects of garlic! It can be fed continuously without danger, and will be of as much benefit to you as it is to your horse. Depending on its quality, garlic varies enormously in price – and when grown in hot dry climates it has a much higher medicinal value than when grown in temperate climates. You get what you pay for – and at the cheapest end of the market you run the risk of buying garlic diluted with onion powder.

In terms of the vitamins and minerals present in it, alfalfa heads the list of herbs readily available to horses. In the USA it is thought of more as a fodder, and is commonly fed instead of grass or hay; in the UK it is more readily available as a chaff or as cubes which are mixed with concentrate feeds. Drying, crushing and leaf loss will inevitably reduce its vitamin content; fed fresh it is unsurpassed as a source of micronutrients, although its high protein content limits the amount which is safe to feed.

Many people will be surprised to realise that after alfalfa, the humble dandelion is one of the next richest sources of vitamins and minerals, for its long tap root allows it to extract nutrients from deep in the soil. Horses have been known to dig for it, and they will also eat the leaves. Both leaves and roots are blood cleansing and act as a tonic, with powerful diuretic effects. The equally humble nettle is another useful herb, although horses rarely eat nettle unless it has been dried. It acts as a tonic and a cleanser, suggesting that it too may help with sweet itch (allergic dermatitis) and other skin disorders, and it also helps in the absorption of iron, implying that it may be useful for the anaemic horse. In itself, it is a rich source of iron, calcium, and potassium. Kelp (a kind of seaweed) is another widely used supplement, which is extremely rich in iron and iodine, and is said to improve the horse's coat and hooves, as well as his general health. Pollution is a big danger here, though: the Irish sea is not a safe source of kelp, and even the Scandinavian sources which were renowned for being clean are now at risk from pollution.

Mint has an antispasmodic effect on the digestive system, and may help gas to be expelled from the bowel. It can be fed regularly to horses, and may help those who are prone to colic. Rosehips are renowned for being rich in vitamin C, and they are also a rich source of natural biotin, which is probably more effective in promoting hoof growth than biotin derived from any other source. My horse eats rosehips with great relish (and also devours roses, much to the consternation of my partner who is attempting to establish a hedgerow between our garden and his field!). Comfrey is another well-known herb, which has recently hit the headlines (and fuelled the cries for more effective regulation of herbal remedies), for it has been linked to the formation of tumours when taken internally in large amounts, and over long periods. It has traditionally been used externally to help in the healing of wounds and bruises, and both externally and internally in the healing of fractures. Because of its powerful properties in this regard it is often known as 'knitbone'.

....

The number of horse feeds, additives, and herbal supplements now available on the market has reached such a pitch that I sometimes wonder if the industry sees us as a gullible bunch of consumers, and is rubbing its hands with glee. In this area, more than any other, commercialism has entered the 'alternative' market, and many different companies have joined the bandwagon, each claiming to have the answer (which is why utilising their 'help lines', and comparing their answers to your queries may give you the best sense of whose advice you wish to follow). Sadly there is no such thing as an independent nutritionist, and everyone has a product to sell – so there will always be different opinions. (This includes the very cynical view of one nutritionist who diagnosed the fundamental problem as: 'We and our horses have been fed so much c--p for so many years that no one knows any longer what's what.') If you trace the evolution of feeding from the traditional diet of 'straights', to the convenience foods, the supplements, and now to the new generation of holistic and herbal products, it becomes clear that the feed companies have 'de-skilled' and confused us so effectively that although the rules of feeding have not changed, its science has moved out of the league of the layman. Horse feeds have supposedly been made for our convenience; but we now need to make far more difficult choices than we did when our only options were oats, barley or maize (corn).

Trading off our desire to do the best for our horses, the feed companies offer seductive, tantalising options; or they make us feel guilty that we are not acting on today's most up-to-date information. So we might for instance, feed a supplement, see no difference, but not dare to stop using it – and some of the marketing used both by the publicly owned companies and by their smaller, more holistically minded opponents can even qualify as 'scare tactics'. As a horse owner facing the dilemma between nutrients and ingredients, you either 'go it alone' or you have no choice but to trust somebody. You can either put your trust in familiar locally grown feeds, or in the world-wide market; in synthetic vitamins or in natural ones, and in drugs or in herbs. Either way, the current trends of greater public accountability (along with the shake-up provided by the BSE scare) are, I think, very positive. The exception to this, however, lies in modern agricultural methods, whose effects are virtually inescapable. It is hard to invoke the wisdom of Hippocrates, especially without good pasture. But – if you are willing to do your homework – it *is* possible to make informed choices, which can only be to the horse's benefit. And if you do change your horse's feeding regime as a result of reading this chapter, please remember the age-old wisdom of making those changes *slowly*.

'Although the rules of feeding have not changed, its science has moved out of the league of the layman.'

Aromatherapy

Aromatherapy is a special branch of herbal medicine, using the aromatic oils which are extracted from the flowers, leaves, branches or roots of plants, herbs, and spices, either by cold-pressing them, or by steam distillation. The essential oils of plants have been used therapeutically in ancient times, in countries as diverse as Egypt, Italy, India and China, and they were first produced commercially in the sixteenth century. The system is now best known in France, where doctors regularly prescribe aromatherapy preparations. These are stocked alongside conventional drugs in French pharmacies. The term 'aromatherapy' was coined in 1937 by a French chemist who was working in a perfume laboratory when he burned his hand. He plunged it into the nearest container of cold liquid – which happened to be pure lavender oil. The burn quickly lost its redness and healed with unusual rapidity, impressing him so much that he began to research the healing properties of lavender and other essential oils. This was the birth of modern-day aromatherapy.

On average, the essential oils are seventy to one hundred times more concentrated than the oils in the plant from which they are derived. Their chemical make-up gives them many desirable qualities, including antibacterial, antiviral and antispasmodic properties. Others are vasoconstrictors (which narrow blood vessels), vasodilators (which widen them), and diuretics (which increase the production of urine). The limbic system – which is the emotional switchboard of the brain – is directly connected to the sense of smell, and also intimately connected to parts of the brain which control breathing, heart rate, blood pressure, stress levels, hormone balance, and memory. (This is why a strong smell can suddenly evoke memories of past years.) This suggests that the oil fragrances may be one of the fastest ways to influence the body, both physiologically and psychologically, and one of the best ways of treating stress-related conditions. Research has shown that they can even alter brain-wave patterns – and thus emotional states – acting simultaneously on the neurochemistry of the brain and the central nervous system.

A study done in 1973 showed that a blend of the essential oils of clove, melissa, cinnamon and lavender, was as effective in treating bronchial conditions as conventional antibiotics. Furthermore, the oils do not have side-effects, and they tend to stimulate the immune system instead of suppressing it. The oils can be taken internally (but only with proper medical guidance, for some can cause toxic reactions), or can be dispersed into the atmosphere through a diffuser or spray. They can be massaged into the skin, in which case they must be mixed with a base oil, such as walnut. Their molecules are so small that they can pass through the skin into the bloodstream, and they easily penetrate bodily tissues. Aromatherapists in the UK are best known for giving therapeutic massage, and this suggests such a mild form of treatment that the general public are often unaware of the clinical uses of the oils, and how effective they are in healing. (They are extremely effective, for instance, in the treatment of cystitis.) In the USA aromatherapy is less well known, for it has no licensing body.

For optimum results, it is important to use top quality oils, and these may be expensive. For example, it takes approximately thirty rose heads to make one drop of rose otto oil, which means that the pure undiluted oil (which is one of the most expensive) will cost about £1 or $1.60 per drop! Crops must either be wild or organically grown, and the yield and the availability of the plant crop will affect the price of the oil. Inevitably, there are many cheaper, adulterated oils on the market, and it is best to

'The general public are often unaware of the clinical uses of the oils, and how effective they are in healing.'

buy oils from suppliers who specialise in aromatherapy essential oils. Avoid labels that use evasive terms like 'pure fragrance essence' or 'pure botanical perfume'. To combat its price, a small amount of a quality oil goes a long way, as long as it is stored in a dark opaque bottle, and kept in a cool dark place with the lid firmly screwed on.

The oils you are most likely to have heard of include eucalyptus, which is the basis of many chest rubs, and is well known for its antiviral and expectorant properties. Lavender has a calming effect, and is useful in treating burns and bites. Tea tree is a non-irritating antiseptic commonly applied to wounds, and is the most widely used antiseptic in Australia. Citronella is also well known as an insect repellent, and since it is one of the cheaper oils you are likely to find it in its pure state.

Caroline Ingraham, a registered aromatherapist who works with horses under veterinary supervision in England, uses the muscle-testing technique of Applied Kinesiology (also used by some chiropractors, and described on page 175) to determine the combination of oils needed. Two horses with the same illness may well – because of their different types and temperaments – respond best to different treatments. The surrogate used in testing will show a positive muscle test as soon as the best combination of oils is found. But even more interesting is the way that the horses themselves will sniff with interest at the oils that are needed, and will turn their heads away from ones which are not. They will even follow someone holding the oils they need in preference to following someone with carrots or their feed! Caroline recommends actively involving your horse in his treatment, allowing him to sniff the oils before they are used in treatment each day – for if he turns his head away the oil is no longer needed. Care should be taken, however, never to let the undiluted oils touch his nose, for some can cause skin irritation especially in strong sunlight.

An aromatherapist working in conjunction with a veterinarian may prescribe oils to be taken by mouth. A couple of drops are then rubbed into the horse's gums, or placed on his tongue, or on a carrot. Many physical and emotional conditions respond to treatment within two days, as evidenced by improvement in the horse, by his loss of interest in the oils, and finally by a positive muscle test. The effects of the treatment may, however, be immediate. Some oils, for instance frankincense and violet leaf – which are often prescribed for fear and nervousness – are blended into a massage gel and massaged around the muzzle. Others, like great mugwort, which is often helpful with allergies, are massaged around the windpipe. Caroline also recommends the use of a spray in your horsebox or trailer, which contains bergamot and garlic oils. These kill airborne bacteria and have an uplifting effect. Similar sprays which deter mites may also may be useful for head-shakers.

Aromatherapy has at times proved useful with horses who have perplexed veterinarians. In one case, a very panicky horse started to lose hair in small patches all over his body. Shampoos, allergy tests, skin biopsies, blood samples, and the combined brain-power of two skin specialists finally led to the conclusion that the causes were stress, and a problem within the immune system which was considered similar to the AIDS virus. This was deemed incurable. Muscle-testing by the aromatherapist also indicated that the horse was stressed, and that the immune system was very weak; but the oils of frankincense and Roman camomile had a strengthening effect.

Frankincense, which is extremely effective in treating fear, was blended into a base oil and massaged around the muzzle twice daily for five days and then once a day until the aroma was of no interest to the horse. Two drops of Roman camomile – which is renowned for treating stress when it manifests in the skin and stomach – were placed on a carrot and given twice a day for five days, and then once a day until it became unappealing to the horse. After one month, the horse still liked the smell of the oils. His temperament had changed dramatically, but the bald patches were still getting worse. It took only another week for the scabs to fall off, and for new hair to begin to grow through.

This case history is a testament to those occasions where a diagnostic procedure which could easily be dismissed as 'mumbo jumbo' proved more useful than all the tests of orthodox medicine; and where an unbelievably simple treatment proved itself over drug therapy. Aromatherapy and herbal treatments are not cure-alls, but they deserve a place beyond that of the last-ditch attempt at treatment. Ironically, although vets often scoff at herbal and aromatherapy treatments, the library at the Royal College of Veterinary Surgeons in London is a mine of information about the herbal treatments of yesteryear. In this great age of technology we have turned our backs on ancient wisdom, preferring – in many cases – to suppress the symptoms of disease, rather than to effect a cure. Our attempts to better nature have led us into all sorts of trouble – from BSE to food intolerances and antibiotic-resistant 'bugs'. We have reached the stage where to go forward, we must glance back.

CHAPTER TEN
Energy Medicine

Homoeopathy, Flower Remedies, Radionics and Acupuncture

Homoeopathy

Homoeopathy is based on the 'law of similars', the belief that 'like cures like'. It was discovered by the German physician Samuel Hahnemann, who lived from 1755 to 1843. However, his painstaking work was actually a rediscovery of more ancient wisdom, for Hippocrates in the fourth century BC stated that 'Through the like, disease is produced, and through the application of the like, it is cured.' In the fifteenth century, the German physician Parcelius utilised the same principle, and Hahnemann's rediscovery of it came after he had abandoned his medical practice, disillusioned with the treatments of his day, and was working as a medical translator. He was a linguist who spoke nine languages, a chemist, a botanist and a doctor – an unusually gifted man who was not afraid to go out on a limb.

Hahnemann was translating a British book about herbal treatments when he became fascinated with the way that bark of cinchona (whose active ingredient is quinine) was such an effective treatment for malaria. He began dosing himself with cinchona bark each day, and found that he developed symptoms just like the periodic fevers which characterise malaria. These stopped when he discontinued taking cinchona. He then proposed that a substance which caused the symptoms of a particular disease in a healthy body could also cure that disease in a sick one. Whilst his 'law of similars' may seem a rather strange phenomenon, it was the theoretical basis of the vaccinations later developed by Jenner, Salk, and Pasteur. (Homoeopaths, however, are not keen on conventional vaccinations, preferring 'nosodes' which are homoeopathically prepared. But since most horses compete sometimes, homoeopathic vets have little choice but to give vaccinations.) The same principle is often also used in the treatment of allergies, with minute quantities of the suspected allergen being introduced into the body to increase its natural tolerance.

Hahnemann continued his experiments by giving various substances to volunteers, who faithfully recorded the symptoms they produced. Each of these 'provings' built up a 'symptom picture' of the substance, which included both its physical and its psychological effects. In this, he was searching for symptoms which matched those of a known disease. By his death, Hahnemann had written one hundred and twelve research papers, and had 'proved' 99 remedies. The current total, which includes substances from animal, vegetable and mineral origins, stands at over 2500. Some remedies – like snake venom, tubercular cow tissue, dog's milk and volcanic ash – sound so bizarre that they could put you off for life; but suffice it to say that these – along with the many remedies of plant origin – are guaranteed to produce symptoms!

Hahnemann demonstrated the efficacy of his system in two desperate situations. When the Battle of Leipzig ended in 1813 with 75,000 wounded and a typhoid epidemic, he treated 180 cases, of whom 2 died. This result would be considered good when compared with our modern-day treatments, but then, a 75 per cent loss would have been typical. In a cholera outbreak in 1831 he treated 154 cases, of whom 6 died – a 96 per cent success rate. Of the 1500 treated by the orthodox methods of the day, only 45 per cent lived.

Hahnemann feared that his subjects might suffer toxic side-effects from the substances he was testing, so during his research he experimented with using more and more dilute tinctures. He began from the 'mother tincture', which was made by soaking the primary plant (or substance) in alcohol, and then utilised the processes of dynamisation and succussion. In dynamisation, the tincture was diluted with either 10 drops of water or alcohol (giving the potencies labelled 'x') or more commonly with 99 drops (giving the potencies labelled 'c'). Then the solution was succussed, or shaken vigorously. This process – which is still used today in the preparation of homoeopathic remedies – is then repeated. In remedies of the potency 6x or 6c, it has been repeated six times; 30c has undergone 30 dilutions each with 100 drops of water, and 200x has been diluted 200 times, each with 10 drops of water. The great surprise – which originally shocked Hahnemann, and which conventional medicine is still struggling to come to terms with – is that with more dilutions, the remedy becomes progressively more potent. This is even more amazing when you consider that after the twelfth dynamisation using the 1:100 method, it is unlikely that a single molecule of the original substance remains.

This leads conventional medics to conclude that any successful homoeopathic treatment is merely the placebo effect, in which a patient's condition improves when they are given a sugar pill and told that it is a potent medicine which is bound to help them. As we have seen, a number of experiments have shown that homoeopathic medicines are more effective than placebos in treating a number of diseases, especially those such as influenza which are acute and self-limiting, and chronic conditions like arthritis and allergies which tend to get progressively worse. On 'QED', a British television programme investigating homoeopathy, the placebo argument was countered through an experiment staged by the British homoeopathic vet Christopher Day. A large herd of cows was divided into two groups of 40, and both were kept indoors during the winter, with one group being given a homoeopathic remedy for mastitis in their drinking water. In that group there was 1 case of mastitis. In the control group there were 19 cases. But cows cannot be influenced by the placebo effect, and it seems reasonable to conclude that the homoeopathic treatment was indeed effective in its own right.

Conventional medicine often regards the symptoms of a disease as the disease itself, and it seeks to eradicate them, bringing down a fever or drying up a runny nose. Chris Day likens this to covering up the oil pressure light in your car when it comes on and signals that all is not well. For homoeopaths believe that symptoms are the body's way of fighting the disease, and are therefore to be encouraged and not suppressed. So a homoeopathic medicine (made of a substance which would produce those symptoms in a healthy individual) stimulates the body which is already producing those symptoms to fight harder and recover faster. This means that homoeopaths do not need to name a disease in order to treat it – and the mystery viruses which stump conventional doctors do not present homoeopaths with a problem. All they need is a detailed inventory of the symptoms, and an understanding of the constitution and lifestyle of the person or animal who is producing them. Then they use their past experience, deduction, intuition, and study of the massive 'materia medica' (and nowadays even computer programmes), to match that 'symptom picture' with a remedy which mirrors it.

So if our two horses (or even you and I) shared the same bug, we might well be prescribed different remedies – for our different constitutions might cause us to manifest different symptoms. Take equine influenza. 'Pulsatilla' would be the treatment of choice for a horse who is friendly but shy, does not drink very much, has itchy eyes, an annoying cough, a creamy or greenish yellow nasal discharge, and whose symptoms improve in the open air. One of the mercury remedies would be chosen for the horse with a short temper whose symptoms worsened at night, and who had a purulent, greenish nasal discharge, swollen glands and difficulty in swallowing, but who also had a dry mouth with a bad odour and bleeding gums. Another horse which showed a dry mouth and marked thirst, a watery discharge from both eyes and nose, irritated nasal membranes which made him snort, and who was restless but more comfortable in

'Conventional medicine often regards the symptoms of a disease as the disease itself.'

warm surroundings, would be a candidate for arsenicum.

This means that a homoeopath must be much more precise than a conventional doctor or vet, for there are no 'broad spectrum' remedies, as there are in conventional medicine. The homoeopath must consider the person who has the disease just as much as the disease which has the person, for the remedies are extremely specific. So an initial consultation can be rather lengthy − and therefore rather expensive − as there is so much to discover about moods, eating habits, diet, condition of the skin or hair, reactions to various stimuli, sensitivity to light and heat, medical history, and so on

Homoeopathic medicines themselves, however, are not expensive, so in the long run treatment can be far cheaper than the use of conventional drugs. This is especially true given that the treatment is a long-term cure, and the condition will not recur − as is likely with an orthodox treatment which is very often a suppression of the symptoms. Obviously, (as in any healing system) acute conditions respond best when they receive treatment as soon as possible, and with chronic conditions, many homoeopaths believe that it takes about one tenth as long to cure the condition as it did to acquire it, with the cure sometimes involving a 'healing crisis', during which the symptoms worsen before they improve.

Homoeopaths consider their patient's constitution when prescribing for acute or chronic illnesses, and they also use 'constitutional remedies', aimed to bring the whole system into balance. So if you have a horse who is extremely flighty, or extremely lazy, his constitutional remedy may well balance out his energy. (I have a theory that people buy horses who are rather like themselves, so you may well benefit from taking the remedy too − but please have a homoeopathic consultation yourself rather than taking my word for it!) When a homoeopathic practitioner takes your case (or your horse's case) she works from such detailed information that she may well not prescribe the obvious remedy which you would find in a chemist or pharmacy or in a health food store. Some practitioners would go so far as to say that there are two types of homoeopathy: the 'cookbook', off-the-shelf prescriptions used (with remarkable success) by the layman, and classical or constitutional homoeopathy, which is based on a knowledge of the sufferer's constitution and on the accurate matching of 'symptom pictures'.

This holistic approach heals the animal on all levels; so the results can include temperamental changes which the owner never expected to see − like a reduction in fear, or in neurotic responses to stress. British homoeopathic vet Mark Elliot, who treats both horses and small animals, has discovered that he can usually find the constitutional remedy for a horse in the first few attempts, whereas finding it for a dog or cat may take more trial and error. Horses are emotionally so open that they are much easier to 'read', and we — their owners — know much more about them than we do about our cats or dogs (or perhaps we are more astute than cat or dog owners).

If your own 'cookbook' prescription does not yield the desired response do not write off homoeopathy; consult a homoeopathic vet whose detailed knowledge will ensure that the treatment has maximum effect. Few people realise that home prescribing can indeed be dangerous, and if used incorrectly homoeopathic remedies can suppress or palliate just like orthodox medicine. Overdosing can also have negative effects, becoming a *proving* through which symptoms are generated. American veterinarian Joyce Harman finds that some of the most confused cases she sees are the result of people trying different remedies without making an appropriate selection. She advises that all chronic problems are seen by a homoeopathic vet, and that home prescribing should only be used in acute conditions. Only a vet can provide you with an accurate diagnosis and a full understanding of the treatment options, so that the type of treatment given becomes a choice which is based on sound knowledge. This not only provides the most beneficial outcome for your horse, it also removes the anxiety factor for you.

....

Hahnemann's discovery was an extremely attractive alternative to the techniques of his day, which included blood letting, and toxic, mercury-based laxatives. Homoeopathy flourished until the turn of the century, but by then the theory that germs were the cause of disease was taking hold, the power of the pharmaceutical companies was growing, and the funds allocated for medical research were channelled towards the fight against microbes. Physicians began to place less and less emphasis on the body's ability to heal itself when given a little nudge. Instead, more and more emphasis was placed on fighting germs with the heavy weaponry which is better reserved for the ultimate crisis.

Researchers focused on disease instead of on health, never considering *why* it is that germs will invade one person's system, whilst another will not succumb to the bug. For a healthy body does not have the (metaphorical) cracks and gaps which allow the bug to enter and set up shop. This approach built the schism which now exists between orthodox and complementary medicine (and which is fuelled by the financial interests of the drug companies). The first wages war on disease, whilst ignoring — or even compromising — the body's in-built healing mechanisms. The second stimulates the body to repair its own defences.

By 1930 homoeopathy had virtually disappeared in America, although in Europe it survived, albeit in much diminished form. Its current revival suggests that people increasingly believe it to be a viable alternative to orthodox treatment. With more and more bacteria becoming resistant to antibiotics, and with 'magic bullets' having so many deleterious side-effects, it is not surprising that our faith is wavering. Meanwhile, the cost of invasive high-tech treatments is soaring beyond the pockets of both governments and individuals. It is a situation which invites some radical new (or old) thinking.

'Another benefit of homoeopathic treatment is that remedies can never be detected in drug tests.'

With horses, another benefit of homoeopathic treatment is that remedies can never be detected in drug tests – for there is nothing there to detect! Here lies the anomaly which makes it so easy for mainstream medicine to regard homoeopathy as 'quackery'. But homoeopathic remedies have been shown to give off measurable electromagnetic signals, and it may be that a homoeopathic remedy stimulates the body's healing response by conveying an electromagnetic message which matches the frequency or pattern of an illness. With its help, the body can produce more energy at the frequency of the illness and thus can throw it off; its response is rather like the resonant response of glass to a tuning fork, which – like a homoeopathic signal – has a very precise frequency that only a resonant body will respond to. (Remember too that practitioners of 'energy medicine' believe that illness begins as a dysfunction in the body's energy field.) Since the electromagnetic energy of a homoeopathic remedy can penetrate cell walls, it is effective against the viruses which do not respond to antibiotics, for these can only work *outside* the cells. The fact that the remedies are essentially energy explains another of homoeopathy's anomalies, which is that you give the same dose to a mouse as you would to an elephant.

Remedies most commonly come in the form of small white pills which have no taste. Remedies for topical application come as creams, and tinctures. When you take homoeopathic pills yourself, you put them under your tongue and allow them to dissolve, for this enables them to enter your bloodstream more quickly than they would from your stomach. You also avoid eating or drinking for twenty minutes before and after taking the remedy, and avoid coffee, peppermint, and other pungent foods which can make the remedies ineffective. So your horse too must avoid garlic, peppermints, and also the topical application of pungent liniments and rubs. When you administer remedies to him you must not touch them, for if you do, you inadvertently dose yourself – as contact with your skin can activate the remedy. (I dosed myself for years before I found this out!) Your choices are to get the pills directly from the lid of the bottle into his mouth, or to gouge a hole in a carrot, tip a pill into it, and then let him eat it. Some vets dilute the remedies in water and squirt them into the mouth with a syringe, or even put them into a small quantity of feed. Whilst this is not the method of choice, it does not seem to inactivate the remedies as it does with people.

As with herbalism, most people seek the services of a veterinary homoeopath when conventional veterinary techniques are not being as effective as they would like, and they have had more than enough of bute, steroids and antibiotics. Often, these chronic diseases are the introduction through which horse owners begin to learn about homoeopathy, and subsequently they start to use it in everyday situations, building up a homoeopathic first-aid kit. The most commonly used potency on sale to the general public is 6c. You may also be able to readily obtain the more potent 30c; but anything above that will need to be ordered from a homoeopathic pharmacy. Although the lower potencies are often used for older or weaker patients, and are given over a longer term, vets will often prescribe the higher potencies of 30c and above, since the dosage given must match the energetic force of the disease. It is common to dose twice a day for three to five days, or to give a 'split dose', on one evening and the following morning.

Probably the best known homoeopathic remedy is arnica, prepared from the plant arnica montana, or mountain tobacco, which is primarily used for bruising, muscle strain, filling in joints, and also shock. It can be taken as tablets, or used topically as a cream, and it can be used alongside conventional treatments – for instance after surgery. Aconite is another treatment for stress, shock, panic, and conditions which are sudden in their onset: so if a homoeopathic vet is called out to a rather gruesome emergency she will often mitigate its emotional effects by dosing herself, the horse, and his owner! Calendula, which is prepared from the leaves and flowers of marigold, is used as a cream on open wounds and cuts, and I have seen tremendously impressive pictorial accounts of the healing of horrible lacerations using this and other homoeopathic remedies. Hypericum, prepared from St John's wort, is useful in healing grazes, cuts, and sole bruises or puncture wounds of the foot, for it is especially effective in reducing pain from the extremities, and the pain associated with nerve damage.

Rhus tox. (made from poison ivy) treats stiffness which is worse in cold damp weather, and which wears off as exercise begins; if given to a healthy person (or horse) it produces rheumatic type pain. The remedy symphytum is homoeopathic comfrey, which can be used to treat bone injuries and bruising without risking the danger which is supposedly associated with taking comfrey internally. Belladonna, prepared from the deadly nightshade plant, is used to treat ailments which involve high fever with sudden onset: this could include laminitis and influenza. Urtica urens, prepared from the stinging nettle, is used to treat hives and similar skin disorders. Ignatia and nat. mur. treat fear, nervousness, and grief – making them useful if a horse is moving to a new place or owner. And so the list goes on, requiring you to obtain sound advice, and ideally to do some background reading as you build up enough knowledge to prescribe sensibly for minor ailments.

George MacLeod's book, *The Treatment of Horses by Homoeopathy*, gives a number of suggestions for each condition, depending on the precise symptoms, and is very clear about potencies and dosages. It is, however, rather daunting for the beginner, and *Horses and Homoeopathy, A Guide for Yard and Stable*, written by Mark Elliot and David Pincus, is very much easier to follow. Chris Day's *The Homoeopathic Treatment of Small Animals* explains the principles of homoeopathy very well, and I look forward to his forthcoming book on treating horses. Miranda Castro's book, *The Complete Homoeopathy Handbook*, may be a good beginning for anyone wanting simple guidelines to get them started, as is *The Complete Guide to Homoeopathy* by Dr Andrew Lockie and Dr Nicola Geddes. I recommend reading some of the broader-based books about human treatment before you look into veterinary homoeopathy. Remember that the major dangers in the home prescribing of homoeopathic remedies are that you fail to realise the presence of a condition which is best treated by orthodox medicine, that you do not understand the effects of the remedies you have given, or that a problem which you think is acute is actually chronic. You can safely use homoeopathy yourself as first aid; otherwise you are best advised to contact a homoeopathic vet.

Flower remedies

Even more subtle than homoeopathy in their effects are the flower remedies, of which the best known are the Bach flower remedies. In the early 1900s Dr Edward Bach was an orthodox bacteriologist working at a London hospital, and he discovered that the presence of certain bacteria in the gastrointestinal tract of patients was associated with chronic illnesses like arthritis and rheumatism. He suspected that the bacteria might be aggravating these conditions, and to test his theory he used them to make vaccines, which he gave by injection. He expected these to boost his patients' ability to immunologically reject the bacteria, thus cleansing the body of the bacterial poisons which might indeed be causing each illness.

As he expected, the vaccines caused significant improvements in the symptoms. But soon after his discovery Bach was given Hahnemann's book on homoeopathy, and since his vaccines frequently produced local tissue reactions around the site of injection, he prepared homoeopathic concentrations of the bacteria which he could give by mouth. The results were far more remarkable than before. Bach identified seven different types of bacteria which were associated with chronic illness, and the homoeopathic preparations he made from them became known as Bach's Seven Nosodes. But he also noticed that these seven types of bacteria were associated with seven different personality types, and he began to prescribe his nosodes strictly according to type, and without reference to each patient's physical symptoms. This resulted in a level of clinical success which exceeded his expectations.

After further investigation Bach concluded that individuals of the same personality type would not necessarily develop the same illness – but that they would respond to whatever illness they *did* develop in the same way. So once he knew about their behaviours and moods he could determine which remedy would cure their chronic illness. Bach had intuitively realised that a relationship existed between illness – or the predisposition to illness – and the emotions, and he reached his remarkable insight over fifty years before the birth of psychoneuroimmunology (which we talked about on page 44). But he was still not content with his nosodes, and he began searching for natural substances which might be even more effective in addressing the emotional precursors to disease. He did not want to wait and treat the established pathology which would become obvious given time.

He found his 'twelve healers' in the English countryside, during the long walks he took when convalescing from an acute illness which nearly took his life. He was a very sensitive man, regarded by some as a psychic. He was so aware of subtle energy changes that he could touch the morning dew from a petal to his lips, and experience the physical symptoms and emotional states which that flower's essence was the antidote for. He realised that the dew from flowers which had been in the morning sun was more potent than that of flowers which had been in the shade. Since he was *not* following the 'law of similars' and he did not want to pulverise his flowers, he sought a method of preparation which would be simpler and more natural than homoeopathic potentisation. He wanted to preserve the life-force within the flowers (considered by many to be the strongest expression of the life-force on our planet). To his delight, he found that if he placed the picked flowers on the surface of a bowl of spring water, and left the bowl in sunshine for a few hours, the water would become charged with the flower's energetic vibrational signature. The charged water was then preserved in alcohol, forming exactly the same solutions that you can buy today.

Bach was also a very spiritual man, who believed in the existence of the 'higher self' or soul. Bach believed that illness occurs when disharmony or conflict are blocking the directives of the higher self from being lived out in the personality. (You can think of the higher self like the conductor of an orchestra, which is composed of the 'sub-personalities' thatconstitute the various roles you play – of wife, mother, rider, business woman and so on. When your conductor cannot be heard over the din of your orchestra, and the various players are trying to out-do each other, you have a problem!) Bach also believed that the appropriate flower essence would have the same wavelength as the energy potential of the higher self which was seeking expression; that it would make contact with this energy, wash over the blockage, and reinforce the potential of the higher self so that it could be realised in the personality.

Not surprisingly, the remedies do not work directly on the cellular systems of the physical body, but on the subtle energy body. If homoeopathy lies at the borderline of the physical and the etheric (or energy) body, the flower remedies influence the more subtle realms of non-physical matter, which vibrate at higher octaves. This means that they have no physical side-effects, that they can be used alongside any other form of treatment, and that taking the wrong remedy simply has no effect.

The Bach Centre in England still produces Bach's original thirty-eight remedies, which are regarded as a complete system, and which are widely available in health food shops and even some chemists. But since the 1970s remedies have also been produced from the flowers native to other countries, including Australian bush flower remedies, American cactus remedies, and even gem remedies, made by leaving gem stones in water. *Bach Flower Therapy, Theory and Practice*, by Mechthild Scheffer, is a good introduction to the remedies, and there are a number of small handbooks about them, including *The Twelve Healers and Other Remedies* by Edward Bach himself.

Each of the remedies can be used as either a 'type remedy', which you or your horse might need at intervals during the course of your life, or as a 'helper remedy', which is useful for temporary states which are not characteristic. Whilst working on this book I have sometimes resorted to taking elm, which is for people who 'feel that the task they have undertaken is too difficult, and not within the power of a human being'! Other remedies address states of fear (both of known and unknown origin), grief, despair, mistrust, jealousy, pride or apathy. The full list cannot fail to include states which you recognise in yourself, as well as in people and horses of your acquaintance!

The best known of Bach's remedies is Rescue Remedy, which is a combination of rock rose for terror and panic, cherry plum for hysteria and loss of control, clematis for the tendency to pass out or feel 'far away', star of Bethlehem for shock and trauma, and impatiens for irritability and tension. It is always worth having Rescue Remedy on hand (for at the very least, it can do no harm), and it can be a useful preventative medicine when you are faced with a big undertaking which will make you and/or your horse extremely nervous. If the worst happens, and you have an accident or upset which calls for emergency measures, I would recommend dosing all concerned – as well, of course, as arranging the necessary veterinary treatment – for you and your horse will be shocked and traumatised.

Dosing your horse is simple: ten drops from the stock bottle can be added to his water bucket, or four drops can be placed on a lump of sugar. To dose yourself, the best procedure is to add two drops from the stock bottle to a 30ml medicine bottle with a pipette, which is three-quarters filled with natural spring water. The mixture can then be topped up with water, or with brandy (if it is to be kept for over three weeks in cool climates, or one week in hotter ones). Vigorously shaking the solution before use makes it more potent, and storing it in the refrigerator is advisable. The dose for humans is four drops put directly into the mouth four times daily, always on an empty stomach, and being careful not to contaminate the dropper. This should include first thing in the morning and last thing at night. In an acute case – when you are most likely to be dosing with Rescue Remedy – four drops can be given every ten to thirty minutes. Animals can be similarly treated. (The dropper must obviously be plastic if you are going to use this method to dose your horse, and a 1ml or 2ml plastic syringe works well.) Animals usually respond faster than us, with more established emotional states often requiring only from three to ten days of treatment. Persistent emotional states in people may require much longer term use of the remedies.

Radionics

Yet more strange in its workings than any of the approaches we have discussed so far is radionics. But in the equestrian world in the UK it has great acceptance, and has become almost an established part of British eccentricity. (An unfortunate court case in America in the 1960s led to radionics being declared illegal there.) Many desperate horsemen have sought help from 'the black box', which has earned a reputation for analysing the underlying causes when a horse is showing symptoms or behaviour which may have perplexed vets, or which has not responded to orthodox treatment. A radionic analysis determines imbalances within the horse's energy system, and it has often been able to pin down a problem where more established methods have failed. Treatment is also given radionically, and often the practitioner also recommends treatment from other sources. These many include chiropractics, homoeopathic or flower remedies, or even orthodox medicine, as well as changes in diet, care and routine.

The practitioner works with the help of a 'witness' – for example, some hair from the horse's mane. For by the holographic principle, every part of the system (including the DNA in the horse's hair) contains information about the total energetic structure of the entire system. Even more strange is the way that this energetic, holographic link between patient and witness is maintained over time and at any distance – even

'A radionic analysis has often been able to pin down a problem where more established methods have failed.'

across the world – so the hair can be used for an analysis no matter how far away the patient is, and throughout the whole of his life.

The instruments used in radionics have been developed and refined since the early part of this century, and with that they have become quicker and easier to use. But the sensitivity and skill of the operator has remained extremely important, for in arriving at her diagnosis she must use her skill in 'radiesthesia' – her psychic sensitivity to subtle radiation of varying vibrational frequency. One of the simplest techniques used by the practitioner in her diagnosis is to ask yes/no questions using a pendulum, which swings in one way for 'yes' and another for 'no'. (This is not dissimilar to the principle underlying the muscle test used by practitioners of Applied Kinesiology and other complementary therapies.)

In the early 1950s the analysis of a patient's condition, using a pendulum in conjunction with the radionics instruments, could take up to a day; now it can be completed in less than an hour. An analysis begins by asking whether the etheric or higher energy bodies are operating at optimum, or whether they are over- or under-stimulated. If the latter, further questions ask if this is due to congestion, infection, blockage, stress, or damage. Each of the energy centres relating to different parts of the body (e.g. the heart centre, which controls the cardiovascular system) is checked to see if it deviates from the norm. Sometimes a problem exists only in the energy body, and has not yet manifested as disease, so it can be treated *before* it appears physically.

Then the physical systems of the body are checked to discover the discrepancy between perfect functioning and actual functioning in each of them, for both the whole system and the worst point within that system. So the practitioner reads down a list of locations within the structure, relying on the pendulum's response to tell her where the worst point is (e.g. the fifth cervical vertebra within the skeletal system). As she measures and records any malfunctions, she builds up an energetic 'picture' of the patient – and her analysis is not complete until she discovers the main cause or causes which underlie the condition, be they physical or psychological.

More questions determine the treatment needed. The practitioner then uses the radionic machines to broadcast therapeutic frequencies of subtle energy to the patient. These may be the functional patterns of organs, the energy patterns of elements, herbs, or psychological states, or the mirror-image pattern of a virus or bacteria. Like homoeopathic remedies, this is a way of matching the frequency of a disease with the frequency needed for healing. The witness provides a two-way energetic link, which not only allows information to flow from the patient to the practitioner, but also enables the patient to benefit from distant therapy. Then, when the fundamental causes of disharmony are identified and corrected, the patient's own natural healing forces take over.

Conditions which appear suddenly and are treated at once usually clear up very quickly, whilst long-standing conditions are much slower to respond. Horses and other animals often respond more quickly and successfully to treatment than people, for we will sometimes have a vested interest in remaining sick. One extremely interesting case history of radionic analysis concerned a number of racehorses in training, who were running extremely well at home, but who never lived up to expectations on the racecourse. No reason for this could be established, until a radionic practitioner discovered that they were suffering from carbon monoxide poisoning as a result of inhaling exhaust fumes in the lorry on the way to the racecourse. With a new exhaust pipe fitted, they ran extremely well.

Acupuncture

Acupuncture is the longest-standing and most thoroughly documented treatment within the energy modalities. Many of the vets who practice it also practice homoeopathy, so the two are often used in conjunction. Like all of the complementary therapies, acupuncture is dismissed by some, and romanticised by others; but whilst it is not a cure-all, there is much experimental evidence for its validity. In Chapter 2 (on page 50) we discussed the lower electrical resistance at acupuncture points, the passage of radioactive isotopes along the acupuncture meridians, and the early formation of the meridian ducts in the developing embryo (preceding the formation of the organs). Researchers into esoteric medicine believe that the acupuncture points and the meridian system provide a pathway for the energy in the etheric body to enter the physical body, and make its way to the internal organs. (Interestingly, the word 'meridian' is a translation from the French of the Chinese word 'jingluo', with 'jing' meaning 'to go through' and 'luo' meaning 'something that connects' or 'a net'.) The Chinese call this energy Qi – a subtle energy which permeates our environment as well as us. It gives us our vitality, and in the Indian system of thought is known as 'prana'.

The Chinese believe that disease manifests firstly within the subtle body, then in the meridian system, and finally in the organs. So the story (which unfortunately documents one of Chinese medicines' failures) is told of an ancient Chinese emperor who went to his physicians feeling unwell. They took his pulses, and made their diagnosis. 'Sir,' they said, 'you have a disease of the energies. We shall treat it using herbs.' So the emperor took his medicine and all remained well for some time. When the symptoms reappeared, he returned again to his doctors. 'Sir,' they said, 'you have a disease of the meridians. We shall treat it using acupuncture.' Again he responded positively to the treatment, and it was quite some time before he returned to them again. 'Sir,' they said, 'you now have a disease

'The Chinese believe that disease manifests firstly within the subtle body, then in the meridian system, and finally in the organs.'

of the organs. We are sorry, but we cannot help you.' His illness might well have reached the stage where only the heroic tactics of Western medicine could have saved his life – for severe pathologies like tumours and diseases of the spinal cord cannot be treated by acupuncture.

Most Western research on acupuncture has centred around its effects on pain, for this aspect of acupuncture made the greatest sense to Western minds. The 'Gate Control Theory' suggests that pain signals cannot reach the brain when there is acupuncture stimulation of peripheral nerves which reach the spinal cord *above* the level where the pain impulse reaches it. Research has also shown that acupuncture stimulates the release of the body's own painkillers, the endorphins and enkephalins which work rather like morphine. By fitting into a 'keyhole' in certain cells of the brain, they prevent neurochemicals which carry the message of pain from fitting in. Interestingly, it is now thought that a twitch placed around the horse's nose has exactly the same effect as acupuncture stimulation, leading to the release of endorphins, and encouraging the horse to stand quietly when one would expect such a painful procedure to make him even more fractious! Neither of these models completely explains the workings of acupuncture, and there are other factors involved which make its effects much broader than pain relief. But the pain control theories have at least stimulated more scientific enquiry, and given Western minds a theory to grasp on to.

'A body which is brought into energetic balance is able to muster all of its innate healing forces, often speeding the healing process by over 50%.'

As well as reducing pain, acupuncture can be used diagnostically, to locate soreness which has not revealed itself to the usual diagnostic techniques. It can stimulate the body to release its own natural chemicals – like the steroid cortisol, which reduces inflammation. It can normalise the body's functions – from blood pressure, pulse and respiration rates, to hormone secretion, and the motility of the gut. Horses who are prone to colic, or to bronchial disorders, and those who under-perform because they do not sweat, have had their body's functioning normalised by acupuncture. It stimulates the immune system, releases muscle spasms, and increases circulation in areas of the body where the healing response needs to be enhanced. In short, a body which is brought into energetic balance is able to muster all of its innate healing forces, often speeding the healing process by over 50% – and there are rarely any of the complications which dog orthodox medicine.

The difficulty that Westerners have with acupuncture (which is the primary health-care system for one quarter of the world's population) stems at least in part from our unease with the Chinese philosophy which accompanies it. Yet many veterinary acupuncturists make it clear that a Westernised 'cook-book' version of acupuncture based on using a certain point for a certain disease is limited in its effects, and that following the Chinese map and philosophy leads to much better results. Qi energy circulates through the entire meridian system once every twenty-four hours. There are twelve meridians on each side of the body, and Qi is concentrated in each of them for approximately two hours. Each of the twelve is named after and related to a specific organ or organ system, and the meridians are paired, with one lying on the top of the body, and the other on the underside. If one of the pair shows an excess in energy, its sister meridian will show a deficiency. Another two meridians bisect the body – the governing vessel running from the upper lip to the underside of the tail, and the conception vessel running from the lower lip to pubic bone, but they are not related to specific organs.

Fig. 10.1 The yin/yang symbol in which each contains a trace of the other.

One meridian in each pair is yin, and one is yang. These are the eternal opposites, which need to be in balance for the body to function normally. Yin and yang do not cause each other, and they are not absolutes, so there is always yin within yang and yang within yin. They co-exist and flow into each other, with each containing a trace of the other – just as day follows night and night follows day, without *causing* each other, and without either being absolute darkness or absolute light. So there can be no yin without yang, just as there is no night without day, no cold without hot, no negative without positive, and no female without male. The traditional yin/yang symbol, in which each contains a small dot of the other (see Fig. 10.1), shows well how they inter-relate. The Chinese consider their imbalance to be due to 'pernicious influences', which can be climatic (including cold, damp, wind and heat), nutritional, emotional, or traumatic. For the horse, this can also include the effects of poor saddling and shoeing, so treatment must view the horse from a holistic perspective, taking these into account.

A normal balance of energy flow between yin and yang is needed in the meridians for body, mind and spirit to remain in perfect health. If the flow of Qi becomes disordered, the normal processes which maintain balance and harmony are also disturbed, and disease (or maybe only dis-ease) is the result. A yin problem shows up as underactivity, so infections or tumours which result from an underactive immune system are yin disorders. A yang problem shows up as overactivity, so auto-immune

conditions resulting from an overactive immune system are yang disorders
The role of acupuncture is to balance that energy; it is not the search-and-
destroy mission of orthodox medicine, and it does not assume that any
one symptom will have *one* cause (an all too common trap in Newtonian
thinking).

The energy flow within the meridians follows the five-element theory,
in which all natural phenomena are categorised as either wood, fire, earth,
metal or water. Each element is related to an organ (e.g. the spleen, which
is yin) and one of the hollow viscera (e.g. the stomach, which is yang),
and with their corresponding meridians. In the Cycle of Generation each
element produces the succeeding element: so *fire* produces *earth* by
burning wood, and creating ashes which are returned to earth. *Earth*
produces *metal* (as mineral deposits), and *metal* produces *water* (since water
sources are often found near mineral deposits, and water condenses on
metal). *Water* produces *wood* (by being absorbed through the roots of
trees), then *wood* produces *fire* and fire produces earth. (See Fig. 10.2.)

In the Cycle of Destruction each element destroys or absorbs the
succeeding element: so wood can injure earth (since roots penetrate the
soil), earth controls water (via dams), water injures fire (by putting it out),
fire destroys metal (by melting it) and metal destroys wood (as an axe cuts
down a tree), and so the cycle begins again. The lungs and the large
intestine relate to metal, and if the lungs are damaged and are using all
their energy to maintain their function, the imbalance will affect water

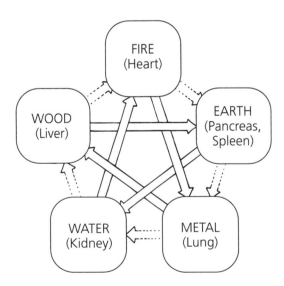

*Fig. 10.2 The five elements of Chinese medicine. The pentagonal pattern forms the cycle of
generation, and the inner star-like pattern forms the cycle of destruction.*

(the next element in the Cycle of Generation). Water relates to the kidneys and bladder, and this connection between lungs and kidneys also exists in the Western medical map. For if blood-oxygen levels are low the kidneys produce a hormone which increases the haemoglobin level in the blood, helping the transportation of scarce oxygen throughout the body.

Despite the apparently fanciful nature of the Chinese explanation for acupuncture, these cycles are really rather complex, and it is probably easiest for us to think of Qi flowing through the meridians like electricity in a circuit. If the energy flowing in the heart meridian is weak, for instance, there is poor circulation, and this can predispose the horse to joint problems. If these lead to lameness, painkillers will only alleviate the symptoms. Drugs or nutraceuticals which enrich the synovial fluid and block the breakdown of cartilage will at least begin to address the problem. But in the Chinese model this has not dealt with the underlying cause – so it is inevitable that the treatment will need frequent repetition. Horses with arthritis respond to balancing the kidney or liver meridian, which relate to bone, and to tendons and ligaments respectively

Another example of imbalance is provided by a friend of mine who was suffering from recurring ear infections, and who became very unhappy about repeatedly taking antibiotics. When she resorted to acupuncture treatment, this revealed a greatly reduced energy flow in the kidney meridian (which ends in the ear). With this rebalanced she has had no more infections – a clear illustration of the difference between a holistic approach which seeks the primary causes of disease, and our Western approach which is so often limited to symptomatic care.

The flow of Qi can be encouraged or reduced in the various meridians by stimulating these, usually with needles, and using points which may be far removed from the seat of the presenting problem. (Severe headaches in people, for instance, are often relieved by inserting a needle into a point on the underside of the big toe which goes by the name of Liver Three.) With people, another form of treatment is the burning of the herb moxa: a small pile of this is placed directly over an acupuncture point and lit. It smoulders rather like a cigarette, warming the point and thus stimulating the circulation and the flow of Qi. This makes it particularly useful in chronic yin conditions in which both of these are blocked. In equine acupuncture, practitioners hold a stick of moxa, rather like a large cigar, near the acupuncture point, and keep one hand beside the point so they can tell when it becomes hot. However, since the technique is a potential fire hazard in stables, many practitioners do not use it at all.

In places, the meridians run deep within the body, whilst at others they reach the surface, and this is where most of the acupuncture points lie. Different classes of point are, in effect, like different classes of electrical boosters or switches. Treatment is then like restoring current flow by

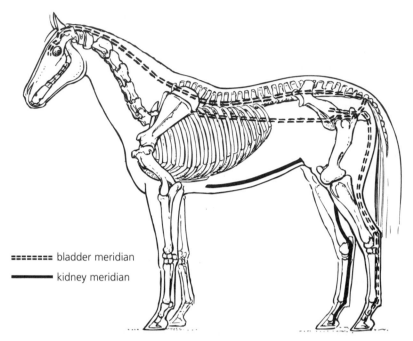

========= bladder meridian
━━━━━━ kidney meridian

Fig 10.3 The bladder meridian on the horse.

turning on circuit breakers, repairing short circuits, or turning up dimmer switches which have caused a reduction in the current. The 'master points' are like main transformers of primary power lines, and they affect a large area of the body or a major system like the muscular system. The twelve 'alarm points' – one on each of the organ meridians – are much more specific, each relating to that particular organ. (Interestingly, Western medicine had found only one of these, which is commonly used in the diagnosis of appendicitis.) These are like the fuses in a fuse box, which tell you which part of the electrical system in your house has shorted out. Then there are the twelve 'associated points', all located along the bladder meridian (Fig. 10.3). These are associated to each of the twelve organ meridians, to the organs themselves, and also to the anatomical structures underlying each specific meridian path.

This makes the bladder meridian extremely useful in diagnosis. Sensitivity in the point which is associated with, for instance, the lung meridian (which is bladder point 13), implies trouble either along the lung meridian, or in the lung itself. If there is no sensitivity in the lung alarm point, then the dysfunction in energy flow must lie somewhere along the lung meridian. This would lead an experienced veterinary acupuncturist to suspect that there could be a problem on the inside of a front leg, at a point exactly beneath the path of the meridian.

Other points used in treatment are the entry and exit points where energy enters and leaves each meridian, and the source points which communicate directly with the organ after which each meridian is named. Then there are the local or trigger points which may or may not be numbered points on the meridians, but which become temporarily sensitive when there is a local injury or imbalance. These are like the electrical switch for a specific appliance in your home. There are several other types of points as well, each with a particular use, and diagnosis follows a specific logic in which one sensitive point leads the practitioner to another until she tracks down the root cause of the problem.

To become sophisticated in her practice, she has to have a very deep knowledge of the meridians, the location and use of their various points, and of the anatomical structures which underlie them. With sixty-seven points on the bladder meridian and between nine and forty-five on each of the others, a veterinary acupuncturist has to know her stuff! She also needs to appreciate the varying sensitivity levels of different horses, knowing that the response shown by a Thoroughbred will be far more obvious than that of a warmblood. The sophistication of acupuncture diagnosis helps to ensure that the original problem is treated: it is all too common, for instance, for a dysfunction in a hind leg to lead to a compensatory lameness in the foreleg which is forced to bear more weight, and for that alone to be addressed by orthodox veterinary treatment. This treats the symptom and not the cause. In contrast, skilled acupuncture diagnosis also detects problems which have not yet manifested as a structural change (even in a distant part of the body), but which are apparent as dysfunctions within the energetic system.

'Skilled acupuncture diagnosis detects problems which have not yet manifested as a structural change.'

Whilst an acupuncturist who treats you will diagnose your condition by taking your pulses, these are more difficult to interpret in animals, so it is palpation of the points themselves which yield the most useful clues. This can become far more subtle than the presence of pain and muscle spasm – sophisticated instruments can be used to detect changes in electrical energy at various points of the skin, but the most sensitive practitioners feel those changes in their fingers. They notice changes in temperature, tension and tissue resistance, and ultimately a sense of an attraction or repulsion which is almost magnetic in its quality. For where there is excess energy at an acupuncture point, there is a build-up of positive charges, and in a case of energy deficiency, there is usually a build-up of negative charges. Learning to sense this obviously takes time, but rest assured that it is possible.

Back in antiquity, the original Chinese needles predate the use of metals, and were made of stone. Later, metallic needles could be up to 12 inches/30cm long, allowing the practitioner to reach deep-seated points. These points and this length of needle are not used in our Western version of acupuncture – sterile, disposable 28 gauge 2 inch/50mm stainless steel needles are the norm for horses. These are much finer than hypodermic needles, and are solid rather than hollow. They are flexible, so it is extremely rare for them to break. Interestingly, after the identification of the AIDS virus, acupuncturists began using disposable needles with plastic handles, and the effectiveness of their treatments on people diminished. When disposable needles were then made with *metal* handles they improved again, suggesting that the practitioner's energy system is somehow involved in the treatment.

There is evidence that ancient peoples used acupuncture with elephants, water buffaloes, camels, horses, oxen, cattle and pigs. Chinese charts which show equine acupuncture points date back over two thousand years, going back at least as far as the Tang Dynasty (AD618-906), during which the first veterinary school was founded. There are over seven hundred acupuncture points on the horse, but these are not so well mapped as in man. Our meridians end on different fingers and toes, and since our five digits have become *one* digit during the evolution of the horse, the positioning of these end points is not so clear, and there are several proposals about their locations. It is important to use the exact points, so it is usually easier to utilise points on the body itself, and these vary in size from pin-points to about 1 inch/25mm in diameter.

Needles are much easier to insert in acupuncture points than they are in other places, where they will often simply not go in. Skilfully used, the needles very rarely draw blood – they push the tissues apart rather than penetrating them. If the horse is fairly relaxed, he feels little more than a pin prick as the needles are inserted, and most horses become relaxed and even drowsy both during and after a treatment. (A dozing horse full of needles makes a bemusing sight, and only a small proportion of horses resent the needles so much that a cold laser is the only viable way to stimulate the acupuncture points.) The effect of needling can be increased by twirling the needles, or by moving them up and down. A resistance may be felt when doing this, which is due to the grasp of the muscle, and it indicates that the correct point has been found. The resistance usually dies away within a few minutes, allowing the needle to be withdrawn easily, and acupuncture treatments usually last from fifteen to twenty minutes.

When compared to other animals, horses are extremely responsive to acupuncture. There may be a visible difference to a horse's condition within a few minutes of the treatment commencing, although it could take hours or sometimes days. Initially the improvement may be short-lived, but after further sessions it should last longer. Treatments are usually

'Compared to other animals, horses are extremely responsive to acupuncture.'

repeated weekly, although this interval could vary from two days to two weeks. If there is no improvement after three weekly treatments, it is unlikely that the horse will respond to acupuncture (not, at least, with that practitioner; another more skilful one may well be able to help). Occasionally the symptoms worsen after a treatment, although this is usually followed by improvement within two to five days. Some horses only experience this healing crisis the first time they are treated; but it suggests that the horse may be hypersensitive to acupuncture, and care must be taken not to overstimulate him in further treatments.

There are a number of variations on the theme of acupuncture, with acupressure and shiatsu (see page 186 in Chapter 7) being two which you can learn to utilise yourself. They are much more non-specific, however, and can interfere with other treatments. If you want to invest money in home treatment you can buy a 'Bioscan', which has a battery-operated box-of-tricks attached to a small metal comb. This is used to scan the body for reactive acupuncture points, emitting a bleep when it finds one. Reactive points can then be treated with a probe which emits either visible red light or infra-red light. (So we now enter the realm of laser acupuncture, which overlaps with the work of some physiotherapists.) The biggest limitation of the system, however, is that it can also respond to damp and/or dirty areas of the horse's skin. There are a number of similar and more sophisticated systems like this in use with people, some of them computerised and able to make very precise diagnoses. On comparison with Western medical diagnoses, the use of these machines has shown that each of the acupuncture meridians is indeed associated with the organ it is named after. This has provided supportive evidence for the Chinese system.

A veterinary acupuncturist may embellish his work with needles by injecting various solutions into the acupuncture points. Vitamin B_{12} is commonly used, as are saline solution and various homoeopathic and herbal solutions. These prolong the effects of treatment, stimulating the point for another ten or fifteen minutes after the needles have been removed. Alternatively, with needles still inserted, the patient can be made part of an electrical circuit to give mild electrical stimulation to the points. (I have had this kind of treatment myself, and it yields a surprisingly pleasant sensation. Again, it is not dissimilar to the electrical treatment used by physiotherapists.) Instead of needling, the points can be stimulated with ultrasound or a cold laser. This is particularly useful for points on the legs – which are harder to find and to insert a needle into – or for very fractious horses.

An interesting study performed at the University of Pennsylvania involved 200 horses from seven breeds whose performance was marred by back pain. This was diagnosed from their history, and from physical symptoms, which included sinking when being girthed or mounted, reluctance to trot, canter or jump, hind leg lameness or dragging toes, teeth grinding and tail swishing. In 14 of the cases X-rays were also used. Some of the horses had previously undergone treatments involving rest and anti-inflammatory drugs, but during the acupuncture treatments they were kept in work. Evaluations were performed before, during and after the treatments by the researchers, and also by each horse's rider or trainer, and by the referring veterinarian. Back pain was considered to be alleviated if (a) examination did not reveal the clinical signs associated with it; (b) if the horse was able to perform normally for its intended use; and (c) if the owner thought the performance of the horse was normal. If *one* of the evaluators did not think the horse had improved enough to fulfil these criteria, it was considered to have no change in its condition.

In the study, 15 horses were treated by traditional needle acupuncture: of these 13 (87%) fulfilled the criteria for the alleviation of back pain. Another group of 15 horses received laser acupuncture, and 11 of these (73%) showed the required improvements. The largest study group, 155 horses, had the appropriate acupuncture points injected with 0.5ml of sterile saline solution without preservatives, and of these 139 horses (90%) met the criteria for improvement. In the most disappointing group, 8 of the 15 horses (53%) injected with 0.5ml of sterile saline without preservatives and 0.5ml of methylprednisolone acetate fulfilled the criteria for improvement. This last group of horses were, however, treated only once, and the researchers recommended *eight* weekly treatments during which the horse should maintain its normal training regime. The results suggest that there is little to choose between the various forms of acupuncture, and although some vets now solely use laser acupuncture, the majority stick to more traditional techniques; but the blending of old and new is bound to lead to proliferation of these treatments, which may well prove to be the medicine of the future.

An overview

The vast majority of the horses seen by veterinarians who practise herbalism, homoeopathy and acupuncture are those who suffer from the chronic conditions that conventional medicine cannot quite cure. Usually this complementary treatment is the owner's last resort, which is unfortunate, given that any treatment is more effective if given at the beginning of a disease process. Very few people use these modalities as they should ideally be used – as preventative medicine, treating imbalances before they manifest as disease in the physical body, or whilst a horse (or person) shows only slight symptoms. The few who *do* use these treatments preventatively believe that treating horses as rarely as twice a year results in fewer injuries, faster healing, and a reduced need for medication.

The conditions which commonly lead us to dose our horses with bute, steroids and antibiotics can very often be treated with herbalism, or with a combination of acupuncture and homoeopathy. The Chinese have never used acupuncture as a complete system in its own right: it is part of their traditional system of medicine, with herbal treatment forming another important component. Combining homoeopathic treatment with the use of herbs is often not advisable, however, for they can 'argue', so when treating horses homoeopathically, care must be taken in the use of herbal feed supplements. It is vitally important not to use conflicting systems of medicine, which means that a vet using complementary techniques must always communicate with the horse's usual vet, and be aware of any drugs which have been used – particularly those which compromise the workings of the immune system. In the UK if you wish to refer a case for complementary treatment you will have to ask your usual vet even if he is not currently treating your horse for that specific condition. However, he is not allowed to refuse your request, and keeping him informed of your progress with the new system may help to bridge the schism which exists between both approaches – which are both valid and helpful when the right choices are made.

As we have seen, acupuncture is particularly successful in treating locomotor and musculo-skeletal disorders. Garrison Savannah, the horse who won the Cheltenham Gold Cup in March of 1990, had seriously damaged a shoulder during a previous race, and early in the year it seemed unlikely that he would run. But two months of acupuncture and careful training brought him back again – and three weeks after the Gold Cup he was second in the Grand National! Some practitioners use acupuncture in isolation; others believe that it will be of limited benefit unless structural problems have first been corrected by chiropractic treatment. Full-blown cases of navicular, spavin, arthritis, and the other degenerative joint diseases also respond well, usually to a combination of acupuncture and homoeopathy. The pessimism of modern medicine, however, leads us to expect that any diagnosis of osteoarthritis will ultimately be the kiss of death, for changes in the bone are commonly regarded as irreversible.

As we learned in Chapter 2, bone is not an inanimate structure, and the bone cells within the body are replaced every two hundred days. This gives scope not only for a condition to worsen, but also for it to improve. If the body is simply conforming to an 'energetic blueprint', the theory of energy medicine predicts that bone growth and/or reabsorption can be guided and stimulated to create healing, and to allow a large percentage of horses to return to full work. In practice this is indeed the case, and the improvement is achieved without the use of anti-inflammatory drugs, whose main aim is to reduce or mitigate the symptoms of the problem.

The treatment of spavin by the orthodox and complementary systems

'Full-blown cases of navicular, spavin, arthritis, and the other degenerative joint diseases respond well, usually to a combination of acupuncture and homoeopathy.'

illustrates well the effects of utilising or ignoring the body's innate healing potential. Under the conventional treatment of spavin, the bones in the affected part of the hock joint are encouraged to fuse; the horse is put on bute and made to work. As the damaged part of the hock seizes up it will usually stop hurting, and the bute is no longer needed. But the 'healing' can put referred stress onto other parts of the joint, and the reduced flexibility of the hock joint may also affect the stifle and fetlock. In complementary treatment, the practitioner would attempt to remobilise the entire joint, remodelling the bones involved and restoring normal function if at all possible. This could require the use of acupuncture and homoeopathy (choosing the remedy most appropriate to the symptoms and constitution of this particular horse).

An holistic approach to the problem also means that saddling, shoeing, work, and nutrition must all be examined so that they too can play a supporting role. Herbal medicine is another viable approach, and one of the (now) leading producers of herbal remedies in the UK began to sell her wares after success with her own horse's developing spavin led to tremendous interest from friends. A multi-national company was spawned from a few bags of herbs supplied to them, followed by contact with a local feed merchant, and a few tiny adverts in the national press. This tremendous success story is testament to a huge demand that was simply waiting for someone to meet it.

Navicular disease must be one of the most dreaded diagnoses of all, but veterinary surgeons using complementary techniques find that 90 per cent of navicular cases respond well to treatment, and horses who were badly affected are often rideable again within a few months! Six months is usually needed to see a lasting improvement – with renewed expansion of the heels and frog, and a reduction in pain. Corrective farriery also supports this process, often with the use of an egg-bar shoe, or by grooving of the wall near the heels. A search is made for any possible contributory factors in saddle fit, exercise routine, diet, teeth, and spinal alignment; and each horse is treated as an individual. With homoeopathic treatment in particular this requires that his temperament, type, likes, dislikes, appetite and thirst are taken into account, along with the particular characteristics of his symptoms.

The minority of horses who do not make a complete recovery are often able to hack out without showing symptoms. The few whose pathology is so far advanced that they do not respond at all to complementary treatment have usually been given high doses of bute or other anti-inflammatory drugs. These seem to inhibit the body's innate healing capacity, as well as damaging internal organs. Low doses given over short time periods do not affect the outcome of complementary treatment, and fortunately, drugs which are used to increase the blood circulation in the foot do not seem to reduce the chances of a complete recovery.

Laminitis is another dread disease, which responds very well to holistic treatment, even when advanced structural changes have taken place in the foot and the horse has been 'written off'. Again, treatment is backed up by strict attention to diet, giving only tiny amounts of quality hay which was made the previous year. This is often mixed with straw to increase fibre intake. Proprietary feeds which contain molasses, sugar-beet pulp, or other by-products of the sugar-refining industry are strictly avoided, and small amounts of 'straights' are given to carry the herbal medicines used. All this can involve the owner in quite an arduous system of care, which is backed up by careful and sympathetic farriery, and sometimes even chiropractic treatment. If a case is caught early, herbal treatments (using willow, devil's claw, and meadowsweet) provide rapid initial relief, and acupuncture has almost immediate painkilling effects. It also begins the longer term healing process, which is often aided by homoeopathy – the exact remedy (which could be hypericum, graphites, aconite, or belladonna, as well as a number of others) being determined by the specifics of the symptoms. Chronic cases obviously take longer to respond to treatment, and again, the few horses which do not respond have almost always received long-term treatment with steroids or other anti-inflammatory drugs.

Head-shaking, an extremely sinister scourge of the modern horse, has been less responsive to complementary treatment, but even a 50 per cent success rate is really quite impressive. The condition is often an allergy, which can apparently have many causes, including dust, pollens, flies, and sunlight. In some horses it is neurotic in origin; other causes are badly fitting tack, skeletal problems which need chiropractic attention, and nose, teeth or ear problems. But the horse's response to all of these causes is indicative of an impaired functioning of the immune system, and it is this which needs to be addressed. Orthodox treatments, which may include antihistamine injections, are an attempt to suppress the symptoms – but often they do not work for very long, and many desperate owners resort to covering their horse's nose with a bag made from a pair of old tights! Very often the onset of the condition can be traced to some initial sensitising stimulus, and reviewing the three months prior to the onset of symptoms can often reveal this – it could be an illness, injury, or even vaccination.

The healing potential of all the complementary systems – as well as of the body itself – is huge. Their use requires a different way of thinking about the body/mind, and about disease, and from an holistic perspective it becomes clear that much conventional treatment is like shutting the gate after the horse has bolted. From this perspective, it seems amazing

'From an holistic perspective it becomes clear that much conventional treatment is like shutting the gate after the horse has bolted.'

that the attempt to suppress symptoms rather than to stimulate healing has gone virtually unquestioned during this century. But most of us have known nothing else, and *culture* is such a hugely pervasive force that we become all but brain-washed into upholding the status quo. Orthodox medicine has increased our life expectancy hugely (although the quality of life of older people who take multiple drugs with multiple side-effects may be very poor); but perhaps history will look back on the rise of the drug companies as a mixed blessing. My only hope is that the powers-that-be appreciate the strength of public opinion, and the capacity of the complementary approaches to help both us and our animals, and to solve the current crises in health care.

CHAPTER ELEVEN

···
'Equus' – The Language of Training
···

SADLY, FOR THOSE of us who want to believe that women are the font of all wisdom, it is *men* who have made the greatest advances in understanding how horses 'tick'. Acting independently, a few notable young cowboys took it upon themselves to follow – and in some cases to live with – the herds of wild mustangs who inhabit the barren lands of the western states of America. This gave them a unique understanding of the ways of the horse. But the best of them took the study of equine behaviour within the herd one step further: they let the horses become their role models in determining how *we* need to 'tick' if we, as humans, are to make sense to horses, and meet them on their own home ground. For by talking to them in the language 'Equus', we save *them* from having to cross the great divide between our species. Traditionally, we have either coaxed or bullied them across, convinced that they – despite their (apparently) lesser intelligence – should learn to speak *our* language.

It is perhaps not surprising that the greatest advances in our understanding of 'Equus' should come from within one of the more brutal equestrian cultures, and be presented as a counterpoint to it. For these people went on to pioneer more humane ways to handle horses; they turned their backs on tradition, and stood up to say that the old ways are not the best. We in Europe would be horrified by some of the methods traditionally used in that culture, especially when breaking horses in, for in cowboy country – with its frontier mentality – the pitting of man against horse took on a very macho significance.

In moving away from this legacy, the leaders in that field have, I believe, surpassed our traditional European ways of handling horses and breaking them in. So, too, from a rather different perspective, has Linda Tellington-Jones. But times are changing in Europe as well, and many people, like myself, now have an ethical objection to the term 'breaking'. It contains the inherent suggestion that in order to produce a horse who is fit for riding, we have to 'break' something – presumably his spirit. A slave subdued by his master might well have been able to do his work on the frontier, but he cannot be a winner in any sphere of today's high-level equestrian competition. Now, he has to *want* to do it. Modern-day riders need an equine partner who genuinely *is* a partner.

Historically, the new wave of Western horse trainers (or behaviourists, as they might prefer to call themselves) probably began with a man called Tom Dorrance. Tom, whom I feel very privileged to have met, is now an old man, with an extremely delightful presence and a wealth of wisdom which he remains happy to share with any interested horse-person. Tom's book *True Unity*, was published in 1987. In it, he talks about his response to the riders who came to him because they thought they had a horse problem. It can be summed up in the phrase, 'I tell them that the horse is having a "people-problem".' He has often been called 'the horses' lawyer' because of his profound search to understand horses, to perceive the world from their viewpoint, and to communicate that viewpoint to their riders.

As far as a rider is concerned, says Tom, the horse may *not* be doing the right thing – but as far as the horse is concerned he always is, for self-preservation is his inevitable motivation. Tom teaches riders to cross the gap between species by 'operating from where the horse is' instead of trying to operate from where *they* are. He seeks an approach which 'can assure the horse that he can have his self-preservation and still respond to what the person is asking him to do.' He suggests that the rider's approach to training should be based on making the right thing easy and the wrong thing difficult – but not impossible, for the horse needs to feel that he has been given a choice. Then, he learns through making that choice, so that his mental, emotional, and even spiritual development are fostered by it.

> 'As far as a rider is concerned the horse may not be doing the right thing – but as far as the horse is concerned he always is, for self-preservation is his inevitable motivation.'

One of Tom's early pupils was Ray Hunt, who wrote *Think Harmony with Horses*, and who has become extremely well known in America as a teacher and lecturer in his own right. John Lyons and Pat Parelli are largely unknown to British readers, despite their books *Lyons on Horses* and *Natural Horse-Man-Ship*, but they too are household names in the *Who's Who* of modern Western horse trainers. Australia (another country with a frontier mentality) also has its share of forward-thinking horse trainers, and has been visited and influenced by these American riders. Each of them takes a somewhat different standpoint within the same broad philosophical approach. These differences – though important to them – seem relatively small when viewed from a completely different horse culture on the other side of the Atlantic ocean, so I hope they will forgive me for not delineating them as clearly as they might like.

The whole ethos of Western riders is to get from A to B whilst staying as comfortable as possible, and, historically, without scaring their cattle. The slow gaits of jog and lope serve this purpose well, and they are a lot less stressful to ride than trot and canter. (I have to confess, however, that watching a Western-trained horse does not excite me like watching the bounding power of a dressage horse.) Although Western riding may not have the same lofty aims as, say, dressage riding, when Western riders handle their horses from the ground they are far more precise than we are. We may want our horses to stand still as we mount, but we are rarely that particular about it – and one thing I can guarantee is that your horse will never become any more particular about anything than you are! We do not expect them to 'ground tie', i.e. to stay put until told they can move. We do not expect them to follow us if we are walking on our feet. We accept behaviour which Western trainers would *not* accept, and if our horses walk all over us we probably either watch out for our feet or lash out at them. We are unlikely to contemplate how we might set about defining the boundaries of our personal space.

....

Here, as I outline the ideas of these trainers, I am not equipping you with enough information to go away and start your young horse in a round pen, to teach him to 'spook in place', or to imprint your newly born foal. If I peak your interest you will have to go to source – to the Western trainers' own writings and video tapes, and ideally to them in person. You will need much more detailed information to ensure the safety of both you and your horse. It is the philosophy and broad general approach of these horsemen which I wish to convey here, and as I do so I am attempting to make you question your own philosophy and realise its limitations. This is an exercise in map-recognition – discovering the presuppositions, the limits, and the pitfalls, of the maps which are so much a part of our equestrian culture that we do not even question them.

The British-born, Western-trained rider Bob Mayhew has brought the teachings of the best Western trainers to the UK. There are a few practitioners qualified in Linda Tellington- Jones' TTEAM work who are resident in Britain, and more are in training. There are many more TTEAM practitioners in Europe, and Linda herself makes regular visits for demonstrations and clinics. But perhaps the greatest impact has been made by Monty Roberts. He was originally invited to England to show the Queen his 'advance and retreat' method of starting horses, and her enthusiasm led to some large public demonstrations. He is now a regular visitor to England, working primarily in Newmarket with racehorses who will not go into starting stalls. Richard Maxwell, who has apprenticed with him, is also making a name for himself as a trainer of difficult horses, and there are more practitioners of Monty's methods currently in training.

Monty grew up as the son of a hard-nosed Western horse breaker, and as a child he was beaten for his insistence that it must surely be wrong to subject horses to such brutality. Experimenting in a round pen (an enclosure of about 16 metres/yards diameter, with good footing and

'When Western riders handle their horses from the ground they are far more precise than we are.'

preferably with solid walls which the horse cannot see through or over), he started his first horse at seven, and by fifteen he had, in essence, developed his method. As an adult, he moved away from the Western tradition and began working with racehorses, and had a very successful business buying unbroken yearlings and selling most of them once they were working well. But throughout his childhood as he developed his method, his mother helped him to keep his unique approach a secret from his father, who never, to his death, believed that a horse could be anything other than 'broken'.

As Monty points out, this attitude is, perhaps, indicative of the inherent difficulties underlying the unlikely marriage of man and horse. It seems instinctively obvious that horses were made to be ridden, and the arguments against this have focused mostly on the horse's physiology, and the strain that our weight imposes on his back and legs. But consider the place that his species and ours each occupy on a continuum of animals, arranged between the extremes of those most likely to flee (mostly herbivores), and those most likely to fight (who are mostly carnivores). Only deer and antelope are flightier than horses; but no creature on earth is more prone to fighting than man. We have attacked virtually every species in existence, and we find occasion to fight each other even when it is clearly not in our best interests to do so!

After us come the big cats. But realise that as long as the big cat's stomach is full, both she and the antelope can co-exist peacefully on the plains of Africa. Man is the predominant predator of horse flesh, and in Italy alone 400,000 horses are eaten per year. But when our belly is full do we just let the horse graze? The answer is a resounding 'No!' – we make him carry us around the countryside, go show jumping, pull a plough, or play polo. The big cats torment their prey only when hungry, but we just cannot leave the poor horse alone.

'At the Equitana horse fair in Germany in 1993, one in three visitors bought whips.'

At the Equitana horse fair in Germany in 1993, one in three visitors bought whips, which were the best-selling item there. This implies that we also cannot resist the temptation to hit the horse as we 'train' him. But pain is the worst possible motivator, and its *least* harmful effect is to take the horse's attention away from what we are trying to communicate and onto the area of pain. Horses continually make it quite clear to us that they will only move away from the stick a limited number of times, and when a horse learns that he is going to live through a beating he often develops the kind of masochistic streak which leaves him standing there, as if to say 'Hit me, go on, do it again...'.

The horse responds to pain in the same way that babies respond to pain within their mouth. The baby who is teething instinctively wants to bite on something, moving *into* pain, not away from it. The horse too is programmed to move into pain: thus he kicks at the wolf who is hanging from his stomach, and does not to run away – which would almost inevitably lead to torn belly muscles, trailing intestines, and ultimately to his death. Similarly, when the bit causes the horse discomfort, he keeps pressing his body weight into it, and does not instinctively slow down and back away from it. There is ample evidence to suggest that violent behaviour with the hand or the stick rarely (if ever) benefits riders. Despite all the evidence of its dangers, we – with our supposed intelligence – continue to operate tunnel vision, and to bring our war-like instincts to bear on the horse.

About 90 per cent of horse-to-horse disagreements within the herd are settled without physical contact, and the communication system belonging to the species Equus is about seventy million years old. Our human communication system, in contrast, is less than two million years old. When we cross into other countries we need an interpreter; but the horse does not. His language is universal, understood by horses worldwide. Furthermore, horses read human body language far more efficiently than we do (remember Clever Hans – page 22), and often they know more about us than we know about ourselves. But we frequently present them with such wildly incongruent communication that we confuse their instincts. Much of my previous writing is about the attempt to be what animal trainer Vicki Hearne calls 'kinaesthetically legible' to the horses we ride. To be *illegible* or incongruent in either our handling or our riding, throws horses into a variety of survival mechanisms (just as it does with children); they 'space out', 'switch off', or become hyperactive.

> *'About 90 per cent of horse-to-horse disagreements within the herd are settled without physical contact.'*

Horses who have *not* been exposed to human contact speak 'horse' in human company more cleanly than the many who have been 'humanised' – especially if they have sold their soul for titbits. Monty Roberts believes that food should never be part of the reward system when training herbivores, for their stomach and their brain do not have the same kind of linkage as they do in carnivores. In either case, if the animal only performs for food, and then one day you have no food, you lied to him. Only when humans begin to read horses like horses read humans can our communication with them be 'clean'; but this is a very new (and perhaps also a very old) phenomenon, practised and taught by only a few individuals. This enables human-to-horse interaction – whether it takes place from the ground or from the saddle – to become a contract in which each party knows their role and bears responsibility for their actions, whether positive or negative in their consequences.

....

'Fight animals' face up to a challenge; 'flight animals' flee from one. The body language which states 'I challenge you' – involving eye contact, an upright posture, squared shoulders, and a projection of your energy – means 'Go away' to a horse. But to a bear it means 'Come on then!'. The converse – with rounded shoulders, lowered eyes, a withdrawal of your energy, and the axis of your shoulders turned away from the animal – tells the bear (with any luck) that you are not worth bothering about. But it invites the horse to come to you. The first action of the trainer in a round pen – even if the horse is virtually unhandled – is to say '*go away*'. Monty and the other trainers I have watched, maintain an aggressive posture as they walk purposefully around the pen in a small circle, throwing the end of a lunge rein towards the horse's quarters so that they keep him cantering. They do not use a whip, as their intent is not to cause pain. The horse begins to run, and the only place he can run is around the edge of the pen.

At this point, the horse is running for his life, and he has not yet realised that the trainer is actually in charge of the situation. When she (the trainer) is ready for this to dawn on the horse, she positions herself closer to the track so that the horse has to change direction to stay away from her. After a number of changes of direction, the horse begins to realise that the trainer is indeed running the show. The cue for these direction changes can gradually become more subtle: when the trainer is behind the line of the horse's wither, moving away from her means moving forward; if she steps in front of that line, moving away from her requires the horse to turn around and go the other way. She can test the sensitivity of her interaction with the horse by picking a spot, and seeing if she can turn the horse at precisely that point.

Meanwhile, as the horse's lungs begin to hurt, he is motivated to find a way out of his predicament. (Since his lungs feel the strain long before his legs, this method is physically much less stressful than many sceptical British trainers have supposed.) He moves his inside ear to the inside, signalling 'I can tell that you're important.' He moves his head and neck to the inside, and he begins to lick and chew, as if to say 'I'm eating, and I would not do this if I thought you were a predator.' His head and neck stretch down towards the ground in an act of subservience, which says, 'If we could have a meeting I'd let you be the chairperson.'

When she has received all of these signals, the trainer can change her message. Instead of being aggressive she becomes submissive. She coils up her lunge rein, looks down at the ground, rounds her shoulders, and does not project her energy. The horse stops running.★ As the horse slows

---

★*When lungeing, I have often noticed that as soon as I lose eye contact with the horse and look down, he will slow down or stop. This is the same mechanism in operation – and lungers who do not project their energy always have difficulty making the horse believe that they really do mean 'Go!'*

down and moves towards the centre of the pen, the trainer stands still; but once he has stopped, her walk follows a rounded, circuitous track, which gradually takes her up to him. If the horse shows any sign of moving away, the trainer backs off before he does; but remarkable as it seems, he will almost certainly remain standing there. Without looking at the horse, the trainer keeps moving towards him, until she can rub him between the eyes. Since this is one of the few parts of the horse's body that he cannot see, it requires a greater act of trust from him. Then she slowly moves away from him, following a figure of eight which has the horse's head at its centre, and each time she reaches his head she rubs him again. But the magical change may already have happened – for if the horse begins to *follow her* as she moves away, she has already achieved what Monty Roberts calls 'join up' and Ray Hunt calls 'hook up'.

Seventy per cent of horses will soon begin to follow the handler; it is as if she draws him towards her by turning her back on him and moving away with her eyes lowered and her shoulders rounded. The remaining 30 per cent of horses will turn and look at her as she moves around, keeping themselves looking squarely at her body. This is good enough. If the trainer has read the horse well and her timing is right, he will *not* move away from her; but if he does, she changes her posture, squaring up to him, becoming aggressive, and throwing the lunge line at his quarters again. Horse and human have both agreed to a contract: when the horse stays with her she will be nice to him; but as soon as he moves away, she will put him to work. When she does, it is as if she says, 'Too bad you did that. Because if you want to move away from me, you're going to have to *really* move away.' And then the whole process begins again.

An experienced trainer working in the round pen is unlikely to need to send the horse away a second time. She is speaking to the horse in his language – and even when she was still in her aggressive posture, the horse had asked her for a meeting. Now that she has taken on a rounded, submissive body posture she has become even more attractive to him, and he *chooses* to place himself at her disposal, following her every movement. Later, he will find a joy in submission which horses who have been coaxed or bullied into their contact with humans cannot share. For this is not the same as the 'progressive desensitisation', which is essentially the basis of our traditional European way of starting horses. In this – an approach which is also commonly used to treat people who have phobias – the frightening stimulus is broken down into small increments. A reward system provides some motivation for tolerating each one, and as each in turn is survived, more fearful ones are added. It is a long, slow, traumatic process.

One proof that the horse has *chosen* his contact with the trainer – rather than being coerced or bullied into it – is the ease with which he is about

....

He [the horse] will find a joy in submission which horses who have been coaxed or bullied into their contact with humans cannot share.'

....

to accept her touch, and the saddle. Once she has established 'join up' the horse will both follow her around the round pen and let her rub his face and neck whenever she stops. She works her way down to his back and quarters, and even picks up his feet. The proof of 'join up' is the way that he stands completely still for this, with absolutely no restraint. As another test, an assistant brings in a saddle and saddle pad, placing them on the ground in the middle of the pen. If the horse goes to break away from the trainer, she may need to put him back to work; but more commonly he follows her up to the saddle, and sniffs at it. She lets him sniff the saddle pad before she puts it on his back, checking that she still has 'join up' by inviting the horse to walk with her around the pen. Then she stops and puts on the saddle, girthing him up carefully, with just one hand on his headcollar or halter. Once the girth is tight enough to be safe she moves away from him, and if the horse does not break away by himself she sends him away again.

The vast majority of horses buck when they first feel the pressure of the girth against the ganglion of nerves just behind the elbow; but this does not alarm the trainer, who deliberately keeps her heart rate and breathing rate slow, delivering the message, 'Everything's fine; there's no cause for alarm.' She also appreciates that the horse *needs to know* if this thing on his back comes off. Once the horse is cantering more quietly round the pen he will signal that he is ready for 'join up' again, and the trainer can make her body submissive, move up to him, rub him between the eyes, and draw him to follow her. Then she picks up the bridle (preferably with a rubber-covered jointed snaffle) and puts it on. At this point Monty Roberts also introduces long lines; he passes an old stirrup leather under the horse's belly and ties the stirrups together. Then he passes the lines through the stirrups on each side, clipping them onto the bit rings. He can then send the horse away from him in canter, and work him on both reins, making several turns and also asking the horse to back up one step.

Now it is time for the rider to enter the round pen. The long lines are removed, the girth is checked, and as the rider leans across the saddle, the trainer holds the horse using a lunge line clipped onto the bit ring. After leading the horse for just a few moments she helps the rider put her foot into the stirrup and mount, sitting up very slowly. Again, the handler leads the horse and encourages him to turn his neck so that he sees the rider out of both eyes. Then she unclips the lunge rein and the rider then walks, trots and canters the horse on both reins. Very rarely does he buck – even when previous attempts to 'break' the horse have been unsuccessful. Once he has made the choice to 'join up' with humans he has a very different attitude to us, and all of our paraphernalia. Every time a new 'bogey' (like the saddle) appears, we are his sense of safety – and he relies on our judgment about whether or not it should be treated as a predator.

When the rider dismounts at the end of this 'traumatic' event, the horse will still demonstrate 'join up' by following the trainer around the pen. Would he do this if he did indeed feel traumatised or betrayed by her? She can take off the saddle and put it on again, moving much more normally this time, and still with no restraint. Monty Roberts usually does this whole process in half an hour to forty minutes, although it has taken him up to two hours. The next day, the horse spends less time in the round pen going through the same steps. Then he can go out for a short ride accompanied by a quiet horse.

If the horse is left unhandled after that first session in the round pen, and brought back into it two years later, he will go through the same steps as if the first time had been yesterday. With 90 per cent retention, he ranks as an 'A' student, and beats most of us hollow. Many people's response, even to the initial round pen session, is one of disbelief, for we all *know* that it takes several weeks to accustom the horse to being ridden. But 'progressive desensitisation' is one of the slowest, least effective ways of creating change in people – for it rarely addresses the root cause of a fear or phobia, and it contains no inherent leverage. Unlike people, the horse has no rational understanding of the process, and we compound his problems whenever we use the language 'human' to lead him into the unknown.

Whenever you speak English to the natives, it takes a very long time to get your message across – and like the horse, the natives may not be *motivated* to understand. The advance and retreat method utilises a very strong, natural motivation – for food, praise, and the reduction of fear all pall beside being able to stand still beside the trainer and *not* run round the pen. The horse's inherent laziness gives us the leverage we need to change his way of thinking, and thus to change his behaviour.

'The horse's inherent laziness gives us the leverage we need to change his way of thinking, and thus to change his behaviour.'

One of the most important and common misconceptions in our work with horses is the assumption that the horse speaks our language (and reads our mind) so well that he *knows our intention*. So let us suppose that we want to ride him over a ditch. He does not know if we want him to stand quietly a couple of feet away from the ditch, put one of his feet in it, all four feet in it, lie down in it, or step over the ditch to reach the other side. This means that many of his possible responses *might have been right*, or are a step on the way towards being right (and remember that as far as the horse is concerned, he is acting from self-preservation and thus he is *always* right).

Ditches and horse trailers must have caused innumerable human/horse

'Trainer John Lyons is adamant that it is always a mistake to start a lesson with your final goal.'

arguments, but there is no need for the long and bitter battles which ensue when we choose to define anything less than our final goal as failure. Thinking of a goal in segments, rather than as one huge chunk, is very liberating – and trainer John Lyons is adamant that it is *always* a mistake to start a lesson with your final goal. Segmenting your goals means that you can always decide to quit, for you are never more than a few seconds away from a small success. When we insist on 'winning' we become so goal-orientated that we completely lose sight of the damage our will can inflict, and we are run by the instinct to fight. We are acting from the standpoint of a one-language animal who believes that the horse can read her mind.

The way we can best define our intention to the horse is by *stopping doing whatever we were doing*, and if possible by moving away. So in the round pen, the trainer goes up to the horse, rubs him between the eyes, and moves away again. That defined standing still and being rubbed as the desired response. Each time she moves away, the horse does the equivalent of thinking, 'Oh, so that was it.' But if he exits before we get close to him, he is left with a lingering doubt about what our intentions really were. So if you were approaching a wild horse in the round pen, and he had not yet signalled that he was ready for 'join up', you could be 15 feet/4.5m away from him when you noticed the first signs of him deciding to run for it. If you immediately walked away, you would have defined your intention as only getting that close, and you would have erased the question in his mind about what you were going to do next. The more questions you can erase, the more confidence the horse gains in both himself and you (especially when whatever you are doing is a more attractive option than running round the pen!). After a number of times of moving away and returning to only the 15-feet/4.5m point, you have continued to reassure him that this is your intention. Then you may be able to move to 14 feet/4.2m.

This is the approach of John Lyons, who thinks more in terms of a 'stimulus-response' training programme than of 'join-up'. So he keeps raising the horse's level of apprehension, and then lowering it again. In our conventional training system, however, we rarely deliberately *lower* it through defining an ending. Instead we keep testing the horse by going one stage further as soon as he appears calm; and as we do this we keep him restrained, thwarting his instinct to flee. When we first put on a roller we probably have someone holding the horse in the confined space of the stable – and if he could run away, he probably would. As we keep doing more and more and more, the horse (if he could talk) might never stop wondering 'What the hell are they going to do next?'

The principle of segmented goals makes a tremendous difference to how you approach many other aspects of horse training. In creating a series of steps, John Lyons asks himself the question, 'What would be easier for the horse than X?', or 'Would it be easier or harder for the horse if we do Y instead of X?' So think of working with a head-shy horse, and touching his ears. Would it be easier or harder for him if we touch his ears for one second or for ten seconds? For ten seconds or a minute? One second is obviously the easiest; yet most of the people I know would move slowly and carefully aiming to touch the ear for at least ten seconds, or even to keep hold of it and refuse to let it go. But if they do this, they are starting with their goal, and risking that both they and the horse – from their opposite ends of the spectrum – become caught in the grip of a 'fight or flight' battle. The more steps we can break the goal down into, the faster we will get there, even though we appear to be travelling slowly. For both we and the horse are far less likely to get hurt, and the horse is far more likely to be calmer at the end of the session than he was at the beginning. To put our final goal in front of the horse is as ridiculous as presenting pre-school children with the classics of English literature and expecting them to read.

Supposing you want to worm your horse for the first time, using a syringe wormer. If you just attempt to stick it in his mouth, you are starting with your goal. Instead, you could put a clean, empty syringe in his feed. Next time you could put some honey on the syringe. When he has made a good job of licking this off in several feeds you could put honey round his mouth with your fingers. Then you could put honey *in* his mouth with your fingers, and honey round his mouth with the syringe. Soon you are putting honey in his mouth with the syringe, and then putting the wormer in his mouth (although he might appreciate a smear of honey to take the taste away and keep the tacit agreement you have made with him). If you plan to clip his ears you could again play the game of 'What would be less aggressive than X?' and break this into a large number of small steps, touching different parts of his body with different materials, until you finally touch his ears with the clippers.

Applying the same approach to trailer loading prohibits us from starting with the goal. There are many ways of getting a horse into a trailer, and all of them work sometimes; but few of them work consistently, even fewer will not endanger either horse or handler. When a method leaves the horse calmer at the end of the session than he was at the beginning, it has solved the problem of loading for a lifetime, and not just for a day. But a horse who is not calm *outside* of the trailer will certainly not be calm *inside* it. He is a danger to himself and others, and he may well be even more dangerous next time.

In his approach to trailer loading, John Lyons prohibits the use of ropes or lunge reins, the use of food (since we are trying to teach the horse to load, not to eat), and the presence of more than one person (since there

'There are many ways of getting a horse into a trailer, and all of them work sometimes; but few of them work consistently, even fewer will not endanger either horse or handler.

will not always be more than one person). He also prohibits the handler from going into the trailer (believing this to be inherently dangerous). Thus the horse must walk *past* her to load. He believes that the worst possible horse should not take longer than four hours to teach to load, although you may accomplish this in ten minutes. But note the wording here – *teaching* the horse to load has very different implications to just simply loading him.

When a horse will not go into a trailer John Lyons' response is to say "That horse ain't broke to lead." '

When a horse will not go into a trailer John's response is to say 'That horse ain't broke to lead.' For the trailer is simply a *distraction*, and the horse who is 'broke to lead' will lead anywhere. To 'lead' into the trailer he must pass the handler, so John's cue for forward movement involves him standing by the horse's left shoulder facing the side of the horse, with his left hand on the lead rope and his right hand holding a stiff dressage whip. He holds the lead rope about 6 inches/15cm from the clip, and wraps the free end around the horse's neck. He begins by raising the hand with the stick towards the horse's hip; then if necessary tickling him on his rump with the end of the whip, hitting with light, slow taps, and if all else fails hitting hard. He does this well away from the trailer. He never uses the rope to pull the horse forward, and does not walk forward himself until the horse walks forward. Whenever the horse makes one step, he stops hitting and pets the horse. After ten minutes or so when this response is established, he heads for the trailer and walks the horse to the point where he stops moving; he waits there and pets the horse. To spend time at this point is important, for this is the place to return to if the horse gets nervous later when he is closer to the trailer.

John suggests that you wait at least three minutes at this point, and only when the horse is completely calm do you again give your cue for forward movement. When he stops walking, you let him stop, and pet him again. When he finally has his front feet by the ramp (or in an American step-up trailer by the step) John suggests that you focus your attention on his back legs, not his front legs. He has specific ways that he uses to block each of the horse's possible escape routes, which lie to each side, backwards, and up on his hind legs. But he specifically does *not* want to beat the horse into the trailer. Instead he rewards any indication of forward movement. This could include swaying – which is the beginning of movement even though each of the horse's four feet still remain planted firmly on the ground. Other indications are reaching down with his head, and lifting one hind leg. John is working on the principle that the longer the horse stands with his head inside the trailer, the more he realises that this is not such a terrible place to have it.

Trailers look a lot like caves – and creatures who eat horses live in caves. Once inside one it is hard to run away – and a floor which looks, feels and sounds so strange may make a standing start extremely difficult. So it is no surprise that to a flight animal a trailer is a daunting place, and that entering one goes completely against a horse's instincts. Linda Tellington-Jones, in her step-by-step approach to trailer loading, deals with this by virtually building a trailer around the horse. Firstly she leads him over wooden planks, and then under plastic sheeting (held by two assistants). Then she takes him between two walls of straw bales – so that when she finally faces him with a trailer, he is familiar with the claustrophobic feelings it may generate.

Once she has a horse standing by the trailer ramp and ready to load, she spends a lot of time stroking the horse's body, hindquarters, and legs with her 'wand'. For she believes that the reluctance of many horses to enter a trailer also centres around their uncertainty about whether they will actually fit in. Stroking the horse with the 'wand' offers him clear kinaesthetic feedback about his edges – helping him recognise where his body ends and air begins, and giving him an enhanced capacity to judge whether this two-horse coffin has indeed been tailor-made for him.

'The reluctance of many horses to enter a trailer also centres around their uncertainty about whether they will actually fit in.'

If John Lyons' suggested focus on the horse's hind feet causes them to move up towards his front feet, the horse will soon get tired, and will want to step with a front foot. He may paw the trailer floor, or leave his foot there for just a few seconds. John is very satisfied when this happens, regarding each time that the horse backs out of the trailer as a new opportunity to teach him the cue to go forward. Also, the horse is learning how to *unload* at the same time as he learns how to load, and he is prevented from feeling trapped inside this 'coffin'. So John considers time in one-minute segments, and expects that the horse will initially have one front foot in the trailer for five seconds out of every sixty, and during the fifty-five seconds that his foot is out of the trailer, he pets him and lets him stand quietly. The idea is to gradually reverse the figures, with the horse's foot in the trailer for fifty-five seconds of every minute. Then, he does the same for each of the other feet in turn. This framework helps the handler to be patient, and it gives the horse the repetition he needs if he is to go consistently in and out of the trailer.

If at any stage the horse begins to back unasked out of the trailer, John keeps tapping him with the whip until he re-establishes forward movement. But at all times he resists the temptation to rush the horse in: he expects the horse to put one front foot in and out of the trailer maybe twenty times; then both front feet go in and out twenty times, and the same sequence is repeated with each foot in turn. Whenever the horse loads, he passes the handler, and once the horse will stay in the trailer, the handler will need to walk into the empty stall, and tug lightly on the lead rope to ask him to back out. Before John considers closing the ramp or doors he bangs and slams them a number of times, and does not worry if the horse backs out in response to all of this noise. He will only close up the trailer when the horse calmly accepts all this commotion, and only then would he tie the horse up.

The horse who is initially bad to load will go through a number of stages during this process. From *bad* – where he may test all the escape routes he can think of – he becomes *good*, and will go partly or completely into the trailer several times. Then, just as we are congratulating ourselves, he becomes '*real bad*', and will fight hard, reinstating the escape routes, and maybe inventing some new ones. We may find ourselves wishing that we had stopped whilst he was good; but instead we have to cut off his escape routes and begin again by loading one front foot into the trailer for five seconds. This will finally make him *better*. He will be better than he was the first time, and better for longer. But then he goes through a period of being '*half bad*', with some rather half-hearted evasions, before he finally becomes '*real good*'. By this time, the trainer can walk towards the back of the trailer and let go of the lead rope several feet from it. The horse will walk in alone.

If the thought of all this time and patience horrifies you, realise that you are viewing the process from the confines of a horse culture which does not pay much attention to good handling. If you were herding cattle in the outback, you would have to be able to guarantee your horse's good behaviour. Traditionally, this has not been important to us: we are willing to have our horses gallop away when we fall off them, and pull back when they are tied. We are willing to push, pull, haul and beat them into trailers. We are willing to have them lay their ears back at us, bare their teeth, and turn their backsides towards us. We simply accept that a proportion of horses are 'just like that'. This is not a good advertisement for the rigour and the appropriateness of our training.

The training methods that John Lyons and Monty Roberts have devised to eradicate these problems are like 'painting by numbers'. John and Monty have no interest in being guru figures who look down upon the masses who just never seem to get it. 'Reproducibility' is one of their highest values, and they believe that if you follow the right steps in the right order the result is guaranteed. In 'training by numbers' there is no magic, and no need for talent. The same is true of my own approach to learning how to ride – and when any approach becomes this reliable and this reproducible, it suggests that our map really is a workable, accurate rendering of the territory.

....

If your horse does not load easily, it means that he 'ain't broke to lead', and that he only ever leads if you happen to be going where he wants to go. There is much more to leading than I want to delineate here, and Linda

Tellington-Jones teaches a variety of different positions which the handler can use for leading, each one with a different purpose. (In the trailer loading example, John was using the position which she calls 'the dingo'.) Linda has made leading into an art form, and a very rigorous exercise. Teaching the horse to tie is also something that should be done with much more thoroughness. Suffice it to say that the horse has to realise (as he does in leading) that giving to the pressure of the rope makes that pressure go away; the horse who pulls back, panics, and *keeps pulling back* has not discovered this. He is also much more likely to pull against the handler in leading, and to head off in his own chosen direction.

This suggests that he considers himself to be higher in the dominance hierarchy, or pecking order, than she is. Any horse which threatens to bite or kick you certainly does, for horses will only invade the personal space of a horse they consider to be of a lower rank than themselves. However, Dr Marthe Kiley-Worthington, author of *The Behaviour of Horses in Relation to Management and Training,* believes that the concept of pecking order – originally devised to explain the behaviour of chickens – is applied too liberally to horses. For their deep and lasting friendships with selected individuals are far more evident, and more impactful on herd life, than aggressive behaviour. A dominance hierarchy is only evident in confined conditions, or where there is competition for a scarce resource.

But let us suppose that you are carrying ten buckets of hard feed, bringing that scarce resource into a field containing ten horses. Horse number one knows that whatever happens he will get his supper, so he does not bother you. It is horse number *ten* who meets you at the gate, because he knows that there may not be much to eat later on. But if horse number nine threatens to bite him, with the result that horse number ten dashes out of the way and knocks you over, you know that you are number *eleven* in the hierarchy. Horses who do the moving are always higher in the pecking order than horses who move away – which is one of the reasons why the work in the round pen is also helpful with horses who are bullies – for it establishes you as herd leader. The horse begins to appreciate that it is a privilege to be in your company, and that any behaviour which is not submissive will result in the dire consequence of being put back to work. When you then touch him in the vulnerable areas between his eyes or under his belly you test and reassert your authority, creating a human-horse team in which both parties recognise that *you* are the leader.

It is similar reasoning which makes John Lyons suggest that if a horse you are leading in hand spooks into you, you should spook him even more to send him away from you. For this re-establishes your personal space and puts you back in control. It also raises his adrenalin level, which will then come back down to a lower level. In a more genteel way, Linda

Tellington-Jones uses her 'wand' to establish and maintain the trainer's personal space. Pat Parelli, too, focuses much of his training on the same issue.

The ultimate invasion of your personal space occurs when the horse bites or kicks you, and John regards biting as a declaration of war. Many people do not take biting that seriously, especially in young horses; but even a half-hearted gesture should not be treated as a game. John makes an interesting comparison when he suggests that if your child greeted you with a surly expression you would not show the same tolerance that you probably would with your horse. You would instead say, 'Hey, don't do that to me!' Whether your horse nips, bites, gets you, misses, or merely opens his mouth one quarter of an inch, John suggests that you immediately give yourself *three seconds* (a very short time) for retaliation, and that you do so with the attitude of wanting to KILL.

Note that your intention is not to punish the horse or to get even with him – your intention is to let him know that he just made a very serious mistake, and that he was lucky to come out of it alive. Since the horse will know if you are bluffing, your attitude is extremely important. A whip can cut into him, so it is not an appropriate weapon, and whatever you do, his head is off limits. But even if you were to hit the horse as hard as you could with a baseball bat (which I am not advocating) realise that you could not hit him as hard as another horse would kick him as he reasserted the importance of his personal space.

After your three seconds are up, John recommends that you pet your horse to reassure him that you still like him. During that short space of time, you raised his fear to a level that he cannot live with, and acted so promptly that the cause and its effect are clearly linked together in his mind. He has experienced the consequences of his actions (for in the wild, actions have *consequences*, not punishments), and he knows what will happen if he oversteps that boundary again. But realise that raising his fear level like this is highly unlikely to make him a nervous horse; fear almost always arises – in horses as well as in people – from concern about what *might* happen, and much more rarely from what *is* happening.

> 'Fear almost always arises – in horses as well as in people – from concern about what might happen, and much more rarely from what is happening.'

If you are a nervous rider, I am sure you will recognise this; for underlying your jitters are fantasies of how the horse *might* shy, *might* buck, or *might* run away with you. You may not like being anxious, but your fears are not so bad that you cannot live with them – otherwise you would not be riding. Commonly, we keep the horse in the state of having just a little fear, both by keeping him restrained, and by never defining our intention and specifying an ending (as we do when we move away from the horse in the round pen). Without this, we leave him in doubt about what we might be about to do next. Then, when this generates fear and the horse learns that he can live with this fear, he can become chronically nervous.

Strange as it may seem, the horse's fear is fed by the handler who moves so slowly, so quietly, and so carefully that she unwittingly conveys the message 'What I'm about to do is really dangerous.' A more matter-of-fact, 'it's no big deal' approach works better, even in the first saddling of the horse in the round pen.

We cannot erase fear from the horse's 'programme' – it is hard-wired into it, and however thorough we are, it is impossible to get horses 'used to' everything they will ever meet. We cannot train for circumstance: for the dog, the car, or the helicopter which will suddenly appear from nowhere – but we can change the horse's *response* to his fear regardless of the situation which generates it. For if he gets frightened with all four feet still planted firmly on the ground, he is not a danger to himself or us, and we will not find ourselves blaming his bad behaviour on external, uncontrollable events. The horse who knows how to manage his fear will be infinitely safer to ride.

John Lyons trains this response in the round pen, often before he ever rides the horse, but after he has established the response of the horse turning to face him when asked. Standing some way away from the horse he says 'Boo!'. If the horse jumps but does not move his feet, John moves up to him and rubs him between the eyes. If the horse takes just a few steps – showing that he thought about leaving but did not actually do so – John will again reward him. As the horse continues to handle his fear John progressively increases the pressure on him by shouting, waving his arms, crumpling plastic bags, waving plastic sheets, and gently flicking a rope over his back. He has, apparently, even started a chain saw in the round pen, and banged dustbin lids together! Again, he cannot get the horse 'used to' everything he will ever encounter in life; but here, in this safe environment (and before he ever gets on the horse's back) he can teach him to control his fear. John does not allow fate to determine his future safety.

If he misjudges the level of threat that he can present the horse with, and the horse does indeed run from the spook, he keeps scaring the horse whilst he runs around the pen, and he makes him change direction every turn or half turn. This gives the horse the opportunity to turn and face him, and makes it clearer that running is not the desired response. In the moment when the horse begins to turn towards the spook, John stops spooking him. Thus the horse discovers that his fear releases the moment he turns to face the object of that fear. At this point, John will move up to the horse and rub him between the eyes, and then move away and begin again.

Trainer Pat Parelli takes a slightly different approach, and accustoms the horse to strange *human* behaviour before he ever rides him. Working the horse in a halter and on the end of a 12 foot/3.6m rope, he makes sure that he can stagger towards the horse like a drunkard, and skip towards him with gay abandon. If the horse moves away, Pat deems him not yet ready to ride. (An awful lot of established riding horses would not pass this test, one of a number of 'pre-flight tests' which Pat considers an essential prerequisite for riding.) He also flips the end of the rope lightly over the horse's back, for as he says, you should be able to 'flog your horse with kindness'. Linda Tellington-Jones also creates opportunities to teach the horse how to handle his fear, and to do this she again uses plastic sheets, which she leads him over, under and through. In her approach too, very much less is left to chance than would be in conventional European ways of working with horses.

....

Pat Parelli describes the horse as "an attitude on four legs". '

All of these trainers, with their somewhat different standpoints, are agreed that lungeing the horse has much less to recommend it than we traditionally suppose. It exercises the horse's body but it does little to train his mind, so, like much of our work, it addresses the wrong issue. Pat Parelli describes the horse as 'an attitude on four legs' – his 'horsonality', like our personality, is so far reaching in its effects that to be effective our work must address his mental and emotional development. In the short term lungeing may render the difficult horse somewhat easier to ride – but at the same time it makes him progressively more and more fit. Soon, this makes him *harder* to ride, and perpetuates the problem it was supposed to cure. Linda Tellington-Jones's response to the fresh, difficult horse would be to work him in hand, leading him slowly and carefully through arrangements of poles (the labyrinth or the star) laid on the ground. This forces the horse to pay attention to where he puts his feet, and instead of staying 'high' he becomes much more focused. As she says, it is much more effective to influence one pound of brain than one thousand pounds of muscle.

'It is much more effective to influence one pound of brain than one thousand pounds of muscle.'

John Lyons also works from the principle that a small controlled movement demands far more mentally from the horse than large scale movement. So if a horse will not stand still, he works him in hand until he will quietly take one step to the right, followed by one step to the left, one step forward and one step back. Initially the horse probably runs to the right, and runs to the left, so that limiting his movement becomes the most important issue. I once watched John do this with a horse for nearly two hours, showing infinite patience coupled with great precision. It took most of this time for the horse in effect to say, 'Can we stop now? I can't wait to stand still.'

If a young horse keeps trying to nuzzle you, and you know that this might lead to biting and barging, you could be tempted just to push him out of the way. But if you invoked the same principle, you would create a situation in which *the horse* decided 'I don't think I want to do that any more.' You might pretend that your hands were cold, and then try to warm them by rubbing them vigorously on each side of his muzzle. Soon it will start to get sore, and the horse is left thinking, 'I'd better keep out of her way.' If a horse stops when jumping, Monty Roberts advocates doing maybe ten quarter pirouettes to each side, whilst keeping the horse just in front of the fence. Very soon he decides 'I think I'd rather jump it next time.'

The bottom line of this approach is that the trainer is making *the wrong thing difficult and the right thing easy* – a philosophy which is used by good riders from many different schools. Early work in establishing the flying lead changes in canter makes the wrong thing (continuing on the same lead) difficult, and the right thing (the flying change) easy. By following this course the rider does not have to overtly punish the horse, for instead of getting out her whip and saying 'Don't do X', she says 'Wouldn't you prefer to do Y?' By instigating rather than scolding she continues to be causal, for it is the *reactive* rider who resorts to punishment, creating yet more unwanted behaviours which will need to be addressed later.

The principle of making the wrong thing difficult and the right thing easy also underlies the work in the round pen, where in effect the trainer says, 'You want to run? Off you go then,' and then bides his time until the horse decides 'I really don't want to run any more.' If the horse breaks away from him after having established 'join up' the trainer again invokes the same principle, sending the horse away so that he reaps the consequences of his actions. But when horses have opted for 'join up', their integrity is tremendous. They know the limits of acceptable behaviour whilst in the handler's personal space, and they know the consequences of leaving that space. They also choose to team up with her and rely on her leadership when faced with new and potentially frightening experiences. As Pat Parelli would say, the human becomes 'a natural leader for a natural follower'.

....

The trainers whose work I have described here undoubtedly have their differences: Monty Roberts talks of 'advance and retreat', John Lyons of 'stimulus-response', and Linda Tellington-Jones of 'cellular memory' and 'non-habitual movement'. Pat Parelli talks of the difference between what is 'normal' and what is 'natural', and Ray Hunt of putting the horse in a bind, and then giving him a way out, letting 'your idea become the horse's idea' so that he can 'respond with respect'. What unites them is that each has a strong philosophy of training which guides all their actions. It is this, along with the practical success of their philosophies, which makes them stand out from the crowd. They share a commitment to working without pain or force. But simultaneously they place much more stringent limits than most of us on the behaviour they will accept from horses.

They impact on horses very quickly, whether they be unhandled youngsters, or older horses in need of retraining. For when we work with horses in the language 'Equus', they show us how quickly they can learn, and force us to reconsider our ideas about their stupidity. I too appear rather stupid if 'taught' in Chinese, and I prefer not to be tied up and restrained. When no fear is involved in learning, and my teacher uses *leverage* instead of *coercion* she is much more likely to find me a willing and intelligent student.

Linda Tellington-Jones began to develop her method after the realisation (born of her training with Moshe Feldenkrais) that by abolishing fear, it should be possible to abandon much of the repetition which we have traditionally supposed to be necessary in our work with horses. In my personal role as a trainer of both people and horses, I have certainly discovered that 'The better I teach, the smarter my students become.' So despite the individual differences in the methods employed by these trainers, the message which I hope comes across loud and clear throughout this chapter is that we have mostly been too stupid to realise that it is our stupidity which makes the horse seem stupid!

One other principle these trainers share is the realisation that anyone who wishes to be in control of her horse must first be in control herself. Consider as an example the trainer who held a public demonstration in which members of the audience brought him very difficult horses to work with. One was a stallion who was a confirmed biter, and who appeared ready to attack anyone in sight. As quick as a flash, and without looking at the horse, the trainer punched him hard on the nose (which I earlier defined as off limits – but this man was undoubtedly masterful enough to break the rules). The trainer then changed his demeanour, became submissive in his posture, and looked down at the ground as if to say, 'Where did that come from?' The horse too reached down, also wanting to know 'Where did that come from?'. Suddenly they were both on the same team searching for the enemy, and soon the horse was following him round like a dog.

In this situation, most people would be intimidated – and those who met aggression with aggression would keep looking the horse in the eye, and keep lashing out at him, perpetuating the contest of man-against-horse. They would want to be one-up, so that they could dominate the horse and put him one-down. How many people would have the self-awareness to change their way of interacting with the horse that quickly? To 'level' with the horse, and to do so with such total self-control is, to me, impressive.

'We have mostly been too stupid to realise that it is our stupidity which makes the horse seem stupid!'

A friend told me recently how she once watched Tom Dorrance, the father of this work, as he and his assistant taught a difficult horse to load. Tom was sitting on his little stool and supervising the process: and at just the right moment, in just the right way, he picked up a small stone, and threw it at the horse's rump. The horse walked straight into the trailer. Immediately some of the audience were at Tom's side, asking 'Where did you get that stone? Have you got any more of them?' In their quest to find 'magic horse-loading stones' they completely overlooked the magic of how Tom read his horse, chose his moment, and applied just the right amount of force. This required an astuteness which they did not recognise; instead they chose to believe that success lay in a magic 'pill'.

In general, we like the idea of magic pills, and want our own learning and our horse's learning to be as fast and easy as possible. By following the right recipe you can indeed make it that way; but as John Lyons suggests, training horses is like baking a cake. If you follow the recipe and put in the right ingredients in the right order, it should come out perfect every time. But the point which so many people fail to realise is that the ingredients have to be put into *us*, not into the horse.

'Training horses is like baking a cake... but the point which so many people fail to realise is that the ingredients have to be put into us, not into the horse.'

....

The approaches to training discussed in these last sections were developed by trainers who have gained a reputation for working well with unhandled or 'difficult' horses. In the process of learning their skill they have undoubtedly become exceptional people – astute observers who are guided by strong philosophical principles. One might argue that perhaps they were exceptional in the first place, and horse owners who do not want – or do not consider themselves able – to develop such expertise may indeed benefit from a little help. To continue our analogy of the recipe, many forward-thinking horsemen consider that 'imprint training' with newly born foals is the best possible way of putting ingredients into the horse, influencing all of his future interactions with people by making him more malleable and easy to work with.

Veterinarian Robert Miller, who for many years had a thriving equine practice in California, regularly intervened in difficult births. Often he had to adjust the foal's position in the womb, pull him out, towel him dry, and give veterinary treatment. Usually, he saw the foals again at three months old when they were vaccinated and wormed. Over time he realised that the foals he had handled at birth were always easier to handle at that later stage, and unusually trusting of human contact. The difference between them and the foals who were not handled at birth remained as they were later started and ridden.

This realisation led Robert to develop the system he calls 'imprint training', to write a book entitled *Imprint Training of the Newborn Foal* (published in 1991), and to produce a video tape of the same name, along with a second tape called 'Early Training'. His ideas seem very new, for many breeders believe that one should ideally not intervene as the newly born foal bonds with the mother. Few people think of the first hour or two of life as a time for learning, and they are probably influenced in this by their experiences of the helplessness of the newly born baby or puppy. But Robert does not believe that he has discovered something new; indeed some Native American tribes and also Bedouin tribes are known to have handled and bonded with their newly born foals, suggesting that his work is a rediscovery of ancient wisdom.

It was Konrad Lorenz, an Austrian scientist, who coined the term 'imprinting', after he discovered that baby goslings would attach themselves to the first thing they saw move after they emerged from the egg. This, he believed, was a pre-programmed response, and if a human foot, or a dog, was the first moving object they saw they would follow it, and it became their surrogate mother. Lorenz originally believed that this phenomenon occurred only in birds, but later work showed that it occurs in many animals.

Baby chicks, ducklings, calves, fawns and foals, will attach to and bond with objects seen shortly after birth, despite the fact that they would otherwise later flee from that same shape. In many species the imprinting period does not occur right after birth, for the young are neurologically and physically so immature. But whilst puppies and kittens are born blind and helpless, flight animals are born so well developed that they can immediately see, hear, and smell – their senses are those of an adult horse. They recognise and follow their mother, responding to her call, and they can run alongside her very soon after birth. In animals for whom the imprinting period is delayed, there are critical learning periods later. During these, as in the imprint period after birth, information is very easily absorbed, and it becomes permanent – hard-wired into the brain/computer, and affecting the attitude and behaviour of the animal throughout life. Subsequent events have very little impact on this input; indeed later responses to stimuli are predetermined by it.

Robert views the four major goals of imprint training as bonding with humans, desensitisation to certain stimuli, sensitisation to other stimuli, and submission to humans. He achieves these goals during the first day or two of the foal's life, ideally doing most of the ground work during the first hour, which – as the true imprint period – is the best learning period of the foal's life. Never again will he be so receptive. Robert believes that the foal can bond simultaneously with his mother and the handler – with anything, in fact, that moves and looms above him in that first hour, and which in the wild would include other herd members.

Very soon after birth, after the mare has stood up and the umbilical cord has broken, she begins to lick the foal, which dries him, warms him up, and stimulates his circulation. This arouses her maternal instincts, and it is important that she is allowed to do it; but a human too can simultaneously rub and stroke the foal, as long as she does not come between him and the mare, whose anxiety will be minimised if mother and baby are kept head to head throughout. The handler's touch can extend to the foal's ears, eyes, nose, mouth, tongue, feet, udder or sheath, and rectal and vaginal area. This desensitises him to the later touch of the farrier who shoes him, or the veterinarian who might examine, worm, or stomach-tube him. If the foal attempts to get up during this procedure the handler gently but firmly keeps him on his side. In doing this she inhibits the flight reflex, and Robert's belief is that 'When an animal is deprived of its emergency survival behaviour it is forced into a more submissive attitude.'

In signalling submission to animals of its own kind, each species takes on the posture of greatest vulnerability. So dogs, who expose their teeth and snarl in defence, lie down and roll over when expressing submission, exposing their throat and stomach. If their mouths are tied shut so that they cannot snarl, they are likely to do this. Cattle who lower their heads and present their horns in defence, raise their heads and lay their horns back against their necks when indicating vulnerability, and if prevented from lowering their head they are again likely to do this. The defensive position for the horse is readiness to flee, with head raised and his body standing squarely on all four legs. By lowering his head he signals submission, and as we noted when considering the work in the round pen, he intensifies the signal by moving his mouth as if feeding, chewing and licking his lips. Whenever we prevent the horse from running away we create an attitude of submissiveness, for the horse who feels dependent and vulnerable seeks leadership. But only if we do not betray the horse by threatening him can we create submissiveness without fear.

Yet, as Robert points out, much of our training system is based on flight deprivation. When we work the horse on the lunge, and even when we first put on a headcollar, lead him, and tie him up, we want him to believe that flight is impossible. In the round pen we negotiate with him by controlling where and how he flees, and making continued flight a less attractive option. In our ridden work we lower the horse's head and create a lateral flexion, which makes flight more difficult. When we displace the hindquarters laterally, we make it impossible for him to make a good standing start. But we can begin this training – in a very humane way – by not letting the newly born foal get to his feet, and whenever he resists any part of the imprint process the handler must persist *until and beyond* the point when the foal relaxes. You cannot do too many repetitions, but

Robert Miller: 'When an animal is deprived of its emergency survival behaviour it is forced into a more submissive attitude.'

you can do too few. For if you were to stop the stimuli whilst the foal were trying to escape you would fix *that* behaviour, sensitising the foal to that particularstimulus rather than desensitising him to it. This would do more harm than good.

After somewhere between thirty and one hundred repetitions of each stimulus the foal will relax and become apparently oblivious to it. This occurs despite the fact that the intensity of the stimuli Robert uses may surprise you when you first watch the 'Imprint Training' video tape. For his touch is very vigorous. He first rubs and massages the foal's head, face and poll, and after rubbing the outside of the ears, he wiggles his finger within the ear canal about fifty times. He then also moves it around inside the nostrils and inside the mouth, rubbing the tongue and the inside of the lips. Again, he usually needs about fifty repetitions of each stimulus before the foal relaxes. He then rubs the shoulder, the chest wall, and the upper foreleg, repeatedly flexing the leg and holding it flexed until it relaxes. He slaps the underside of the hoof fifty times, making a loud noise as he does so. He then moves to the hind leg and foot, the tail, the perineal area, and the udder or sheath, before turning the foal over and repeating the whole process on the other side. The only part of the foal he does *not* rub and desensitise is the part of the abdomen where the rider's leg will lie, for this will later be sensitised to touch.

He then goes one stage further, rubbing the foal's body with electric clippers whose motor is running, paying special attention to the ears and face. This desensitises the foal to the sound and the vibration of the clippers. (He does not, however, actually clip the foal.) He also rubs the foal over with crackling white plastic, whose colour and noise make it an exceptionally frightening stimulus. If the weather is good he will spray the foal lightly with warm water from a spray bottle, simulating fly spray.

This process of 'flooding' the foal's nervous system with stimuli takes about one hour, including short rest periods where the foal just bonds with the mare, who will also continue to bond with him as Robert works. He does imprint training alone, but recommends that inexperienced people do it in pairs, so that one can hold the foal whilst the other does the procedures. Also, two people can roll the foal over more easily, giving access to both sides of his body. During the desensitisation procedures, bringing the foal's head around to the side so that his nose comes towards his withers makes it impossible for him to get up. But at the same time it facilitates lateral flexion, and eases the introduction to the halter and to leading which Robert will do the following day.

After the foal has nursed and is strong enough to stand for a while, Robert continues the session, accustoming him to light pressure on his back by rhythmically pressing in the saddle area with the flat of his hand about fifty times. By wrapping his arms around the girth region and clasping his hands beneath the foal's chest he desensitises the girth area, rhythmically squeezing it at least fifty times. He picks up the foal's feet and taps them, which should present no problem if the earlier work was done well. He even suggests that someone who is tall enough should straddle the foal without placing weight on his back; then when a rider first sits up on his back he will remember seeing that large shape looming up above him.

When the foal is first standing, Robert also uses a surgical glove and a lubricant to desensitise the anus and rectum, so that it will later be easy to take the horse's temperature or do a rectal examination. Robert also sensitises the foal, so that he backs up one step on response to chest pressure, which is then immediately released. He also moves forward from pressure on his backside, and moves his hindquarters in response to flank pressure, and his forehand in response to neck pressure. Unlike all the earlier work, these responses need only a few repetitions to train. This session, and any subsequent ones done with the foal standing, must not last more than fifteen minutes. Should the handler not be there during the first hour of the foal's life, she can either work with the standing foal for fifteen-minute time periods, or wait until he is lying down and do exactly the same procedures as above, keeping the foal on the ground for one hour.

Depending on the strength of the foal, Robert does the second session with him at about one day old, putting on a halter, starting to lead him, and even beginning the work which will lead to him tying well. Throughout this process he always keeps the foal very close to the mare, and he asks nothing which is beyond his capabilities. But for the detail of this I will refer you to his book; suffice it to say that he sets up a situation in which the foal is immediately rewarded for giving to the pressure of the lead rope. This is critical, for the horse who always does so will never pull back when tied, and will never try to escape the handler like the horse who 'ain't broke to lead'.

Over the first two weeks of the foal's life Robert reinforces the procedures each day, and adds loading both mare and foal into a trailer, and leading the foal from the mare. His experiments with imprint training began in 1967, and over all the time since then neither he nor anyone else using the method has, to his knowledge, had a mare reject a foal. Indeed, he believes that the nervous first-time mother is more likely to bond easily with her foal when she sees the handler with him, and that she is also less likely to become protective of him, and aggressive towards humans over the next few days.

Foals who are petted excessively or who are bottle-fed, are renowned for growing up believing that they can walk all over people, and Robert has found that horse owners are frequently worried that the imprinted foal will do this same. But he has proved that his training creates responsive, obedient, submissive foals, who show neither fear nor contempt for human beings; instead they respect and trust us. The few novice handlers who have used foal imprinting and later criticised the system for producing bossy foals, have perhaps failed to make the distinction between *petting* the foal and *training* him. For it is extremely important that the foal is not allowed to invade the handler's body space by nosing or nibbling: we want him to learn that we can touch him in any way and any place that we want, but that he may not touch us without permission. Any invasion of the handler's personal space needs to be dealt with firmly, and Robert recommends that a foal which begins to bite has a finger flicked on his nose so quickly that action and reaction are firmly linked in his mind.

'Imprinted foals have become exceptional performers in many equestrian spheres.'

Imprinted foals have become exceptional performers in many equestrian spheres. Historically, American racehorse trainers believed that a horse should be flighty and nervous to run well; but many have discovered the truth of Robert's belief that the frightened horse is more likely to choose to run in the centre of the pack. The people-orientated horse is more likely to be motivated by his jockey, for he is willing to try for people – as Monty Roberts would say, he and his rider are 'on the same team'. He is also a much safer horse to be around, and to do things to, which is particularly helpful when he has to have routine but invasive veterinary treatment, or in those awful moments when you need him not to panic. If he were ever to become caught in wire, for instance, you need him to trust you implicitly, and to know that flight is not the best answer.

On his first video tape, Robert demonstrates how he handles the foal who has not been imprint trained, and who, even at a few days old, has proved himself pushy, aggressive, and difficult to handle. In the herd unruly foals are disciplined by older herd members, so he speaks to the foal as they would, in 'Equus'. After catching the foal and putting on a foal-slip he imitates the cry of an enraged stallion, and he uses his whole leg to kick at the foal's belly (undoubtedly less hard than another horse would kick him). He has to do this only three times for the little horse to undergo a character change which has always proved lasting. Robert presents this technique, as I do, with some trepidation, for it is obviously open to abuse; yet it is a superb example of the way that 'Equus', in this context, is a far superior language to 'human'.

CHAPTER TWELVE
Animal Communicators

THERE ARE YET more dimensions to speaking 'Equus' which lie beyond handling and riding, and there is another small group of speakers whose credentials lie solely in their effectiveness. Animal communicators make telepathic contact with animals, offering advice to people who want to know whether a horse (or other animal) is in pain, why he is behaving so strangely, and what historical experiences have caused these patterns. Inevitably, the only evidence I can offer you of their effectiveness is anecdotal – and you could be forgiven for the kind of healthy scepticism which may leave you feeling that I have finally gone off my head! But whether these people really do communicate with animals is in many ways not the issue. To study their approach teaches us a lot about communication, and the questions which people repeatedly ask tell us about ourselves, and the assumptions we make about horses.

The first few animal communicators who have spoken out about their gift and begun offering their services, have, in effect, given permission for others to follow. For their message to 'closet communicators' is 'You may not be crazy after all,' whilst their message to the rest of us is 'You could learn to do this too.' For now you can train in the craft, learning, in the first place, to put aside your scepticism. Many young children show tremendous empathy with animals, talking *to* them – and perhaps even *with* them – only to be told by their parents that of course the family dog cannot speak! Many of the animal communicators I have spoken to say that they did, as children, have two-way conversations with animals. Some never lost that gift (although they learned to remain silent about it), whilst others say that they recovered it in adulthood once they gave themselves permission to be that 'crazy'.

It all began for American Beatrice Lydecker when she was waiting by a traffic light and heard a cry for help. ('The call was strangely soundless,' she says in her book *Stories the Animals Tell Me*, 'yet I heard it anyway.') Looking around, she saw only a Dobermann Pinscher, standing behind a warehouse fence. She cautiously approached the dog – who she knew was trained to guard – and as she did so, she felt a strong sense of loneliness, and a hunger for affection. The dog licked her hand and nuzzled her wrist, leaving her feeling confused, for she had only ever seen him snarl at anyone foolish enough to go near.

It all began for American Kate Reilly when someone came to look at a horse she was selling, and said, 'I want my psychic to talk to him before I decide about buying him.' Kate's initial sense of amusement was abruptly halted when the prospective purchaser came back with an accurate rendering of the horse's history, including facts no one else could possibly have known. Very soon, Kate was on a training course with Penelope Smith, whose book *Animal Talk* was published in 1982. Kate Solisti spent her early childhood with a cat whose company and conversation she found preferable to that of the humans around her; but when he died she turned away from animals and nature, and it was much later in life that she re-found a way to talk with other animals. British animal communicator Nicci Mackay swears that, 'I've always been able to do it. It's really hard for me not to.' Nicci was a 'closet communicator' for many years; but within weeks of plucking up her courage to 'go public' she had been featured in two major newspapers and appeared on breakfast television!

....

My favourite book in this general area is J. Allen Boone's *Kinship with All Life*, which was written way before its time. Much of the book tells of his experiences when asked to look after Strongheart, a German Shepherd dog who, in the early 1950s, became one of the stars of Hollywood. Strongheart was an exceptional dog, and he soon proved to the author that he could read his mind, even at a distance. It also became clear that the dog was forced to resort to play-acting his wants and needs out of a desperate desire to get them across to such a dumb human. In a bid to see if he could discover how Strongheart knew and understood so much, J. Allen Boone decided to 'reverse the customary procedure of 'man trains dog' and instead make it 'dog trains man'.

J. Allen Boone also knew that his training programme required that he give up the superior position of 'human', looking down from such elevated heights on a less intelligent dog. But this was not as easy as he had anticipated, for inevitably, he failed to appreciate the ways in which he was so entrenched in this superiority that he was blind to its effects. As all his efforts to communicate with the dog came to nothing he became increasingly frustrated, and he gradually began to sense that the factors which were blocking communication must lie inside himself.

Finally he realised that he was trying to solve the problem solely with his intellect, and that 'There had been altogether too much of ME as a self-appointed knower, and not enough of Strongheart and what he might have to share as an intelligent expression of life.' The turning point began for J. Allen Boone when he started to list all of Strongheart's character qualities, and this led him to the recognition that Strongheart was a mental and spiritual being as well as a physical body. He then realised that he had never actually 'seen' a dog, but only merely 'looked at' it, and he began to appreciate that he was watching 'not a dog expressing great qualities, but rather, great qualities expressing a dog.' From this spiritual perspective, he found himself sharing a profound sense of kinship with the dog who had previously seemed an enigma.

When he sensed that the dog was communicating with him it happened very suddenly, in a quiet moment of stillness and receptivity which occurred when he had essentially given up, abandoning the frenzied attempts of his ego and his intellect to master the situation. He found (and subsequently verified) answers to all the questions he had mentally been asking the dog. The experience was like 'suddenly remembering something I had always known but temporarily forgotten in the fogs and confusions of human experience.' But whenever he fell into the trap of perceiving himself as superior, their communication system temporarily broke down, and he 'dropped to the relatively low level of just another dumb human trying to appear important in the shadow of an intelligent dog.'

His encounter with the dog was a life-changing experience which left him believing that there were times when 'the Mind of the Universe' communicated through both of them, and he likened this to the closeness of any two people who are in such rapport that they share thoughts and feelings without needing to speak. His time with Strongheart paved the way for many other animals with less obviously impressive credentials to become his teachers, enriching his life and honing his philosophy just as Strongheart had done.

....

Modern animal communicators share this spiritual perspective on life, operating from a belief system which is based on the equality of different life forms. Each species shows aptitudes and behaviours which are appropriate for his body and nervous system, with the more complex forms of life having more choices programmed into their brain-computer. (This is often not apparent, however, when watching the many riders who are constantly outwitted by their horses!). But having these capabilities does not necessarily make us or other animals *better* – although the purely behaviourist stance would argue that we humans are superior, and that animals are instinctual beings who function like robots and have little or no intelligence. This is a belief system which would make communication with them both philosophically and practically impossible. This was the mindset which J. Allen Boone struggled to change in himself when faced with the contradictions offered by an exceptionally intelligent dog.

If we measure intelligence by how closely an animal can imitate human behaviour, we use an extremely biased view of it, assuming that manual dexterity and the ability to read and write are its most important forms. (Perhaps we should be regarded as an unintelligent species because we cannot fly like a bird or smell like a dog.) Many animals are far more perceptive and aware than the people who attempt to understand them; they adapt to change far better than us, and they more easily learn from experience. By many definitions, this makes them more intelligent. Animals beat us hollow, as well, in their ability to detect human incongruity. They may, in fact, appear 'dumb' simply because of this; for if we approach a jump with a mental picture of the horse refusing, can we blame him when he does so? If we call our dogs but we mentally picture them running away, are they in fact disobedient if they do so?

The differences between the pictures we make in our mind's eye and our external words or actions are certainly not lost on animals as they so often are on people, who are blind to our insincerity. So one of the first rules of animal communication is that the pictures you make and the words you say must match up: you must 'walk your talk', saying, acting, and meaning what you are thinking. The sensitivity of animals to the inner workings of our minds suggests that they understand far more than we give them credit for. Even in speech, the exact meaning of our words may not register, but our voice tone and our attitude certainly do (and 90 per cent of human communication, the psychologists tell us, is *non-verbal*, so we tend to vastly overestimate the importance of words). Our intentions, emotions, images, and thoughts get through to our animals, but the random thoughts of the 'butterfly brain' have so little meaning that any self-respecting human who wants to make sense to animals must be able to still her mind, and think only the thoughts she means to convey.

Penelope Smith, in her book *Animal Talk*, suggests that you practise sitting quietly with animals, just as J. Allen Boone did with Strongheart, stilling the chatter in your mind, and appreciating their presence. Becoming aware of your judgments and preconceptions about animals enables you to become more perceptive about who they are on a level deeper than their physical form, and this opens the doors of perception. Penelope also suggests that you practise making visual images, and develop the ability to send them to your animal friend. (You could think of tossing them like a ball, or of just having them hang in space at a point of your choosing.) As you do this, you can also verbalise the content of the image either to yourself or out loud. Beatrice Lydecker suggests that you ask a question by sending your animal friend a picture representing the

'Many animals are far more perceptive and aware than the people who attempt to understand them.'

'Any self-respecting human who wants to make sense to animals must be able to still her mind, and think only the thoughts she means to convey.'

information you want – perhaps of where he used to live. The content of this is actually immaterial, for if the picture is wrong, he will send you back a corrected picture. The beauty of this is that it frees you from the need to get it 'right'.

Penelope also suggests that you say 'Hello' to your animal, and imagine that he says 'Hello' back. This may sound like making it up, which of course it is: but bear in mind that unless we can first *imagine* something happening, we cannot manifest it in reality. So if you cannot imagine getting a reply from your animal you will never get one. For an animal to 'hear' you, he must be paying attention, and not be distracted by food or by another of his own kind. Your intuitive sense of whether he is 'with you' is a better guide than vision, for animals can at the same time pay attention to you *and* to their environment. Or like two people sitting quietly together, you can be in very close rapport without there being any outward expression of attention.

Being able to still your mind and think in pictures has the advantage of stopping you from *talking to yourself* about what your animal could or should say, and wondering whether in fact you did just get an answer. If your mind is preoccupied with this, you are trying to solve the problem with your intellect, and like J. Allen Boone, you will feel blocked. Instead simply 'listen' (with all of your senses) and you will finally receive your answers in a quiet, still frame of mind – perhaps as an idea, a picture, a feeling, or as the 'Aha!' of sudden knowing which then needs to be unpacked and expressed in language. Do not try and change it, add to it, or qualify it. Just acknowledge it, even if it did not tie in with your expectations. Then you might continue by asking 'Is there anything you want to tell me?'

....

Even if you doubt the efficacy of these steps, and the validity of telepathic communication in general, realise that you probably know far more about your animals than you acknowledge consciously. For whether they are happy, sad, bored or distressed is usually obvious to anyone who is astute enough to notice the moods of the *people* who surround her. Like people, each animal has his own individual character, and within each species some are more talkative, bright and aware than others. Some (like some people) are preoccupied with their stomachs, and will follow their genetic heritage and body impulses more strongly than those who enjoy adapting their ways to a life with people. Our animals thrive in an atmosphere of respect and appreciation, but like children, they often fulfil our prophecies and play the game we expect them to play, acting dumb in ways that have hidden pay-offs for them! So one way to get animals to act intelligently is to treat them as if they are intelligent; but they may not immediately respond to a change in the status quo. For this can require them to give up the abdication of responsibility which either their dumb-act or our dumb-act has previously allowed.

If it is too far-fetched for you to accept the idea that animals can become our teachers, guides, and healers, realise that this is only a map – you do not actually have to believe it for you and your animals to reap the benefits of thinking in this way. For if you act *as if* it is true, your behaviours will come from much different motives than they would if you viewed yourself as master and animals as your servants. For this gives you permission to 'walk all over' them.

The role of teacher has greater ramifications for horses than it does for any other species, since we interact with them so closely, and commit so many sins in the process. Yet according to the animal communicators horses have very altruistic values, working from the assumption that when we are cruel, it is simply because we know no better. They offer themselves in the hope that we will learn compassion, wanting us to respond to them in ways which are life-enhancing – for their and our 'higher good'. They remain ever hopeful, and are more than willing to endure the various forms of torture we administrate. 'Horses will show me a picture of the whip,' says Kate Reilly, 'but never of the person who hit them.' Rarely do they place blame, and become aggressive or vindictive in response to us. Mostly, 'They believe that everything they endure simply makes them bigger and stronger – that it's part of what they need to do. Whether the relevant lessons are learned by the people who abuse them is actually irrelevant to them.'

Professional animal communicators can work at a distance, using a photograph of the animal, or even (outrageous though this may sound) through a telephone conversation with the owner. Kate Reilly reports that horses always give her some piece of information which identifies them, and convinces the owner that she is indeed giving an accurate reading about the right horse. The stories of the successes of these people are legion, and I will share just a few with you.

A friend of mine consulted Beatrice Lydecker one day when all the horses in her barn had obviously been very disturbed during the night. Her stable manager had heard a commotion and had gone outside, but had seen nothing. She did, however, have a strange feeling that she was being watched – so strange that the hairs on the back of her neck stood up on end. The horses in one row of small outdoor runs were particularly distressed, and they became the participants in Beatrice's investigation. The first horse would not talk to her. ('Not surprising', said my friend when she told me the story, 'in every day life he's a really uncommunicative old so-and-so.') From the next horse she pieced together that they did not know what it was, but it had frightened them horribly, and it smelt very bad. It walked on four legs, but could also stand up on two, as it did by the side of their runs. When the girl with yellow hair had come out to see what was happening it had hidden behind the shed, but it watched her every move. Finally Beatrice concluded, 'You know, I think it must be a bear.' My friend was incredulous, since bears had long since disappeared from her urban area in California. But the next day her local newspaper carried the headline, 'Bear caught at local garbage dump' – less than half a mile from her barn.

Samantha Khury, an American psychic who was featured in the television programme 'I Talk with Animals', was consulted by a racehorse trainer in New York. One horse who was extremely bad-tempered and not training well insisted that he needed a rest, despite the fact that he had recently returned to his owner's home for a spell at grass. The horse insisted that this had *not* been a rest, that he had been treated badly and made to work exceptionally hard. When the owner was asked about what had really happened he revealed that he had indeed kept the horse in training. But the horse was willing to negotiate: he would try his hardest in the next race in return for a spell of genuine time off. He kept his part of the bargain (as did his people), and ran well in the race.

Animal communicators are consulted most often when a horse is not performing well, and many are particularly good at discovering the origins of pain in a horse's body, even when both conventional and complementary techniques have failed. Animal communicators (like radionics practitioners) are often the last port of call for horse owners who have dangerously disobedient horses. They are also useful if you have the kind of horse who – if he were a car – would be jokingly diagnosed as having come off the assembly line on a Friday afternoon! The owners of these horses commonly reach a point of desperation at which they have nothing to lose, and the cost of a consultation is minimal compared to that of scanning the horse from head to foot with all the technology available. Some of the psychics also perform hands-on healing work, finding places where the horse's energy is blocked and releasing it so it moves freely through his body.

Some animal communicators have described their diagnostic ability by saying 'It's as if I step inside the horse's body and feel what he feels.' They believe that very few horses do *not* have aches and pains, with backs and feet as the more commonly sore places. Often these are the small, livable-with aches which beset many people, and frequently there is more than one sore place. But often their pains are more significant than that, and the generosity of horses is such that the rebellious, difficult horse is almost certain to be in pain. To think of him as wilfully disobedient is to take a very blinkered view. As dressage rider Kyra Kyrklund points out, horses do not spend twenty-three hours a day standing in their stables thinking, 'How can I make her really angry tomorrow? How can I get her so enraged that she'll beat me black and blue?'.

Kate Reilly impressed veterinary surgeons at the Tufts veterinary hospital in Boston, when she had been consulted about a horse who was not performing well, and had told the owner exactly which vertebra was affected and precisely how it had been rotated. X-rays then revealed this precise problem. She also hit the nail on the head with a horse who was due to be put down, following seven independent veterinary opinions. He was thought to have the equine equivalent of motor neurone disease, which is untreatable. But instead she diagnosed that a back injury was putting pressure on nerves to his front legs so that he was intermittently unable to feel them. There was indeed some damage which was not repairable; but chiropractic treatment enabled him to live a quality life, and to return to light work.

Many people also consult animal communicators when they are trying to decide whether to sell or keep a horse. However, if you contact one saying 'I own a horse who...' she is likely to reply, 'You cannot *own* a horse...', insisting that if you want to think of him as *your* horse, then you will have to think of yourself as *his* person. Horses, we are told, are often very curious about where they might go next, and are often less attached to us than we imagine. They also (like our other animals) appreciate knowing how long we are going away for when we leave them. All animals like having a job to do, and we are advised to tell them clearly what that job is – whether your cat is there to bring 'good vibes' to the house, your dog to cheer you up when you feel sad, or your horse to give you feedback about your riding and to share the joys of galloping in the countryside.

Nicci Mackay finds that the most common question which people ask her is 'Does my horse love me?'. Since horses do not wag their tails and jump on our laps, their signs of love are less evident than those of most companion animals, yet we are more to them than bringers of food. One normally undemonstrative horse walked over to his person and licked her face in response to the question; another admitted that he was still pining for a previous owner whose smell, touch, environment and way of riding had suited him perfectly.

Most people will ask an animal communicator 'Why does my horse do X?' But some people want their horse to know how upset they are by X, working on the principle that if only the horse *knew* this, then surely he would stop doing it. This is a tactic which is often used to harangue both spouses and children, although it rarely works. Its chances with the horse are equally slim, for horses need to be horses – to feel, act, and think like horses – and it is when we do not respect their horse-nature that we stress them beyond the point of tolerance.

It is the beauty, grace and power of horses which attracts us to them, often as very young children. The juxtaposition of their strength and their gentleness touches many people's hearts, creating a bond even greater than the affinity they feel for other animals. There is often a sense of longing involved too, and psychologists (headed by the noted psychoanalyst Dr Sigmund Freud) have struggled to explain the attraction that horses have for us. But their theories have certainly never rung true for the avid riders amongst us. (Perhaps the psychoanalytic interpretation of riding is best summed up by the bumper sticker which one of my pupils brought back from America. It read 'Put something exciting between your legs – ride a horse.') From a slightly different viewpoint, philosophers have argued for centuries about whether animals have souls, but philosophers have rarely related their thinking to human/animal relationships.

My personal map of this territory is based around the idea that animals rarely lose touch with their spiritual essence – with the qualities which J. Allen Boone saw in Strongheart. As young children, though, we often lose touch with the most spontaneous, spirited, and vulnerable parts of ourselves. As we learn to use language and become socialised, so we are 'tamed', and the pressures of education and growing up exact their price. The roles we are expected to play become the dominant forces in our lives, our 'sub-personalities' develop their strengths and conflicts, and we may get so out of kilter that we no longer recognise our true '*self*'. (This is reminiscent of Edward Bach's philosophy, discussed on page 241.) But we can experience this again in meditation, and through riding – or any other activity which generates such complete absorption that we have no sense of time passing, or of ourselves as separate from the action we are performing. Perhaps part of the challenge of living on this planet is that having *lost* contact with our spiritual essence we have to go through the process of *finding* it again – or of not finding it, as the case may be.

We can pressurise our animals – and particularly our horses – so that they too are in danger of losing that connection (and some psychoanalysts would suggest that our envy would lead us to do this); but I think that as very young children some of us see in animals, and in horses in particular, a wholeness which we know we are losing, and which we long to regain. Hence the strength of our attraction to them. So one possible choice is to let our horses become our teachers as we re-find our own wholeness, and seek to develop the beauty and the power of theirs. Or we can compromise it in both them and us through our egotistical and heavy-handed ways of demanding their obedience. Some fight animals will

'One possible choice is to let our horses become our teachers.'

undoubtedly never learn, and some flight animals will never stop fleeing; but our ways of crossing this great divide between our species *are* changing, bringing with them a respect for horses – for their integrity, for their needs, and for their role as partners in the endeavour of horsemanship. The animal communicators tell us that horses are eternal optimists – despite our appalling record in learning from the mistakes which inevitably compromise them. I am an optimist too.

Epilogue

WHETHER WE LIKE it or not, we are all, collectively, in the midst of a paradigm shift which embraces the way we treat, ride, and keep our horses. It has become an unstoppable force, pioneered by people who have been brave enough to go out on a limb, often working alone as they honed their skills. To you, these changes may seem sudden in their onset; but they have been a long time coming. Monty Roberts used his 'advance and retreat' method for over thirty years before he ever showed it to anyone. Robert Miller spent forty years attempting to convince people of the value of 'imprint training'. New ideas always need a non-judgmental atmosphere in which to develop – which can mean hiding from the contempt of your peers, and waiting until your findings mature into ideas 'whose time has come'.

If you take the traditional bell curve which shows the population as a whole and describes its acceptance of any new idea, the first 6 per cent at the beginning of the curve are the innovators. The 6 per cent at the other end are known as the laggards, and the vast majority of the population lie somewhere in between. We are working our way up the bell curve at an amazing rate, with books, videos, and international travel allowing a faster dissemination of knowledge than ever before. And knowledge is a one-way door; once you know something and can work with the greater sophistication which it gives you, it is hard to go back, and to pretend you do not. In this 'information age', knowledge brings responsibility. We might wish for the good old days in which ignorance was bliss, when you just saddled up and went for your ride without thinking (for instance) about the ramifications of your saddle fit or the implications of foot balance. But for many, those days are gone.

I spoke recently to a researcher who had studied the history of man's involvement with the horse. 'I think we are really coming out of a dark age of the horse,' she said. 'When horses were kept by nomadic people they were their *currency*, and were valued as such. Since then we have used horses in so many ways which have been to their detriment. But I think it's all beginning to change now, thanks to the work of a few people who are taking a much more holistic viewpoint.' In 1996 Robert Miller wrote to me saying, 'I predicted a decade ago that by the turn of the century, horsemanship as we have known it for thousands of years, based on pain and force, will be changed for ever.' He feels that he is now really seeing this happen, and part of the change is being catalysed by his methods which, after a lifetime's work, are finally gaining worldwide acceptance. (He is still wondering, however, why it is that the British can be counted amongst the laggards – especially given our tradition of caring so well for horses.)

Individually, those of us on the upward slope of the bell curve struggle with these changes: if our horse begins to look lame do we go down the conventional medical path as we would have done a few years back? Do we seek out a remedial farrier? Do we turn our back on the established drug treatments and opt to use herbs, acupuncture or homoeopathy? It is all too easy to fall between the two approaches, especially if you 'go it alone' and do not seek qualified veterinary opinion. If you dabble in both, you do justice to neither, and as more vets become qualified in the complementary treatments – and enthusiastic about their efficacy – the schism between the approaches will abate. So will the ambivalence and confusions of horse owners, for we are currently 'caught between the devil and the deep blue sea' and we need the help of vets as we chart new territory and rechart the old.

No one person can be an expert in every sphere of horsemanship. I have learned a tremendous amount through writing this book, but will never have the skill of the Masters who have learned their craft through hands-on experience, devoting their lives to the horse, and to the astute observation through which a new approach develops. Gleaning quality knowledge requires a tremendous number of comparisons, and Monty Roberts, for instance, has started over nine thousand horses. I have spent more hours than I could possibly count watching riders, and piecing together the determining factors of their skill. The best saddlers, farriers, bodyworkers and vets have all undergone a self-imposed training course. The people who learn from these Masters do not need to reinvent the wheel – but they do need to appreciate that if they are to become practitioners who can do more than just regurgitate what they have learned, then they too need to become astute observers who can process information and learn from experience. For this is the Master skill.

'We consumers need the skills to differentiate between the practitioner who has fifteen years of experience, and the person who has had one year of experience repeated fifteen times.'

As laymen, we consumers need the skills to work our way through a tangle of possibilities, and to differentiate between the practitioner who has fifteen years of experience, and the person who has had one year of experience repeated fifteen times! Distraught horse owners are very vulnerable people, and the emotional turmoil of having a lame or sick horse can cloud our judgment. (As one of my pupils who is a vet once commented, 'I have to call in the vet when my horses are lame; I just can't cope.') To remain pragmatic we need to feel that there are people and approaches with a proven track record in whom we can put our trust – whether their skills are based on high-tech medical advances, or on the complementary approaches which the medical world would regard (from within the limits of its own map) as 'mumbo jumbo'. Just as moving to a new area requires you to find a team of tradesmen to do minor repairs on your house, so you need to find a team of practitioners to take care of your horse. Neither is an easy task.

....

The vast majority of innovators within equestrianism have relied on their own senses, not the high-tech equipment of the laboratory. But along with those who have no accepted scientific credentials, the academics within the new sports science and equine studies departments of the universities are bound to make their contribution. Fortunately for us, many of the people in them are determined to disseminate their knowledge to the riding public rather than confining it to those who read the scientific journals.

We now have photography which uses 250 frames per second, giving us precise data on movement patterns which we have never had before. We have force plates, which measure with tremendous precision the forces generated when the horse's foot impacts on the ground. We have treadmills and optoelectronic cameras, coupled to computers which can analyse the movement patterns of the horse's limbs. It is a revolution akin to the beginning of photography, which showed that prior assumptions about how horses moved were simply not true. We lag way behind other sports, where the computer analysis of the technique used by talented performers has impacted on the teaching of the sport as a whole. But we will soon know much more about the movement patterns used by the talented horse and also by his rider.

More and more, practitioners from the various disciplines (both high and low tech) are teaming up and referring to each other, sometimes within a clinic setting, and sometimes less formally. They may need to work together over a significant period of time to unravel complex patterns, and instigate the changes that are needed. It can become a costly venture, and the high-tech options will always remain beyond the resources of many. But there are always low-tech alternatives, and for horse owners, it is the ability to make wise choices which pays the highest dividends.

So the horses who pose tricky, unsolvable problems may require case conferences (or 'summit meetings' as one of my physiotherapist friends calls them) held with a number of professionals:

'Well,' says the vet, 'we shall need to X-ray the feet.'

'The left fore twists as it lands,' says the farrier, 'and the right hind will also need some drastic rebalancing.'

'There's a lot of muscle wastage in the right hind quarter,' says the physiotherapist, 'and the right hind moves out to the side instead of stepping beneath the body.'

'The saddle slips to the right,' says the saddler, 'and it's causing significant damage to the muscles along the left side of the spine.'

'The rider sits crooked,' says the biomechanics expert, 'and I think she is bringing the saddle over with her. That could be affecting the right hind.'

'There are several problem areas in the neck,' says the chiropractor, 'and until we release these I don't think the crookedness behind can alter.'

'Those sharp edges on the teeth in the right jaw are definitely related to that crookedness,' says the dentist, 'we really need to fix those.'

'To think that you have one problem with only one solution is clearly naive – and is the product of reductionist Newtonian thinking.'

Each practitioner sees the (or a) problem lying within her own domain, and is likely to believe that fixing this will prove to be the key which unravels the whole puzzle. You, as the horse's concerned owner, could be left in the middle wondering who to believe; but to think that you have *one* problem with *only one* solution is clearly naive – and is the product of reductionist Newtonian thinking. It is an approach which no longer holds water.

Inevitably, some ways of looking at the problem will not bring the expected gains, and some horses will confound and surprise us. I recently attended a symposium at Bristol University, and was fascinated by a case which was also fascinating the staff there. For in a treadmill analysis of the gaits of two horses, the horse with nearly perfect gaits had been going intermittently lame, and no one could work out why. Meanwhile, the horse which had strained a flexor tendon and had every reason to be lame was contriving to keep himself sound. His tactic was to manoeuvre his legs into a 'tripod' formation, bringing his opposite hind leg more under his body mass so that it could bear increased weight and relieve the foreleg. So perhaps we should be looking for the *inventive*, rather than the perfect horse...

The next few years are not going to be easy, as we marry knowledge gleaned from disparate sources and from maps which may well conflict with each other. But, if we can manage not to get bogged down in 'map battles' I think – like the people I quoted above – that we could be entering a new age for the horse. The holistic viewpoint, when married with technological advances, gives us an overview we have never had before. But all of this back-up only exists because horses represent such an enormous investment in time, love, energy and money, and because we want to *ride* them. Increasingly, people do this not just to fulfil their ego needs or for recreation; they see their riding and their learning process as a way to learn the larger lessons of life. If this idea were to catch on, times would become very good for the horse.

Bibliography

Chapter One – The Map is Not the Territory
Bandler, Richard, and Grinder, John, *The Structure of Magic*, Science and
    Behaviour Books Inc, 1975, USA
Covey, Stephen R., *The Seven Habits of Highly Effective People*, Simon &
    Schuster, 1989, USA
Grandin, Temple, *Thinking in Pictures*, Doubleday, 1995, USA
Hillenbrand, Laura, 'Leading the Blind', *Equus* 229, USA
Kiley-Worthington, Dr Marthe, *The Behaviour of Horses in Relation to
    Management and Training*, J. A. Allen, 1987, UK
Laborde, Genie Z., *Influencing with Integrity*, Syntony Publishing, 1983,
    USA
Morris, Desmond, *Horsewatching*, Jonathon Cape, 1988, UK
Sacks, Oliver, *The Man Who Mistook His Wife For a Hat*, Pan Books,
    1986, UK; Alfred A. Knopf, USA

**Chapter Two – Body/Mind/Spirit – Challenging Our Accepted
    Notions**
Brennan, Barbara Ann, *Hands of Light*, Bantam Books, 1988, USA
    – *Light Emerging*, Bantam Books, 1993, USA
Burr, Harold Saxton, *Blueprint For Immortality*, Neville Spearman, 1972, UK
The Burton Goldberg Group, *Alternative Medicine: The Definitive Guide*,
    Future Medicine Publishing Inc., 1994, USA
Chopra, Deepak M.D., *Quantum Healing*, Bantam Books, 1989, USA
Dacher, Elliotts, M.D., *P.N.I. The New Mind/Body Healing Program*,
    Paragon House, 1991, USA
Gerber, Richard, M.D., *Vibrational Medicine*, Bear & Co., 1988, USA
Goody, Peter C., BSc, PhD, *Horse Anatomy*. J. A. Allen, 1976, UK
Heller, Joseph, and Henkin, William A., *Bodywise*, Wingbow Press, 1986,
    USA
Hillenbrand, Laura, 'Drugs and How They Work', *Equus* 214, USA
Riemersma, D. J. *et al.*, 'Tendon Strain in the forelimbs as a function of

gait and ground characteristics and *in vitro* limb loading in ponies',
Equine Veterinary Journal, 1996, **28** (2), UK

Watson, Lyall, *Lifetide – The Biology of Consciousness,* 1979, Simon &
Schuster, USA

Weil, Andrew M.D., *Spontaneous Healing*, Alfred A. Knopf, 1995, USA

Chapter Three – Equine Dentistry

Goody, Peter C., *Horse Anatomy*, J. A. Allen, 1976, UK

Hayes, Captain M. Horace, FRCVS, *Veterinary Notes for Horse Owners*,
edited by P. D. Rossdale PhD, FRCVS, Stanley Paul, 1987, UK; Simon
& Schuster, USA

Webber, Toni, *Mouths and Bits* (Threshold Picture Guide), Kenilworth
Press, 1990, UK

Chapter Four – Farriery and Gait Analysis

Gonzales, Tony, *PBM: A Diary of Lameness*, REF Publishing, 1986, USA

Jackson, Jaime, *The Natural Horse*, Northland Publishing, 1992, USA

Jurga, Fran, 'Fancy Footwork', *Equus* 205, USA

Kilby, Emily, 'No Bad Hooves', *Equus* 212, USA

Mackay-Smith, Matthew P., DVM and Kilby, Emily, 'Land Flat, Fly True'
Equus 197, USA

Price, Hayden and Fisher, Rod, *Shoeing for Performance*, Crowood Press,
1995, UK; Trafalgar Square, USA

Richardson, Robbie C. RSS, *The Horse's Foot and Related Problems*,
Greatcombe Clinic, 1994, UK

Ryan, Tom, FWCF, 'Lateral Medial Foot Imbalance', unpublished paper,
UK

Williams, Gail PhD, 'The Role of the Foot in Equine Locomotion',
PhD thesis, University of Bristol, 1996, UK

Video Tapes

Redden, Ric, DVM, 'The Four Point Trim', available from Advance
Equine, PO Box 54, Versailles, KY 40383, USA

Chapter Five – Saddles and Saddle Fit

Bennett, Deb PhD, 'Who's Built Best to Ride', *Equus* 140 and 141,
USA

Kilby, Emily, 'Choosing Saddle Pads', *Equus 223,* USA

Murdoch, Wendy, 'Selecting the Right Saddle', *Equus* 213, USA

Smith, Karen, 'Easing Mounting Pressures', *Equus* 214, USA

Chapter Seven – Equine Bodywork

Britton, Vanessa, *Alternative Therapies for Horses*, Ward Lock, 1995, UK;
  Sterling, USA

Bromiley, Mary FCSP, RPT(USA), SRP, *Natural Methods for Equine
  Health*, Blackwell Scientific Publications, 1994, UK & USA
  – *Massage for Horses* (Threshold Picture Guide), Kenilworth
  Press, 1996, UK

The Burton Goldberg Group, *Alternative Medicine: The Definitive Guide*,
  Future Medicine Publishing Inc, 1994, USA

Gatterman, Meridel I. MA, DC, *Foundations of Chiropractic*, Mosby-Year
  Book, Inc., 1995, USA

Kaselle, Marion and Hannay, Pamela, *Touching Horses*, J. A. Allen, 1995,
  UK

Meagher, Jack, *Beating Muscle Injuries for Horses*, Hamilton Horse
  Associates, 1985, USA

Snader, Meredith L. VMD, Willoughby, Sharon L. DVM, DC, Khalsa,
  Deva Kaur VMD, Denega, Craig BA, Basko, Ivor John DVM, *Healing
  Your Horse*, Howell Book House, 1993, USA

Tellington-Jones, Linda and Bruns, Ursula, *The Tellington-Jones Equine
  Awareness Method*, Breakthrough Publications Inc, 1988, USA

Tellington-Jones, Linda and Taylor, Sybil, *The Tellington TTouch*, Viking
  Penguin Inc, 1992, USA; Cloudcraft Books, UK

Zidonis, Nancy A. and Soderberg, Marie K., *Equine Acupressure, A
  Treatment Workbook*, Equine Acupressure Inc., 1991, USA

Video Tapes

Bromiley, Mary, 'Hands On', Equestrian Vision, UK; Trafalgar Square,
  USA

Tellington-Jones, Linda, 'Touch of Magic for Horses', available from
  TTEAM offices in USA & UK
  – 'TTouch for Dressage Horses'
  – 'TTouch for Head and Neck'
  – 'TTouch for Body, Legs and Tail'

Chapter Eight – High- and Low-Tech Approaches to Injury

Bromiley, Mary FCSP, RPT(USA), SRP, *Equine Injury and Therapy*,
  Blackwell Scientific Publications, 1987, UK & USA
  – *Physiotherapy in Veterinary Medicine*, Blackwell Scientific Publications,
  1991, UK & USA

Denoix, Jean-Marie and Pailloux, Jean-Pierre, *Physical Therapy and
  Massage for the Horse*, Trafalgar Square Publishing, 1996, USA; Manson
  Publishing, UK

Malven, Pennsylvania, *Equine Wound Management*, Lea & Febigor, 1991, USA

Porter, Mimi, 'Equine Sports Therapy', Veterinary Data, 1990

Chapter Nine – 'Let Food Be Thy Medicine'

Allison, Keith, *A Guide to Herbs for Horses*, J. A. Allen, 1995 UK

– *A Guide to Equine Nutrition*, J. A. Allen, 1995, UK

Anthony, Christine, 'Can Supplements Calm Horses?', *Equus* 213, USA

de Baïracli Levy, Juliette, *The Complete Herbal Handbook for Farm and Stable*, Faber & Faber, 1984, UK

Bromiley, Mary FCSP, RPT(USA), SRP, *Natural Methods for Equine Health*, Blackwell Scientific Publications, 1994, UK & USA

Burton Goldberg Group, *Alternative Medicine: The Definitive Guide*, Future Medicine Publishing Inc., 1994, USA

Grosjean, Nelly, *Veterinary Aromatherapy*, The C. W. Daniel Company Ltd, 1994, UK; National Book Network, USA

Hillenbrand, Laura, 'What's for Dinner?', *Equus* 224, USA

Houghton Brown, Jeremy and Powell-Smith, Vincent, *Horse and Stable Management*, Blackwell Scientific Publications, 1994, UK and USA

Ingraham, Caroline, *Treating the Emotional and Physical Body Through Applied Kinesiology and Essential Oil Therapy*, published privately by the author

– *Aromatherapy for Horses* (Threshold Picture Guide), Kenilworth Press, 1997, UK

Moor, Jack, 'Shattering Myths About Feeding', *Equus* 284, USA

Morgan, Jenny, *Herbs for Horses* (Threshold Picture Guide), Kenilworth Press, 1993, UK

Pagan, Joe PhD, Duran, Steven PhD, Jackson, Steven PhD, 'Balancing Micronutrients', *Equus* 206, USA

Ryman, Daniele, *The Aromatherapy Handbook*, The C. W. Daniel Company Ltd, 1984, UK; Beekman Publishers, USA

Self, Hilary Page, *A Modern Horse Herbal*, Kenilworth Press, 1996, UK

Pilliner, Sarah, *Horse Nutrition and Feeding*, Blackwell Scientific Publications, 1992, UK & USA

Chapter Ten – Energy Medicine

Britton, Vanessa, *Alternative Therapies for Horses*, Ward Lock, 1995, UK; Sterling, USA

Bromiley, Mary, *Natural Methods of Equine Health*, Blackwell Scientific Publications, 1994, UK

Castro, Miranda, *The Complete Homoeopathy Handbook*, St Martins, 1991,

USA; Pan Books, 1996, UK

Dower, A.L.D., *Healing With Radionics*, The Keys College of Radionics, 1980, UK

Day, Christopher, *The Homoeopathic Treatment of Small Animals*, The C.W. Daniel Company Ltd, 1984, UK; Beekman Publishers, USA

Elliot, Mark, BVSc. MRCVS and Pincus, Tony, BPharm MRPharmS *Horses and Homoeopathy, a Guide for Yard and Stable*, Ainsworths Homoeopathic Pharmacy, 1994, UK

Gerber, Richard, M.D. *Vibrational Medicine*, Bear and Co 1988, USA

Kilby, Emily, 'Acupuncture' *Equus* 200, USA

Lockie, Dr. Andrew, and Geddes, Dr. Nicola, *The Complete Guide to Homoeopathy*, Dorling Kindersley, 1995, UK & USA

Macleod, G. MRCVS DVSM, AFHom *The Treatment of Horses by Homoeopathy*, Health Science Press, 1977, UK; Beekman Publishers, USA

Sellnow, Les, 'Acupuncture', *The Horse*, Jan, Feb, March 1997, USA

Snader, Meredith L.VMD, Willoughby, Sharon L. DVM, DC, Khalsa, Deva Kaur, VMD, Denega, Graig, BA, Basko, Ivor John, DVM, *Healing Your Horse*, Howell Bookhouse, 1993, USA

The Burton Goldberg Group *Alternative Medicine: The Definitive Guide*, Future Medicine Publishing Inc., 1994, USA

Chapter Eleven – 'Equus' – The Language of Training

Dorrance, Tom, *True Unity*, Give-It-A-Go Enterprises, 1987, USA

Hunt, Ray, *Think Harmony With Horses*, Pioneer Publishing Co, 1991, USA

Kiley-Worthington, Dr Marthe, *The Behaviour of Horses in Relation to Management and Training*, J. A. Allen, 1987, UK

Lyons, John with Browning, Sinclair, *Lyons on Horses,* Doubleday, 1991, USA

Parelli, Pat, *Natural Horse-Man-Ship*, A Western Horseman Book, 1993, USA

Roberts, Monty, *The Man Who Listens to Horses*, Hutchinson, 1996, UK

Tellington-Jones, Linda, *The Tellington-Jones Equine Awareness Method*, Breakthrough Publications Inc., 1988, USA

Video Tapes

Miller, Dr Robert DVM, 'Influencing the Horse's Mind', Palomine's Blue Ribbon Series, Millers Harness Co., Rutherford, New York
– 'Imprint Training the Foal'
– 'Early Training'

Lyons, John, 'Round Pen Reasoning', John Lyons Symposiums Inc.,

USA
– 'Leading and Loading Safely'
Parelli, Pat, 'The Natural Horsemanship Video Course', Parelli Natural
   Horsemanship Center, USA
   – 'Natural Trailer Loading'
Roberts, Monty, 'Starting the Young Horse', Flag is Up Farms, 1989,
   USA
   – 'Join-up'
Tellington-Jones, Linda, 'TTEAM Learning Exercises I and II', avaiable
   from TTEAM offices in USA & UK

Chapter Twelve – Animal Communicators
Boone, J. Allen, *Kinship With All Life*, Harper & Brothers, San Francisco,
   1954, USA
Hearne, Vicki, *Adam's Task*, Vintage Books, 1982, USA
Lydecker, Beatrice, *What the Animals Tell Me*, published privately by the
   author, USA
   – *Stories the Animals Tell Me*, published privately by the author, USA
Miller, Robert M. DVM, *Imprint Training*, A Western Horseman Book,
   1991, USA
Smith, Penelope, *Animal Talk*, Pegasus Publications, 1982, USA
   – *Animals, Our Return to Wholeness*, Pegasus Publications, 1993, USA

Useful Addresses

United Kingdom

**Ainsworth Homoeopathic
 Pharmacy**
38 New Cavendish Street
London, W1M 7LH

Andrew Foster
22 Station Road
Walsall
West Midlands, WS2 9JE

Animal Therapy Ltd
Tyringham Hall
Cuddington
Aylesbury
Bucks, HP18 0AP

**Association of British
 Veterinary Acupuncturists**
East Park Cottage
Handcross
Haywards Heath
Sussex, RH17 6BD

**Association of Chartered
 Physiotherapists in Animal
 Practice**
Moorland House
Salters Lane
Winchester
Hants, SO22 5TP

Bach Flower Remedies
Customer Enquiries
Broadheath House
83 Parkside
Wimbledon
London, SW19 5LP

Balance
The White House
East Claydon
Bucks
MK18 2NH

**British Association of Holistic
 Nutrition**
Borough Court
Borough Road
Hartley Witney
Hook
Hants
RG27 8JA

**British Association of
 Homoepathic Veterinary
 Surgeons**
Chinham House
Stanford-in-the-Vale
Faringdon
Oxon
SN7 8NQ

The British Herbal Medicine Assocation
PO Box 304
Bournemouth
Dorset
BN7 6JE

Cotswold Grass Seeds
The Barn Business Centre
Great Rissington
Cheltenham
Gloucester
GL54 2LH

Equine Aromatherapy Association
PO Box 19
Hay-on-Wye
Hereford
HR3 5YP

The Fragrant Earth Co. Ltd
PO Box 182
Taunton
Somerset
TA1 1YR

The Herb Society
134 Buckingham Palace Road
London, SW1W 9SA

Hilton Herbs Ltd
Downclose Farm
North Perrott
Crewkerne
Somerset
TA18 7SH

Osteopathic Information Service
PO Box 2074
Reading
Berks, RG1 4RY

The McTimoney Chiropractic Association
21 High Street
Eynsham
Oxford, OX8 1HE

Pat Parelli – PNHMS (UK)
The Natural Animal Centre
Rushers Cross Farm
Tidebrook
Mayfield
E. Sussex, TN20 6PX

Proteq Saddle Pads
Graingers
West Ashling
Chichester
W. Sussex, PO18 8DN

National Association of Animal Therapists
Tyringham Hall
Cuddington
Aylesbury
Bucks, HP18 0AP

The Radionics Assocation
Bearlin House
Goose Green
Deddington
Banbury
Oxon, OX15 0SZ

Register of Qualified Aromatherapists
PO Box 6941
London, N8 9HF

Monty Roberts (UK agent for)
Ms Kelly Marks
Lethornes
Lambourn
Berks, RG17 8QS

Roe Richardson Co. Ltd
North Sutton Farm
Sutton Grange
Ripon
N. Yorks
HG4 3JE

**The Royal College of
Veterinary Surgeons**
32 Belgrave Square
London
SW1X 8QP

TTEAM UK
Sunnyside House
Stratton Audley Road
Fringford
Bicester
Oxon, OX6 9ED

Mary Wanless
Chapel Plaister's Cottage
Wadswick Lane
Box
Corsham
Wilts, SN14 9HZ

USA

**The Academy of Veterinary
Homeopathy**
1283 Lincoln Street
Eugene, OR 97401

American Botanical Society
PO Box 201660
Austin, TX 78720

American Herb Association
PO Box 1673
Nevada City, CA 95959

American Herbalists Guild
PO Box 1683
Sequel, CA 95073

**American Veterinary
Chiropractic Association**
P.O. Box 249
Port Byron, IL 61275

**The American Holistic
Veterinary Medical
Association**
2214 Old Emmerton Road
Bel Air, MD 21015

**California School of Herbal
Studies**
PO Box 39
Forestville, CA 95436

Echo Publishing Inc
(The Chamisa Ridge Catalog)
Rt 9 Box 72-8
Santa Fe, NM 87505

**The Equine Trigger Point
Myotherapists Association**
259 Mountain Road
North Granby, CT 06060

Herb Research Foundation
1007 Pearl St, Suite 200
Boulder, CO 80302

**International Association of
Equine Dental Technicians**
PO Box 6103
Wilmington, DE 19804

**The International Veterinary
Acupuncture Society**
2140 Conestoga Road
Chester Springs, PA 19425

John Lyons Symposiums Inc.
PO Box 479
Parachute, CO 81635

Ortho-Flex Saddle Co.
RT 2 Box 132
Nevada, MO 64772

Pat Parelli
PNHMS Center
Box 5950
Pagosa Springs, CO 81147

Monty Roberts
Flag is Up Farms
PO Box 86
Solvang, CA 93464

San Fransisco Herb Co.
250 14th Street
San Fransisco, CA 94103

TTEAM
Animal Ambassadors International
PO Box 3793
Santa Fe, NM 8750100793

Australia

Pat Parelli (Australian agent for)
PNHMS Centre Australia
PO Box 2232
Gosford
NSW 2250

**National Herbalists Assocation
of Australia**
287 Leith Street
Coorparoo
Queensland 4151

Canada

**World Wide Association of
Equine Dentistry**
PO Box 807
Turner Valley
Alberta
TOL 2AO

Index

Page numbers in **bold** denote illustrations